{340}

RAJARAJA CHOLA

KING *of* KINGS

KAMINI DANDAPANI

ALEPH

ALEPH BOOK COMPANY
An independent publishing firm
promoted by ***Rupa Publications India***

First published in India in 2022
by Aleph Book Company
7/16 Ansari Road, Daryaganj
New Delhi 110 002

ISBN: 978-93-91047-92-4

3 5 7 9 10 8 6 4 2

Printed in India

To

My very own Rajaraja: My father, Raja,

The bright suns of my personal galaxy:
Vasanta, Vijay, Aditi, and Rohan,

And my beloved Roger Roger Cholan, provider of unconditional love, laughs, and tail-wags galore.

The world is like the impression left by the telling of a story.

Yogavashishta, 2.3.11

And every dead king had a story
Of ancient glory, sweetly told.

Francis Ledwidge, 'The Dead Kings'

CONTENTS

Book Three: The Sun at High Noon

Book Four: The Son Also Rises, and the Moon Too

THE DYNASTY DIRECTORY

A veritable revolving door of dynasties left their impact on the Cholas and influenced their fortunes. Some endured through the bitter end and most rose, and then faded away (some several times), felled by the relentless passage of time and history. This is the dynastic milieu of the Cholas, presented in brief.

THE BANAS (EARLY 4th TO MID-16th CENTURY CE)

A relatively minor dynasty that nonetheless played a key supporting role to powers stronger than themselves. They claimed descent from the demon-king Mahabali and occupied the lands surrounding the Pallava and Western Ganga domains.

THE (EASTERN) CHALUKYAS OF VENGI (7th TO 12th CENTURY CE)

In the seventh century, a breakaway faction of the Chalukyas established itself independently in the eastern Deccan and ruled out of the capital Vengi. In time, the rulers of this Vengi line became a part of the Chola universe through marital alliances. Rajaraja Chola's daughter was married to a Vengi prince called Vimaladitya, an alliance that set in motion a far-reaching chain of reactions. A child of this union, Rajaraja Narendra, married Ammanga, the daughter of Rajaraja's son Rajendra. Their child, Kulothunga, would cross the matrilineal line to become the ruler of the Cholas, resulting in the fusion of the Chola and Vengi dynasties.

THE (WESTERN) CHALUKYAS OF BADAMI/KALYANI (6th TO MID-8th CENTURY CE FROM BADAMI; LATE 10th TO END 12th CENTURY CE FROM KALYANI)

They ruled from Vatapi, known today as Badami, in northern Karnataka, and rose to prominence in the sixth century. As they notched up victories over rival chieftains and kingdoms, particularly the Rashtrakutas, their rule extended to the entire Deccan region that included large swathes of today's Maharashtra, Andhra Pradesh, Telangana, and Karnataka. The Chalukyas' great and long-standing rivals were the Pallavas, and therefore, by association, the fledgling Cholas as well. Starting in the mid-eighth century, their star dimmed for a couple of centuries as the Rashtrakutas took over their lands. They came back to prominence in the late tenth century with the fall of the Rashtrakutas and ruled from Kalyani, some 300 kilometres north of their old capital, Vatapi. They became a major Chola rival and one of Rajaraja's greatest foes was Satyasraya, the Western Chalukya ruler. Later, too, this dynasty caused no end of trouble for the Cholas; the son of the great ruler Rajendra died in a battle against the Chalukyas. Eventually, they came to an end at the hands of the newly risen Hoysala dynasty.

THE CHERAS (3rd CENTURY BCE TO 12th CENTURY CE, WITH PERIODS OF SERIOUS DECLINE IN BETWEEN)

They were an ancient dynasty and Chola rivals at least from Sangam times. Their kingdom lay to the far west, in parts of present-day Kerala and western Tamil Nadu. They ruled out of Karur. They frequently joined hands with the Pandyas in an effort to subdue the Cholas, but they were also valued allies, a perfectly normal situation for the times. By the tenth century, they were effectively absorbed into the Pandya fold. The Cheras, Sangam Cholas, and Pandyas formed the ancient triumvirate known as the Mooventar or The Three (Kings), the oldest known dynasties who ruled over southern India.

THE HOYSALAS (10th TO 14th CENTURY CE)

A Kannada power whose earliest records date from the mid-tenth century, a couple of decades prior to Rajaraja's ascension to the Chola throne. They ruled from Belur, and then Halebid (some 200 kilometres to the west of Bengaluru), where some of the most sculpturally stunning temples in the world endure. Early on, they suffered a defeat at the hands of Rajaraja's troops, but later, from the twelfth century onwards, they gained over the fading Western Chalukyas. The Cholas lost some territory to the Hoysalas, but later, in the thirteenth century, the two joined forces against the Pandyas, and the Hoysalas provided vital friendship and help to the Cholas. At their peak, they ruled over much of Karnataka, and made inroads into some Tamil lands (north of the Kaveri) and bits of western Andhra and Telangana. They eventually fell to the Vijayanagar forces, and their lands were merged into that empire.

THE KALABHRAS (3rd TO 6th CENTURY CE)

A dynasty that ruled over parts of southern India after the Sangam Cholas from approximately the third to the sixth centuries. They are often described as mysterious, because very little is known about them. The Pallavas and Pandyas were suppressed during their rule, and in the literature and inscriptions of these regimes, they were portrayed in unflattering terms.[1] They followed the Buddhist and Jain faiths, a fact that might have encouraged the popularity of the Hindu Bhakti movement that followed soon after their dissolution and downfall. They left no trace of their presence.

THE PALLAVAS (LATE 3rd TO END 9th CENTURY CE)

Relative newcomers to the Tamil dynastic landscape, they emerged on the scene at the end of the third century and remained in power through the ninth century. In between, they were eclipsed by the Kalabhras. They occupied the northern regions of Tamilakam, and their domain was called Tondaimandalam. Kanchipuram and Mamallapuram were their main cities. Their most productive period was in the sixth and seventh centuries after the fall of the Kalabhras, when they built marvels like the Shore Temple, the cave temples and rathas at Mamallapuram, and the Kailasanatha Temple in Kanchipuram; their power extended as far south as the Kaveri River, into Chola domain.

THE PANDYAS (POSSIBLY AROUND 4th CENTURY BCE TO MID-16th CENTURY CE)

They were an ancient power, a mighty dynasty whose domain was further south of the Chola lands. Their capital city, Madurai, is one of the oldest continuously inhabited cities in India. They were ambitious and fearless, the Cholas' oldest, fiercest, and toughest rivals, and their fates were intertwined from at least as early as the Sangam era and continued through the entirety of Chola rule. They, too, faded into the shadows during the period of the Kalabhra rule, and their revival happened simultaneously with that of the Pallavas. The Cholas' end came at the hands of the Pandyas. The Pandyas lost much of their territory to the Madurai sultanate which established itself in their capital of Madurai in the fourteenth century. The once mighty Pandyas clung to a vastly diminished area and ruled out of Tenkasi. Their end came in the sixteenth century as an upstart regime—the Vijayanagar empire—that would go on to attain great heights, swept through their lands.

THE RASHTRAKUTAS (MID-8th TO LATE 10th CENTURY)

A Karnataka-based powerhouse dynasty that caused untold misery to the Cholas. They rose to prominence in the mid-eighth century, snuffing out the Chalukyas and taking over their lands. Their core territory was around Gulbarga in northern Karnataka, and their capital was Manyakheta or Malkhed but at their peak their empire stretched to lands far to the north and south of their heartland. One of the most devastating losses faced by the Cholas came at the Battle of Takkolam in which the army of the Rashtrakuta king Krishna III destroyed the Cholas; the crown prince Rajaditya, son of the ruling Chola emperor, Parantaka, was killed in this battle, and their fortunes took a nosedive. It took over three decades, and the ascension of the greatest of the Chola monarchs, Rajaraja, to steady the helm and take the Cholas to great heights.

THE SINHALA KINGDOMS

The rulers of the emerald isle of Ceylon (Sri Lanka) across the waters of the Palk Strait were bitter enemies of the Cholas from very early on, in the tenth century. They sought the help and protection of the Cholas' greatest rivals the Pandyas, which the Cholas could not leave unavenged. In addition, the island's ports lay along the lucrative maritime trade route between East and West, and besides, it was rich in resources like copper. The pearl fisheries in the Gulf of Mannar between Sri Lanka and Tamil Nadu were another attraction; vast numbers of pearls were used for temple jewels to adorn their sacred bronzes. Chola troops made repeated attacks on the island, wreaking havoc, but Ceylon proved a difficult territory to subdue and maintain and the twelfth-century emperor Kulothunga finally cut territorial ties.

THE SRIVIJAYAS (7th CE TO 13th CENTURY CE)

A thalassocracy across the Bay of Bengal, in modern Indonesia and Malaysia, they were a loosely aligned confederacy of city states led by Srivijaya (modern Palembang in Indonesia). Their location made them a key player in the trade nexus between China and the countries to the west of India, and therefore, a prime threat and rival to the Cholas who were after a piece of the same pie. From the reign of Rajaraja, the relationship between the Cholas and Srivijayas was both friendly and hostile, the double-faced diplomacy necessary to hedge all bets and keep matters from spiralling out of control. Rajaraja endowed the revenues of a village for the upkeep of a Buddhist vihara built by the Srivijaya ruler in Nagapattinam; his son Rajendra launched a massive naval raid against this kingdom not very long after.

THE WESTERN GANGAS (MID-4th CE TO END 10th CENTURY CE)

They ruled from Talakad, and their kingdom was in the region around Mysore in southern Karnataka. They remained a largely regional dynasty, and often played a subordinate role to regimes bigger and more powerful than themselves. They proved a vital ally to the Cholas against the Rashtrakutas, with two kings, Prithvipati I and his grandson Prithvipati II, distinguishing themselves on the battlefield on behalf of the Chola kings Aditya and Parantaka. However, in a switch-about that proved disastrous to the Cholas, one of their rulers, Butuga, allied himself with the Rashtrakutas, and was a key factor in the devastating Chola loss at the Battle of Takkolam.

And our protagonists:

THE SANGAM CHOLAS (APPROXIMATELY 4th CENTURY BCE TO 4th CENTURY CE)

The earliest Cholas, they lived and ruled from approximately 400 BCE to 300 CE. Their domain was a narrow belt around the Kaveri delta that included Uraiyur near present-day Tiruchirappalli, and Kaveripoompattinam, 160 kilometres away, on the coast. Much of the extant oeuvre of what is known as Sangam poetry was created during this time, and the kings of this era are often identified by this label. Among the best-known kings of the Sangam Cholas were Karikala, the King of the Charred Leg, and Kochengannan, the King of the Red Eyes.

THE IMPERIAL CHOLAS (850 CE TO 1279 CE)

From Vijayalaya who became ruler in 850 to Rajendra III who ruled until 1279, the Imperial Chola dynasty included a remarkable cast of characters and some not-so-remarkable ones. The well-known kings include Rajaraja and his son Rajendra, many others like Parantaka and Kulothunga, and queens like Sembiyan Madevi, whose lives and achievements are no less fascinating. They ruled from Thanjavur and Gangaikondacholapuram in the deltaic region of the great Kaveri River and their legacy lives on in a variety of ways to this day. The scale and grandeur of their achievements earned them the Imperial appellation.

This is their story.

TIMELINE OF RAJARAJA'S LIFE

947 CE: Rajaraja is born, the third child of Sundara Chola and Vanavanmadevi.

985 CE: Rajaraja is crowned king of the Cholas.

989 CE: Defeats Chera warriors of Kandalur Salai (present-day Kerala), one of Rajaraja's earliest military successes.

990s CE: Rajaraja directs his attention to long-time foes, the Pandyas.

991 CE: Rajaraja sees early military victories in his conquest of Ganga territory.

993 CE: The trademark epithet 'Tirumagal Pol' appears in Rajaraja's Tamil meykkirti.

993 CE: Rajaraja leads the invasion of Sinhala lands (Sri Lanka).

999 CE: Vengi prince Vimaladitya is married to Rajaraja's daughter after the victory at Vengi.

1000s CE: Pandya Mandalam is renamed Rajaraja Mandalam, Pandya lands fall under Chola control.

1000 CE: Rajaraja earns the title Ulagalanda Perumal (the great king who measured the earth) for commissioning a gargantuan land survey of his entire kingdom.

1003 CE: Rajaraja captures Rattapadi (Western Chalukyas), former Rashtrakuta domains under Satyasraya's command.

1004 CE: Rajaraja becomes lord of Talakad, the Ganga capital.

1004 CE: Building of the Brihadeeshwara Temple begins.

1005 CE: The Cholas conquer the Mysore region.

1005 to 1010 CE: Conquers the Maldives.

1010 CE: The Brihadeeshwara Temple is completed. The main deity of worship is a giant stone lingam named Rajarajeshwara.

1012 CE: Rajaraja's son Rajendra is appointed yuvaraja.

1012 CE: Rajaraja sends a trade delegation to the Song court in China.

1014 CE: Death of Rajaraja Chola.

◆

A timeline like this is rather misleading, giving the appearance of a neat chronology with victories, events, and territories stacking up in a linear, orderly fashion. The reality could not be more different. It was common practice to boast of military success based on minor victories; quite often, both sides claimed to have won the same battle. Subjugating the Pandyas, and winning over present-day Kerala, Karnataka, and Andhra Pradesh/Telangana took years of fighting even if victory was declared early on.

Imperial Cholas Family Tree

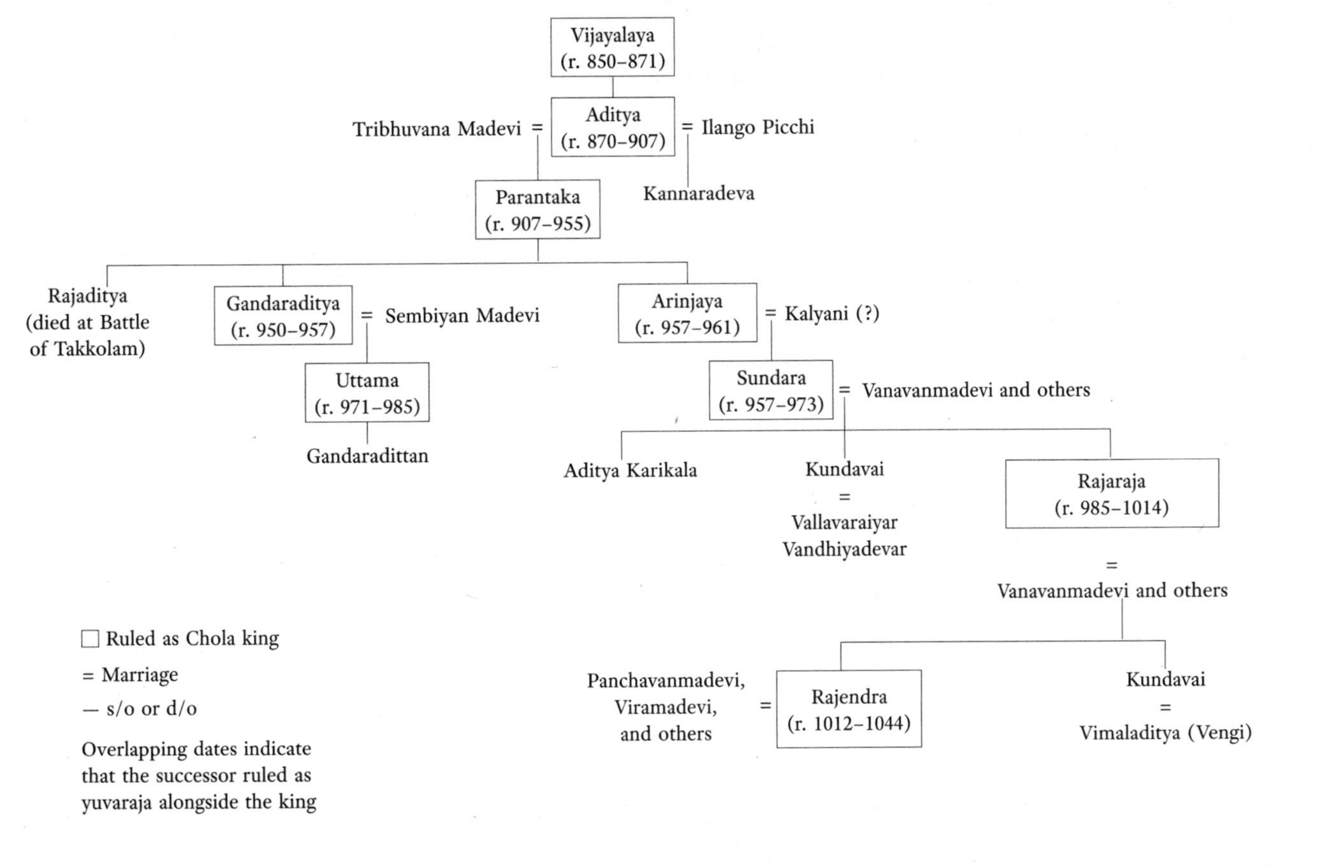

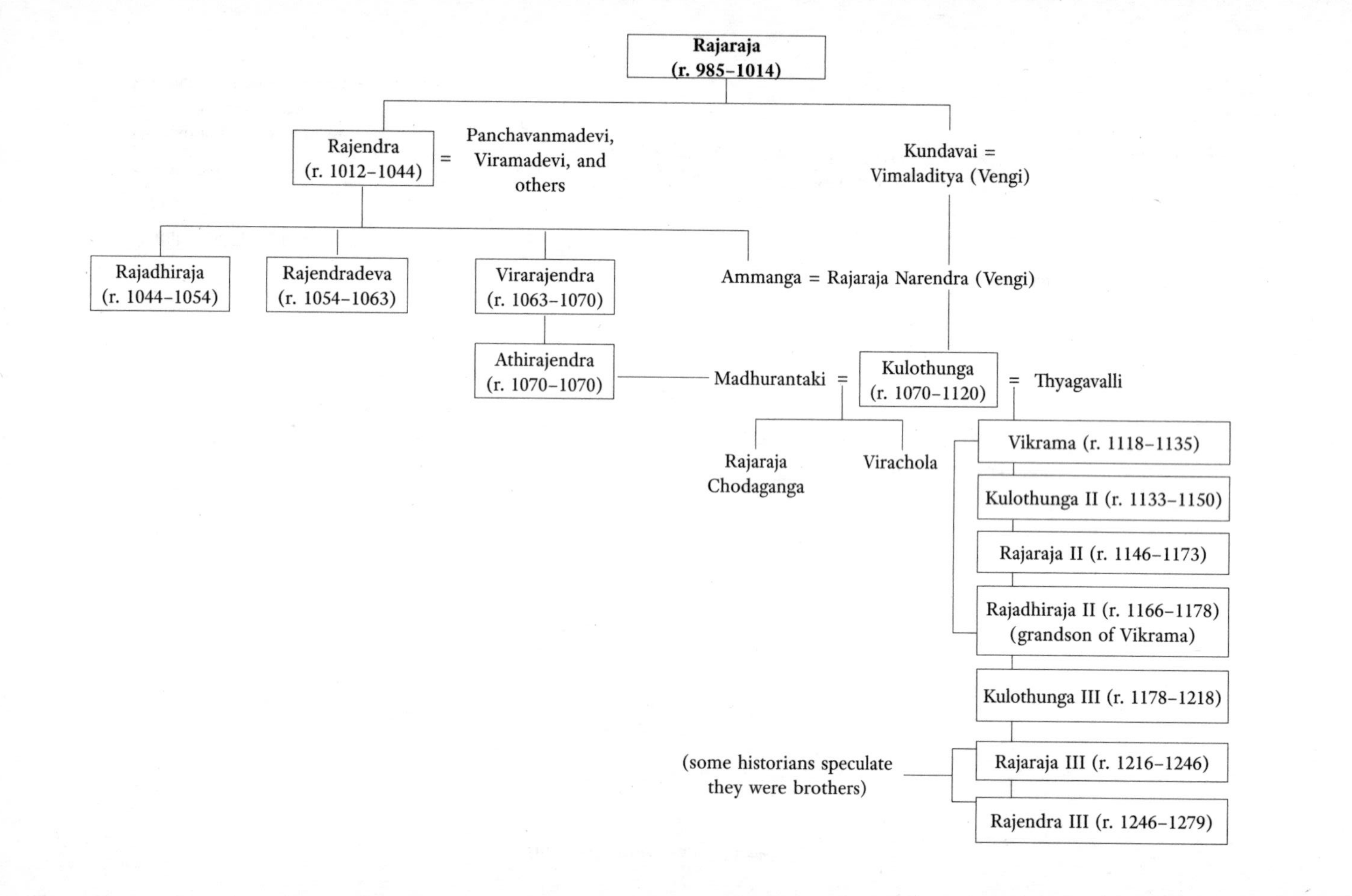
Rajaraja
(r. 985–1014)
Rajendra
(r. 1012–1044)
=
Panchavanmadevi,
Viramadevi, and
others
Kundavai =
Vimaladitya (Vengi)
Rajadhiraja
(r. 1044–1054)
Rajendradeva
(r. 1054–1063)
Virarajendra
(r. 1063–1070)
Ammanga = Rajaraja Narendra (Vengi)
Athirajendra
(r. 1070–1070)
Madhurantaki =
Kulothunga
(r. 1070–1120)
= Thyagavalli
Rajaraja
Chodaganga
Virachola
Vikrama (r. 1118–1135)
Kulothunga II (r. 1133–1150)
Rajaraja II (r. 1146–1173)
Rajadhiraja II (r. 1166–1178)
(grandson of Vikrama)
Kulothunga III (r. 1178–1218)
(some historians speculate
they were brothers)
Rajaraja III (r. 1216–1246)
Rajendra III (r. 1246–1279)

PROLOGUE

Long before sunrise on 18 July 985, Arulmozhi Varman awoke after a restless night. It was the day of his coronation, the culmination of over a quarter of a century of apprenticeship under his father and then his uncle. In the early years of that period, the one destined for the throne, the star that had shone brightest in his father's eyes had been his brother, Aditya Karikala. But fate dictated otherwise. Aditya Karikala was murdered, hacked to pieces, and his killers were still at large. Arulmozhi Varman shuddered when he remembered the day his brutalized body had been found. Almost as bad as seeing his brother in that state was watching the life ebb out of his parents' eyes. They never recovered from the shock; his father had died a broken man, and his mother, unable to bear the thought of living on, had flung herself on to her husband's funeral pyre. Just like that, Arulmozhi became an orphan.

This date for his coronation had been chosen with special care. It was the month of Karkataka, past the blazing heat of the summer months and before the drenching monsoons set in. It was the day the moon travelled through the domain of the twin stars of Punarvasu. Restorers of harmony, heralds of light and goodness, emissaries of prosperity, success, and good fortune, these bright stars, nurtured by the mother of all gods, Aditi, would watch over him and ensure a reign that matched their brilliance.

That day, the sun rose with extraordinary radiance, casting a golden glow over the land. In the distance, the Kaveri twinkled and sparkled like a sea of diamonds. The dewdrops on the paddy fields glinted before vanishing gently into the limpid air. The streets of Thanjavur, the Chola capital, had been swept to an immaculate spotlessness, perfect canvases for kolams of staggering beauty and complexity.

The hub of activity was the great Thanjavur Fort. It looked resplendent in the early morning sunshine, with flags and banners fluttering in the breeze and flower garlands adding bursts of colour and an intoxicating aroma. The heady fragrance of jasmine hung heavy in the air. Electric energy rent the air as the war drums thundered, bells and bugles, tambourines and kettle bells pealed, clanged, boomed, popped, and crackled shrilly.

In and around the fort was a sea of people—singing, dancing, laughing, cheering, going in and out of the fort, revelling in the freedom from the customary rules and restrictions. Everywhere in the city, homes were full of guests who had come from the ends of the kingdom, from the Chola lands and beyond, to witness the coronation. People who were old enough to remember reminisced about the days of endless fighting, the darkness that descended upon their lands after the brutal attacks by one Chola rival after another. But now, things were looking up and happier days were surely ahead. After all, the man who would soon be their king, Arulmozhi Varman, had been born with the most auspicious of auguries and omens; hadn't the Naga women exulted and danced with joyous abandon when he was born and, wonder of wonders, his arms had borne the marks of the conch and the wheel, incontestable proof that he was descended from none less than Lord Rama!

Inside the fort compound, the coronation hall had been adorned and had never looked grander. The world needed to be shown that there was no greater power than the Cholas. There were still a few hours left for the coronation, but the hall was full. Those who couldn't make it inside—because they were not important enough, or because they had arrived too late—would have to wait until much later to see their beloved Arulmozhi, when the newly crowned king made his way through the streets, greeting his subjects from atop his elephant.

Those who lived in the palace—among them Uttama Chola, the retiring king, his wives, Arulmozhi's wives, his sister

Kundavai—made their way into the coronation hall through a private entrance and took their seats. The prime place of honour was reserved for the diminutive yet formidable grande dame of the kingdom, Arulmozhi's great-aunt and mother of Uttama Chola, Sembiyan Madevi. She and Arulmozhi shared a special bond that had grown into an unbreakable attachment through the years, fuelled by fierce loyalty and mutual admiration. They were both people of exceptional intelligence and vision and saw in each other the potential to lift their land to its highest glory. Arulmozhi's face lit up with a warm smile when he thought of the old lady. What travails she had endured, and yet, she had never succumbed to self-pity, never shied away from her duty to her god and people. Through everything, her faith in her beloved Lord Siva never wavered, inspiring her to create ever more stunning images to worship him and adorn his temples. She had navigated the treacherous tightrope of family politics with grace and dignity. It was his immense respect for her that drove him to step aside nearly fifteen years ago and let her son, Uttama, take the reins of power. It was a wise move, he realized now, in retrospect. He would have been far too young and impetuous had he become king then. Sembiyan Madevi's wisdom had served the kingdom well, and would serve him well, too.

Arulmozhi felt the excitement surge in him as he climbed on to his lotus-flower chariot alongside his beautiful wife, Vanavanmadevi, mother of his cherished son, Rajendra. The boy was bold and daring and already showed tremendous promise.

The religious rites that ensured a prosperous reign and kingdom under the all-powerful gaze of Lord Siva were performed with soul-stirring devotion by the priests. Then, the ancient golden crown of the Chola clan, worn by every king since Vijayalaya, the nine-gem encrusted necklace, the sword and the sceptre, were placed on a giant plate and taken around the hall to be blessed by all present there.

It was now the turn of the court poet, who recited in sparkling verse the epic tale of the Chola origins and ancestry.

Arulmozhi's chest swelled with pride as he listened. What a glorious story it was, what a glittering lineage of ancestors, and now, he, Arulmozhi Varman, was going to add his name to that slate of heroes.

The one who begat the Chola line was no less than the most effulgent one of all, the Sun. A smile played about Arulmozhi's lips as he listened to the poet expound on his unmatched luminescence. The poet moved on to other great forebears, a whole slew of outstanding kings. He told the story of King Sibi. Arulmozhi listened attentively; it resonated with him, this tale of a king for whom justice and equity were all important.

The poet was an excellent raconteur. His words fell like a cascade of gems as he recounted the legend of the Chola ancestor Sibi, a just and righteous king who ruled many years ago in a faraway land. The gods wanted to test his character, to see how his principles would hold up in a difficult situation. The gods in this story were Indra and Agni. The former took the form of a hawk, who set about chasing Agni, who had transformed himself into a gentle dove. The dove, at the moment of certain capture and death at the hands of the hawk, flew into King Sibi's lap, begging for protection. Sibi cradled the terrified bird in his hands and promised to keep him safe. Soon after, the hawk flew up to Sibi and accused him of depriving him of his meal. Sibi saw that both birds had a point. But he had promised the dove he would guard him from harm, and he was a man of his word; at the same time, he realized that this meant the hawk would go hungry. A compromise was reached: he would carve out a piece of his own flesh, equal to the weight of the dove, and give it to the hawk. A scale was produced, with the dove on one side, and a growing pile of Sibi's flesh on the other. No matter how much of his flesh he gouged out, it never equalled the weight of the dove! In pain and agony, and yet determined to keep his word, Sibi mounted the scale. Still it did not tip over. At that point, the Indra and the Agni revealed themselves, blessed Sibi, and praised his tremendous integrity and courage.

Next, the adventures of a lustrous king named Chola were recounted, about how he established his kingdom on the banks of the divine river Kaveri. The great kings of the Sangam age, Karikala and Kochengannan, were praised. And then it was on to Vijayalaya, who birthed the newest chapter in the Chola book with his daring conquest of Thanjavur from the ruling Muttaraiyars. Familiar names followed, names Arulmozhi had heard from ever since he could remember: Aditya, Parantaka, Gandaraditya, Arinjaya, his grandfather, Sundara, his father, and then across patrilineal lines to Uttama and now, him. Such heroism, much bloodshed, so much catastrophe, struggle, triumph, and success.

And then, at last, it was time. Old Uttama Chola walked slowly up to him, bearing the heavy crown. With a smile, he placed it upon Arulmozhi's head. From every direction multi-coloured flowers came flying through the air, landing softly on and around him. Outside, the war drums, bugles, kettle drums, tambourines, and bells erupted into a frantic crescendo. A howl of triumphal jubilation ululated through the warm, sticky air. It could be heard for miles around.

Arulmozhi Varman was the king of the Cholas. Long live the king!

INTRODUCTION

A thousand and some years ago, there arose in southern India an empire that was among the most remarkable the world has seen. It grew atop the tottering scaffolding and shifting sands of fading dynasties and fierce rivalries, ruthless kings and double-crossing aspirants, myth-burnished, propelled forward by the slow burn of faith and the blazing fires of boundless ambition. It defied a myriad obstacles that came its way, and yet, through all the struggles and violence, it also cultivated and refined an aesthetic sensibility of breathtaking beauty.

This was the Chola empire. And in a dynasty that did not lack for larger-than-life characters, there was one in particular who stood head and shoulders above by the standards of any day.

He was Rajaraja Chola. King Squared, King of Kings, a fitting name for this multifaceted man who built one of the world's most glorious empires, for whom a single 'raja' would be pitifully inadequate, wholly unequal to the magnitude of what he accomplished. He made his mark on the vast and messy canvas of the convoluted sociopolitical dynamics of his time, no mean feat in an era teeming with ambitious and brutal rulers. He fortified the foundations of what was till then a ragtag kingdom, put into place a meticulously organized system of administration, and led the empire into a period of magnificent splendour and grandeur that reigned supreme in military might, as an economic powerhouse, and in art, architecture, literature, music, dance, and religion.

And yet there is very little accurate information about this king for the lay reader of history. Most books cede a paragraph to him and his reign; more generous ones dedicate a couple of pages. They sing his praises, but don't delve into any depth to get the measure of the man, to explore the milieu, the confluences of time, place, people, and psyche that made Rajaraja what he was, what he made of his world. There are movies on him in which imagination has run riot; there are websites that shine a spotlight on just one aspect of what must have surely been a complex, fascinating personality.

Who was this man, this King of Jewels, Incomparable Chola, Great Saviour, Jewel of the Solar Dynasty, Lion Among Kings?

He was born Arulmozhi Varman in 947, the third child of Sundara Chola and Vanavanmadevi. His older brother, Aditya Karikalan, the crown prince, was killed in suspicious circumstances, and so the younger son ended up being crowned emperor in the year 985. He was close to his older sister, Kundavai, and had a great deal of respect for his great-aunt Sembiyan Madevi. This alone must have set him apart from the typical male of his time. Rajaraja was clearly a remarkable man with an extraordinary outlook and vision, a Jupiter in a universe of small planets. Narcissistic, ambitious, power-hungry, ruthless, far-sighted, shrewd, compassionate, generous—he makes for a fascinating character study.

When Rajaraja became king in 985, he inherited a kingdom that was reeling from a shattering military defeat at the hands of a foe that rivalled the Cholas in drive and ruthlessness—the Rashtrakutas. This defeat, in 949, suffered by Rajaraja's great-grandfather Parantaka, led to a thirty-year period of Chola instability, a tangled mess of brief reigns and internal strife, with foes rearing their heads in every direction.

The supremely ambitious Rajaraja was undaunted. He aimed to reconquer every province that had been part of his predecessors' domain and even extend the empire. His vision and his ability to execute that vision set him apart and enabled him to break away from the countless petty chiefs and their little fiefdoms that his ancestors had been a part of. Over the course of his reign, he fortified and expanded what had been a collection of local villages and districts and stitched this patchwork into an imperial whole. Military campaigns until his reign had been ad hoc affairs. Rajaraja upped the ante and conducted his campaigns in a highly organized manner. He sent his troops out in all directions, pushing the Chola boundaries ever further out with his ambition and vision. He notched impressive and important wins against his dynasty's old enemies, the Pandyas and Cheras. Further north, his armies engaged in bitter fighting against the Chalukyas. Rape, looting, and plunder were the order of the day; there are reports of the 900,000-strong Chola troops (a face-saving exaggeration, perhaps?) creating havoc.[1] The Chola coffers swelled with the spoils of war.

Some of his most brutal campaigns were in Ceylon (present-day Sri Lanka). The island was drawn into the conflicts between the Pallavas and Pandyas, with the emergence of the Cholas stirring matters up still further. Rajaraja took advantage of the infighting and launched a savage attack on the capital, Anuradhapura, looting and plundering with impunity. Buddhist chronicles of the incursions highlight the devastation wrought by his troops.[2] Later in his reign, he conquered 'old islands of the sea numbering twelve thousand' thought to be the Maldives, which were staging points in the maritime trade routes of the time.

But mere conquest would not make a king worthy of superlatives. Rajaraja was interested in more than merely notching up wins against his enemies. And so, his most fascinating achievements were not his military ones, but everything he did to organize his empire, to make his kingdom an integral part of the thriving trade nexus in the lands to the east and west, to ensure that music, dance, literature, art, and architecture thrived. He was probably very conscious of leaving behind a legacy.

Among the most remarkable relics and sources of knowledge about Rajaraja's reign are the inscriptions carved on the walls of the Chola temples. There is an amazing profusion of them that provide copious, detailed facts about a multitude of aspects of the life of the times. It was quite common in other earlier dynasties to have inscriptions that narrated an emperor's family lineage and sometimes his achievements. Poetic licence often ran rampant, and the historian had a difficult task separating fact from hyperbole. Rajaraja conceived of a standardized format for the inscriptions, and this has left researchers with an unprecedented wealth of information on the chronology of events of his reign, the transactions and events of his years in power. His brilliant innovation was to add and systematize a section eulogizing the reigning monarch, a feature, taken at face value, that is of immeasurable benefit to the historian. This shows a man who was aware of the import of the position of the ruler and of his empire, and of the need to make it known. He ensured that it was updated regularly. This section, called the meykkirti, was in Tamil, and laid emphasis on historical accuracy rather than poetic flourishes.

Meykkirti, 'true fame', is invaluable as a chronological record of the king's achievements, but is also full of colourful flourishes.[3] In this new format, inscriptions had the Sanskrit prasasti (a section of the inscription in praise of rulers) with its mythological beginnings segueing into genealogical flights of fancy followed by the actual historical lineage; next came the meykkirti in Tamil listing the military and other achievements of the ruler responsible for the inscription; and finally, the actual business of what the inscription was recording, also in Tamil. New verses were added to the meykkirti as the king's reign progressed and he had more achievements, whether military, religious, or economic, to record. Rajaraja's meykkirti began with the words 'Tirumagal Pol', a distinct way to identify him.[4] Each king had his own particular meykkirti and the reigning king's name was indicated at the end. Rajaraja's meykkirtis were brief but his son Rajendra's grew increasingly longer with the years until, by the end of his reign, they were mammoth undertakings. Those of his sons became more complex and lengthier still, full of rhetorical flourishes and brimming with details of people and events connected with the king.[5] From these inscriptions, we get an idea of the structure and administration of Chola society, the various classes and castes of people, information on taxation, land revenue, village constitution, and dispute resolution. They present a picture of a well-organized society, a product of Rajaraja's vision and regulatory skills. There are disputes of opinions (as we will see later)—not surprisingly—about how centralized or decentralized the Chola bureaucracy was, but it is clear that there was a structured organization in place that resulted in a well-administered and governed kingdom.

Before, during, and after Rajaraja's time, the maritime trade routes between China and the Arab lands were busy with ships that plied these seas, laden with silks, ceramics, spices, pearls, and metals. Rajaraja realized the strategic importance of having ports along the eastern coast of his kingdom that could serve as way ports for these ships. He imposed heavy taxes on the cargoes of ships that called at his chief port, Nagapattinam. He mobilized a fleet of vessels that could have numbered as many as a 1,000 at the peak—they were used for war, trade, and distribution of supplies.[6]

Rajaraja recognized the importance of strategic friendships and alliances; brute force was fine when needed, but goodwill and large-heartedness were also very much at play. The Leiden plates, a set of inscribed copperplates that are now at Leiden University in the Netherlands, tell of the grant by Rajaraja of a village, Anaimangalam, to a Srivijaya king for the upkeep of a Buddhist vihara in the port city of Nagapattinam, where Buddhist visitors (many of them traders from the Srivijaya confederacy) could worship.

Taxes were a major source of revenue in Rajaraja's empire, and we have records, mainly from temple inscriptions, of the processes in place to collect them. The inscriptions show us once again that he believed strongly in a well-ordered, methodical way of going about things. Tax collectors collected money from a variety of businesses based on a highly codified system. Duties and penalties also contributed to the king's revenue stream, which was spent on the royal family, salaries, charity, and of course, the temples and the rich and varied life and rituals associated with them.

The most magnificent living gift that Rajaraja left behind was the striking Brihadeeshwara Temple in his capital city of Thanjavur. Completed towards the end of his reign in 1010 AD, the temple is one of the most stunning monuments anywhere in the world. At the time it was completed, it was the tallest temple in all of India.[7] What a spectacular sight it must have been—and still is—rising in majestic glory over the flat Kaveri plains, with its vast expanse of grounds, profusion of stunning sculptures, and tall vimana with its massive crown—an engineering feat in any era.

Rajaraja single-handedly created a new religious centre by building the temple where he did and in so doing, gave himself a divine seal of approval. Through its size, majesty, and beauty, he announced to the world his greatness and prestige, the dazzling achievements of his reign, his ability to harness the best to create the best temple in the known universe of his people. He poured his war booty into the temple, as did many of his subjects, eager to please him, to please their god. Rajaraja proclaimed his larger-than-life devotion to Siva with this temple; the glory, power, and munificence of Siva rubbed off on him and further enhanced his sheen and allure.

The temple became the epicentre of the kingdom, its cultural and economic heart. It was the grand unifier of Rajaraja's empire, a land of a volatile diversity of people who followed disparate cults, worshipped a variety of gods, belonged to different castes, and followed an assortment of occupations like chieftain, warlord, farmer, merchant, artisan, and priest. This grand temple served to establish his sovereignty and conferred a spiritual halo on him and his actions.

A great emperor like Rajaraja established his might and gained tremendous respect not merely because of his military prowess; he presented himself as the exemplar of the ideal ruler, one who had the moral authority and divine approval to rule over his lands and people. This did not stop him from the very essential acts—from his point of view, to shore up his finances and keep in motion his grand actions of temple building and donations—of looting and pillaging the towns in the outer borders of his empire, where the not-so-long arm of his bureaucratic machinery did not quite reach.

He had many wives but only a few children that we are aware of. His only known son, Rajendra, was an able inheritor of his legacy, and expanded the kingdom still further, invading parts of Southeast Asia and other territories. He was the yuvaraja, or king-in-training, under his father, for several years, before he became the king himself.

Rajaraja and his son believed in their own greatness, and they ensured that their subjects believed it too. They viewed themselves as more elevated royals than their foes. Their kingship had a strongly symbolic and ceremonial character to it, imbued with cosmic significance, soaked in myth and extolled in hyperbolic eulogies. They anointed themselves with grandiose titles, far loftier than what their ancestors just a few generations back had used. They elevated the idea of the god-king to a high art, worshipping images of deceased kings and erecting temples for them. This was a common mindset of kings in much of India at the time; however, Rajaraja and his son, true to form, operated on a scale grander than most.

Of course, Rajaraja did not rise in a vacuum, and the exploits and adventures of his forebears were often no less thrilling than his own. There were Cholas before him; well before him, in fact, going back a thousand years to the very earliest Cholas, whose story we know about through the brilliant poetry of their time, the poems of the Sangam poets. Those stories need to be told, too, and we will journey deep into the past, to learn about the earlier Chola dynasty, from whom the latter-day Cholas claimed descent. Then we will move forward in time to cover the events and characters that set the stage for the resurgence of the Chola dynasty and for the reign of Rajaraja and his descendants. This sparkling kingdom lived on for two and a half centuries after Rajaraja and even today we see vestiges of their greatness around us.

◆

The Cholas considered themselves kings of the solar dynasty, descendants of the most radiant one of all, the Sun himself. A vast and glittering constellation of gods, sages, and eminent kings formed their lineage. Their destiny was greatness, and they did everything in their means to achieve it, to soar to ever greater heights. Later, they joined forces with the rulers of the lunar dynasty, and together, the sun and the moon rose high in the sky before their eventual and inevitable descent into darkness, and then oblivion.

In Hindu mythology, many great kings are from solar and lunar dynasties. Interestingly, the solar dynasty features royal progenitors and characters from the Ramayana and the lunar dynasty from the Mahabharata.

The solar dynasty begins with the Sun, of course. As Rajendra Chola's Thiruvalangadu copperplate inscriptions put it so evocatively:

> The eye of the three worlds was the Sun from whom sprang the sprouts of all (families of) kings. From him (i.e. the Sun) was born by concentration (manana), Manu, the first of kings, whose name became (thus) conformable to (its) meaning.[8]

From the Sun and Manu came a line of (mythical) kings who feature in Hindu epics and the Puranas (including the family that Rama was a part of); following this, a potpourri of names that were mythical, but not necessarily from the epics or Puranas.

This is where we encounter Sibi, a just and righteous king who ruled in a faraway land—Baluchistan, in present-day Pakistan. But what does Sibi have to do with our Chola kings?

Thousands of miles and a universe away from Baluchistan, these kings claimed descent from this very Sibi. The Anbil copperplate grants, issued by Rajaraja's father Sundara Chola, tell us:

> ...from this ornament of kings was born Sibi who out of compassion protected the dove's young by offering the flesh cut out of his own body and weighed in a scale.[9]

Several of the poems of Sangam literature address a Chola king thus: 'Thou scion of the Chola line who saved the dove from woe...(*Purananuru* 37) and Descendent of him who to save a dove did enter the weighing scale....(*Purananuru* 39).'[10]

The descendants of Sibi were called 'Saibya' in Sanskrit; in Tamil, this became 'Sembiyan', a common moniker for the Cholas.[11] Other sobriquets are Killi and Valavan.

The genealogies next move on into quasi-historic territory, drawing from Tamil myth and tradition. A lustrous king named Chola enters the picture, who, after a series of adventures, establishes a kingdom on the banks of the river Kaveri.

> Then came king Rajakesarin who conquered all (*his*) enemies. After him came Parakesarin who was bent on destroying the towns of hostile kings. The name of Rajakesarin and (*that*) of this Parakesarin became alternately the order of kings born in their family.[12]

And so indeed it was—the Chola kings alternated between Rajakesari (Lion among Kings) and Parakesari (Lion to Outsiders or Enemies), and had a tiger on their emblem.

From this point, actual Chola kings follow, from the Sangam age, and then, finally, the Imperial Cholas, starting from Vijayalaya, and going on until whichever king issued the inscription.

These mythological elements serve as a way to validate and substantiate a royal family's lineage and to establish and sanction their authority. It established the king as larger-than-life, one who was descended from gods and heroes, and therefore being possessed of their qualities of divinity and heroism. The historian Romila Thapar has proposed that during periods of political fragmentation and rapid or sudden ascent to power (such as before the Imperial Cholas rose to power) fashioning lineages that demonstrated divine, solar or lunar origins played a critical role in establishing legitimacy and even erasing the family's low-caste origins. These genealogical fables drew from a common and interconnected well of stories—the Mahabharata, the Ramayana, the Puranas.[13] The myriad variations of the stories from these sources allowed for different versions of the same stories to be accepted without question. Thus, genealogical narratives that are repetitive and sometimes contradictory, and often quite obviously fabricated and far-fetched are quite common. Somewhat counterintuitively, each version can reinforce and enhance the other. Credibility, literalness, and accuracy are not the point here. Creating an idealized image, placing that image in a cultural context that is understood and revered, directing our vision through a prism of impressions and judgements—that was the aim, and surely, the Cholas succeeded.

The real-life empire arose from a divinity-touched mythic past. The medieval view of the universe was one where god, king, and commoner inhabited the world and kept it in functioning harmony.

◆

Unlike most empires, the Cholas enjoyed two separate periods of glorious efflorescence, the first in the early centuries of the first millennium, and the second, starting several centuries later and peaking high and strong in the early centuries of the second millennium.

During their first incarnation over two thousand years ago around the dawn of the first millennium, the known world stretched from the powerful Roman empire in the west to China in the east, which had expanded greatly under the Han dynasty. In between lay notable kingdoms like Parthia, Gandhara, and

Magadha. A few centuries earlier, the great Mauryan emperor Ashoka had ruled over almost the entire subcontinent of India. His kingdom lapped at the borders of the lands of the early Cholas, and his rock edicts mention the southern kingdom.[14] And many centuries later, the closing decades of the tenth century during which the Cholas succeeded in rising to prominence once again and gained a measure of stability were ones in which major events were stirring all over the world. In Europe, an unwieldy conglomeration of states seethed under a cycle of near-perpetual border wars. Amidst this chaos, a succession of Frankish kings followed the footsteps of their great ancestor Charlemagne and consolidated their hold over Rome, adding a new chapter to the history of this great city. In faraway South America the once great Mayan civilization was crumbling into ruin. Across and beyond the Arabian Sea the Fatimids of Egypt edged out the Abbasid caliphate which had ruled out of Baghdad and enjoyed a golden age of arts and learning. In China, the Song dynasty led the nation to a period of high economic prosperity and its trade policies ignited a ferment of activity that our Cholas were keen participants in.[15]

And closer to home, kings and dynasties, big and small, rose and fell much like elsewhere in the world. The Rashtrakutas, who had loomed large in the Deccan and beyond, were eclipsed by the Chalukyas. The Pala dynasty which at its peak in the early ninth century controlled much of today's Bengal, Bangladesh, Nepal, and the Gangetic plains, commenced on a long period of disintegration, finally sputtering to its demise in the twelfth century. In the north and west, a knot of Rajput tribes was engaged in constant struggle for dominion and status; of these the Gurjara Pratiharas who, one legend goes, were once lowly doorkeepers to the mighty Rashtrakutas, succeeded in breaking ahead of the pack and in seizing control over much of present-day Rajasthan and more.[16]

Through all this, the Cholas made their own history.

Their first incarnation saw some of the loveliest poetry the world has ever seen. That alas, is almost the only remnant of that time. When they rose to prominence again, they created permanent mementos of stunning beauty in their temples and sculptures, along with historical records that are unparalleled in their profusion and detail. They managed to hold together a patchwork of territories, subduing and bringing into their fold squabbling chieftains and petty kings, a dizzying mélange of sociocultural diversity, the urban elite, fiercely independent tribals, and a knotty assortment of castes. They reeled all of this into their net of bureaucracy and administrative organization that was conceived of and established with breathtaking attention to detail, creating order out of a hopeless jumble. For all this and more, historians conferred on them the Imperial designation.

What drove them? Did they operate with the vision or ambition to create an 'empire', as we understand it today? Perhaps not. Fighting and conquering were a way to establish their hero credentials, which they reinforced with their extravagant proclamations on their inscriptions. Their conquests made them richer, and they poured their booty into the most glorious and awe-inspiring temples of their time. By providing jobs and grandiose titles to distant vassals, rulers ensured that they would continue to be under their control. If anything, all their grand gestures only sat atop a constantly agitated current of uneasy and restless uncertainty. Maintaining the image and status of supreme protector and champion of the people, the chosen representative of god in their realm, the patron of poets and priests, the one whose task was the ultimate, the most exalted, the very upholder of the cosmic order, took every kind of endeavour, from fighting to conniving to praying to benevolence to largesse.

In this book we will journey through the triumphs and travails of the Cholas over their many centuries of rule and explore their multifaceted genius. The book is divided into four sections, each of which covers a particular period in Chola history.

Book One sets the stage and introduces us to the world of the earliest Cholas. We will voyage along the great Kaveri River, the life-force that provided abundant sustenance and nourishment and has borne witness to millennia of Chola history. We will read about the luminous poetry of the Tamil Sangams that captured in unparalleled fashion the ethos and events of the ancient Chola kings. We might have but a fractured knowledge about these kings, like Karikala and Kochengannan, but that makes them no less fascinating. Their names and legacies were evoked and revered long after the curtains fell on the Sangam era.

Book Two picks up the Chola story several centuries after the Sangam period. Out of a turbulent whirlpool of kings and dynasties fighting for power and dominance, a young chieftain named Vijayalaya won a crucial battle that set into motion the emergence and efflorescence of the Imperial Cholas. Through almost constant fighting and heart-crushing losses, he and his heirs managed to establish the shaky foundations of what would eventually become one of the world's truly great empires. We will read about the soaring heights and subterranean lows that Vijayalaya and his successors Aditya, Parantaka, and others experienced, paving the way for the greatest Chola of all.

Book Three is about Rajaraja, the most illustrious king of this dynasty, under whose reign the Cholas achieved their greatest glory. We will read about his military successes, how he strategically and methodically expanded and consolidated his kingdom. The rest of this section examines the many aspects of Chola life that are relevant, to varying degrees, to every Chola ruler, much of it honed under Rajaraja. We see how the society, land, and the army were organized and how crime and punishment were handled. We learn how the geopolitics of the time shaped and influenced the fascinating world of merchants and trade and how this spurred Rajaraja's daring and visionary expedition to China. Everything the Chola kings did was for their beloved Lord Siva and the Bhakti movement that took root in Tamil lands shaped the lives of Chola kings and their subjects in a myriad ways. The glorious Brihadeeshwara Temple was Rajaraja's magnificent offering to his lord. Stunning bronze idols were created that enriched the lives of the innumerable temples that dotted the land. We'll read about the lives of the Chola women, who were strong and accomplished. And we will take a brief look around Rajaraja's capital city, Thanjavur.

Book Four explores the post-Rajaraja Chola world. Rajaraja's son, Rajendra, strove to outdo his father in every measure, and he succeeded. His temple at Gangaikondacholapuram, the capital city he established, perhaps to set himself apart from his father, is one of the loveliest anywhere, a softer, gentler counterpart to his father's soaring behemoth just a few kilometres away. No empire lasts forever, and while the Chola kings enjoyed many military victories and continued to build beautiful temples, the inevitable decline started to take place in fits and starts and the once powerful Chola empire started to fracture, fragment, and then be destroyed all together. Their end came at the hands of their greatest rivals, the Pandyas.

The book ends with an Epilogue in which we will read about Rajaraja's legacy and the many ways that the Cholas are still part of the culture and life of the regions they ruled.

BOOK ONE

Setting the Stage

CHAPTER 1

THE MOOVENTAR (OR THREE CROWNED KINGS) A STORY

Once upon a time, southern India was ruled by three dynasties: the Chola, the Pandya, and the Chera.

The *Chola Purva Patayam* (Ancient Chola Record) is a palm leaf manuscript of uncertain but assuredly ancient vintage. In it is the story of a person named Salivahana, who was born in Ayodhya in a potter's hut. Salivahana acquired great power which he put to ill-use, and there was disorder and anarchy in the land. He defeated the local ruler and went about persecuting those who did not follow his ways. His wickedness caused great suffering and drought and famine ravaged the country.

The people prayed to Lord Siva for help, but his initial efforts were thwarted by the wily Salivahana. Siva realized that ordinary measures would not suffice. He went into a deep meditation; out of this first came Vira Cholan, born of the mind of Siva, followed by Ula Cheran, and Vajranga Pandiyan. Each of them was assigned a domain, and to Vira Cholan was designated the formidable task of slaying Salivahana.

A great many twists and turns followed but in the end Salivahana was vanquished thanks to the joint efforts of Vira Cholan and his cosmic brothers Ula Cheran and Vajranga Pandiyan. Vira Cholan had to pay for his crime—however evil the villain and however noble the cause of getting rid of him, killing is wrong, and he suffered various maladies on that account. He was advised by a fortune teller to build multiple temples to Siva, Vishnu, and Muruga as well as dwellings for Brahmins and ascetics. His maladies disappeared just on hearing the words of the fortune teller. The undertaking of ridding the world of Salivahana accomplished, the three kings returned to their respective domains and established their dynasties.[1]

The Cholas settled and built their kingdom around the delta of the great Kaveri River; the Pandyas, deeper south near Madurai, and the Cheras, to the west around Kerala. Together, they are referred to as Mooventar, the Three Crowned Kings.

CHAPTER 2

BEHOLD THIS KAVERI, GRACEFULLY FLOWING

Hail, Kaveri!
Robed with flowers, swarmed by singing bees,
you roam, sinuous and fanciful,
casting dark glances from your swift
and carp-like eyes.
Your gait and charming looks are the pride of your
lord, whose virtuous sceptre's never gone astray.
Hail, Kaveri!

Shilappadikaram[1]

The Kaveri originates in the forested heights of the Brahmagiri Hills of Coorg in Karnataka. Nearby, a small temple at Talakaveri marks her genesis, a humble beginning for a river worshipped and celebrated by generations of kings and commoners alike.

Here is a tale about how this great river came to be. The wedding of Siva with Parvati was imminent, and a huge crowd had gathered to celebrate in the Himalayas. Their combined weight was so much that the mountains started tilting and sinking precipitously. At this time, the southern regions teemed with cruel demonic creatures who were wreaking havoc in the land. Something had to be done, and soon. Siva ordered the pot-bellied sage Agastya, one of the original saptarishis or seven sages of Vedic lore, to go south. His mandate: to act as a counterbalance, level the land, set the demons right and restore order.

Agastya and his wife, Lopamudra, set out, armed with a pot filled with water from the Ganga. Lopamudra was the daughter of Kavera, and she was sometimes referred to as Kaveri. (In some versions of this story, Agastya carries his wife, Lopamudra /Kaveri, in his pot.)

Along the way, Agastya tamed the mighty Vindhya mountains which, jealous of the stature of the Himalayas, were growing ever taller, interfering with the cosmic workings of the sun and the moon. Once he reached the south, Agastya emptied out his pot of water which became the river Kaveri, the Ganga of the south, Dakshin Ganga.[2]

Agastya, who is called Agatthiya in the Tamil country, is revered in the south as the seminal figure who was the creator of the fertile Kaveri delta region. Even more important, he is believed to have brought the gift of the Tamil language, entrusted to him by none less than the great Lord Siva, and accounts of the first Sangam, an esteemed academy of poets, have him presiding over it, conferring his wisdom and knowledge of the language on its members. He is considered to have been the guru and mentor of the author of the *Tolkappiyam*, who relied on Agatthiya's now lost work, *Agatthiyam*, for his own.

Agastya or Agatthiya is fascinating for the multiple, somewhat conflicting perceptions there are of him; one as the bearer of Sanskrit and Vedic traditions to the south of India; the other (primarily in Tamil lands) as the father of the Tamil language and culture and of crucial importance to the Cholas, the person who blessed their land with the life-endowing waters of the Kaveri, the river goddess who 'meanders through the countryside, swinging her hips to rhythms of a flower wreath... who has fed the fertile land just as a mother feeds her child'.[3]

The Kaveri, south India's most sacred river, flows southeastwards across Karnataka and Tamil Nadu, through lush vegetation and twisted gorges, cascading in a series of spectacular waterfalls, for over 700 kilometres before emptying itself into the Bay of Bengal, south of Cuddalore in Tamil Nadu. Ancient systems of irrigation and modern hydroelectric dams dot the river and combine to make the over 72,000 square kilometres of the Kaveri basin one of the most bountiful regions of India. The great Krishnarajasagar Dam, which was completed in 1932, is a feat of engineering from more recent times. It straddles the river 20 kilometres northwest of Mysore. Abutting the dam, the Brindavan Gardens with its magical coloured fountains provides a verdant, tranquil counterpoint to the muscular might of the dam.

A further 10 kilometres on, the river splits into two and girdles the island of Srirangapatna. The story of this little rocky isle for the past several centuries has been one of siege after siege. It is home to the fort, summer palace, and tombs of Haidar Ali and Tipu Sultan, who were the bane of the British.

The Kaveri continues its journey southeastwards, past Somnathpur with its thirteenth-century Kesava Temple adorned with stunning carvings of Hoysala art, and past Talakad, once the seat of the Ganga empire in the eighth and ninth centuries and now a favourite spot for pilgrims. A little further east is Sivasamudram where the Kaveri plunges through a series of wild and narrow gorges and where the thunderous force of her descent is harvested at the hydroelectricity power plant located there.

The Kaveri River enters Tamil Nadu in the district of Dharmapuri and announces its arrival in the most spectacular way at the Hogenakkal Falls. Here, a drop in the elevation of the land, combined with the growing volume of the river, results in these breathtaking falls with their huge plume of mist and booming roar. The waters here are thought to have healing properties, as the river has flowed through forests filled with medicinal plants. The richly wooded forest all around, the towering trees, the rocky outcrops in the river, and the exhilarating mist make this one of the most beautiful places in Tamil Nadu. The carbonatite rocks in the area are believed to be among the oldest of their kind in the world.

The wild river is tamed after its thunderous incarnation at Hogenakkal. The dam at Mettur, an engineering marvel that harnesses the Kaveri's waters for irrigation and electricity purposes, subdues and tempers the river as it widens and grows in its journey through the plains, joined by the rivers Bhavani, Noyyal, and others. After sweeping past Tiruchirappalli, the river divides itself into a northern stream called the Kollidam (or Colleroon), and a southern stream which retains the name Kaveri, as it flows around the sacred island of Srirangam. On this island stands one of the holiest shrines to Lord Vishnu, the Ranganatha Temple, with its towering gopuram, thousand-pillared mandapam, and golden vimana, all celebrated in song and poetry. Nearby lies Uraiyur, capital city of the earliest Cholas, renowned during their reign for its prosperity and written about in glowing terms by the great polymath Ptolemy.

A few kilometres further on, the Kaveri and the Kollidam reunite. Here, the beds of the two rivers are at different heights; left alone, this would mean all the water from the Kaveri would get drawn into the Kollidam, leaving the delta parched and barren. It is at this point that we can see an ancient, still functioning dam, the Kallanai, also called the Grand Anicut. Literary and inscriptional evidence tell us that it was built by the early Chola king Karikala around 2,000 years ago. It is a remarkable feat of engineering. Large granite boulders were sunk into the riverbed for over a thousand feet across the river, held together by mere clay. That a stone and clay structure could control the waters of the Kaveri for so many centuries is testament to the skills of the builders of antiquity. In the early nineteenth century, the dam received a facelift and modern touches thanks to the suggestions of a British military engineer who was commissioned to look into improving the irrigation of the Kaveri delta region. The Kollidam continues its lonely journey gently northwards; dry during much of the year, it is not used for irrigation purposes. The grand temple built by the Chola monarch Rajendra Chola graces its northern bank, a reminder of a great era, rising tall in the quiet countryside.

The Kaveri flows on, and a little further downstream, near

the ancient temple city of Thanjavur, the now expansive river breaks up into innumerable streams and channels that wend their way through the verdant paddy fields of the plains, forming a massive delta. Here, in one of the most fertile places in the world, as it nears the end of its long journey, the river delivers its final, most abundant gifts, visible in the rich green that ripples as far as the eye can see. Villages and towns, each with their own temple, many dating back a thousand years and more, dot the riverbanks. The lushness seen here is one of the most soothing sights anywhere.[4]

The luscious green paddy fields and open expanses of banana, sugarcane, mango, and coconut groves come alive with the soil and waters of the Kaveri delta. In Chola times, around 70,000 acres were under cultivation. Today, over a million acres of this immensely fertile land are used for the cultivation of paddy, earning Tamil Nadu its sobriquet 'Rice Bowl of India'. Two rice crops are harvested annually, thanks to the river enjoying the bounty of both the summer rains of the southwest monsoon as well as the rainfall from the northeast monsoon that blows in from the Bay of Bengal later in the year. The dense, viscous alluvial clay of these plains, called kalimann, is ideally suited for the cultivation of rice, allowing the ideal balance of soil aeration and water drainage that is necessary for this crop.[5]

This abundant agricultural bounty was the backbone of the Cholas' prosperity. They recognized that their beloved river was like a cache of diamonds, but like any diamond, its true worth shone through when it was treated right. The river had to be harnessed, tamed, diverted, and coaxed into its best form. And here the Chola genius showed itself yet again. They built a veritable labyrinth of numerous channels and canals that crisscross the deltaic region. These range from those that are practically rivers themselves to those just a few feet across, dividing one field from the next. These canals, with their multiple sluice points ensured that the land received just the right amount of water to ensure the best output.

This ancient river has the bounce and swagger, the twinkle and vivacity of youth. It has enriched the lives of our earliest ancestors; artefacts from Stone Age dwellers have been found along its banks as have remnants of a multitude of human civilizations since. Its journey ends quietly, tamely, at Puhar, that once bustling renowned port where people from distant lands rubbed shoulders with the locals and where all enjoyed its delights. Parts of it are now lost to the sea, buried away from sight, a victim of the vagaries of time and nature.

The Coromandel coast at the Kaveri's end point is named for the Chola dynasty that drew its sustenance from its waters and soil. This is the Coromandel of Edward Lear's delightful nonsense verses, 'On the coast of Coromandel/Where the early pumpkins blow/In the middle of the woods/Lived the Yonghy Bonghy Bo'. This is the Coromandel that inspired John Masters, who wrote of the City of Pearl by the sea with its red temple towers, hump-backed bulls, perfumed flowers and spices. This is the Coromandel that was once Chola Mandalam, the realm of the Cholas.

Here the lovely Kaveri has been a silent witness and spectator to the sweep and thrust, the ebb and flow, the grandeur and the quiet moments, of millennia of history. Generations of kings bowed to her divine power and her munificence, creating and ruling kingdoms from along her banks. Today, she might be poisoned by industrial effluents, raided by the sand mafia, and choked by weeds, but she is the Eternal Kaveri, who, according to the *Shilappadikaram*, 'neither angry Saturn, nor the comets wandering in the sky, nor brilliant Venus whose descent towards the southern star is a sign of drought, can perturb....'[6]

CHAPTER 3

RED EARTH AND POURING RAIN
SANGAM LITERATURE

When you go way back, deep into the cobwebbed recesses of Indian history, dates, lifespans, and timeframes assume fantastical dimensions. History and legend, fact and mythology, humans and gods rub shoulders and bleed into each other. Meticulous accuracy is not the point here. Conveying a sense of ancientness, wonder and grandness is. And so it is with accounts of the earliest Cholas and the Tamil Sangams.

Let's start with a story that begins in the far north of India in the holy city of Varanasi. The lord of creation, Brahma, was performing a series of horse sacrifices, and once he completed the rites, he went to bathe in the river Ganga. Accompanying him were his three wives: Saraswati, Savithri, and Gayathri. Along the way, Saraswati heard the divine music of a group of celestial apsaras and stopped to listen. The music done, she hurried to the river, only to find that her husband and co-wives had completed their dip in the river and stepped out. She was furious to see that they had not had the courtesy to wait for her. The inevitable ensued: a marital spat. She snapped at Brahma. He snapped back and took matters a step further: he issued a curse. Since she had spoken in anger, Saraswati would have to repent and endure the penance of undergoing forty-eight human births.

Both Brahma and Saraswati knew the curse was excessive, but the words had been uttered, and could not be retracted. He tried to soften the blow by sketching out an attractive scenario of how things would unfold. He told her that of the fifty-one phonemes that lived in her body, forty-eight would become poets in the world and form a Sangam or academy. The great lord of Madurai, Siva, would participate with them in the Sangam and would dwell as knowledge in the hearts of all the poets, ensuring that the wisdom of poetry would be nurtured and safeguarded.

And thus, born of a quarrel, a curse, and the phonic pieces of Saraswati, the goddess of speech, the Sangam and its poets came into this world. They studied a multitude of languages including Tamil and Sanskrit and achieved proficiency in all of them.[1]

But what were the Tamil Sangams, really? And what is Tamil Sangam poetry? Popular belief and historical evidence suggest different things. The word 'Sangam', which means an organized body or academy, was first used by Nakkirar, a seventh-century commentator of a grammar of love poetry.[2] He recounted an elaborate tale about three great Tamil Sangams that thrived in the three capitals of the Pandya empire. Its members included gods, sages, kings, and regular citizens, who wrote poetry that had to fulfil high standards and requirements in order to be published. In Nakkirar's telling of the tale of the three Sangams, they lasted an improbable 4,440, 3,700, and 1,850 years, respectively. Still more far-fetched are the ages of the poets he has written about. A mythical Great Flood makes an appearance. There are many other flagrant absurdities. They do make for an interesting read, a fable dotted through with nuggets of fact.[3]

Alas, the works of the first two Sangams are almost entirely lost to us. What remains is a collection of over 2,000 poems from the third Sangam that are of breathtaking sophistication and beauty and make up the corpus of what we call Sangam literature. And borne on the timeless words and emotions of these poems, we are transported directly into the minds, landscapes, and chronicles of the early Cholas who lived, loved, fought, traded, and ruled in the region around the delta of their beloved Kaveri. They are our primary source of their history that took place two millennia ago. We might not have hard facts and figures but instead, a whiff, a delectable fragrance, an essence, that is evocative and educative in a very different, but no less enlightening, way.

Pinning down dates for the Sangams from Nakkirar's account is well-nigh impossible. Fortunately, we are not entirely awash in a sea of inconsistency. There are accounts from other ancient historical works like the *Periplus of the Erythrean Sea* and Ptolemy's *Geographia* that have many points of similarity with the descriptions and accounts in Sangam poetry. Archaeological discoveries of Roman coins as well as evidence of a linguistic and prosodic nature lend further clarity. Many of the people and events written about are of a historical or quasi-historic nature and can be compared against other accounts. Taking all these together, it is now generally agreed that the era of the third Sangam was between 100 BCE and 250 CE.[4]

Sangam poetry probably began as an oral tradition. These poems have all the informal charm of something that is to be enjoyed aurally in contrast to a more formally composed poem that aims for a different kind of impact with written words. Several centuries after they were written, probably during the eighth or ninth century, they were gathered into anthologies. Medieval scholiasts further anthologized and codified the poems, which were the subject of elaborate commentaries, annotations, and interpretations.

For many centuries after that Sangam poetry languished in dusty oblivion, etched on to crumbling palm leaves, keeping company with white ants, mould, and mouse-droppings in lofts and attics in towns and villages scattered over Tamil Nadu. In the nineteenth century, as the printing press became popular in India, several people did stellar work in lifting these poems from obscurity and building awareness about them beyond the milieu of experts and scholars. Among the most prominent was U. V. Swaminatha Iyer, a legendary figure in the world of Tamil literature who went by the affectionate appellation of Tamil Thatha. In his autobiography, he described a momentous meeting that took place on 21 October 1880, a Thursday, that forever changed him and his life's work and the fate of Sangam literature.

Swaminatha Iyer had been recently appointed the Tamil pundit at the Government College in Kumbakonam. He had been the star student of Meenakshisundaram Pillai, a Tamil scholar and poet with outstanding intellectual credentials and accomplishments and was in good measure proud of this fact. Also recently arrived in Kumbakonam was a Ramaswamy Mudaliar, who had been transferred there as munsif or judge. He had a reputation of being a brilliant and learned young man, highly knowledgeable in Tamil, Sanskrit, and classical music. Swaminatha Iyer was advised to meet the newcomer and he did, his reluctance notwithstanding. He went in there, confident and secure in his knowledge, certain that he would impress. He came out a changed man, humbled by his discovery of a world far more vast, ancient, and complex that he had all this while been in the dark about.

The meeting got off to a cool start. The munsif 'spoke with the indifference one shows to a stranger in whom one has no interest'. Swaminatha Iyer was disquieted to see that his host was unimpressed by his educational pedigree and by what he had read (he considered himself, until that point, to be supremely well-read and well-informed on Tamil literary matters). It didn't seem to matter how many, or how difficult, were the works that Swaminatha Iyer claimed expert knowledge of; Ramaswamy Mudaliar remained unmoved by the litany of names. His reaction was, 'What is the use of all these books?' and 'Is that all? Haven't you read any old books?' He then proceeded to name a few: *Jeevaka Chintamani. Manimekalai. Shilappadikaram.*

Swaminatha Iyer had to confess, in shame and dismay, that no, he had not read them, or even heard of some of them. And talking to Ramaswamy Mudaliar, he realized that there was an entire universe of Tamil literature, older than anything he had encountered thus far, but of a sophistication, beauty, and style that boggled his mind. He changed the course of his life and work to track down these works, and edit, annotate, and print them. He devoted the rest of his life to travelling throughout the Tamil lands, leaving no stone unturned in his efforts to ferret out manuscripts from attics, monasteries, and storerooms.[5]

Swaminatha Iyer and his peers—foremost being his peer and friendly rival, Damodaram Pillai—rescued old manuscripts and brought these ancient works into the modern world and into wide circulation.

Today, what we know as Sangam literature consists of a 'grammar', the *Tolkappiyam*, from the Second Sangam, and two anthologies from the Third Sangam. These are the Eight Anthologies (*Ettuttokai*) and the Ten Idylls or Long Poems (*Pattupaattu*). There are some scholars who include the great epics *Shilappadikaram* and *Manimekalai* in the Sangam corpus, though those who are not in this school of thought point out the difference in language as well as the entire ideological, social, and cultural milieu of these as proof that they were written at a later date, after the sun had set on the Sangam era.[6]

The *Tolkappiyam* has been described as one of the most brilliant works of Tamil literature. Calling it a 'grammar' of the Tamil language is to do it great injustice as we probably imagine something along the lines of what a modern grammar textbook covers. This most ancient of all Tamil literary works is exhaustively wide and deep. In its present-day form, it consists of three books, each with nine chapters. The first book deals with the sounds of ancient Tamil and their production—phonetics, phonology, and graphemics. The second book is all about words and is concerned with etymology, morphology, semantics, and syntax. The third book covers the subject matter of literature and is therefore of tremendous value from a sociological, psychological, and cultural viewpoint.

It is in this third book of the *Tolkappiyam* that we encounter the broad categories of ancient Tamil literature—Akam and Puram—and their literary conventions.

Akam poetry deals with the inner landscape of the mind.

These poems are tender, intimate and private, and recount the trials, tribulations, and joys of that eternally and universally popular emotion—love. Five different geographical landscapes that form the topography of the Tamil lands are each linked to a particular emotional state, a brilliantly evocative literary device that connects the outer world to the inner one. The landscapes are named for a flower that grows in the region; each landscape serves as the setting for a particular type of love story or situation.

Thus, the worlds of love and longing, trysts and separation, infidelity, heartbreak, and resentment come beautifully alive in the Akam poems. With photographic clarity and vibrant, descriptive language full of details and metaphors, they invite us into the world of the Sangam lovers. These lovers, and sometimes their friends, or close relatives, speak directly to us; it is their voice we hear, not the poet's. The level of detail of the landscape—the flora, the fauna, the seasons, and so much more—is breathtaking; more stunning still is how these are used to evoke the complexities of human relationships.

The hills and mountainsides of the kurinci (kurinji) flowers are where lovers meet, often clandestinely, in the delicious flush of early love. The forests and pastures where the mullai (jasmine) spreads its fragrance are the setting for patiently waiting lovers and domestic contentment. As the relationship progresses, there are the inevitable scenes of sulking and even unfaithfulness. Sangam poetry sets these in the agricultural croplands and plains, the abode of the marutam or queen's flower. We have the poems of restless, angst-filled waiting and secret meetings at nightfall on the seashore with its neytal or blue lily flowers and seagulls, crocodiles, and sharks. And finally, the barren stretches that many relationships have to endure, perhaps due to family disapproval, the (male) lover's call to battle or travel to a faraway place, find expression (aptly) in the bleak environments of the palai (desert tree), the parched wastelands laid bare by the scorching heat of summer.[7]

These beautiful poems are anywhere from three to 800 lines in length. We know of over 400 poets, although more than half the poems are composed by a very prolific group of just sixteen poets. Among the best known of the Sangam poets are Kapilar and Ammuvanar. The poets were masters and mistresses of metaphor, and many of them came to be known and identified by a particular turn of phrase or striking metaphor. In one of the loveliest of the Sangam poems, from the anthology called *Kuruntokai*, a man tells his lover,

> What could my mother be
> to yours? What kin is my father
> to yours anyway? And how
> did you and I meet ever?
> But in love our hearts are as red
> earth and pouring rain:
> mingled
> beyond parting.[8]

The poet is called Cempulappeyanirar, which means the Poet of the Red Earth and Pouring Rain.

Sangam poetry is largely secular, although there are occasional religious references. In fact, it is the only example of secular Indian literature from such an ancient age. The poems describe a world that is achingly real, with people who could have lived anywhere, anytime.

The majority—around three-quarters of the total corpus—of Sangam poetry belongs to the Akam genre. In contrast to the intimate, private world of the Akam poems are the Puram poems. These deal with the outside world, the realms of politics and war, kings, and heroes. Where the voices in Akam poems belonged to nameless, anonymous, everyday people, Puram poems are often about specific people, places, and events. Court poets and war bards wrote about the lives and incidents of their rulers and patrons and gave vivid descriptions of daily life, food, festivals, trade, and commerce in the towns, villages, and countryside of the time.

And it is through these Puram poems that we get a glimpse into the people, places, and events that made ancient Tamil—and Chola—history.

CHAPTER 4

THE KING WITH THE CHARRED LEG AND OTHER EARLY CHOLAS

Karikala Chola is one of the greatest of the early Cholas who lived sometime during the latter part of the second century CE. It is impossible, so many centuries later, and peering through the murky lens of accumulated myths and exaggerations, to know exactly when he lived and reigned. There are some who believe that there were two Karikalas, grandfather and grandson, which is impossible to prove or disprove.[1]

Karikala's reputation loomed so large even during his time that he has been written about in both Akam and Puram poems. A lady potter, a lame weaver of flower garlands, and war and court bards are among those who have written about him. Piecing together these fragments, we have learned what we know about this greatest of the early Cholas. He was a fierce and fearless warrior, a far-sighted and visionary promoter of trade and agriculture, a lover and generous patron of literature, music, and dance and a fine musician himself, a true renaissance man, one who enjoyed life's pleasures and lived it to the full.[2]

Life was not easy for Karikala. One of the long Puram poems, *Porunaraatruppadai*, the Guide for War Bards, tells us that he inherited the throne while still in his mother's womb. His father, Ilancetcenni, praised for 'being bright as the sun in his chariot, the owner of many spears of victory, and with a triumphant army of foot-soldiers, cavalrymen, charioteers and those who fought mounted atop elephants',[3] had an untimely demise while his wife, a princess from a nearby minor royal family, was pregnant with Karikala.

The situation was ripe for intrigue and plots and Karikala's early years were filled with upheaval and uncertainty. Loyalties and ties were tenuous and in constant flux. Karikala was thrown into prison. He may have burned his leg in a fire in the prison, one reason for his moniker: kari means charred; and kala, leg. The story of his gutsy escape and subsequent rise to power is a favourite with several poets.

Kannanar, the author of *Pattinappalai*, one of the longer Sangam poems, writes:

> Like the tiger cub with its sharp claws and its curved stripes growing (strong) within the cage, his strength came to maturity (like wood in grain) while he was in the bondage of his enemies. As the large-trunked elephant pulls down the banks of the pit (in which it has been caught) and effects its escape by filling in the pit, and joins its mate, even so after deep and careful consideration, he drew his sword, effected his escape by overpowering the strong guard (of his prison), and attained his glorious heritage in due course.[4]

Through sheer grit, Karikala prevailed and is believed to have ascended the throne at a very young age. He set about fortifying and protecting his kingdom and defeating those who dared turn against him. His military prowess struck terror through the land. *Porunaraatruppadai* tells us that his enemies, who had not known his strength at first, bowed to him later, and that those who did not obey suffered great distress. Karikala was reputed to be fierce in appearance, like an angry Lord Murugan.

Then came the big event of Karikala's reign, the one he is best known for—the Battle of Venni. Today Venni—called Kovil Venni—is a little village a few kilometres east of Thanjavur. Here, nearly 2,000 years ago, raged a battle that has been written about in so many Sangam-era poems, that it almost certainly took place, and was of great import. To quote one poem,

> On the plain of Venni where fine toddy is made, the great Karikala met the famous kings in battle. On the battlefield he destroyed their drum and put down the two kings and eleven Velir chiefs.[5]
>
> Karikalan wearing a garland sweet to behold ruined the two Great Kings with his fierce effort at Venni—Pandiyan wearing a strand braided with beautiful, tender, saw-edged leaves of neem with black branches, and Cheran wearing a tender palmyra frond strand, on their lifted, large heads.[6]

We know nothing of the circumstances that led to this battle, but it represented a turning point in Karikala's life. Southern India at the time was ruled by the Pandyas in the deep south, the Cheras to the west, and the Cholas in and around the delta of the Kaveri River, in addition to countless chieftains who controlled small territories and constantly shifted allegiance to one or other of the major rulers. Several poems tell us that the Chera ruler, rather than submit to the ignominy of defeat, committed suicide, possibly by starvation.

> The valiant king got a wound on his back from one whom he regarded as a king equal to him in status and (so) slew himself.[7]

There was no looking back after this. Karikala's reputation as a fearsome fighter was established. He further consolidated his position and reputation at a battle at Vahaiprandalai in which he defeated a coalition of chieftains who had ganged up against him. He ravaged the towns of his enemies, looted and destroyed their fields, ponds, prayer and concert halls. One by one, he vanquished them all—the Oli chiefs, the Aruva kings, the Tennavan and Irunkovel kingdoms, the kings of the north and west. A few centuries on, the legends of his heroism remained undiminished, and his 'northern' conquests found mention in the great Tamil epic, the *Shilappadikaram*.

> Once King Tirumavalavan [Karikala] wandered along all the frontiers of his realm, vainly seeking a monarch deserving the honour of battle. In the far north, he thought, he might meet adversaries more worthy of his sword. So on an auspicious day he ordered that his lance, his parasol, and his war drum be brought. He prayed to his genie, asking for the favour of an opponent mighty enough for his shoulders. Then he marched northwards and ever northwards until only the Himalayas, the abode of the gods, was able to stop him. There he carved on the face of the king of mountains his own emblem, the lion, and returned in glory.[8]

Did Karikala march all the way north to the Himalayas? Is this another instance of the myth overtaking the man? Does it actually matter, because what these tales and poems really tell us is that Karikala's image and reputation was larger than life. And that showed in so many aspects of his reign. He was not intent on fighting and conquering alone. He established a kingdom that was known for its prosperity, trade, music, dance, food, and festivals. He converted forests into arable land, encouraging agriculture and the fertile abundance of crops that made the region so prosperous. He tried to tame the Kaveri, prone to flooding and destruction during heavy rains, by shoring up its banks. He is believed to have been responsible for an ancient dam across the Kaveri called the Kallanai (Grand Anicut), a series of boulders that controlled the flow of water to ensure even and balanced irrigation.

In the early years of his reign, his capital was at Uraiyur. It is on the banks of the Kaveri, near present-day Trichy, around 60 kilometres from the later Chola capital of Thanjavur. Sangam-era poems provide us with vivid descriptions of a vibrant, prosperous place: a big town with vast landing and unending prosperity. Trade and commerce were brisk and a wide range of items were up for barter—honey, yams, fish oil, toddy, sugarcane, flattened rice, meat, and wine.

The poet Mudathamakkaniyar who wrote the *Porunaraatruppadai* describes Karikala's generosity of spirit, his hospitality towards him, an impoverished poet. He likens his arrival at the palace of Karikala in Uraiyur to that of a bird that flies to a fruit-bearing tree. He describes his entrance into the palace grounds through the beautiful gateway that was never closed to those in need. When he met Karikala, he writes, he was treated like a relative, and his kindness and warmth made him melt like warm wax. The king himself removed his torn, sweaty, louse-infested clothes and gave him new clothes that were so fine that the weave was invisible to the eye. The royal treatment continued as our poet was plied with liquor, served in gold bowls by beautiful women, and serenaded by lutes and drums. He was fed rich meat, perfectly cooked rice that looked like jasmine buds, sweets, and many other dishes and was urged to keep eating, even after he was full. Night and day he ate, this once starving poet, until he could barely breathe and hated the very idea of food![9]

Later in his reign, Karikala moved his capital from Uraiyur to the port city of Kaveripattinam, which was also known by various other names like Kaveripoompattinam, Pattinamam, Puhar, and Poompuhar. This ancient port city, situated in present-day Nagapattinam district near where the Kaveri empties itself into the Bay of Bengal, enjoyed tremendous renown in its heyday. It was involved in trade to and from places near and far. Its fame was such that it finds mention in the *Periplus of the Erythrean Sea* (circa 50 CE), an account of a Greek merchant who travelled and traded around the Erythrean Sea, which in the Greco-Roman world included the Red Sea, Persian Gulf, and Indian Ocean. Around a century later, Claudius Ptolemy an Alexandrian mathematician, produced his *Geographia*, his mapping of the world based on, among other things, peripli (travel documents), many of which were highly unreliable, the tools of mathematics and science of his time, and the extremely limited knowledge that was available then. Still, his work is invaluable in giving us a wealth of information and detail that we would otherwise not have. He describes 'Khaberis' (widely acknowledged as Kaveripattinam) as an emporium, and while his geographical coordinates for the place are off, and his references to the nomad tribe of Soras (Cholas) hazy, the fact they have merited mention in this ancient work by an esteemed scholar who had never set foot in India is telling and points to the widespread renown Kaveripattinam must have enjoyed at the time.

For the most detailed and delightful accounts of Kaveripattinam, we must turn once again to our Sangam poets.

One of the best sources for this is the *Pattinappalai* by Kannannar. Palai poems, as we saw in the previous chapter, are those that deal with the separation of lovers. Pattina(m) refers to Kaveripattinam. In (presumably) telling his lover that he needs to go to Pattinam, Kannannar narrates the glories of the place which was surely the centre of the Chola universe then. So lifelike and comprehensive are the details that it reads like an eyewitness account.

Pattinappalai describes a city that consisted of a dynamic harbour and port area, as well as an urban centre further inland. The harbour bustled with the activity of ships loading and unloading their precious cargoes. The customs house, watched by loyal guards who safeguarded the wealth of their king, stamped the royal ensign of the Chola tiger on all goods before they crossed into Chola territory. The area near the sea and harbour was where the fisherfolk, foreign traders, and shipbuilders lived; further inland were the homes—nay, mansions—of the wealthy, that were so tall that they touched the clouds and needed many stairs to reach the upper levels. The streets of this prosperous town, guarded by the gods, were filled with akil and sandal from the Western Ghats, pearls from the southern seas, corals from the east, and products from as far away as the Ganga, Lanka, and Burma! In this fertile land blessed by the bounteous Kaveri where sugarcane, paddy, coconut, areca nut, turmeric, mango, and palmyra grew in fecund abundance, the people, under Karikala's benevolent rule, enjoyed music and dance, and worshipped Lord Murugan in joyous street festivals.

A few centuries after *Pattinappalai*, another exemplar of classical Tamil literature, the great epic *Shilappadikaram*, had many verses of praise on Kaveripattinam or Puhar. The city lacked for nothing, with its vendors of unguents, bath powders, cooling oils, flowers, perfume, fine silks coral, sandalwood, pearls, gold, precious gems. People made a living as traders, washermen, bakers, vintners, fishermen, coppersmiths, carpenters, goldsmiths, tailors, shoemakers, and musicians; in the centre of the city was the wide royal street, the street for the temple cars, the main bazaar, and the homes of the rich merchants; in other parts lived the less wealthy coachmen, bards, dancers, clowns, prostitutes, florists, servants, and others. What a testament it is to both Karikala and his times that such a place did exist, and with such an esprit de la vie that it ignited the imagination of the best poets and chroniclers of its time.

Today, Kaveripattinam, or Poompuhar, is an unassuming seaside town, a far cry from the major urban centre it was in the ancient world. While there is nothing on land to show for its one-time greatness, underwater excavations have revealed evidence of buildings, wharves, and piers of an ancient harbour.

As for Karikala, the greatest of the ancient Cholas, nothing is known about the circumstances of his death, but his passing was mourned in poetry:

'He who stormed his enemies' forts dauntlessly, who feasted his minstrels and their families...performed sacrifices, according to Vedic rites...He, the great and wise king is alas! no more.'[10]

After Karikala, the frayed and sparse threads that we have in the ancient literature are too meagre to weave together a coherent narrative. It appears that there was a great deal of civil strife and the old rivals—the Pandyas, Cheras, and assorted chieftains—were at each other's throats again. Many of Karikala's hard-fought gains came to naught as the Pandyas and Cheras regained some of their lost territories, and the Cholas themselves broke up into several sections that each claimed dominance over a particular territory.

There were the synchronously named Nalankilli (the Good Killi) and Nedunkilli who may or may not have been brothers and who may or may not have been Karikala's sons. But it does appear that they belonged to rival factions of the Cholas, one who ruled from Uraiyur, and the other from Kaveripattinam. The Cholas, who had barely come together as what could be considered a cohesive unit in Karikala's time, split into battling groups. These were not peaceful times, with the constant fighting for power and domain.

Nalankilli, who ruled from the booming port city of Kaveripattinam, appeared to have had the upper hand. He has found mention in no fewer than fourteen Sangam era poems, most of which tell of the great amount of time he spent on the battlefield, fending off enemies and trying to keep his kingdom together. Nedunkilli, in the meantime, seized control of Uraiyur.

Poems portray Nedunkilli as possessing a doomed and distasteful combination of ambition and cowardliness, an unheroic and indecisive leader who shut himself up behind high walls which resulted in the suffering of his citizens.

> Children cry for want of milk, women tie their hair without flowers, people weep and wail for want of water to drink.[11]

Internecine warfare is never a good thing. The constant conflict and upheaval begat unhappiness and gloom. The poet Kovur Kilar addressed Nedunkilli and Nalankilli thus:

> Your enemy is not the kind who wears
> the white leaf of the tall palmyra
>
> nor the kind who wears garlands
> from the black-branched neem trees.
>
> Your chaplets are made of laburnum,
> your enemies are made of laburnum too.

When one of you loses
the family loses

and it is not possible
for both to win.

Your ways show no sense of family:
they will serve only to thrill
alien kings

whose chariots are bannered,
like your own.[12]

In the end, piecing together accounts from the epic *Manimekalai* and the *Purananuru* poems, it has been inferred that Nalankilli defeated Nedunkilli at a battle in Kariyaru. And with that the civil strife between the rival Chola branches appears to have come to an end.

Nalankilli was now the acknowledged ruler, but his reign was not a success. The country was in a shambles after the civil war. Nalankilli might have been a good man, but he was an indifferent ruler, and suffered the flaw of excessive pride and a tendency to boast. He did manage to capture several fortified towns in the Pandya country, and died after a short and not particularly noteworthy reign.

The next emperor after Nalankilli was Killivalavan. His path to the throne was not easy. No fewer than nine Chola princes joined forces, revolted, and sought to knock him out of his position and divide up the kingdom. Fortunately for Killivalavan, his cousin, Chenguduvva Chera came to his aid, dealt all nine princes a stinging defeat, and helped consolidate Killivalavan's position.

It was now time for revenge, to punish those who had dared support the breakaway princes. A chief named Malayaman had done just that, and he paid the price with his life. Killivalavan did not stop there. Malayaman had two young sons, and Killivalavan, a hot-headed young man, was all set to have them trampled to death under the feet of elephants, when the poet Kovur Kilar stepped in and stopped the brash young king.

> You come from the line of a Cola king
> who gave his flesh
> for a pigeon in danger,
> and for others besides,
>
> and these children also come
> from a line of kings
> who in their cool shade
> share all they have....
>
> Look at these children,
> the crowns of their heads are still soft.
>
> As they watch the elephants,
> they even forget to cry....
>
> Now that you have heard me out,
> do what you will.[13]

Kovur Kilar's words moved Killivalavan sufficiently; the little children were spared.

We imagine poets as being a world apart from the seamy, bloody realms of politics and war, and yet the Sangam poets were in the thick of it, not merely as chroniclers, but also as mentors and philosophical guides. Were their words addressed directly to the king? Or conveyed through a messenger? We have no answers, but we do have a fascinating insight into the influence the poets and their poetry might have wielded.

Killivalavan made an unsuccessful attempt at capturing Pandya territory. The Pandya commander Palayan Maraiyan roundly trounced his forces. The *Purananuru* poets are silent about this defeat, but a poem by Nakkirar in the *Ahananuru* makes a trenchant reference to his loss.[14]

Killivalavan next trained his sights on the Chera capital of Karur. It was a great military success for the king but the city of

Karur, laid to siege, was subjected to brutal attacks. The buildings, walls, fields, and gardens outside the city walls were destroyed. Once again, a poet tried to intercede to stop the carnage. He was unsuccessful and the fair city of Karur was ravaged.

Killivalavan had multiple wives. One of them, Sithathakai, was the daughter of a king who claimed descent from Mahabali, the king who was humbled and subdued by the dwarf-god Vamana. Killivalavan and Sithathakai had a son, Udaya Kumar, a handsome and promising young lad who was killed one night in the prime of his life. Killivalavan had another son, by another wife who was a Naga princess who lived in Manipavallam. He sent for this son, who was put on a merchant vessel which set sail on a dark and stormy night. When the storm cleared, the young price was found to be missing. Frantic searches were conducted up and down the coast, to no avail.

Killivalavan heard the news of his son's tragic fate just as the festival to the king of gods, Indra, was getting underway. The grief-stricken king abandoned the festival and set out in search of his son.

That night, a terrible tsunami storm tore along the coast and crashed over Kaveripattinam, Killivalavan's capital, and destroyed it. This was the terrible revenge of the ocean goddess Manimekalai, her punishment to the people of Kaveripattinam for failing in their duty to honour the god Indra.

Legend tells us that Killivalavan had a son, Tondai, by the Naga princess. It is unclear if this was the son who vanished at sea or another one. This prince went on to rule Tondaimandalam, in the northern part of present-day Tamil Nadu. Tondai's descendants would later come to be known as the Pallavas.[15]

Killivalavan died soon after his capital city was destroyed. His large-hearted spirit lives on in the words of the poet Alattur Kilar:

He is Killi Valavan,
    he wears perfect garlands,

his ornaments are flames
of yellow gold.

Go to him,

and you don't even have to stand
at his great door.

Go, fill your eyes
with the chariots he gives away
in broad daylight.
Once you've seen him,
you'll wear lotuses of gold, flowers
no bee will touch,

and you don't even have to stand
there, at that door.[16]

After him, there followed a slew of minor kings, and then came the last known of the great Sangam Chola kings.

This was Kochengannan, the King of the Red Eyes. What we know of him is a mix of the fantastical and quasi-historic, and the two have become inextricably woven together. Much of what we know of Kochengannan's actual history is from a poem called 'Kalavali' that is part of the *Purananuru* anthology, written by the poet Poigaiyar.

Kalavali is a forty-verse poem that contains gruesome descriptions of a battle near Karur, which was then a part of Chera territory. Kochengannan defeated the Chera king and took him prisoner. The poet Poigaiyar, a friend of the Chera king, sang the praises of Kochengannan and his valour on the battlefield (the substance of much of 'Kalavali') and by appealing to his vanity succeeded in getting the Chera king released from captivity.

This great king who distinguished himself on the battlefield was also a deeply religious man. And this is where his story takes a turn into the terrain of fantasy.

The great Saivite Nayanmar poets of the seventh and eighth centuries, Sambandar and Sundarar, sang of Kochengannan building multiple temples to Siva. Centuries after he died, his name would make its way into a tenth-century copperplate inscription by another Chola king called Sundara Chola who wrote of 'the king called Kochengannan, who built temples for the lord of Gauri (that is, Siva) in all the countries'.[17]

Fast forward to the twelfth century, and Kochengannan's story morphed beyond all recognition. In a book on the lives of the sixty-three Saivite saint-poets or Nayanmars called the *Periya Puranam*, he joined their elite ranks, complete with a story that could only have been conjured up by the liveliest imagination.

The story weaves an intricate web. Prior to his birth as a king, Kochengannan was a spider, supremely devoted to Lord Siva. Every day, he wove a web around the Siva lingam at the local temple, to protect it from insects and other detritus. And every day, a zealous white elephant pulled the web apart. One day, in an unfortunate encounter with the elephant, the pious spider lost his life. Lord Siva blessed his faithful devotee and with his divine benediction caused him to be born again, in human form.

And thus, Kochengannan was born, but not without a struggle. His parents, who had prayed long and hard for a child at the temple at Chidambaram, had their prayers answered at last, but realized that the child's birth would happen during an inauspicious time. In order to postpone the delivery until a propitious time came around, his mother suspended herself upside down. As a result, when Kochengannan was born—at a felicitous hour, after all—his eyes were bloodshot giving him his name, which means the King of the Red Eyes.[18]

The story of the early Cholas comes to a close here, but the Chola dynasty would rise again. Many centuries later, they would be reborn with a new line of ambitious, fearless kings. Rising to greatness seemingly out of nowhere, they claimed descent from great Sangam Chola kings like Karikala and Kochengannan.

These names found their way into the later Chola genealogies alongside the Sun, Manu, and a whole host of mythical and quasi-mythical people.

In the centuries that passed between one line of Cholas and the next, other regimes rose to power, and the inevitable march of time and history pushed them into the shadows. There, they waited, the once-renowned Cholas, living small, unremarkable lives.

Until a fateful day in 850.

BOOK TWO

Dawn's Early Light

CHAPTER 5

BEFORE DAWN
SOUTH INDIA ON THE EVE OF THE CHOLA RESURGENCE

Before we begin the story of the Imperial Cholas, let us set the stage by seeing what was afoot in southern India, to try and make sense of the churning turbulence out of which they emerged.

The Sangam Cholas had faded into obscurity by the third or fourth century. After that there was a period of around three hundred years about which very little is known. Historians refer to it as the Kalabhra Interregnum.[1] The Kalabhras are a bit of an enigma. When and whence they came remains largely unknown. A fifth-century writer named Buddhadatta wrote in glowing terms of a Kalabhra king Achutta Vikkanta who 'ruled the earth'.[2] Literature says this Achutta kept the Pandya, Chera, and Chola kings in confinement.[3]

The Kalabhras were roundly denounced as evil interlopers who upset the existing order (such as it was), dethroning the rightful rulers of the land and helping themselves to funds intended for religious or charitable purposes. The Pandyas had a particularly biting view of the Kalabhras, unsurprising considering the havoc that the latter's army wreaked on their lands. The Velvikudi grant of the Pandyas writes of a 'Kali king named Kalabhran [who] took possession of the extensive earth driving away numberless great kings'; it refers to them in the plural and mentions their 'oceanlike' army.[4] They are reviled as uncivilized, for having destroyed the Pandya kingdom around the third century. This is a somewhat harsh characterization; it is very likely that it was during their time that some seminal works of Tamil Jain and Buddhist literature were written, including the epics *Shilappadikaram* and *Manimekalai*.

These Kalabhras have always been referred to as 'mysterious'; perhaps they were a warlike tribe rather than dynastic rulers with an interest and ability to form an empire. They made inroads into Pandya and Pallava lands. They appear to have inspired terror in those they conquered, going after local chieftains and Brahmin priests with ferocity. They were Buddhist; some of their leaders might have followed the Jain faith, and during this period these religions enjoyed the support of people of wealth and power.

Around the end of the sixth century, the reign of the Kalabhras came to an end, and the Pallavas and Pandyas slowly made their way back to dominance, the Pallavas in the northern Tamil region, and the Pandyas far down south. Evidence of this is in the copperplate grants and inscriptions that write of their re-emergence under Simhavishnu and Kadungon respectively.[5] They were each other's greatest and most irksome rivals. In between, in the deltaic region of the Kaveri, a messy conglomeration of petty and not-so-petty chieftains were locked in a pitched struggle for territory and supremacy. The entire region was a swirling mass of rivalries between dynasties whose power waxed and waned, dependent on the support of an assortment of principalities.

The Cholas at this time barely bear mentioning. As bit players on the landscape, reduced to the ignominy of occupying a mere buffer zone, they inhabited the turbulent frontier land between two rival powers. This once dominant power had to suffer the indignity of its lands being trampled over by the upstart Pallavas and old foes Pandavas. Their territory, encompassing some of the most fertile lands in the region, was sought after for its agricultural fecundity, among other things. The Pallavas and Pandyas were by no means secure; not for a moment could they assume that their position was stable. These kingdoms had their spheres of power and influence but further out in the hinterlands, their control was tenuous at best, and loyalty had to be secured and maintained with muscle, threats, guile, and gifts and marital alliances.

There was the constant push-and-pull of conquering, looting, and pillaging, along with generous offerings to temples as well as sharing the spoils of war with allies and important people. We have no idea if a guilty conscience spurred the generosity, or a fervent hope that it would restore cosmic justice, but this was the order of the day.

Hiuen Tsang (Xuanzhang), a Buddhist monk, scholar, and traveller from China visited south India during the first half of the seventh century. He visited Kanchipuram, the Pallava capital around 640 CE. At that time, the Chola country, which he referred to as Chu-li-ya or Chulya and its capital, Uraiyur, covered a small area. The land was one of jungles and marshes, wild and rugged, and with brigands operating freely. He made no mention of a king, which probably meant that there was no one of consequence in power. He has nothing nice to say about it; his words are, in fact, harsh:

> The country of Chulya [Chola] is 2400 or 2500 li in circuit; the capital is about 10 li round. It is deserted and wild, a succession of marshes and jungle. The population is very small, and troops of brigands go through the country openly. The climate is hot; the manners of the people dissolute and cruel. The disposition of the men is fierce; they are attached to heretical thinking. The sangharamas are ruined and dirty as well as the priests.[6]

From Chulya, Hiuen Tsang carried on north, past a wild forest district, to what is assumed to be Kanchipuram. His opinion of the place is striking, especially for the contrast to what he wrote of the Cholas and their country. 'The soil is fertile and regularly cultivated and produces an abundance of grain. There are also many flowers and fruits. ...[T]he character of the people [is] courageous. They are deeply attached to the principles of honesty and truth...and highly esteem learning.'[7]

The decades from the last quarter of the eighth century through the beginning of the ninth century saw a restless, seething land caught in the grip of multiple power struggles. Two great powers who had been at each other's throats were now exhausted: the Western Chalukyas were fading into the shadows, and the once mighty Pallava dynasty was beginning to fragment and shrink, and would linger a little while before joining their old foes in the graveyard of once great dynasties. The Rashtrakutas rose to prominence and power, taking over the erstwhile stomping grounds of the Western Chalukyas. And deep to the south, the mighty Pandyas ate away at each other from within. Internal dissensions spelled doom for their prospects, although it would be a long while yet before their star set.

Into this messy strife stepped the Cholas.

It is customary to write of the resurgence of the Cholas as a bursting forth from a prolonged period of darkness. The reality is more nuanced. To use the historian Nilakanta Sastri's words, they emerged from a state of 'suspended animation'.[8] Their rise to dominance, far from suddenly emerging from total obscurity, came from a slow consolidation of power. They advanced, sometimes creeping forward, pawn-like, sometimes through a series of knight's moves, zigzagging in bishop's fashion and with confident Queen-like victories.

CHAPTER 6

A GLIMMER ON THE HORIZON
PARAKESARI VIJAYALAYA (R. 850–871)

> There was then the crest-jewel of kings, named Vijayalaya, who had powerful arms and who was the abode of victory in battle.[1]

The middle of the ninth century saw the dawn of a new era for the Cholas after all those centuries in the shadows. At that time, they were confined to a narrow band of land around Uraiyur from where the ancient Cholas had once ruled. Dormant, but far from extinct, they survived while playing minor roles in helping those in power. In the early decades of the ninth century, they were dependent on the largesse and protection of the Pallavas. The western Deccan was under the Rashtrakutas who ruled from their capital Manyakheta; they had snuffed out the Western Chalukyas. The eastern area was under the Eastern Chalukyas. South of the Rashtrakutas and Chalukyas were the Pallavas, with the Gangas at the western edge of their territories and the Banas to their west. Each of these empires had to employ Janus-faced tactics and never let their guard down. Strategic alliances were key.

The Pallavas were fraying at the edges. There had been an internecine struggle and they had split into two factions. One, headed by Nripatungavarman, had sided with the loathed Pandyas and had entered the southern part of Chola territory. The other side was led by Aparajita, who ruled over Tondaimandalam, the traditional Pallava lands in the northern Tamil region. Parts of their kingdom fractured and broke away into a collection of chieftaincies. Only a small core of their formerly great empire remained theirs.

Interspersed among this motley collection of kingdoms was an even more variegated assortment of chieftaincies whose loyalties could make or break the tenuous hold these empires had over their domains and people. The Kaveri River valley and delta—the once and future province of the Cholas—was under the decentralized control of local landlords.

These chieftains and landlords were important players in the politics of the age. Not quite powerful enough to command large kingdoms, they cast their lot with more dominant rulers, gaining, in return, both protection and scraps of territory. Allegiances shifted frequently and the fragmented and sometimes nebulous nature of inscriptions makes it difficult to pinpoint exactly who was on whose side when.

To emphasize their dependent status, they often assumed the titles and surnames of their overlords. Matrimonial alliances often helped to build and consolidate their position. Cross-cousin marriages along multiple generations was common practice, and family trees were terribly tangled. It behoved each side to treat their daughters-in-law well; it was they who would produce the next generation's spouses.

This was the milieu, one of fading empires and those hungry for growth, of chieftains jostling for power and position, ready to switch loyalties the moment the situation demanded it, of which a certain chieftain named Vijayalaya was a part. And there were many chiefs, some friendly, others not, that he had to contend with.

South of the Kaveri River near Trichy, in modern-day Pudukkottai district, occupying the uneasy zone between the Cholas and the Pandyas, were the Irukkuvels. Also called Velirs, their power centre was Kodumbalur. In the ninth century, they cast their lot in with the Cholas, entering into marital and military alliances with them and proving themselves a crucial ally against the Pandyas. For a few centuries they enjoyed the status earned by having friends in power, but by the twelfth century they suffered the same fate as many clans before them, sinking into obscurity and obsolescence.

Then there were the Paluvettaraiyars. They were very loyal to the Cholas and were of great help both politically and militarily once the latter started accumulating and consolidating power. They also built temples and made generous endowments for their upkeep. There is uncertainty about where they came from, perhaps Paluvur near Trichy. There was also a connection to today's Kerala; they gained sufficient importance to give one of their daughters as a bride to the royal family of Kerala; around half a century later, a Chola ruler named Parantaka I married the daughter of a Kerala king who was called the Paluvettaraiyar.

Then there were the Muttaraiyars, who were key players in the story of the (re)birth of the Cholas. Their main base was a town called Sendalai; Thanjavur was also an important city in their domain. Their leader, in the mid-ninth century, was Elango Muttaraiyar.

The Muttaraiyars were enterprising chieftains who controlled part of the fertile Kaveri delta region, the region formerly ruled by the ancient Cholas. There is scant inscriptional evidence on the Muttaraiyars. There has been some speculation that they might have been linked in some way with the Kalabhras who, having been uprooted by the Pallavas, drifted south into what would become Chola lands. Inscriptions at Sendalai (their headquarters) describe them as ruling over Thanjavur. Like the Cholas at the time, they lacked the size and power to be fully independent. What they lacked in power they made up for in smarts, and they managed to hold on to their territories by shifting their allegiance, depending on how the winds blew, between the Pallavas and the Pandyas. In the mid-ninth century, they cast their lot with the Pandyas.

At some point—historians disagree about the exact date because there is no firm evidence—probably around 850 CE, there was a battle between the Muttaraiyars and the Cholas; the latter were led by an upstart chieftain out of Uraiyur named Vijayalaya.[2] We know nothing of Vijayalaya's antecedents, but he must have been a man of tremendous ambition and vision. He won, and Thanjavur became his. Over a century and a half later, his feat would be memorialized on a copperplate inscription made by one his most illustrious descendants, the son of the great emperor Rajaraja.

> In the illustrious family...was born Vijayalaya of praiseworthy prowess, whose footstool was battered by the diadems in the rush for precedence (ahamahmika) of kings desirous of prostrating.... He, the light of the Solar race, took possession of (the town) Tanchapuri (i.e. Tanjore) which was picturesque to the sight, was as beautiful as Alaka (the chief town of Kubera)....[3]

Half a century later, a further embellished version would appear on another inscription, and claim that Vijayalaya built, in the Chola country, a town named Thanjapuri (Thanjavur);[4] we know this to be untrue as Thanjavur was already in existence, occupied by the Muttaraiyars.

The battle must have been a fierce one; Vijayalaya is said to have received ninety-six battle scars. The poet who wrote the historical ulas (a genre of Tamil poetry that describes the king in procession, and which includes, in quite hyperbolic language, his genealogy and details about his court and activities) to the later Chola kings, Vikrama Chola, Kulothunga Chola, and Rajaraja Chola II, praised 'the victor of many a battlefield who bore on his person no less than ninety-six scars gained in battle' and 'he who wore ninety-six injuries like ornaments on his body'.[5]

It was a small step for Vijayalaya, a giant leap for the Cholas.

Vijayalaya moved his capital from Uraiyur to Thanjavur. To give thanks for his victory he built a temple to the goddess Nisumbhasudani in his new capital. The goddess—radiating fierceness with her fangs, gruesome weapons dripping blood and gore—was the ideal war deity, an apt power to worship and thank for victory on the battlefield. The Thiruvalangadu plates put it beautifully: 'Having consecrated the image of Nisumbhasudani whose lotus feet are worshipped by gods and demons, he, by the grace of that goddess bore like a garland the whole earth, resplendent with her garment of the four oceans.'[6]

One can imagine Vijayalaya praying to her before setting out to battle.

Chola genealogies tell us that early on, Chola kings were called, alternately, Parakesari and Rajakesari.[7] Vijayalaya was the first Parakesari of the Imperial line. We don't know if the later Cholas created the genealogies and retrofitted Vijayalaya with the Parakesari moniker or if Vijayalaya started the trend or if it was already in existence. If Vijayalaya did indeed pick the Parakesari title, he must surely have been attracted to the qualities evoked by the name: Lion to [One's] Enemies.

Not much else is known about Vijayalaya, except that he likely shrugged off several aggressive threats by the Pandyas. An inscription in a town in South Arcot district, a good distance north of Thanjavur, refers to a cattle raid by him early in his reign—clearly Vijayalaya had ambitions to gain land further afield from Thanjavur.

Vijayalaya's victory in Thanjavur set the ball rolling for the resurgence—or emergence—of one of the most splendid and powerful dynasties not just in south India, but anywhere in the world. He might not have known what he set in motion, but he certainly had ambitions and took steps to achieve his ends. Kinship alliances were crucial in securing loyalty, and Vijayalaya married off his daughter to the Irrukavel chief from Kodumbalur and for several generations after that there was a reciprocal exchange of brides between these families.

Vijayalaya appointed his son Aditya as yuvaraja or ruler-in-waiting. A fearless warrior himself, Aditya took an active part to recapture what he could of Chola country. Thus Vijayalaya expanded his sway up to Pudukkottai in the south and Tiruttani in the north, with the help of his courageous son. The existence of two temples, one at Narthamalai (16 kilometres north of Pudukkottai) called Vijayalaya Cholisvaram and the other,

Vijayalisvaram, at Vilakkannapundi near Tiruttani (around 40 kilometres north of Kanchipuram), confirm the southern and northern boundaries of his kingdom.

However, his foothold on his newly won territories was tenuous, to say the least. There is inscriptional evidence that the Pandyas and Pallavas were in Chola lands through the latter part of the 860s and much of the 870s until Vijayalaya died, which shows that their presence there was very much a fact of life in the region. But, however shaky and precarious his control, Vijayalaya had set into motion the emergence of the greatest power of the region.

CHAPTER 7

BUILDING TOWARDS GREATNESS RAJAKESARI ADITYA (R. 870–907)

> The son of this Vijayalaya was Adityavarman, better known by the name of Kodanda-Rama. He fell on the Pallava monarch, who was seated upon a maddened elephant, and killed him in battle.[1]

Vijayalaya was succeeded by his son Rajakesari Aditya. The date of his ascension is uncertain. The only information we have hinges on an inscription at Takkolam that mentions a solar eclipse that took place in Aditya's twenty-fourth regnal year. Naturally, there are several solar eclipses that make likely candidates. There was one in 894 and another in 895, and twenty-four years prior to that would make his year of ascendency to the throne 870 or 871. The problem with these dates lies with the long gap between Aditya's last-known inscription and the year his son, Parantaka, took over. The last inscription that we have from Aditya's reign is from his twenty-seventh year as king, which, if he ascended the throne in 870 or 871 would be in 897 or 898. His son, Parantaka, became king in 907, which leaves a long gap during which we have no information about any Chola ruler. So we have to consider another eclipse, one that took place in the year 913. If we take this as the eclipse referred to in the inscription, Aditya would have become king twenty-four years before that, in 889. And his final known inscription, twenty-seven years into his reign, would have been in 916, and this means that his reign and that of his son Parantaka's overlapped by around ten years. Due to irreconcilable discrepancies between several other inscriptions, most historians have chosen to accept

870 as the more likely date.[2] Aditya inherited a small kingdom from his father as well as a large measure of ambition.

Vijayalaya's victory over the Muttaraiyars (around 850) had stirred up a hornet's nest. The Muttaraiyars had aligned themselves with the Pandyas, and this meant that the Pandyas had to avenge the loss. To add fuel to the fire, Vijayalaya was an ally of their bête noire, the Pallavas. Years of serving the Pallavas (who were the Cholas' overlords) must have left some vestiges of loyalty. This, along with shrewd political calculation, must have prompted Aditya to continue to support the Pallavas.

The Pandya ruler was Varaguna, also known as Maranjadayan, ruling from his capital city of Madurai. An aggressive ruler, he was alarmed by the many implications of the defeat of his allies, the Muttaraiyars, at the hands of the upstart Cholas. They were considerably weakened after their loss, and Varaguna sought revenge, determined to cut the Cholas down to size.

He gathered his forces and made his way north. The date is uncertain as is the length of the campaign, but some scholars believe that Vijayalaya was still the Chola ruler at this point. The campaign began promisingly, and he succeeded in reaching Idavai, a village on the north bank of the Kaveri, which was part of Chola territory. After capturing Idavai, he made his way further north where he destroyed the fortifications at a place called Vembil. Inscriptions show that Varaguna even advanced as far as Araisur, which was on the Pennar River in Tondaimandalam, the ancient Pallava dominion. By this time, Vijayalaya's son, Aditya had become the Chola ruler. At this point, it appears that Varaguna was confronted by the combined forces of the Pallavas, Gangas, and Cholas, and was forced to retreat, driven back towards the south.

The year was 880, and the Chola ruler was now Aditya, a full decade into his rule. At a village called Sripurambiyam a decisive battle was fought. Sripurambiyam, also known as Thirupurambiyam, is a small village midway between the

Kollidam River to the north, and Kumbakonam to the south. Fighting on one side was the Pandya Varaguna, aided by the Muttaraiyars and possibly the breakaway Pallava Nripatunga (although there is no consensus on this). On the other, were the Pallavas, straitjacketed by the Chalukyas to the north, led by Aparajita, fighting bitterly and desperately for territory, pride, revenge and, as it turned out, their very future. He was aided by Aditya Chola and the Ganga king, Prithvipati I. The Gangas were in a pitched struggle against the Rashtrakutas who kept a close eye on their activities and nipped in the bud any hint of rebellion. Naturally, the Gangas bristled at this. They also had their hands full with the Chalukyas threatening their territory. The understanding was that the Pallavas would help the Gangas with this situation in return for their loyalty. There was a family connection as well: Aparajita's mother was a Ganga princess, a matrimonial alliance made perhaps with just such a political bond in mind. The alliances were like a row of precariously set dominoes, highly unstable, any movement or change could set off a chain reaction of consequences.

The Battle of Sripurambiyam represented a turning point—the Pandya and Pallava fortunes took a turn for the worse, which in turn helped pave the way for the Cholas to gain territory, power, and fame. The Pandyas suffered a bitter loss. Of Nripatunga, the breakaway Pallava who allied himself with Varaguna Pandya, nothing was heard of again. This was a huge blow for the Pandyas, and while the Pallavas were, in theory, the victors, their success was more due to the efforts of their allies than their own.

In the fierce fighting, the Ganga king, Prithvipati I, lost his life. Prithvipati's grandson, Prithvipati II, described it thus in his Udayendiram inscription:

> Having defeated by force the Pandya lord Varaguna at the head of a great battle of Sripurambiya, and having (thus) made (his) title Aparajita (i. e. the unconquered)

> significant, this hero entered the heaven of his friend (viz. Indra) by sacrificing his own life.[3]

The Pallavas lost a faithful ally in Prithvipati, but they won the battle, in large part thanks to the efforts of Aditya and his army. The tottering Pallava empire managed to cling on. The grateful Aparajita gifted a large part of the Chola dominion to Aditya, greatly increasing the latter's power and influence. This was, as Sastri put it so evocatively, like 'training a tiger cub to a taste of blood'.

After his success at the battle of Sripurambiyan and with precious lands added to his domain, Aditya headed west to the hilly Kongu territory, or Kongudesa.

The Kongu region, as is evident from its name which is a geographic, not dynastic, designation, was not the homeland of any dynasty in particular. Surrounding it were the Cheras to the west, the Pallavas on the north-east flank, the Gangas to the north, the Pandyas in the south, and the Cholas to its east. It is a hilly region, and somewhat remote. In the ninth century, when the Cholas were gaining in power, the Kongu lands were a troubled frontier region to the west of the Chola and Pallava heartlands and, consequently, were sought after by both these powers. Although it was an isolated area, it lay along an ancient trade route that connected the Coromandel and Malabar coasts as far back as during the Sangam era. A veritable treasure trove of Roman coins has been found along this route.

The *Kongudesa Rajakkal*, a sixteenth/seventeenth-century chronicle,[4] tells of Aditya's conquest of Kongudesa and Talakad, lands to the west of Chola territory. Aditya's conquest would have been between 870 and 894.

The *Kongudesa Rajakkal* states that Aditya conquered Kongudesa and Talakad.

> In the *Chola-desam*, *Aditya-verma-raya*, son of *Vijayadi-raya*, being crowned in *Tanjavur-patnam*, he came to *Congu-desam*, and conquered the *Vardar* (huntsmen or

> wild people) of the king of *Congu-desam*, and took the town of *Talicad*; and, giving many free endowments to many *agraharas*, he governed that country, in addition to his own.[5]

Sundara Chola's Anbil plates write of Aditya's generosity in constructing and endowing temples in the Kongu region, which most likely means he had territorial rights in the area.[6]

Sastri has surmised that when Aditya Chola conquered Kongu, these were Ganga lands that he added to his growing kingdom. The Gangas became feudatories of Aditya Chola after this as stated in inscriptions at Udayendiram and Takkolam. Also, while there are records of the presence of Aditya's son Parantaka in the region, there is no record of his conquest, leaving us to assume that it had already been conquered by Aditya. Parantaka was probably the yuvaraja at the time, being groomed to follow his father as ruler.

Aditya's military general in the Kongu battles was Vikki Annan. He likely belonged to the Velir clan from Kodambalur, who had been, and continued to be, key Chola allies. A ruler as perceptive as Aditya must surely have realized the importance, both political and commercial, of good ties with this clan. Kodambalur, in the Pudukkottai region, formed a buffer zone with the Pandyas to the south, and also lay along the significant land trade routes of the day. Further strengthening the Velir–Chola bond were matrimonial ties; Aditya's daughter, Anupama, was married to a Velir chieftain. He was a successful military leader, responsible for the Chola victories in the region.

Vikki Annan was richly rewarded, by both Aditya and his ally, Sthanu Ravi, of the Kerala Cheras, for his pivotal role in this victory. He was showered with an unprecedented assortment of gifts and honours including a palace, an army of male elephants, a fly-whisk—an important symbol of power and authority—a palanquin, drums, bugles, and a new title, that his descendants could inherit—Sembiyan Tamilavel. To give thanks for this bounty and the enhanced status, Vikki Annan's wife Kadamba made generous endowments at a newly built stone temple to Siva on the north bank of the Kaveri, in a little town called Thillaistanam. Her donation of a hundred sheep for a lamp[7] was recorded in an inscription at on the south wall of this temple, in the year 875.

There is a cluster of seven temples around Thanjavur, that are referred to as the Sacred Seven—Saptha Sthala—that show evidence of the close involvement of Chola monarchs in their upkeep and management, starting from Aditya. These temples were already held in high regard by Siva worshippers and several of the Nayanmars wrote enchanting verses in their praise in centuries past. Near the Kadamba inscription at Thillaistanam is another one dated 878 by Aditya's son Adittan Kannaradeva, who never attained the throne, making note of his gift of gold for a continuously burning lamp at this temple. These were among the earliest inscriptions from Aditya's reign and make a strong case for the involvement of Aditya in the upkeep of the temples. From this point on, there are many inscriptions from Aditya, and a corresponding paucity of inscriptions in Chola lands by the Pallavas and Pandyas indicating that Chola power had been consolidated and strengthened there. Patronage to these temples continued well after Aditya's time, with inscriptions showing donations by his grandsons.

Aditya was a religious man and a great devotee of Siva. He built many temples along the Kaveri. In the words of the Anbil plates, his temples, built of stone, lined the banks of the Kaveri all the way from the Sahya mountains to the ocean.[8] He converted old mud and brick temples into more permanent structures of stone. The original idol and sanctum likely remained but the rest of the temple was rebuilt. Some of the finest gems of early Chola temples are from the reign of Aditya. Many of them stand to this day. They are small, single-storeyed affairs, a far cry from the soaring creations of future Chola kings. These temples lack any foundation inscriptions, which probably means that these were already in existence, and upgraded in what came to be known as the Chola style. Temples built or rebuilt during Aditya's reign have been found from Kannanur (near Trichy) in the south to Takkolam, showing the extent of his empire.

As stone temples became popular, so too did the first portable bronze procession images, which became an important part of the temples. A very popular icon was that of Siva as Tripurantaka, the destroyer of the three citadels, a manifestation of Siva as one victorious in battle. This must have surely resonated with the Cholas as they battled to vanquish their rivals and establish themselves. The constant fighting did not inhibit the creative urge. The choice of imagery might have been inspired and influenced by the conditions of the time, of frequent warfare.

Later in his reign, Aditya fought directly against the Pandyas too, in his own capacity rather than as a Pallava ally. He defeated the ruler, Parantaka Viranarayana, who was the younger brother of Varaguna II who had lost the Battle of Sripurambiyam (and had died not long after).

This constant battling decimated both the Pandyas and the Pallavas.

Aditya, like most of his contemporaries, employed an active network of spies to keep abreast of what was going on in both his own lands as well as in kingdoms near and far. The Udayendiram plates of Prithvipati II state that:

> ...Aditya, who overcame the whole crowd of exalted kings; whose splendour, being emitted to enter various countries, dispelled the darkness (*which were*) troops of enemies; who learned the true state (*of the affairs of his enemies*) from his spies; who made the excellent wheel (of his authority) roll with incessant speed; (and) to whom, the continually rising, joyfully bowed the four regions.[9]

Aditya amassed tremendous wealth from his Kongu conquest, including a vast horde of gold. He used some of this to gild the roof of the sanctum sanctorum at the ancient hallowed Nataraja temple at Chidambaram (according to a memoir of the sixty-three Nayanmars).[10] However, other sources, like the Anbil, Leiden, and Thiruvalangadu plates, credit Parantaka with the laying of the gold on the roof of the Chidambaram Temple.

It is likely that Aditya began the gilding of the roof, which was then completed by his son. Another possibility is that Parantaka, as Aditya's yuvaraja, fought in the campaign in Kongu and had a hand in collecting the booty of gold and gilding the temple's roof.

Aditya continued to gain greatly in wealth and territory. The early years of the tenth century saw his biggest triumph in a stunning betrayal of an old ally. As the Kanyakumari inscriptions put it, Adityavarma, well known by the name Kodandarama, seated on a furious elephant, jumped upon and killed the Pallava king in battle.[11] With this victory, he added to his kingdom the lands that had once belonged to the empire of his friend, Aparajita Pallava, and thus the region of Tondaimandalam came into Chola hands. Aparajita was unconquered no longer. This prized region, once a Pallava bastion, was the newest feather in Aditya's cap. His capture and annexation of Tondaimandalam was his most important achievement, expanding, for the first time, the Chola lands and power into territory that had never been theirs to command thus far. For this, he earned the title 'Tondai Nadu Pavina Rajakesarivarman' (the Rajakesarivarman who overran Tondai Nadu)—according to an inscription on a temple wall in Thillaistanam.

Having taken over these Pallava lands, the Cholas now had a dangerous enemy as their neighbour to the north: the Rashtrakutas.

Aditya, like almost all monarchs of his era, married multiple women. One of them, named Illango Picchi, is believed to have been a daughter of the Rashtrakuta king Krishna II who was also known as Kannaradeva II. No doubt this alliance was made with political and territorial benefits in mind. This marriage produced a son, Adittan Kannaradeva. As Illango Picchi was the senior wife of Aditya, this son should have been the heir to the throne.

However, for reasons that are not known, another son, Parantaka, succeeded Aditya as king. Perhaps Adittan Kannaradeva died before he could gain the throne, perhaps Parantaka schemed his way to the kingship. Whatever the reason, it soured relations between the Rashtrakutas and the Cholas and the two would come into conflict early in Parantaka's reign.

Another wife of Aditya was a Pallava princess, a smart move that ensured that the Pallava territories became part of his own.

The Cholas clearly cared about their legacy and about appearing righteous and just. The Thiruvalangadu plates describe Aditya as wise, scholarly, and knowledgeable, full of energy, and 'always bent upon removing evil, adhering himself to the path of the righteous and protecting the earth'.[12] His sense of fairness is evident by the fact that he respected the grants made by previous Pallava sovereigns whose territories were now part of Aditya's domain (as seen in the inscriptions at Thirukkalukunram in his twenty-seventh regnal year).

Aditya, a devout and successful warrior king and a smart and strategic diplomat, took the Chola dynasty towards an empire. He began his royal career as little more than a feudatory; by the end of his reign, he had replaced the Pallavas as one of the two great powers in southern India. The Gangas became his allies as did the Cheras. He was aptly described in his son's inscription at Sholinghur as the great king who 'was able to bear, free of trembling and agitation, the globe of the earth, [who] was created with care by the Creator, in order that the crowd of serpents, and all the elephants of the regions, who are supporting the earth, might not feel tired',[13] words that conjure up an image of a south Indian-style Atlas shouldering the weight of the world—an exaggerated but not wholly untrue claim.

It is believed that Aditya died in the northern reaches of his kingdom, near present-day Kalahasti. A stone inscription found in North Arcot district refers to him as Tondaiman Aatrur Tunjinadeva, which means that he died at Tondaiman Aatrur, which has been identified as Tondamanad. This village is around 10 kilometres from Kalahasti in Chittoor district. Here there is a temple, variously called Kodandaramesvaram (Kodandarama was one of the names he was known by), or Adityesvaram. This is probably the only temple before Rajaraja's Brihadeeshwara Temple that was built entirely by a reigning Chola monarch, Parantaka, Aditya's son and successor. It is a pallipadai or sepulchral temple, built on or near where Aditya was buried or cremated. On the north base of the central shrine is an inscription by Parantaka, dated 941. It records endowments of gold and paddy to the temple that would cover the costs and supplies for a seven-day festival celebrating the natal star month of Aditya. A thousand people from all classes of society would be fed every day during the weeklong festival, and lavish arrangements were made for the worship of the temple's deity.[14]

It was a grand gesture of filial piety and devotion, one appropriate for a great father and king.

CHAPTER 8

THE GRAND OLD MAN
PARAKESARI PARANTAKA (R. 907–955)

> To Aditya was born a son named Parantaka, who was the abode of the goddess of valour.... Parantaka destroyed the Pandya king with his whole army, took all his wealth and burnt his capital Madurai.[1]

Parantaka Chola, the son of Aditya, became the third ruler of the Imperial Chola line in the year 907, on a day between 15 January and 25 July that year. This is the first year of ascension that can be verified. An inscription on a wall of the Sivalokanathar Temple in Gramam in Villipuram district mentions the thirty-sixth year of Parantaka's reign, which happened in the Kaliyuga year 4044 along with the name of a star and month.[2] The Chola historian needs to be well versed in not only the language of the period, but also in astrological and astronomical matters!

After centuries of operating from the shadows while ruling over a few odd tracts of land and villages and having to endure the indignity of being mere secondary players in the ever-swirling power struggles of southern India, the Cholas were finally poised to step into the fray as a power to be reckoned with. Both the Pallavas and Pandyas were considerably weakened after the Battle of Sripurambiyam, and both depended heavily on the backing and loyalty of their feudatories, something that could hardly be relied upon.

Parantaka inherited a kingdom that his father, Aditya, had worked hard to win and expand. The stretch of land from Kalahasti in the north to the region around the Kaveri delta in the south was his to govern. The Gangas, now ruled by

Prithvipati II, the grandson of the first Prithvipati who had lost his life fighting the Pandyas at the Battle of Sripurambiyam, were under his control. The Cheras to the west were, after a fashion, a friendly force.

With the defeat of the Pallavas, much of the Tondaimandalam region, the Pallava heartland, came under Chola rule. The Pandyas had been dealt a hard blow at Sripurambiyam. It was a good moment to strike, and Parantaka struck.

In 910, the third year of his reign, Parantaka awarded himself the title Madurakonda Parakesari—the Parakesari who defeated (the Pandya capital of) Madurai. This meant that he must have led a military expedition to Pandya lands around 909–910. However, there are no inscriptions of his found anywhere in the Pandya lands, which most likely means that there was a raid or battle of sorts, and while Parantaka might have made some minor gains, his grand title of Madurakonda was vastly exaggerated and was perhaps more an indication of his ambitions and intentions. Nonetheless, Parantaka was relentless and was possessed of grand ambitions. With his attack on Madurai, he had issued the Pandyas a warning.

In the meantime, trouble was brewing along Parantaka's northern frontiers. Here, a potentially dangerous coalition of dynasties had banded together hoping to stop the growing Chola threat in its tracks. The Rashtrakutas of the Deccan, headed by Krishna II, and aided by the Banas and Vaidumbas, invaded the Chola territory from the northwest. Krishna II's daughter had been married to Aditya; she was in fact his senior and chief wife. They had a son, Adittan Kannaradeva. Clearly, this was a marital alliance with a larger objective—that Kannaradeva would follow his father as king, and thus achieve a consolidation of Chola and Rashtrakuta territories. If matters had proceeded according to protocol, that would have been the case. But Kannaradeva was sidelined, and henceforth, vanished from the records. There is no mention of what became of him. His half-brother Parantaka was made king. Krishna II very likely wanted him ousted, so that he could seize what he believed was rightfully his.

A battle was fought in the year 911 at Thiruvallam in North Arcot district. It ended badly for Krishna II and his allies. Parantaka's Ganga ally Prithvipati II was instrumental in the victory at this bloody battle, where he was 'the fire of death to his enemies'.[3]

◆

Immediately surrounding the Pallava country was an ancient clan called the Banas. They claimed descent from the demon king Mahabali, who had been made a doorkeeper to the temple of Lord Parameshwara. Chola control over Pallava lands and its surroundings would not be complete without quashing the persistent menace of minor clans like the Banas. Their power and reach might have been small, but by means of labyrinthine networking and independent cunning, they ensured that the Cholas were never truly the masters of all they conquered.

After the Battle of Sripurambiyam and the death of Aparajita, Pallava power was an anaemic shadow of its former self. The Banas, who had been loyal vassals of the Pallavas, realized that the time was ripe for them to assert their independence and make the best of the situation. Their inscriptions, found in places in and around the Pallava country, make no mention of their feudatory or vassal status. Putting up inscriptions in places indicated control and ownership of those places. For those with a conquering and expansion mindset like Parantaka, this meant that those signs had to be destroyed.

And so, early in his reign, between ongoing skirmishes and battles with the Pandyas, Parantaka targeted the Banas and their territory. That was a necessary step for him to gain complete control over Pallava lands.

We tend to imagine that all territorial conquest happened through large-scale wars and battles. However, inscriptions indicate that a lot of the action took place in the form of plundering raids in which cattle, jewels, and other loot were seized. So it was with the Banas. There were losses on both sides but, eventually, Parantaka prevailed. His victory, yet again, was in large measure thanks to his faithful vassal, Prithvipati II.

Prithvipati II, also known as Hastimalla, was a ruler of the Western Ganga dynasty, with territory around present-day Mysore. This dynasty was riven with infighting and had splintered into rival factions. Prithvipati headed one of the blocs. His grandfather, Prithvipati I, had sided with the Pallavas, along with the Cholas, against the Pandyas at Sripurambiyam. At that point, the Western Gangas were a mere subsidiary power that had command over only those lands granted to them by their overlords.

In large part due to Prithvipati II's efforts, the Banas' lands were conquered. As a reward and in gratitude, Parantaka gifted these lands to Prithvipati. In addition, around 912, he was showered with adulatory titles like 'Banadiraja'—lord of the Banas; a further title, Sembiyan Mahabali Vanarayan, was bestowed upon him. His loyalty had reaped rich rewards.

With this victory the Banas now became one of the constellation of vassals in the Chola firmament. Prithvipati II was richly rewarded but that he was still very much a feudatory is clear from an inscription that mentioned that he 'amply showed that a particle of the sun was inherent him'—i.e. he was a mere speck of the powerful brilliance of the solar king of the Cholas.[4]

In celebration of his victory over the Banas and the Rashtrakutas, Parantaka awarded himself a new title —Virachola, the Brave Chola.

Parantaka had made a strike against the Pandyas very early in his reign, and had even awarded himself the Madurakonda title, but the reality was that the Pandya lands were not under his control at all. The complete absence of any of Parantaka's inscriptions in those areas from the early period of his rule is ample proof that his work there was far from done.

The Cholas' rivalry with the Pandyas hit a new high during Parantaka's reign and set the stage for many ensuing battles through his reign and those of his successors. He waged battle twice against the Pandyas. The first might have resulted in a minor victory, but it merely whetted Parantaka's appetite for further success in the region.

Parantaka's conquest of the Pandya lands was a prolonged affair. Methodically, he laid siege and started annexing bits and pieces of Pandya lands starting from the west and slowly encircling it. The Pandyas were tough foes. But while the Pandya king Rajasimha had his back to the wall, he was not ready to concede defeat.

Across the water, the wise and just King Kassapa V ruled on the emerald isle of Ceylon. King Rajasimha sent numerous gifts to him, hoping to gain his favour and military aid. Kassapa knew of the growing might and threat of the Cholas and was probably all too aware that if the Pandya kingdom fell, his would be next in the Chola line of fire. After consulting his ministers, he sent a military contingent to help the Pandya king, with his sakkasenapathi, a very high-ranking military official, as their leader. The king himself went to Mahatittha, on the coast, and sent his men off with a stirring speech. When the army from Ceylon arrived on Pandya shores, they were greeted by a relieved King Rajasimha, who announced that he was sure that by acting together, the two forces would be victorious.

His optimism proved misguided. Initially, judging from inscriptions that described the battles, it appeared that both sides enjoyed victories. Rajasimha's Sinnamannur inscriptions boast of the king of Thanjai (Thanjavur) fleeing after surrendering his arms, of pierced bodies shedding blood.[5] But in the end, it was utter disaster for the Pandya and Ceylonese forces. A pitched battle with elephants, horses, and soldiers took place at Vellur. Parantaka had a strong force, and his loyal friends the Cheras, the Paluvettaraiyars, and the Irrukavels all pitched in. The armies of the Pandyas and the Ceylonese were crushed. The Sakkasenapathi succumbed to a local plague. Inevitably the soldiers too fell ill and started dying in large enough numbers that their king ordered their return to Ceylon.

The Kanyakumari plates state excitedly:

> Parantaka destroyed the Pandya king with his whole army, took all his wealth and burnt (his capital) Madhura; for this achievement he received the title of Madhurantaka.[6]

This vitally important victory earned Parantaka further grand titles: Maduraiyum Illamum Konda ko-Parakesari—the king who gained victory over both Madurai and Ceylon; and Samgramaraghava—resembling Lord Rama in battle, apt as both kings defeated their Lankan rivals.

This battle took place around nine years into Parantaka's reign. However, inscriptions bearing his name as ruler appeared in Pandya lands a good ten years after the event. The Vellur battle was a decisive one for paving the way for the downfall of the Pandyas and for Chola annexation of their territory, but it was just one of many hurdles that Parantaka had to push past before he was fully and truly the ruler of the territories of that proud and ancient dynasty.

Rajasimha must have realized that staying on in his kingdom would be foolish. He remembered the generosity of the Ceylonese king, and he made his way to that island again. His friend, King Kassapa V was no more, and the ruling king was Dappula IV. Dappula greeted Rajasimha warmly and set him up comfortably in a home in the countryside along with a generous income. But Rajasimha was restless; what he wanted was more troops with which to fight his loathed Chola rival Parantaka in order to regain his kingdom and his pride. While Dappula appeared to be ready to oblige, the nobles of his court protested vigorously. Rajasimha realized he had outstayed his welcome and, leaving behind his crown and other royal paraphernalia, made his way to Kerala, the homeland of his mother. And thus a chapter in the story of this once proud and great dynasty came to a close.

Parantaka spent the next two decades surrounding, closing in, and annexing the Pandya territory until around 940 when the crown jewel of that dynasty, Madurai, passed into Chola hands. Parantaka was a man who did not believe in half measures. He must have been possessed of a monumental ego and pride. If he was to be crowned king of the Pandya lands, he wanted to do it wearing the Pandya crown and the Pandya royal regalia. He sent his messengers across to Ceylon, demanding that the Pandya crown jewels, left behind by Rajasimha, be sent to him.

The Lankan king then was Udaya IV, a slothful man who was too fond of alcohol for the good of his subjects and himself. He might have been an idle inebriant, but he was no pushover, and he denied Parantaka his request. In a fury, Parantaka sent an army to Lanka. King Udaya summoned his senapathi (army chief) who had been busy quelling rebellious uprisings elsewhere in the country. The battle that followed ended badly for the Lankans. The senapathi was killed while attempting to flee. King Udaya, his alcoholism and laziness notwithstanding, still had his wits about him, and fled, Pandya crown jewels in hand, into the hills of the Ruhuna region. The Chola troops tried, unsuccessfully, to follow him. They gave up and returned home, empty-handed. The Pandya crown jewels remained in Lanka. It would take around a hundred years, and the efforts of another great Chola ruler, Rajendra, to seize the jewels and bring them to the Chola mainland.

It is ironic indeed that the Pandyas sought the help of the kings of Ceylon. The *Mahavamsa*, a chronicle of over 2,000 years of Ceylonese history, describes how, during the reign of King Sena I of Lanka (r. 846–866 CE) the Pandyas launched a massive attack on the island and wrought widespread destruction. The king was forced to flee, and took refuge in Malay country. The yuvaraja slit his own throat while seated on his elephant at the battlefield, preferring to die by his own hand, rather than by the hand of the enemy. The Pandyas helped themselves to a substantial quantity of loot, leaving the island with 'none value whatsoever'.[7] Eventually, an agreement was reached, and the king was able to return to his capital. Later, Sena I's successor

Sena II, cleverly allied himself with a rebel Pandya prince and with his help killed the reigning Pandya monarch, collected a vast amount of loot (including that which had been taken by the Pandyas during their invasion—sweet revenge!) installed their ally the rebel prince as king of the Pandyas, and returned home, well satisfied.

There is much disagreement about the veracity of this account; and inconsistencies abound. In florid language it tells a colourful, much embellished, and sometimes questionable saga of the island, but it is invaluable as it is the only document of its kind, covering the breadth and depth it does. It might seem utterly incomprehensible to us that a regime that was so brutally plundered should offer solace and assistance to the very aggressors who had so humiliated and wrecked them. But in that era of ever fickle and volatile coalitions, this was politics as usual.

Why did the Pandyas turn to Ceylon for aid? They were probably running out of options for possible allies, with the Cholas having suppressed the Pallavas, the Banas, and the Vaidumbas and adding more feudatories into their fold. The Ceylonese, just across the water, were a logical choice, and they, in turn, very likely alarmed at the growing power of the Cholas, recognized that helping the Pandyas would be to their benefit should the Cholas turn their attention southwards once again.

However, the Pandyas were tough foes and had not been crushed for good. The Kaveri delta region was easy enough to truly subdue and bring into the Chola fold. Further south, towards Pandya lands, the rudimentary administrative structure as well as the large tracts of wild forested lands that were home to hostile tribal chiefs made it almost impossible to get firm control over those areas. The availability of nearby Ceylon as a hideaway for conquered enemies and as a place from which revenge attacks could be launched added to the Cholas' problems. Conquering the Pandya territory was a long drawn-out process, and the first inscriptions by Parantaka in this region began after twenty-four years of the start of his reign.

Around three decades into his reign, Parantaka was at the height of his powers. He had subdued the Pandyas, made victorious inroads into Ceylon, befriended the Cheras and enjoyed the feudatory loyalty of the Western Gangas. His territory extended from Nellore in the north to Kanyakumari in the south. He ensured that inscriptions in his name were installed all over the lands he conquered, showing his authority over them. Over 700 inscriptions have been found from his reign, many of which are in and around Thanjavur, his seat of power, as well as throughout Tamil Nadu, and a handful in Andhra and Karnataka, giving an idea of the extent of his dominion.

But Parantaka was never able to rest on his laurels and enjoy a peaceful contemplation of his achievements. There wasn't a moment when there wasn't a threat looming somewhere that he had to attend to. While he was fighting the Pandyas to the south, he was aware that along his northern frontiers, trouble was brewing.

The never-say-die Rashtrakutas remained a persistent threat and thorn in the side of the Cholas. They prowled the northern boundaries of Parantaka's dominions, particularly Tondaimandalam, the fertile precious former territories of the Pallavas.

The Banas seethed under the overlordship of the Western Gangas and the Cholas. They had sought the aid of the Rashtrakutas, led at the time by Krishna II, which had resulted in heavy losses for both them and the Rashtrakutas at the Battle in Thiruvallam early in Parantaka's reign around the year 911. The years went by and the Western Ganga ruler, Prithvipati II, who had so loyally and unflinchingly served and aided Parantaka, died. The new ruler, Butuga II, must have been possessed of a cold-blooded ambition—he murdered his older brother and hijacked his territories and the kingship. And in the geopolitical manoeuvring of that time, he had, as his ally, a king whose ruthless ambition, political astuteness, military acumen, and vision exceeded his by a wide margin. This was the Rashtrakuta king, Krishna III, who had ascended the throne around 939.

Krishna III had had it tough from the very beginning. His father was an old man when he became king, and as yuvaraja, Krishna III had had the chance to be a lot more active, therefore imbibing larger and more lessons in survival, warfare, and diplomacy. Krishna III's path to the throne had involved a healthy dose of machination including scheming, fending off a usurper, and possibly bloodshed as well. In this he was assisted by the Ganga king Butuga, who had married Krishna III's sister. Theirs was therefore a close familial as well as political bond. He was fully aware of the importance of being surrounded by friendly powers and his approach to achieve that end was very often to kill those he felt were hostile to him and put into power someone whose support he felt he could depend on. In addition to the Ganga king Butuga, he had the backing of the Bana king Vikramaditya.

Krishna III was in the prime of life when he became the Rashtrakuta king, a master politician who was skilled in the art of pitting one side against the other and revelling in the resulting discord and disarray. At the height of his power, practically the entire peninsula south of the Vindhya mountains was under his control. With Krishna III and Butuga II in power, Parantaka faced troubles far worse than anything he had experienced thus far. They were major thorns in his side along his northern frontiers. The duo was ruthless and aggressive. They were determined to expand their domains and Parantaka's hard-won lands to their south were their main targets. It was also very likely that there was an element of personal animosity and resentment and they wanted to curtail the Chola king's growing power. We saw earlier that Parantaka's father, Aditya, had married a daughter of the Rashtrakuta king Krishna II. She was his senior wife, and bore him a son, Adittan Kannaradeva who, by normal ascension protocol, should have succeeded his father as king. For reasons unknown, it was Parantaka who became king. So perhaps Krishna III felt compelled to conquer and own what he felt belonged rightfully to a Rashtrakuta.

In addition, Parantaka had done the unforgivable in interfering in Krishna III's internal family politics. His son-in-law, Govinda IV, had ruled briefly as the Rashtrakuta king. He was an ineffectual and unpopular leader; his feudatories had revolted and pulled him off the throne. He was replaced by his nephew, Amoghavarsha III. Amoghavarsha was followed by his son, the reviled Krishna III. Parantaka, following the time-worn custom of winning over his enemies and their territory through familial ties, attempted to restore Govinda IV to the throne. This probably only served to incense Krishna III and strengthen his resolve to destroy the Cholas. Those who had dared shelter Govinda IV after he was dethroned also faced the wrath of Krishna III as he wreaked havoc amongst the Banas and Vaidumbas.

Parantaka was well aware of the danger posed by Krishna III. He was a worthy rival and the two were probably evenly matched for their ambition, ruthlessness, and need for revenge. Besides, the Rashtrakuta threat was not a sudden one that came out of nowhere. There had been regular skirmishes and cattle raids along the northern frontiers and the Cholas had suffered losses. Parantaka's kingdom had enjoyed a steep growth, from a relatively small local realm to one that now occupied the lands that had long belonged to other powers. This came at a price, with the inevitable rumblings of discontent and dissension, as well as the growing difficulty in maintaining control over an expanding kingdom.

Parantaka knew that the Rashtrakutas would not take kindly to his growing successes and the shifting balance of power. From around 935, he fortified the area to the north, between the rivers Pennar and Vellar, with a strong military presence. The location provided swift access to the northern boundaries, and served as a zone of protection for Cholamandalam.

◆

Rajaditya was Parantaka's oldest son, and heir apparent or yuvaraja. The yuvaraja played a critical role in helping the ruler maintain control over his kingdom, particularly in trouble-torn areas. He served as an extra pair of eyes and ears, helped with administrative affairs, warfare, and defence, and was the most trusted right-hand man of the king. As it was a position of such importance, demanding complete confidence, reliability, and dedication, tradition dictated that it was the eldest son of the chief queen who should be awarded the title of yuvaraja.

Rajaditya was put in charge of preparations to deal with the Rashtrakutas and their allies. He was fully equipped with a battle-ready army including elephants and horses. The army was based in a village on the banks of the river Pennar that he named Rajadityapuram after himself. This was in the northern reaches of his father's kingdom, in the former Pallava heartland of Tondaimandalam. The family's old allies, the Cheras, sent assistance; a general named Vellan Kumaran was both a top flight military officer and a close friend of Rajaditya's. Rajaditya also had the support of his younger brother, Arinjaya.

Sometime in the year 938, Krishna III decided that it was time to wage war against Parantaka. At stake was Tondaimandalam, part of the old Pallava dominion. He wanted to start by capturing the northern reaches of the Chola kingdom, where Rajaditya was based, armed and ready. He set off with his army from his capital Malkhed, joined along the way by Butuga II. The Banas and Vaidumbas, sensing an opportunity for revenge and retaliation, added their muscle. Parantaka's men took on Krishna III and enjoyed some initial victories. These merely served to toughen Krishna's resolve.

The little village of Takkolam is around 10 kilometres north of Kanchipuram, in the heart of Tondaimandalam. Today it is a minor station on the Arakkonam–Chengalpattu line of Indian Railways. In the mid-tenth century, it enjoyed some renown, as its temple, dedicated to Siva, found mention in the hymns of the great bard Sambandar. Many Chola inscriptions line its walls.[8] It was here, in the year 949, that a bitterly fought battle took place, over ten days of bloody fighting. On one side were Rashtrakutas, with the Ganga leader Butuga II pitching in with his men and military prowess; on the other side, the Cholas, with Parantaka's son Rajaditya in charge. Elephants and horses in both armies added to the violence and destruction. Hundreds of lives, of man and beast, were lost in the fierce fighting.

Rajaditya, the son and heir-in-training of Parantaka, fought bravely, but lost his life in the battle. Butuga's trusted aide-de-camp, a warrior named Manalera cleared a path for Butuga to approach Rajaditya—he split open the forehead of Rajaditya's elephant, forcing the beast and the prince to drop to the ground. Butuga then attacked the howdah upon which Rajaditya was seated and assaulted him with a barrage of sharp arrows, and, finally, stabbed him. The mighty warrior's heart was pierced, and he died a hero's death, fighting to defend his father's empire.

The Larger Leiden plates describe his death movingly:

> That heroic Rajaditya, the ornament of the solar race, having agitated in battle, the imperturbable Krishnaraja along with his army, with his sharp arrows falling in all directions, while (*seated*) on the back of an excellent elephant, had his heart split by the thrusts of his (Krishnaraja's) sharp arrows and mounting a celestial car went to the world of heroes (*viraloka*) praised by the three worlds.[9]

Another account of this battle is found inscribed on a 'hero stone' found at Atakur in Mysore district. The stone was inscribed shortly after the Takkolam battle. The inscription is attributed to the reign of Krishna III and his henchman Butuga.

The inscription at Atakur is hardly flattering to Butuga for its description of the manner in which he killed Rajaditya.

> At the time when Kannaradeva was fighting against the Chola, Butuga (II), while embracing Rajaditya,

> treacherously stabbed him with a dagger, and thus fought and killed him....

The inscription goes on to describe the generous gifts that Kannaradeva showered upon Butuga as reward for killing the enemy.[10]

The Takkolam battle would have been a major event of the time. It has found mention in the Jain poet Pushpadanta's *Mahapurana*, in which he wrote that in the course of his travels, he arrived at Melpati (Manyaketa), the Rashtrakuta capital. Here, he noted, he encountered the glorious and charming King Tudiga—none other than Krishna III himself, who was in his palace there, having cut off the head of the Chola king.[11]

The Chola empire, held thus far with fragile alliances, stumbled but held on. The Rashtrakutas, headed by Krishna III had some more years of hard fighting as they butted their way south. Their inscriptions started appearing in the Tondaimandalam region only several years later. A grant issued by Krishna III from North Arcot district (in Pallava domain) boasts about him erecting a pillar of victory all the way south at Rameshwaram. There is no way to tell if this was true or mere empty boasting, as no inscriptions of his have been found there. Krishna III continued to rule for almost another two decades, through the reigns of several more Chola emperors, until his death in 967.

The Chola fortunes fell after this loss. Their hard-fought gains evaporated; the Chola vassals in the south, seeing the disarray to the north, reasserted their power.

There are a handful of inscriptions issued by Parantaka in the heart of the Chola domain, near Thanjavur. The last inscription that has been found is from his forty-eighth regnal year, 955. He must have been an old man then, filled with memories of the great triumphs he enjoyed and the terrible losses he suffered, having reigned for nearly half a century as one of the great Chola rulers.

Parantaka's long reign was not all dedicated to fighting. He was supremely devoted to Lord Siva. The roof over the sanctum at the Nataraja Temple in Chidambaram was covered with gold tiles. Some sources ascribe this to his father, Aditya; some give the credit to Parantaka. It is likely he was involved in some way, as he played a pivotal role in his father's victory in the Kongu region which won them the huge booty of gold that was used for the Chidambaram temple's roof. The Leiden plates unequivocally attribute this deed to Parantaka:

> With the pure gold brought from all the quarters which were subdued by the prowess of his own arm, this banner of the solar race (i. e. Parantaka) covered the mansion of Indramauli (Siva) at Vyaghragrahara (i. e. Chidambaram).[12]

The Thiruvalangadu plates praise him effusively as a true follower of Siva: 'Parantaka...who was a bee at the two lotus feet of Purantaka (Siva).'[13] He performed the tulabharana ceremony several times, and donated his weight in gold to the temple at which it was done—another sign of his devotion and generosity.

Parantaka's religious devotion was not restricted to Siva. Nathamuni, a great Vaishnavite guru lived during his reign, and it is believed the two were closely associated. It was Nathamuni who recovered the Tamil hymns (*Pasuram*) of the twelve Vaishnava saints (Alwars) which had virtually been lost.

During his reign, the arts of peace received as much attention as deeds of war. Old brick temples continued to be converted into more permanent structures of stone. Two of the finest temples built during his time and that still stand today have exquisite stone carvings—they are at Thiruvaduthurai and Punjai. During his reign, Nataraja—whose Tamil name was Adavallan—became the family deity of the Cholas. Poetry, art, and music flourished.

An inscription from 1019 mentions Parantaka's creation of many channels with clear water for irrigation.[14] Irrigation is a topic discussed in depth in many epigraphs. Pallava and Chola inscriptions provide the important information that three ways of irrigation were known and practised by the agriculturists of the north Chennai region—by damming rivers, by using hand picotahs, and by using baskets. As there were not many rivers in this area, the use of methods two and three seem to have been widely prevalent. The inscriptions frequently mention tanks for irrigation purposes. Epigraphs from Koyambedu mention the lake (eri) of that village.

The soil of the Kaveri delta—rich, alluvial, dense yet allowing for percolation—provides the ideal fertile environment for rice crops to flourish. It is a crop that makes arduous demands of the farmer, from transplanting the delicate young sapling a few at a time to having to ensure frequent flooding of fields alternating with dry spells. Water is a critical component of a successful rice crop, and an abundance—but not excess—of it has to be available through nearly the entire growth process. The Chola kings were well aware of this right from the days of Karikala, who dammed the Kaveri to protect villages along its bank from inundation, to Parantaka and beyond. With the reclamation of large tracts of land along the Kaveri, agriculture thrived.

Parantaka was a leader who understood the value of administering well the lands that came under his rule. One of the most interesting and important of any Chola inscriptions are from his reign, found on the walls of a village named Uthiramerur.[15] We will look into this in more detail later.

Parantaka was a man of many wives. As many as eleven wives have been named in his inscriptions. A growing empire needed strategic alliances, and marrying the daughters of rulers, chieftains, and others of importance was a way to secure and ensure loyalty. Two of his more important wives (in that they bore the successors to the throne) were Chera princesses from Kerala. The Cheras had been, and continued to be, faithful and dependable allies, and trusted members of his military and political retinue were from Chera country.

Parantaka had five sons: Rajaditya, Gandaraditya, Arikulakesari, Uttamasili, and Arinjaya. The greatest tragedy of his life was the loss of his oldest, Rajaditya, on the Takkolam battlefield; he was the son he had so carefully groomed to succeed him. It was Gandaraditya, a man of many virtues, but ill-suited for the particular rigours and stresses of kingship, who next ascended the Chola throne. Parantaka had several daughters, one of whom was married to a Velir chief from Kodambalur.

It is probably fair to call Parantaka the first of the truly great Chola emperors of the Imperial line. He left his mark where no Chola had before. In his long reign of nearly fifty years, he enjoyed exhilarating triumphs and suffered excruciating losses. His achievements made him a man on whom a rich passel of adulatory titles was conferred. There were those that highlighted his military prowess: Maduraiyum Illamum Konda—defeater of Madurai (the Pandyas) and Lanka; his respect for scholars (Pandita Vatsala); his religious generosity (Pon Venda Perumal—having gilded the roof of the Pon Ambalam of Chidambaram); as brave and valiant (Vira Cholan); a great ruler (Chakravartin) who was so strong and fearless that he wrestled with elephants (Kunjara Mallan).

For all the tumult during his reign, the inscriptions make it appear that he was held in high regard by his subjects who treated him as a father, the embodiment of the boundless joy of his subjects.

Let us bid adieu to this great king with the glowing words that his grandson, Sundara Chola, had inscribed on the Anbil plates:

> In him, valour had its goal, skill was incarnate, courage had a (steady) hold, goodness found a protector, the earth had good king, poetic art a proper seat, skill in the (fine) arts found a common shelter, and his fame caused astonishment in all quarters.[16]

CHAPTER 9

CHAOS AMIDST CHAOS
GANDARADITYA TO UTTAMA CHOLA
(950–985)

The three decades that followed the death of Parantaka are mired in confusion. The evidence, such as it is, is unclear and historians disagree about who reigned, and when.[1] Stone and copper inscriptions, our only sources of information, appear to contradict each other on who reigned and in what order. Overlapping and missing dates, names that don't match up, the confusing Parakesari/Rajakesari nomenclature with multiple possibilities for each one, and over-eager prasasti poets who sacrificed accuracy for poetic eloquence are some of the problems historians have to deal with.

The Leiden grant from Rajaraja's reign states unequivocally that after Parantaka, the kings were Rajaditya (killed at Takkolam), Gandaraditya (Parantaka's second son), Arinjaya (Parantaka's third and youngest son), Sundara Chola (Arinjaya's son), Aditya Karikala (the oldest son of Sundara Chola), Madurantaka Uttama Chola (the son of Gandaraditya), and finally, Rajaraja. That makes six kings squeezed into a short period of thirty-three years; but adding up the highest possible regnal years from inscriptions produces a number far higher. Most scholars agree that Rajaditya and Aditya Karikala didn't actually reign, but served as yuvarajas under their fathers, when it was accepted to have their names in inscriptions along with their (yuvaraja) regnal year. It was not an orderly father to son succession, but rather a zigzag procession across the family tree, suggesting internal strife. The very foundations of the fledgling Chola regime were rocked by Parantaka's defeat at Takkolam.

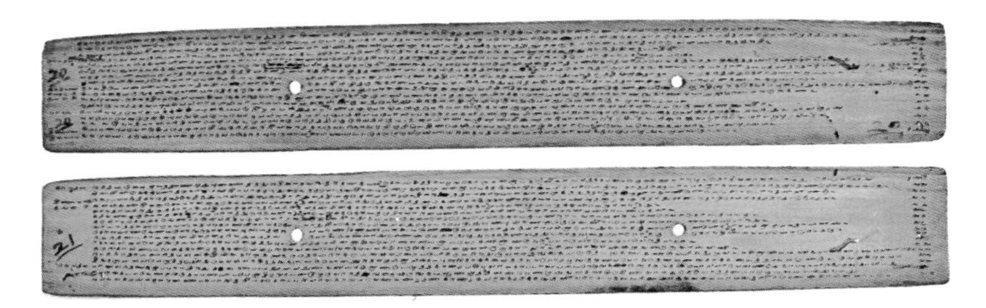

Top: The River Kaveri at Tiruchirapalli, from the British Museum, Company School painting, 1820–30.
Middle: A mural of the Kaveri River at the Panchanadishwara Temple, Thiruvaiyaru. Probably 10th century CE. Siva's bull Nandi is believed to have been born here.
Bottom: Palm leaf manuscript that includes Sangam-era literature. Manuscripts like this are a few hundred years old. At the U. V. Swaminathan Library, Chennai.

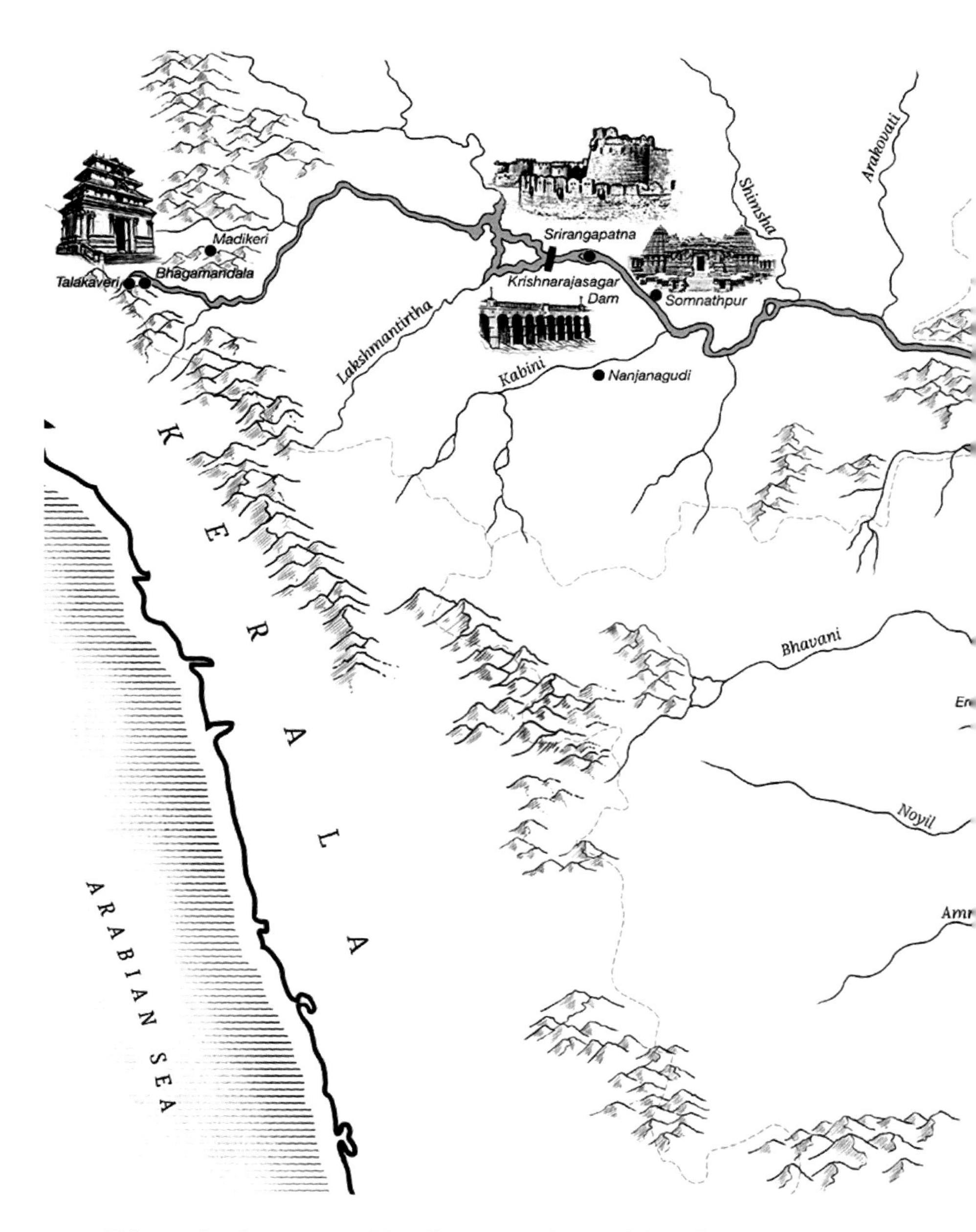

This map has been prepared in adherence to the 'Guidelines for acquiring and producing Geospatial Data and Geospatial Data Services including Maps' published vide DST F.No.SM/25/02/2020 (Part-I) dated 15th February, 2021.

THE KAVERI RIVER

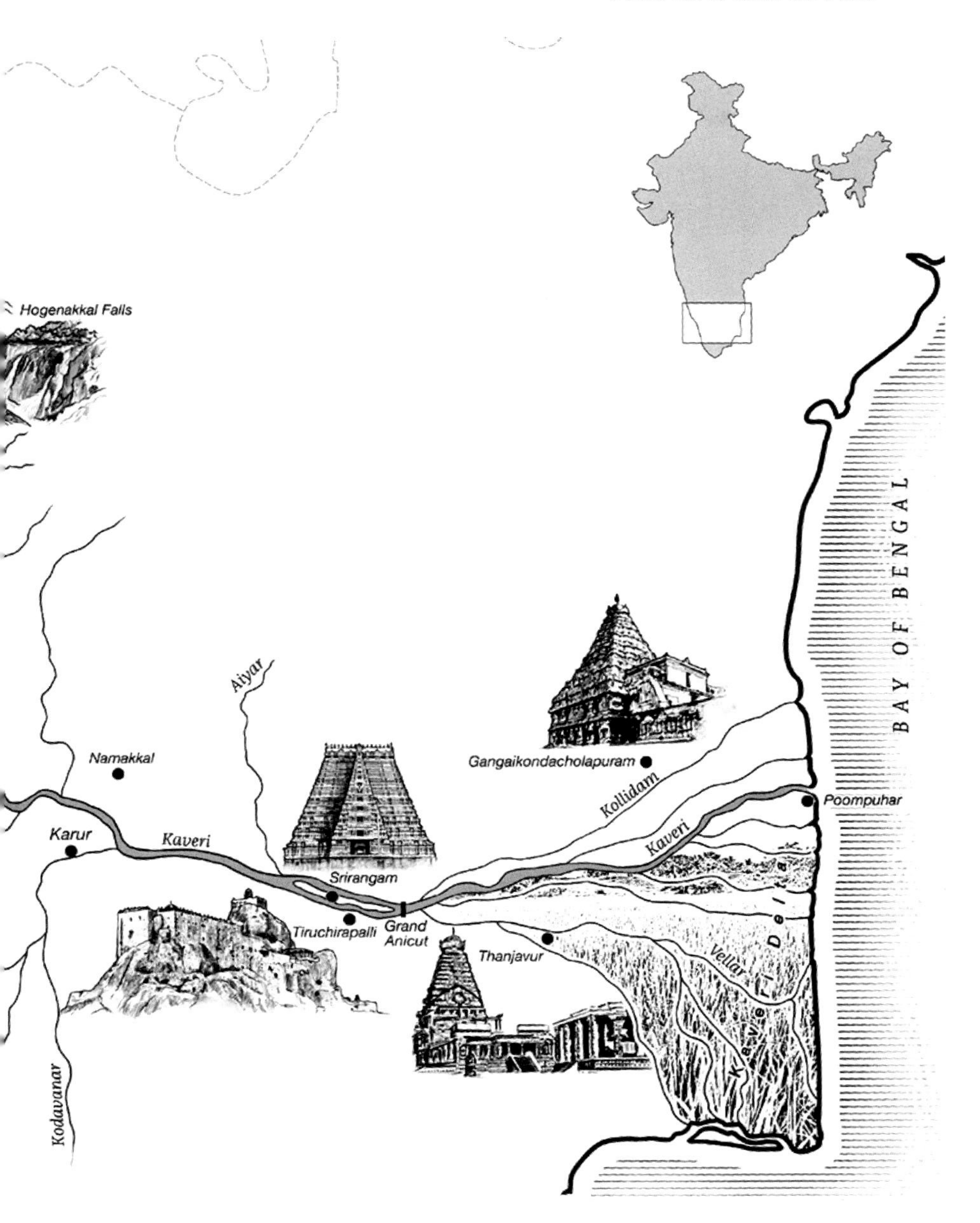

0 50 100 Kilometres

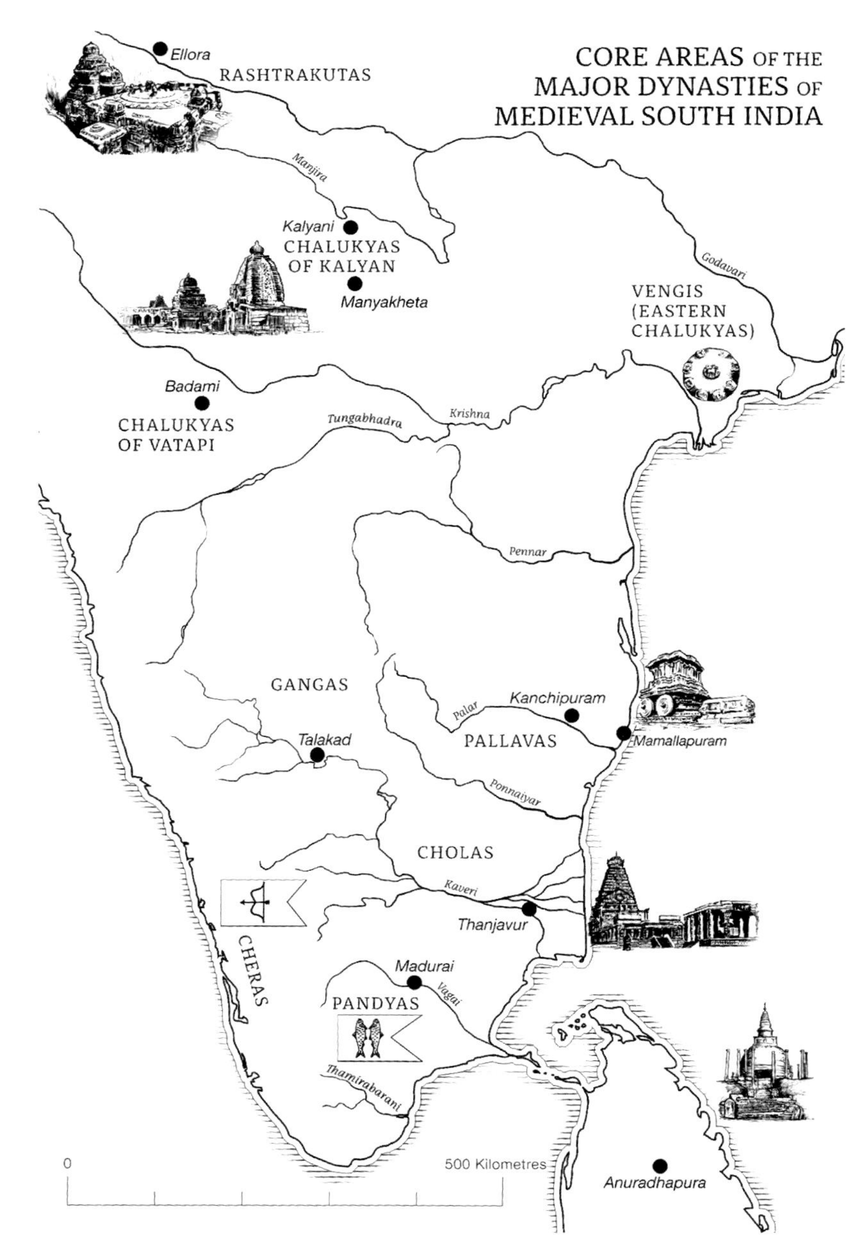

This map has been prepared in adherence to the 'Guidelines for acquiring and producing Geospatial Data and Geospatial Data Services including Maps' published vide DST F.No.SM/25/02/2020 (Part-I) dated 15th February, 2021.

Top: Vijayacholeshwara Temple in Narthamalai, probably late 9th century CE. An example of early Chola temple architecture. There is no agreement on who built it; some say it was a Muttaraiyar chieftain, others claim it was Vijayalaya Chola. *Bottom*: Moovar Koil in Kodumbalur, likely built by an Irukkavel chieftain who was friendly with the Cholas. An important example of early Chola-era temple architecture, probably from the 9th century CE.

Top: Stone carvings and inscriptions at the Brahmapurishwara Temple, Pullamangai, built by Parantaka I, early 10th century CE.
Bottom left: Bronze idol of Queen Sembiyan Madevi, 10th century CE, now at the Freer Sackler gallery of the National Museum of Asian Art, Washington D.C.
Bottom right: Konerirajapuram village. The Uma Maheshwara Temple, built by Queen Sembiyan Madevi in the 10th century, is here.

Top: Rajaraja I's Brihadeeshwara Temple, Thanjavur, completed 1010 CE. The 65-metre high vimana and capstone of the Brihadeeshwara Temple are visible.
Bottom: The Rajaraja Tiruvasal or entrance gateway (gopuram) at the Brihadeeshwara Temple. The vimana is visible in the background.

Top: Mural of Siva as Nataraja on the wall of the sanctum sanctorum of the Brihadeeshwara Temple.
Bottom: Mural on the walls of the sanctum sanctorum of the Brihadeeshwara Temple. This is believed to be a painting of Rajaraja and his guru Karuvur Devar although scholars have differing opinions on who these figures might be.

It would not be until Rajaraja that the kingdom's golden age would begin.

THE PIOUS ONE: RAJAKESARI GANDARADITYA (R. 950–957)

> ....Gandaradityavarman protected the whole earth dispelling the dense darkness (viz.), all (his) enemies.[2]

Gandaraditya, the second son of Parantaka I became heir-apparent in 950 after the death of his brother Rajaditya in the Battle of Takkolam. He ruled alongside his ageing father for a few years and became the monarch after his father's death in 950 but ruled a mere seven or eight years.

Very little is known about his reign. Gandaraditya inherited a kingdom that was in disarray and sadly shrunken after the disastrous loss at Takkolam and the ongoing struggles with the Pandyas. The Rashtrakuta king Krishna III was very much a force to reckon with, and he was busy consolidating his kingdom and rewarding his allies to ensure their continued loyalty.

Gandaraditya appears to be a man more inclined to piety and worship than warfare and empire building; the fiery, ambitious Chola spirit seems to have bypassed him.

An inscription in Udaiyarkudi from 972 describes him as the 'lord who rose and went west'.[3] This has excited a variety of interpretations. The most dire one sees the 'west' as being a euphemism for death. Gandaraditya was reputed to be an extremely spiritual man of a scholarly bent, and some historians are of the view that he possessed these traits to such an extreme that he chose to escape the earthly realm and worldly bonds by undertaking a fast unto death. Others have, however, attributed a rather more benign and literal meaning, saying that perhaps he actually went in a westerly direction to devote his life to Lord Siva, renouncing his empire, and taking on the life of a religious recluse. The land to the west could be Karnataka or

Kerala. Either way, it is taken to refer to his extreme piousness.

Offered as proof for the more literal understanding of Gandaraditya going west is an inscription in Karnataka from the eleventh-century emperor Rajendra Chola's time that mentions a Sivagnana Gandaradithar (Gandaraditya the Siva aficionado).[4] The inscription records the donation of icons of Uma Parameshwari and Gandaradita Vidangar to the temple in Channapatna in Karnataka. And in a Siva temple in another town in Karnataka is a sculpture of a man in the act of doing penance. Some scholars say there is a similarity between this image and that of Gandaraditya that his wife Sembiyan Madevi commissioned at her temple in Konerirajapuram. As with much of Chola history, we have to weave our stories out of the thinnest and most fragile of threads.

We have the barest snippets about Gandaraditya's activities. He built a village on the north bank of the Kaveri that he named Gandaradittam, after himself. He also excavated an eponymous tank. In keeping with his pious nature, and perhaps also showing a tolerant bent of mind, he sponsored both a Vaishnava and a Jain temple, or at the very least, permitted the use of his name on them.

Gandaraditya is best remembered for his remarkable wife Sembiyan Madevi. There is far more to write about her, than him. We will read more about her later.

PARAKESARI ARINJAYA (R. 957–961?)

> Arindama *(i.e. the destroyer of enemies)* bearing indeed a name which was full of meaning, became the best of kings...[5]

For an emperor whose very kingship has been questioned and about whose reign almost nothing is known, the Anbil plates are fulsome in their praise of Arinjaya:

> Like unto victory born of prowess and policy, and like the unequalled heaven, the outcome of sacrifice and sacrificial gifts, a son named Arinchika of unequalled fame was born to these two[6] [Parantaka and his wife who was the daughter of the Paluvettaraiyar Kerala king]

The Leiden plates, not to be outdone, say:

> ...the heroic Arinjaya, a very conflagration in the...forest of enemy kings, ruled the whole earth.[7]

After Gandaraditya, the throne should rightfully have gone to his son, Uttama. However, convention dictated that the king had to be at least fourteen years of age and married, and Uttama fell short on both counts. The throne thus went to Gandaraditya's younger brother, Arinjaya.[8]

One of Parantaka's wives was the daughter of a Kerala king who was called Paluvettaraiyar, and Arinjaya was their son. He assisted his brother Rajaditya when he was the yuvaraja posted to patrol Parantaka's northern borders. It is very likely he fought at the disastrous Takkolam battle as well. Interestingly, there is no mention of Gandaraditya's presence there; perhaps Parantaka judged this son, so pious and gentle, as unfit for the savage realities of building and defending an empire. Arinjaya might have even assisted Gandaraditya during the brief period he was king.

His priority must have been to start the arduous work of reclaiming Tondaimandalam, now in the hands of the Rashtrakutas, who had entrusted their feudatories, the Banas and Vaidumbas, to take control of these lands. To this end, Arinjaya resorted to the tried-and-tested tactic of marrying his daughter to a Bana chief (there is an inscription that refers to the daughter of Arinjaya as the Queen of the Banas) thus (hopefully) seducing them away from their alliance with the Rashtrakuta Krishna III and securing the loyalty of at least one branch of the Banas. There must have been the inevitable battles and perhaps Arinjaya lost his life in one of them. He died in a town called Aatrur, which was in the Tondaimandalam region to the north. Perhaps he had gone there on an ill-fated quest for territory. His grandson, Rajaraja, built a temple in his memory, over his remains, in this village. Rajaraja named the temple Arinjigaishwara; now known as Choleswara, it lies deserted. The village itself seems to have been renamed Rajasrayapuram, after Rajaraja. An inscription there, made in Rajaraja's last year as king, his twenty-ninth, records the donation of land to this temple 'which Sri Rajarajadeva had been pleased to build in our city as a resting place for the king who fell asleep (died) at Aatrur'.[9]

RAJAKESARI SUNDARA CHOLA/PARANTAKA II (R. 957–973)

> While that emperor Sundara was ruling the circle of the earth, the syllable *ha* (indicative of sorrow) was heard by people only in words like *hara*.[10]

The Chola line had moved to Arinjaya, the youngest son of Parantaka, and after his death the next Chola to become king was his son Sundara Chola or Parantaka II. Sundara's mother was a Vaidumba princess (possibly named Kalyani), the only queen of Arinjaya mentioned in the Anbil plates. His names—Sundara and Parantaka—are explained:

> ...he possessed a multitude of good qualities which belonged to his grandfather, and his name as well....
>
> (a son) who quite surpassed Cupid in beauty and who received (therefore) the auspicious name Sundara-Chola (the handsome Chola).[11]

The Pandyas, perennial thorns in the Cholas' side, remained a menace that had to be dealt with. This was where Sundara Chola trained his attention first. From as early as five years into his reign, Sundara Chola was called Madurakonda Rajakesari (the Rajakesari who conquered the Madurai–Pandya ruler).

There was a bloody battle against the Pandyas at Sevur (Chevura) in which both Sundara Chola and his oldest son, Aditya Karikala, acquitted themselves brilliantly. This Battle of Chevura was fought against the old Chola foe, Vira Pandya (son of Rajasimha II who had faced defeat at the hands of Sundara Chola's grandfather Parantaka). Apparently, so resoundingly was he defeated that he was forced to 'flee and climb the peaks of the Sahyadri mountains'.[12] Sundara Chola joined the ranks of his relatives who claimed the title 'Madurai Konda' or 'Madurantaka'—vanquisher of the Madurai ruler.

The Leiden copperplate grant of Rajaraja describes how, at the city named Chevura, Sundara Chola filled the land with 'heaps of sharp and pointed arrows sent forth from his beautiful bow and caused to flow manifold rivers of blood springing from the high mountains i.e., the enemies' elephants cut asunder by (his) sharp sword'.[13]

The Battle of Chevura was hard-fought and bloody. Sundara Chola's Irrukavel ally from Kodambalur, Bhuti Vikramakesari proved to be a reliable friend, and distinguished himself in the battle. However, despite the claim made by the Thiruvalangadu plates that Aditya Karikala 'took the head of Vira Pandya', it's likely that the Pandya ruler was not actually killed, but rather, merely badly humiliated. There are no inscriptions of Sundara Chola's in Pandya country, indicating that the threat had not been fully extinguished at this time.

Sundara Chola appointed his oldest son Aditya Karikala yuvaraja and co-regent, sometime between 956 and 966.[14] As co-regent he was apparently entitled to one of the alternating appellations the Cholas gave themselves, and as his father was a rajakesari, he was a parakesari. His mother was Sundara Chola's chief queen, Vanavanmadevi.

There appears to have been another battle against Vira Pandya, who had presumably returned from atop the Sahyadri mountains. What's more likely is that the Pandyas were driven south, with another Kodambalur chieftain called Parantaka Siriyavelur leading the charge and chase. It appears, based on inscriptional evidence, that he killed Vira Pandya in gory fashion, brandishing his head atop a pillar of victory. The Thiruvalangadu plates boast that Aditya Karikala 'played sportively in battle with Vira Pandya, just as a lion's cub (does) with a rutting mad elephant proud of his strength'. However, it appears that he himself suffered losses at this battle, because the very same Thiruvalangadu plates of Rajendra Chola state:

> Having deposited in his (*capital*) town the lofty pillar of victory (*viz.,*) the head of the Pandya king, Aditya disappeared (*from this world*) with a desire to see heaven.[15]

Aditya Karikala has been called 'Pandiyanai Talaikonda Parakesari'—the Parakesari who took the Pandyan's (Vira Pandyan) head. There has been much debate about the exact significance of the phrase 'talaikonda' (taker of the head). There are multiple candidates for this title; both the Pandyas and Cholas, as well as others, lay claim to it. Vira Pandya has, for his part, called himself 'Solantalaikonda' (he who took the head of the Chola). Who was the Chola who had his head taken by the Pandya? And how could it be that both sides could take this title?

It appears that the moniker talaikonda is not to be taken literally. Rather, the likeliest interpretation is that it is a form of extreme humiliation in which the vanquished king bowed his head down before his conqueror as a sign of subjugation and defeat. The victorious king might have added to his enemy's shame by placing his foot upon the proffered head. In the case of Aditya Karikala, Rajendra Chola's Thiruvalangadu plates stated in no uncertain terms that he killed Vira Pandya and displayed his severed head at his capital. Was this an exaggeration, a legend that came into being and grew with the passage of time?

The Pandya menace was very much a factor during Sundara Chola's rule. The inevitable battles followed and both sides suffered defeats and losses. The Pandyas were fierce adversaries and refused to be quelled. Sundara Chola and Aditya Karikala might have boasted about their Pandya triumphs but when it came to the acid test of inscriptional evidence, they failed. No inscriptions of theirs have been found in Pandya country, and it took a later Chola king, Rajaraja, and fierce fighting on his part to finally subdue them and establish his presence there. In fact, Rajaraja crowed about how he vanquished the Pandyas while they were powerful and illustrious, which probably goes to show that for all their claims, Sundara Chola and Aditya Karikala did not really make much headway against the Pandyas.

Nine years into his reign, Sundara Chola sent troops into Ceylon. This might have been an act of revenge—Vira Pandya had requested help from the Ceylonese, and the ruler, Mahinda IV, had obliged. Parantaka Siriyavelur, the Kodambalur chief who had proven himself an able fighter against the Pandyas, led the Chola forces. The battle ended badly for the Cholas and Siriyavelur, who lost his life. The Sri Lankan chronicle *Mahavamsa* has an account of the battle in which the king dispatched his chief general to fight the Chola troops, which he did successfully, after which the Cholas, unable to vanquish the Ceylonese king, made peace with him thus spreading Mahinda's fame across the water.

Even as Sundara Chola struggled against the Pandyas, matters started looking up for him at his kingdom's northern frontiers. The Rashtrakutas, who had wreaked such havoc earlier, finally started succumbing to the exigencies of constant warfare. Again, Sundara was aided by his Kodumbalur allies, particularly Bhuti Vikramakesari who claimed that he turned the waters of the Kaveri red with the blood shed during the fighting.[16] Slowly but surely, the inscriptions of Krishna III were edged out, and those of Sundara Chola and Aditya Karikala grew in number.

At some point during his campaigns in the northern regions of his kingdom, Sundara Chola suffered a terrible blow. His beloved son, Aditya Karikala, the designated heir, was assassinated. We know nothing more about this. There has much speculation about the manner of his death. It seems very likely that he was murdered; we know this from a few lines of an inscription at a temple in the little hamlet of Udaiyarkudi. This inscription was made several years later in the early years of Rajaraja's reign. Among other things, it names three brothers and accuses them of treason for the assassination of Aditya Karikala (according to the inscription, they were guilty of treason because they murdered Karikalasolan who took the head of the Pandya) for which act the perpetrators were punished by having their lands, and those belonging to a specified list of family members, confiscated and sold.[17]

This inscription raises a whole host of questions. Who were these men? And why did they murder Aditya Karikala? Were they hitmen employed by Uttama Chola, keen on reclaiming the throne he believed was rightfully his, since it was his direct line of forebears who had ruled until his father abdicated the throne? Or could it have been Rajaraja himself, ambition overcoming fraternal sentiment? Or might it have been the Pandyas, smarting under their losses and at the humiliation of having the head of their ruler displayed on a stick, to the jeers and laughter of the reviled Cholas? Or could it have been somebody else altogether, who had his own reasons to do away with him? Alas, over a thousand years later, all we have are the possibilities that the imagination can conjure up.

Sundara Chola himself took an active part in affairs in the north and, in 973, he died at Kanchipuram, in the golden palace built for him by his son Aditya Karikala, and became known as 'Pon Maligaittunjina Deva', the lord who died in his golden palace.[18] His chief wife Vanavanmadevi, the mother of his three children—Aditya Karikala, Kundavai, and Rajaraja, committed sati on his funeral pyre. It appears that she might have feared that her handsome husband would fall prey to the allures of the beauties of the celestial realm; the Thiruvalangadu plates express her thoughts and actions thus:

> 'I am determined to follow my lord Sundara (i. e. the beautiful) before (*he*) is coveted by the celestial damsels' so saying zealously, his devoted queen the glorious Vanavanmadevi, a very Arundhati in (*her*) manifold good qualities abandoned her own people and followed him as [night] does the day to heaven, afraid as it were of the allurement (*of her husband*) by celestial nymphs and (*desirous consequently of*) being near (*him*) even there.[19]

Sundara Chola was known to have been a connoisseur and patron of literature in both Sanskrit and Tamil. The Thiruvalangadu plates of Rajendra say he was believed to have been an avatar of Manu himself, come to earth re-establish the laws and justice, which had suffered during this age of Kali.[20]

The earliest extant Chola copperplate grant, the Anbil plates, that record the grant of a village 'out of affection' to a Brahmin minister named Aniruddha, is from his reign.[21] The Anbil copperplates record the grant of a village named Anbil, or in its Sanskritized form, Premagrahara, to a minister of Sundara Chola's, called Aniruddha. This minister, a learned Brahmin from a family of pious devotees of Ranganatha of Srirangam, made a request for this land, which was buttressed by an order from a Muttaraiyar chief. Clearly, it behoved Sundara Chola to heed this request-order, and the grant was made, with all the measurements, methodology, and other details inscribed on copperplates as a permanent record. The dimensions of the land were determined by the path taken by a female elephant, and the new owner Aniruddha and his household were free to enjoy everything Anbil had to offer: its plants, trees, gardens, tanks, wells, without having to pay any taxes on the land and its produce. The ceremony of allowing a female elephant to mark the borders of the gifted land was an ancient one and was called pidi suldal in Tamil.[22]

The Anbil plates are one of only four copperplate grants that we are aware of that include Chola genealogical information. It is largely thanks to these that we know anything at all about the kings who established and consolidated the newly risen line of Cholas. Each of the grants has a portion on the genealogy of the Cholas, from the mythical to the protohistoric to the current lineage; each was written by a different author, and therefore tells a somewhat different tale, reflecting the imagination and inclinations of the author. There is quite some discrepancy in the different accounts of the early genealogies, as the authors have taken ample liberties in their interpretations of literary and mythological sources. The genealogies are just the preamble to the actual business of the grant, which while full of laborious detail about practical issues, nonetheless lets us picture what everyday life in the Chola realm must have been like. Without these inscriptions, we would be mostly in the dark and the glorious world of the Cholas would remain a closely guarded secret.

PARAKESARI UTTAMA CHOLA/MADHURANTAKA UTTAMA CHOLA (R. 971–985)

> ...the son of Gandaraditya, (i.e) king Madhurantaka, he, of powerful arms and famous as Mahendra (Indra), protected the earth which had the ocean for its girdle.[23]

Uttama Chola, the son of Gandaraditya, had been a young child when his father's reign ended, far too young to become the ruler. A full two decades later, following the reigns of his uncle Arinjaya and his cousin Sundara, the reins of power came into his hands. He ruled for sixteen years, all the while assisted by his nephew Rajaraja.

There is scant information on him in the Larger Leiden plates; all we learn was that he possessed powerful arms and that he protected the earth, which had the ocean as its girdle.[24] The Thiruvalangadu plates make generous mention of his piety and devotion to Siva but other than the briefest mention of his showing his wrath only in the killing of enemies, there is nothing to shed light on his military or political efforts.[25] There is, however, a tantalizing hint of something amiss, but no details, inviting us to read between the lines and guess at the power politics, strategic thinking, or practical reasoning that must surely have prevailed. The reins of power had swung from the son of one son of Parantaka to another, and this was a situation ripe for jealousy, covetousness, and backstabbing.

By the normal order of succession, Sundara Chola's son Rajaraja should have become the next Chola king. Why did Uttama Chola become the king after Sundara Chola? Why did Sundara Chola's son, Rajaraja, not succeed his father? The Thiruvalangadu plates hint darkly at an ominously brewing Kali Yuga. The people, in order to stop it in its tracks, were eager to enthrone Rajaraja and restore order. Rajaraja, however, the noble Kshatriya that he was, would not take the reins of power as long as his uncle coveted it.[26] There is so much left unsaid in the inscriptions which might be interpreted in any number of ways, depending on how one views the dramatis personae. The historian Nilakanta Sastri minces no words in painting Uttama Chola as the villain who murdered Aditya Karikala and ensured that the throne came his way: 'Uttama Chola furnishes an instance, by no means unique in history, of selfish and perverse offspring born of parents distinguished for piety and right-mindedness (Gandaraditya and Sembiyan Madevi); and his rash and bloody self-seeking stands out in striking contrast to the true nobility and statesmanship of the future Rajaraja.'[27]

We don't know how things worked out the way they did. Perhaps there was a mutual understanding and compromise. It is likely that Sembiyan Madevi, Uttama's mother and a lady who commanded respect across the generations in her family and the kingdom, mediated an arrangement. Uttama was the senior in age and in the relationship and had belonged to the 'main' branch which then became a collateral one during Arinjaya and

Sundara Chola's reigns, and thus he did have a legitimate claim to the throne. And so it was, by whatever means it happened, that Uttama Chola became the next Chola monarch, with Rajaraja appointed as his yuvaraja, a position he had for all sixteen years of Uttama's rule—ample time to observe and learn.

The very first Chola coin we know of is from the reign of Uttama. The coin itself is lost to us now, but it was once in the possession of Sir Walter Elliot, a Scottish civil servant of the nineteenth century who worked primarily in the Presidency of Madras. He was a man of many interests and abilities: he was a keen naturalist, linguist, and numismatist, among other things. Sadly, towards the end of his life, he began to lose his sight, and eventually became completely blind. It is remarkable that even with his failing eyesight he continued to indulge in his fascination for coins, and had to resort to feeling the coins in order to describe them to a scribe, who then wrote down what he had to say. Thanks to his description, we have an idea of what the Uttama Chola coin looked like. The two sides were identical. In the centre was a seated tiger with a fish to its right; Uttama Chola's name was inscribed in the Grantha script along the circular margin, along with a ring of beads. The coin was made of gold.[28]

After the precipitous ups and downs of Parantaka's reign and the near non-stop battles and skirmishes that followed, Uttama Chola inherited a kingdom that was relatively stable in its northern reaches. Much of the old Pallava lands that had been lost to the Rashtrakutas were now back in the hands of the Cholas. The sheer number of inscriptions in these regions from the years before Uttama, and the nature of the transactions recorded—about mundane, everyday undertakings—are testament to the fact that the years of fighting and wars were over in that region, for that period at least, and it was back to life as usual.

The Pandyas, alas, had proven themselves troublesome again during Sundara Chola's rule, and Uttama Chola must have felt obliged to send his forces to quell them and to Ceylon as well. We know nothing of what transpired there, but several of his coins found in those parts are evidence of the Chola presence there during his reign. He added more soldiers to his armies and also provided them with coats of armour to protect them.

There are a number of stone inscriptions as well as a set of copperplates from Uttama's reign. They provide scant details on his political and military affairs, as the vast majority deal with temple-related activities, apt, perhaps, for a man who was said to be of a pious bent of mind. The copperplates are in the museum at Madras (referred to as the Madras Museum Plates), and while several plates are missing, the remaining plates provide details about the management of the temple of Uraka near Kanchipuram. The plates also give a host of interesting information about Kanchipuram. We learn the names of the four quarters where the weavers, who were patronized by the king, lived. These weavers enjoyed a high status, as several silk weavers were appointed as temple managers, had the privilege of conducting certain festivals, and were exempted from paying taxes in return for their services. There is information on two irrigation canals that watered certain districts. And, we also know that Uttama Chola had a palace in Kanchipuram, as it was while he was seated there that his minister approached him with a request that some of the income from the temple be spent for certain services at the temple.[29] The plates also refer to him as the Chola king who was the destroyer of Madura, but with no substantiating evidence, there is not much more we can say on this.[30]

Uttama Chola, like his ancestors and descendants was a pious man, a devout worshipper of Lord Siva. With tranquillity restored in the kingdom, temple-building picked up during his reign, aided in large part by the passion and vision of his mother, Sembiyan Madevi. He donated generously to temples and made endowments for worship during special festivals. Uttama's officers gave plentifully to temples. One, called Ambalavan

Paluvurnakkan who served under both Uttama and, later, Rajaraja, was a member of the king's council and was awarded the title Vikramasola Maharajan for his services. In gratitude, he built a stone temple on the north bank of the Kaveri in a village called Govindaputtur, and endowed an entire village as well, so that its income could sustain the temple.[31]

Uttama had at least five wives, who were mentioned together in an inscription. The chief wife, Orattanan Sorabbaiyar, maintained her primary position through Uttama's years as king, as seen by her title 'Tribhuvana Madeviyar', that indicated that she was ranked first among his queens. She, along with her co-wives, including Kaduvettigal Nandippottairaiyar and Siddhavadavan Suttiyar, made donations to a temple in a village named for their mother-in-law, the grande dame Sembiyan Madevi.[32]

Uttama Chola died in 985. He had at least one son that we know of, Madurantaka Gandaradittan. But he did not follow his father on to the throne. Perhaps there had been an agreement that Rajaraja would succeed Uttama; he had been the king-in-waiting throughout his reign, after all. Perhaps Uttama's mother, Sembiyan, a lady of high honour who enjoyed a relationship of mutual respect with Rajaraja, ensured that the better man prevailed. Perhaps Gandaradittan possessed the same gentle qualities as the grandfather he was named for, and had no interest in the harsh world of ruling.

In any case, the stage was set for the greatest Chola ruler to make his mark.

BOOK THREE

The Sun at High Noon

CHAPTER 10

THE KING OF KINGS
RAJAKESARI RAJARAJA CHOLA
(R. 985–1014)

> Arunmolivarman was himself then installed in the administration of the kingdom...and the ends of the quarters heavily roared with the tumultuous sounds of the war-drums, rows of bells and bugles, kettle drums, tambourines and conches.[1]

The emperor who would be known as Rajaraja (king of kings) was born Arulmozhi Varman in the year 947. He was the second son of Sundara Chola and his queen Vanavanmadevi. Naga women danced when he was born, delighted because they believed that this emperor would relieve their husband, Adisesha, of the weight of the world on his head. It was proclaimed that, like Vishnu, Arulmozhi was born with the auspicious marks of the conch and the wheel.[2] Such signs could only mean that he was destined for greatness. His birth star was Sadayam, a fact mentioned in inscriptions recording his endowments to temples.[3] Astrological texts inform us that those born under this star are caring and brave, visionaries with a commanding personality and strong likes and dislikes.

He had an older brother, Aditya Karikala, and a sister, Kundavai. When he was born, the ruling Chola monarch was Parantaka, Rajaraja's great-grandfather. It was the final decade of Parantaka's reign, and the empire was in free fall. The disastrous Battle of Takkolam, in which Parantaka's beloved son and his heir-apparent, Rajaditya, lost his life, happened just a year or two after Rajaraja was born. Parantaka never recovered from this blow. All the work of his early years slipped away as the Rashtrakutas to the north and the Pandyas to the south regained what they had lost. Was this the topic of conversation in the Sundara Chola household? Were Rajaraja's early years filled with talk of what had been, what might have been?

He was just ten years old when his father, Sundara Chola, became king. Young, yes, but not too young to watch, absorb, and learn. Sundara Chola inherited a decimated kingdom, but he worked hard to recover lost territory in the north, and enjoyed a major victory over his Pandya foe, Vira Pandya. As we've seen, Aditya Karikala was believed to have been responsible for the Pandya king's death, earning him the epithet 'Pandiyanai Talaikonda Parakesari' (he who captured the head of Vira Pandya). Knowing of his brother's valour on the battlefield must surely have inspired the young Arulmozhi. Things were on track for Aditya Karikala to succeed his father as king; he was being groomed for the role, and displayed great promise.

Tragedy struck the Cholas yet again when Aditya Karikala's life of promise and future kingship was rudely cut short. All we have are the plaintive words from the Thiruvalangadu plates. Having deposited in his capital the lofty pillar of victory—the head of the Pandya king—Aditya disappeared from this world with a desire to see heaven.[4] As we saw in an earlier chapter, we know he was assassinated and that his assassins were caught and punished.[5] We can also gather that he was murdered, and not killed in battle as there are no inscriptions eulogizing his bravery, as there were for his grand-uncle Rajaditya.

No more than a couple of years after the death of Aditya Karikala, Sundara Chola, stricken with grief, died in his golden palace in Kanchipuram. His wife, Vanavanmadevi committed sati. At the age of twenty-two or twenty-three Rajaraja became an orphan.

Through all the turmoil of his youth, his older sister, Kundavai, and his grand-aunt, Sembiyan Madevi were a constant and steady presence. They were both strong, intelligent women, devout and astute, and they must have been a strong influence on the young Rajaraja.

After the death of Sundara Chola, Rajaraja should have become king. He was certainly old enough to assume the reins of power. He fulfilled the conditions necessary to be king: he was over fourteen years of age, and he was married. The Chola line of kings had shifted to his branch of the family, and his own brother had been slated to be next in line. However, for reasons unknown to us, but which therefore invite all manner of speculation, Rajaraja's uncle, his father's cousin Uttama, son of Gandaraditya and Sembiyan Madevi, became the next ruler of the Cholas. The year was 970. We have only inscriptions which, with their rosy-eyed description of events, tell us that though requested by the subjects to occupy the Chola throne in order to destroy the persistently blinding darkness of the powerful Kali (yugam), Arunmoli Varman, who understood the essence of royal conduct, desired not the kingdom for himself even in his mind, while his paternal uncle coveted his dominions.[6]

Conjecturing what the 'persistently blinding darkness' might be, or wondering about Uttama's covetousness, are pointless here. Whatever the reasons for Rajaraja stepping aside, it probably speaks for a high level of maturity, understanding, selflessness, and patience—qualities that are rarely found in someone so young. It is very likely that there was an agreement that Rajaraja would become king once Uttama's reign ended. According to the Thiruvalangadu plates: 'having ascertained by the marks (on his body) that Arulmozhi was the lotus-eyed (Vishnu) himself, the able protector of the three worlds that had incarnated (on earth) Madhurantaka (Uttama Chola) installed him in the office of heir-apparent, and (himself) bore the burden of (ruling) the earth.'[7]

Once again, Rajaraja had the opportunity to observe and learn, for the fifteen years that Uttama Chola ruled, this time with the added advantage of being a bit older and wiser.

Finally, after the death of his uncle, Rajaraja became king, the next Rajakesari, on Saturday, 18 July 985, the day of the star Punarvasu in the dark fortnight in the month of Karkataka; he would go on to become the greatest of the Chola monarchs.[8] It would have been a grand occasion, with the tumultuous sounds of war drums, bells and bugles, kettle drums, tambourines, and conches ringing through the land, likely for days.

Rajaraja was a man with ambition, and he reached for the stars. He wanted all of southern India under his control. He wanted his foes in every direction subdued, once and for all. He must have envisioned himself at the helm of a grand kingdom, where peace reigned, where everything worked like clockwork, where religion, music, and beauty reached their highest calling.

He had his work cut out for him. He utilized, brilliantly, the very important element of communication, using it for royal publicity and self-glorification. He established a royal cult of personality, building the largest temple in the land at the time and naming it after himself. He took official communication to a high art, making sure all his victories were made known to everybody, and for posterity. Symbolism and ceremony meant a great deal to him, and he ensured that his deeds were made known through his inscriptions throughout his kingdom. These inscriptions could not have reached all the places they did if the Chola apparatus did not have the ability to place them there. The appearance mirrored the reality.

The kingdom he inherited was not large, and had not yet fully recovered from the constant battling with the Rashtrakutas and the Pandyas. Rajaraja knew that he needed to secure his western borders and subdue the Pandyas. To the north lurked the threat of the Chalukyas who were gaining ground and could spell trouble.

Rajaraja must have absorbed the lessons learned by his predecessors. Judging from the absence of inscriptions about military expeditions for the first eight years of his reign, it has been assumed that he spent this time building up and training his army, and also working out his strategy. There might have been battles fought and won, but perhaps none decisive enough to be inscription-worthy.

And then 'this king—a pile of matchless prosperity, majesty, learning, strength of arm, prowess, heroism and courage—invaded and conquered all the quarters, commencing with the direction of Trisanku (the south)'.[9]

Four years into his reign, his inscriptions started to include the phrase 'Kandalur Salai-Kalamarutta' before his name, proclaiming his victory at Kandalur, part of the Chera territories in present-day Kerala. This phrase has excited much scholarly debate on what exactly it was that he defeated. To begin with, there were multiple interpretations of what the 'salai' in Kandalur could mean. They span an interesting range from a Brahmin feeding hall, an armoury, a naval base, and a military training centre.[10] And because of this there have naturally been differences in opinion about what Rajaraja did there to award himself the 'Kandalur Salai-Kalamarutta' label.[11]

In 2009, a hero-stone dating from the fourteenth year (999 CE) of the reign of Rajaraja was found in a lake bed in a village called Chengam, around 35 kilometres from Tiruvannamalai, and 250 kilometres north of his capital city, Thanjavur. Hero stones are found all over India. They are memorials that honour someone who died a hero's death, usually in battle or while fighting a tiger or other wild animal. This particular hero stone is unusual for multiple reasons. The inscription describes how a man was killed, for the unacceptable behaviour of pulling the saris of several women who belonged to the family of an oil-monger. More interesting, and more pertinent to the story of Rajaraja, are the other inscriptions on this stone. There is a eulogy to Rajaraja, in which he is praised for 'beheading the Malai Alargal'. These were the Chera warriors of Kandalur Salai, a seaside town near Thiruvananthapuram in present-day Kerala. In addition to the beheadings, the hero-stone inscriptions tell us that he also split the Chera king's naval vessel in two, destroyed a number of boats, and built a mandapa (hall) there.[12] It is clear from this inscription that what happened at Kandalur Salai was a violent military victory for Rajaraja.

The battle at Kandalur Salai appears to be one of Rajaraja's earliest military successes. The likely trigger? The rude behaviour meted out to a diplomatic envoy of Rajaraja by the Chera king Bhaskara Ravi Varma, an insult that could not go unavenged. In addition, and more importantly, the Chera ports along the west coast were rival participants in the booming trade with Arab lands including the prosperous Fatimids of North Africa. Capturing those ports would ensure that control of and profits from that trade would fill not the Chera, but the Chola coffers. It would take several more years and attempts before the territory was fully conquered by Rajaraja. It took a full eight years after he began his reign for his inscriptions to appear in the region.

Rajaraja trained his sights next on the Cholas' long-time foes and perennial thorns in their side, the Pandyas. The Pandyas had caused untold misery to every Chola emperor. At the best of times, there had been a sullen submission on the part of the Pandyas, but even then, they resisted being incorporated into the Chola kingdom and this reluctance posed a state of regular danger that could erupt into disaster at any time. The Pandyas appear to have formed an alliance with the Cheras in Kerala and the Sinhalas in Ceylon to deal with their common foe—the Cholas.

It is hard to tease out the exact chronology and order of Rajaraja's conquests from his inscriptions. It is generally accepted that after his victory at Kandalur Salai he took on the Pandyas. The Pandyas were tough and wily old foes who would not go down without stiff resistance, and it took several attempts on the part of Rajaraja's forces to finally subdue them completely. The Pandya king was Amarabhujanga, and the Thiruvalangadu plates are scathing in their dismissal of him and his allies: 'Amarabhujanga being seized, other dissolute kings, whose rule was secretly mischievous, being much afraid of him

(Rajaraja) at heart, wished to hide themselves, like serpents with sliding crooked bodies.'[13]

We do not know what became of Amarabhujanga after this. If he survived Rajaraja's military depredations, he would have had to swallow the ignominy of seeing his ancestral lands in the hands of the enemy and would have been a helpless spectator as Rajaraja emblazoned his mark all over the land. As the Pandya lands slipped into Rajaraja's control, he renamed villages, temples, and districts, making it known that they were now under Chola control. Pandya Mandalam was now renamed Rajaraja Mandalam. Inscriptions were made in the Vatteluttu script that was prevalent in those parts. A mere ten years into his reign, his inscriptions appeared at the far extremes of the once-Pandya territories, in Ambasamudram and Suchindram, and inscriptions continued to be added in the coming years. One inscription made in the year 1000 at the Sthanunatha Temple in Suchindram gloated: 'Rajaraja...deprived the Seliyars (Pandyas) of their splendour at the very moment when Udagai...was most resplendent.'[14] In addition to inscriptions, large numbers of copper Chola coins have been found in Pandya lands, including in Madurai, further establishing the fact of their conquest of the region.

Rajaraja was well aware that he could not rest easy after his Pandya conquest. After all, they had risen like the proverbial cat with nine lives, time and time again. He posted troops in the territory to put down any rebellions. One troop, called the Munrukaimasenai was stationed at Tiruvalisvaram (near Tirunelveli, deep in Pandya territory) which in some inscriptions is called Rajaraja Chaturvedimangalam, a subdivision of Rajaraja Valanadu. Judging from inscriptions at the temple there, the troop enjoyed many military successes. They also took a proprietary interest in the temple, ensuring its eternal protection under their care.[15]

It is interesting to note that one of Rajaraja's queens—believed to be his first—is Panchavan Madevi. Panchavan was a title adopted by Pandya kings, indicating that she was very likely a Pandya princess.[16] Her name features first in the list of his many wives, which probably meant that she was his first wife. It is likely that he married her after Sundara Chola's or Uttama Chola's victories against the Pandyas.

It was after his initial Pandya victories, eight years into his reign, that Rajaraja introduced the Tamil meykkirti to his inscriptions, a standardized ode to himself listing his achievements that included his trademark epithet, Tirumagal Pol. As his triumphs grew, so too did the length of his meykkirtis, adding his newest victories to those already there. These official introductions made it easy to know who the inscriptions referred to, a relief after the records of earlier rulers where it was often unclear which Parakesari or Rajakesari they were referring to.

Rajaraja continued westwards into the hill country called Malai-nadu. This area, part of present-day Coorg, was probably under joint Chera–Pandya custody. Here, he launched a fierce attack on Udagai, the 'resplendent' town mentioned in an earlier inscription. The impetus for the attack appears to have been an insult meted out to Rajaraja's diplomatic envoy. It is not certain if this was the same insult that prompted the battle at Kandalur Salai, but in any event, Rajaraja was not one to take an insult lightly and he unleashed the full force of his wrath upon Udagai and the surrounding Malai-nadu. Eighteen princes were killed in this retaliation and the city was set on fire. This event clearly captured the imagination of the twelfth-century Chola court poet Ottakoothar, who wrote about it in all his three ulas.[17]

CONQUEST OF SOUTH-WEST DECCAN

The Thiruvalangadu plates did not exaggerate when they stated that Rajaraja 'conquered...all the directions'.[18] To the north-west lay Gangavadi, the kingdom of the Western Ganga dynasty, occupying the region in and around Mysore. Their capital was Talakad, situated on a bend in the river Kaveri. They were the earliest dynasty to establish control over a large portion of present-day Karnataka, starting in the fourth century. A couple of centuries later they fell victim to the inevitable ferment of rival dynasties vying for power, and had to settle for subordinate status, as feudatories of a newly rising power, the Chalukyas. Then followed a dizzying rollercoaster ride of internecine fighting and shifting allegiances. From being the sworn enemies of the Rashtrakutas and friends of the Cholas, they did an about-face due to some shrewd marital matchmaking. The Gangas were now staunchly allied with the Rashtrakutas. It was a Ganga king, Butuga II, fighting on behalf of his Rashtrakuta friend Krishna III who dealt the Cholas one of their nastiest blows when he killed the young king-in-waiting, Rajaditya, at Takkolam in 949.

Rajaraja set out on his conquest of Ganga territory quite early in his reign. The great Rashtrakuta empire had succumbed to the slings and arrows of outrageous fortune, and bereft of their support, the Gangas were imperilled and vulnerable. He must have enjoyed early success, as his inscriptions have been found in the area, from as early 991. Another inscription dated two years later mentions that he was the lord of Rattapadi, Talakad, Pirudinagar, and Nolambapadi, all towns and districts in Gangavadi. The Nolambas, a minor power who were vassals of the Gangas, calculated correctly that it would serve them better to switch their loyalties to the Cholas, and turned against the Gangas. They helped the Cholas in their efforts to conquer the Mysore region. Inscriptions mention a general (or generals) named Nolambadhiraja Corraya (the name indicates that they were from the Nolamba clan) who led Chola troops against the Gangas. Talakad, the Ganga capital, was captured in 1004.[19] In this Rajaraja was ably assisted by his son and yuvaraja, Rajendra.

Following in the tradition of grooming the crown prince for the role that awaited him, and having lived and learned under two kings, Rajaraja took good care to fulfil this responsibility. He had just one son, Rajendra, a man who would prove a worthy successor in every way to his illustrious father. As a young boy, Rajendra was given extensive training in riding horses, elephants, and chariots, and in the use of multiple types of weapons. He proved an excellent student, excelling in the true test of the real-life battlefield. He was also well versed in the Vedas and other religious scriptures.[20]

Around the year 996, Rajendra was appointed the mahadandanayaka, or viceroy, of Gangavadi and the surrounding regions. He distinguished himself brilliantly. The plan was to close in on the Ganga capital of Talakad, but the flanks had to be secured first. Within two years, Kilalai-nadu, to the immediate east of Talakad, had fallen into Chola hands. At the Battle of Panasoge he, along with a general called Panchavan Marayan (some scholars believe that this was Rajendra himself), defeated the Coorgi chief, thus getting rid of a vital ally of the Gangas. Like his father, he possessed both brawn and brain, and was a canny strategic thinker. He sowed dissent in Coorg by appointing as a vassal a rival chieftain who had been loyal to the Cholas—an act that left Coorg riven in conflict long after the Cholas had vanished from power.

The Coorg loyalty secured, Talakad was attacked, and fell to the Cholas. Strangely, there are no inscriptions from either the Cholas or the Gangas about the battle, but the *Kongudesa Rajakkal*, a chronicle of the region written in the sixteenth or seventeenth century, mentions that Rajaraja changed the name of a village near Talakad to Rajarajapuram. Rajaraja set about putting into place a system of administration and drawing the region into the workings of his realm. He retained the local system of land apportionment of padis, which were similar to the Chola mandalams, merely changing their names to make it clear who was in power. Nolambapadi became Nigarila Chola Mandalam; Tadigaipadi (in modern-day Bangalore) became Vikrama Chola Mandalam, and Gangapadi became Mudigonda Chola Mandalam. He founded mercantile towns to promote trade and commerce in the region. Grants were made to villages in the area, and several temples to Vishnu were built, showing Rajaraja's respect and consideration for their religious preferences. An inscription refers to him as Chola Narayana, which must have been one of the names he was known by in the Mysore country.

When Rajaraja ascended the throne, the Rashtrakutas, who had been the Cholas' fiercest foes to the north, had faded from the scene. In their place, trying hard to absorb the Rashtrakuta territories into their fold were the Western Chalukyas of Kalyani, in the western Deccan. The early Chola victories of 991–92 in Gangavadi spurred the Chalukyas to greater efforts. Their king at the time was Tailapa II, who had been the beneficiary of a generous grant of territory by the Rashtrakuta king Krishna III a couple of decades earlier. He had been biding his time, watching and waiting patiently, and now he sensed that the time was right to strike the final blow to the Rashtrakutas and put himself in a stronger position to expand his territory. He succeeded in suppressing his former overlords the Rashtrakutas, and went about establishing himself in the western Deccan, in the area between the Narmada and Tungabhadra rivers. He even claimed a victory over Rajaraja's troops in 992, capturing 150 of his elephants. However, a few years after this, Tailapa II died, and was succeeded by his son Satyasraya.

In Satyasraya, Rajaraja met a formidable foe. He was a young king with the vigour and ambition of one with a kingdom on the rise. He ruled over the territory called Rattapadi, or country of the Rattas, in other words, the Rashtrakutas.

At this time, there was trouble brewing to the east in Vengi country, in present-day Andhra. This area was ruled by the Eastern Chalukyas, a branch of the original Chalukyas who had split away in the sixth century and established themselves independently. The ruler, Danarnava, had died in battle in 973 at the hands of an ambitious chieftain called Jata Choda Bhima. Bhima declared himself king and took control over the Vengi dominion. Danarnava's sons fled the kingdom and were forced to live in exile. Bhima ruled for twenty-seven years, assisted by his son Saktivarman. Chalukya records (not surprisingly) describe this period as aswamika, anayaka, and arajaka*:* without god, governance, or king.[21] In other words, they claim this was a period of anarchy. However, there was no anarchy in the real sense of the word, but from the point of view of the deposed Eastern Chalukya family, it was certainly a state of doom.

In 982, Jata Choda Bhima and his army launched an attack on Kanchipuram—which was then in Chola hands—and succeeded in capturing it. The victory appears to have been short-lived, as just a year later, Chola inscriptions were back in the city. Not much is known about Bhima and his Vengi kingdom in the immediate aftermath of the Kanchipuram expedition, and it is assumed that he continued to rule without serious opposition. But now Jata Choda Bhima had marked himself as an enemy of the Cholas.

When Rajaraja came to power in 985, he recognized that the Vengi situation—an independent and unfriendly power on his north-eastern frontier—spelled trouble. It would be necessary to bring it under his control and into the Chola fold. Also, Vengi, rich, green and fertile, would be a prize well worth winning.

Here is where Rajaraja's brilliance in strategic thinking, honed during his years of observing his father and uncle at work, came into play. He recognized that Jata Choda Bhima was a seasoned warrior, a tough opponent. Pure brute force could backfire. So instead, Rajaraja took the route of stealth diplomacy, befriending the sons of the dead king Darnarnava, and offering them protection and possibly the promise that he would help restore to them what was rightfully theirs.

To this end, Darnarnava's younger son, Vimaladitya, was married to Rajaraja's daughter Kundavai, named for his sister. Together, Rajaraja, along with Darnarnava's older son, Saktivarman, went to war against Jata Choda Bhiman. The exact course of events is not known, but it appears that the fighting dragged on for several years. Saktivarman's records state that he killed a great warrior, Ekavira. Next he killed two powerful chiefs, Baddema and Maharaja. Finally, in the year 999 the Chola team declared victory. Copperplate inscriptions from Pabhubarru sing the praises of Saktivarman: 'His youth shone like that of a lion when in the Tamil battle he attacked the formidable elephants (of the enemy). He performed a wonderful feat when with his own hands he killed the sharp and peerless hero sent by Choda Bhima. He dug up the wide-spread tree of Jata Choda to its very roots....'[22] Rajaraja himself dealt the death blow to Jata Choda Bhiman—the Thiruvalangadu plates say that he killed him with a mace.

Saktivarman was crowned the Vengi king, but expectedly, the position came with strings attached: he remained firmly under the guidance of Rajaraja, operating strictly under his supervision. The Eastern Chalukyas functioned as loyal vassals of the Cholas. Saktivarman ruled for twelve years, and in the year 1011, his brother Vimaladitya, Rajaraja's son-in-law, became king. The fates of the Eastern Chalukya and Chola empires became further intertwined. A mere sixty years later, Rajaraja's great-grandson, the son of Rajendra's daughter, an eastern Chalukya prince named Kulothunga, took over the reins of the Chola empire.

But back in Rajaraja's time, the Western Chalukya king Satyasraya had been observing Rajaraja's activities in the Vengi kingdom and must have been deeply disturbed. He had successfully subdued enemy forces in parts of the Konkan and Gujarat regions and wanted to spread this dominion eastwards as well, and wrest Vengi away from the Chola grip.

As the new millennium dawned, some of the most dramatic, savage battles took place in the Deccan. The battles must have been closely fought, and on a colossal scale, and each side claimed victory over the other.

Rajaraja's inscriptions from the year 1003 assert that he captured Rattapadi, the former Rashtrakuta domains that were now in Satyasraya's command.[23] Revealing his multifaceted skill and expertise as well as his fearlessness, he single-handedly controlled the oncoming onslaught of the Chalukya army just like the great Lord Siva controlled the headlong descent of the river Ganga on to the earth. Wielding a sword while seated on horseback, he withstood the attack by the leader Satyasraya.[24] A Chalukya general, Kesava, was taken prisoner. As for Satyasraya, he was said to have fled the battlefield to avoid facing Rajaraja's army again. The Thiruvalangadu plates wrote about this in its inimitable manner: 'This is strange that though Satyasraya fled to avoid misery from the attack of his (Rajaraja's) ocean-like army, still, misery found a permanent abode in him. But this is not strange, that his flight is due to his birth from Taila.' The word Taila can be interpreted in two ways: it is both the name of his father, and also means oil, which flows, or runs.[25]

Despite the claims of the Chola inscriptions, Satyasraya was not a foe who would concede defeat so easily. There are accounts of a massive battle at Donur, in the Bijapur district of Karnataka. This would have been a part of Rattapadi, and indicates that Rajaraja's conquest of the area was far from complete, and that both sides faced losses and victories. Inscriptions provided wildly exaggerated accounts, each king vying to outdo the other in a medieval game of political propaganda.

There is a stone inscription, belonging to Satyasraya, dating from 1007 that was found in a village called Hottur in Dharwad district in Karnataka. The rectangular block has a carving of an archer (presumably meant to denote Satyasraya or one of his men) shooting at two men; at his feet, pierced by arrows, lies a fallen warrior. The inscription sets the stage and speaks of the time when a king, Rajaraja Nityavinoda (one of the many titles of Rajaraja), came accompanied by 900,000 men and halted at Donavura (Donur). This king ravaged the whole country, perpetrating murders of women, children, and Brahmins, seizing women and overthrowing the order of caste. The inscription now calls our attention to the auspicious king of kings, supreme lord, supreme master, the ornament of the Chalukya race, the auspicious king Satyasraya who drove away the Chola, captured his trains of baggage waggons, and made a triumphal progress through the south.[26]

Soon after, in the year 1006, Satyasraya sent an army to Vengi. An inscription on a slab in the Nageshvara Temple in Chebrolu in Guntur district crows that Satyasraya's general Bayalanambi destroyed the forts of Dhanyakataka and Yanamadala, reducing them to ashes.[27] Rajaraja could not ignore this provocation and dispatched an army to Vengi. His son Rajendra, who had been appointed viceroy of the newly acquired Gangavadi territory, left that region and went to Vengi in order to deal with the situation there and restore order. The same Panchavan Marayan who had distinguished himself in Gangavadi (who, as mentioned earlier, some scholars believe was Rajendra himself) was also present.

Back in the west in Gangavadi, it was too early yet for Rajaraja to rest on his laurels. The Hoysalas had been gathering strength and power in the region, and in the year 1006, a fierce battle took place in Kaliyur, across the Kaveri from Talakad, on its south bank. Inscriptions on a stone victory pillar tell us the story. A Chola general named Aprameya distinguished himself exceptionally, and was clearly the hero of the battle, defeating the Hoysala general Naganna and handing the Cholas a major victory. A band of feudatory chieftains also met their end in the fighting, and his valour 'won him a name to last as long as the sun and the moon'.[28] Aprameya seems to have been a remarkable character who wore many hats: inscriptions describe him as a great minister (mahamatya), a loyal feudatory (samanta), and a governor (kothamandala nathan). He must have been a fierce fighter and a terror to the enemy, as he is also called 'Malapa Kula Kalam', a form of Yama to the hill-folk. The victory pillar, which had been embedded into the ceiling of the Gopalakrishna Temple of Kaliyur, also gives us a vivid pictorial enactment of the battle. There are elephants, trunks lifted high, fleeing the scene, given hot chase by men on horseback; the air is thick with flying arrows.[29]

Around twenty years into his reign, Rajaraja's conquest of the Mysore (south-west Deccan) region was completed. All of southern Karnataka comprising the modern districts of Kolar, Bangalore, Mysore, Mandya, Tumkur, and to some extent Coorg were firmly under Chola control.

It is impossible to present history neatly. Multiple events happen simultaneously and often there are several, quite often conflicting, narratives of the same event. Both factions in a war claim victory. Each side exults in the other's annihilation. This is particularly true of Rajaraja's conquest of the territories of the Deccan.

RAJARAJA'S INVASION OF SRI LANKA

In the late tenth century, the island of Ceylon was ruled by the Sinhalese king Mahinda V. He became king just a few years before Rajaraja, in 981, but the two kings could not be more different from each other. According to the *Culavamsa* (a historical record of the monarchs of Sri Lanka covering the fourth through the nineteenth century), Mahinda was 'of very weak character', and had 'wandered from the path of statecraft' and his kingdom was in shambles.[30] His fortunes had evaporated, there was no money to pay his troops. The Pandyas, once a friendly power who could be relied upon to help, had been trounced and humiliated by the Cholas. Mahinda's troops consisted of mercenary soldiers from Kerala, who were difficult to deal with even under normal circumstances. Mahinda employed them nevertheless, as he considered the local Sinhala soldiers insufficiently aggressive. With no salary forthcoming, matters reached a mutinous state with the soldiers beating down the door of the king's palace and issuing threats. Mahinda proved to be a coward. He escaped via a secret underground passage to the remote hills of Ruhuna, in the southern part of the country, and set up camp there.

There was now complete anarchy in the country.

The time and circumstances were perfect for an invasion.

Ceylon was rich in copper and spices and was part of the lucrative trade route that included China, Southeast Asia, and West Asia. In addition, the Pandyas had been on excellent terms with the kings of Ceylon, which made them natural enemies to Rajaraja. Rajaraja heard about the state of affairs in Ceylon from a horse-dealer who had been there and witnessed the disorder.[31] It must have been a mutually beneficial communication: for Rajaraja, this was critical and strategically important information; and the horse-trader might have benefited monetarily and commercially both immediately as well as down the road.

Rajaraja wasted no time in sending his troops to Ceylon. In describing this expedition, the Thiruvalangadu plates went so far as to say that Rajaraja's feat surpassed that of Lord Rama:

> The Lord of the Raghavas (Rama) constructing a bridge across the water of the ocean (with the assistance of) able monkeys killed with great difficulty the king of Lanka (Ravana) with sharp-edged arrows; but, this terrible General of king Arulmozhivarman crossed the ocean by ships and burnt the Lord of Lanka (Ceylon). Hence, Rama is surely surpassed by this Chola general.[32]

What followed was utter and complete annihilation of the long-time capital, Anuradhapura. Rajaraja's own inscriptions are coy about the details, but the *Culavamsa* minces no words. 'They violently destroyed here and there all the monasteries, like blood-sucking yakkhas they took all the treasures of Lanka for themselves.'[33] The four great Buddhist monasteries of Anuradhapura were very prosperous from gifts and endowments from the royalty and wealthy of the island. Each monastery also had a stupa built over a relic chamber; these too were ransacked by the Cholas in their search for treasure. A large portion of this booty went to fund Rajaraja's masterpiece, the Brihadeeshwara Temple. He gave as devadana (a gift, most commonly land, to god), several villages in Ceylon to the temple, and their tax revenues were used towards its expenses.

Even allowing for the exaggeration of the *Culavamsa* chroniclers who were Buddhist monks who would have been justifiably upset at the large-scale desecration, it is clear that Rajaraja's troops decimated the city. Anuradhapura, reduced to nothing, was no longer a viable capital, and the Cholas used the city of Polonnaruwa as their headquarters in Ceylon, until they were driven out of the island in 1070.

Rajaraja's conquest covered the northern part of Ceylon, which now became a mandalam under his regime, called Mummudi-sola-mandalam. The southern areas, which were unruly and lacked the prosperity to seriously tempt the Cholas, remained out of their control. A lovely granite and limestone temple to Siva was constructed in Polonnaruwa. It stands to this day, a relic of the triumphs of a great ruler of bygone times.

Rajaraja had now truly earned the moniker Mummidi Chola, or the triple-crowned Chola, as the monarch of the Chola, Pandya, and Lanka lands.

Rajaraja's final conquest, mentioned only in inscriptions late in his reign, was that of the 'old islands of the sea numbering 12,000'.[34] This has been generally accepted as meaning the Maldives, an archipelago on the Arabian Sea, around 700 kilometres from the southern tip of India, south and west of the mainland. This conquest must have been a major feat, involving a fleet of ships travelling a good distance across the seas to conquer an unknown place. Why the Maldives? They were likely important waystations in the highly lucrative maritime trade route between the lands to the west and India. Capturing the Maldives would bring into Rajaraja's fold a good measure of control and the profits from this sea lane, adding to what he already commandeered from his eastern ports.

Rajaraja enjoyed some of the most spectacular military victories the likes of which the region had never seen, nor would see again for several centuries, until the Vijayanagar dynasty came into power in the fourteenth century He was a fearless leader and a highly skilled and versatile warrior, equally at ease and adept with a mace, sword, on horseback, and more. He planned and executed his conquests with a brilliant strategic vision, and he played the geopolitical game as well as the best. His many titles—Kshatriya Sikhamani, Rajendra Simhan, Uyyakondan, Pandya Kulasani, Keralantakan, Nittavinodan, Rajasrayan, Sivapadasekharan, Jana-nathan, Ravikula Manikkam, Nigarili Cholan, Cholendra Simhan, Chola Marttandan, Raja Marttandan, Telunga-kula-kalan, Kirti Parakraman, Mummudi Solan, Chola Narayanan, Jayangonda Solan, Singalantakan, Taila-kula-kalan were just some—spoke to the range of victories he enjoyed. He was enormously fortunate to have a son as brilliant, ambitious, and fearless as himself, and whom he could trust to carry out difficult military expeditions. There are no accounts of mutiny or disloyalty among his men, which spoke to his being a leader who won their respect and fealty. With his conquests, all of peninsular south India came under his control, as well as northern Sri Lanka and the Maldives.

Twenty-seven years into his reign, in the year 1012, Rajaraja appointed his son Rajendra as co-ruler. Two years later, after twenty-nine unforgettable years as the Chola king, he died, sometime between the middle of 1013 and 1014. He was sixty-seven years old.

CHAPTER 11

THE LAND BENEATH THE CHOLA SUN
CHOLA ORGANIZATION

An old Buddhist text, the *Aggnana Sutta* (The Knowledge of Beginnings) of the *Digha Nikaya* (Collection of Long Discourses), tells a simple but fascinating story. It is a creation myth of sorts, but one that also travels far forward in time. In it, the Buddha, in conversation with two Brahmins who left their caste to become Buddhist monks, tells them how humankind and human society came to be. Here is one part of the tale, in which he describes how they evolved from their earliest days and how, eventually, there came a time when the rice plant appeared on earth. The first grains of rice were sweet like honey and without husks and the people devoured them. They couldn't get enough of this wonderful food and they became fat and lazy. As their gluttony grew, they consumed more than they needed, and they craved yet more and then they began to hoard the rice. The situation turned ugly as the once-smooth process of production, consumption, and storing of rice was disrupted. The elders tried to alleviate matters by allocating shares of the rice amongst the people, but this did not solve the problem. The rice, which had flourished in abundance, became a difficult crop and the people had to work hard to grow and harvest it. They grew rice in their own plots of land which they divided from those of others and guarded these plots closely. Their greed and gluttony continued to grow, and they began stealing from their neighbours' land. Things turned dark, with crime and punishment now part of the fabric of society. Something had to be done to control matters before they spiralled into chaos. They appointed an arbitrator, and called him the Maha Sammata, the People's Choice, and it was his duty to ensure that peace and justice prevailed.[1]

The story is instructive because it could serve as a parable for how society came to be formed in medieval times, with the redistribution of surplus, the emergence of private property, the appointment of a person or persons to oversee the affairs of the community and the beginnings of a social and political hierarchy. From this grew the 'state', with its king and ministers, revenues and taxes, trade, military, and grand projects.

Southern India under the Cholas underwent a remarkable transformation. From a collection of chiefdoms, it evolved, under the first rulers of the Imperial line, into a kingdom of sorts—fragile, unstable, in a state of constant flux, but a kingdom, nonetheless, eventually becoming a true imperial kingdom under Rajaraja. As the kingdom developed, so too did the king ruling it, from a raja (king) to a maharaja (great king), to kinghood's highest calling: the maharajadhiraja (supreme king of great kings).

As with anything else about the Chola empire, we have as our main source of information the thousands of inscriptions etched on to temple walls and copperplates. Around half of the inscriptions that have been published deal with land organization of some sort and through these we get a picture of everyday society and how those at the top of the social hierarchy—wealthy peasants, the priestly class, and the ruling elite—shaped and moulded society to their advantage. A lot of the organization of districts, towns, and villages in Tamil Nadu today dates to Chola times, persisting through centuries of social, economic, and political changes.

When we attempt to envisage the shape and structure of the state and society a thousand years ago, we are naturally grasping at a few threadbare straws as we desperately try to glean some sense, create a picture, build a model of what things must have been like. And it is no surprise that opinion has been divided and several scenarios have been presented, each with its enthusiasts and critics. Was the Chola kingdom a meticulously organized bureaucracy that controlled all aspects of governance from the centre; or was the central power in name alone with the reality being that each region took care of itself with whatever systems it implemented or had in place? Scholarly opinion has been sharply divided. Nilakanta Sastri thought it was the former; Burton Stein disagreed strongly.[2]

In Sastri's reading, the grand byzantine bureaucracy was yet another assertion of the control and power the king wielded over his domain. Stein, on the other hand, had quite the opposite view, that the king and his core team were but a small entity, surrounded by many segments, each minding their own affairs. He believed that the real territorial authority of the king was limited to the core segment—the area surrounding the capital, Thanjavur—of the kingdom. Elsewhere, the king's authority was merely ritualic and custodial, as he had no real political jurisdiction over those segments. It was the king's moral and sacred authority, tied together with the allegiance of local chieftains, that allowed the king to maintain his power and control over his territories; it was not a matter of the all-prevailing influence of military might, but rather, the ethical and honourable principles that the king supposedly stood for, that enabled him to rule. Naturally, such an extreme point of view was challenged, particularly since it seemed counter-intuitive that the king should have no power over the lands he conquered. Stein himself softened his stance over the years, admitting that the king had both political and ritual authority, but he maintained the notion of the segmentary state.[3]

Whether one believes in Sastri's vision of a gloriously organized centralized officialdom or Stein's notion of a multi-headed, multi-armed collection of divisions, there is no disputing the fact that there was an organization and that there were policies governing how these worked. There is also a third model, the integrative model, proposed by Hermann Kulke in 1982, in which the state is seen as arising from the integration of localized territories into other localized territories, through conquest, and also the integration of local political structures and hierarchies into the larger state apparatus. Broadly, he envisioned it as the territorial, cultural, social, and economic integration of smaller units into a larger one.[4]

The rich trove of epigraphical information points to a movement, primarily from the eleventh century on, from a scattered, inconsistent jurisdiction over the agrarian villages to a more centralized, organized, and successful control.

One of the ways Rajaraja proclaimed his greatness and control over his dominion was through the construction of the Brihadeeshwara Temple. The main deity of worship, a giant stone lingam, was named Rajarajeshwara—one of Siva's many appellations, yes, but surely no small coincidence that it was also the emperor's appellation. Using such a religious symbol to flaunt his greatness does give the nod to Stein's idea of the king's ritual sovereignty over his kingdom, but this temple also demonstrates very clearly that Rajaraja's influence was very real and far exceeded anything suggested by tokenism. The walls of the Brihadeeshwara Temple swarm with inscriptions that lay out in minute detail the contributions to the temple's coffers by villages from all over Rajaraja's kingdom, not just those belonging to his core segment, as well as specifics about each of these villages. For a king to have such clout, and such knowledge, implies strongly that he had the influence.

The king was the central figure, the supreme head of the government, the person whose word and authority was absolute. Kings had to play multiple roles—war leaders and heroes, representatives of god on earth, dispensers of patronage, wealth and land, enablers of trade and prosperity.

The early Chola kings were little more than exalted chieftains, and this was reflected in the titles they gave themselves. As the king rose in stature to the position of a full-fledged emperor holding sway over an impressively sized domain, the titles grew apace, matching the king's growing eminence with ever more grandiloquent labels. The Chola kings alternated between the parakesari and rajakesari titles. As they conquered new territory, the name of that territory was often appended to their name; the Madurantaka or Madurakonda title (victor over the Pandya capital of Madurai) was a particular source of pride, as it indicated victory over their toughest foes. Rajaraja had the most impressive titles of all, and a lengthy list it was (as we've seen), given the vast range of his achievements.

Great leaders need people by their side who are smart, trustworthy, and capable of executing plans and orders in a manner true to the vision of their commander. Rajaraja was fortunate to have several such men that he could rely on. Foremost was his son, Rajendra, a fearless warrior and brilliant strategist who won him major victories in the Vengi and Ganga domains. There was Madhurantakan Gandaradittan, the son of the previous king Uttama, who played a major role in temple affairs. As the son of a former ruler, he might have resented his subordinate role, but he appears to have been a faithful and hard-working deputy. Inscriptions at the Brihadeeshwara Temple mention a Senapathi Krishnan Raman (called Rajendrasola Brahmamarayan in the Larger Leiden grant, indicating that he worked for Rajaraja's son Rajendra as well) who played a key role in the building of the temple. Then there was Senapati Kuravan Ulagalandan, also called Rajaraja Maharajan, who earned his Ulagalandan moniker thanks to his efforts in the mammoth undertaking of the land and revenue survey during Rajaraja's reign. Rajaraja was also on friendly terms with many chieftains, in particular the Paluvettaraiyars who were a part of his trusted network and played important roles in maintaining peace and harmony in his lands.

As the kingdom grew along with the web of complexities inherent in its operation, so too did the size of the king's retinue. Executing a royal order, called the tiru-aanai (sacred command), took numerous officers who between them held a dizzying array of titles and who ensured that the work was done exactly according to the king's words. So intricate was the web of the bureaucratic apparatus that it was well-nigh impossible—in theory—for a forger or a defrauder to sneak in.

Heading the officialdom were the adhikaris. Meaning 'the one who wields authority' the adhikari was, presumably, the king's most trusted officer, and assigned to act on behalf of the king. The number of adhikaris grew greatly during Rajaraja's rule, hardly surprising considering his administrative ambition and vision. Some of them accompanied the king everywhere while others were entrusted with travelling around the kingdom, executing his orders. The adhikaris are referred to in inscriptions by their titles that were bestowed upon them by their king; the titles signified high honour and recognition. Among the most common titles found in inscriptions are muvendavelan and brahmamarayan, with the name of their emperor prefixed to it. Because of this, however, we often do not know their actual names, or any personal details about them. However, these titles do disclose other interesting facts about the people who were awarded them. The muvendavelan title was given to high-ranking Vellala (land-owning/chieftain) officers in the revenue and executive departments. Brahmins with an exemplary service record were awarded the brahmamarayan honorific. There were a whole host of other officers, many endowed with impressive sounding titles. In endowing a diverse range of people across the kingdom with the same titles and honorifics, Rajaraja proved himself yet again a far-sighted king. Men across the kingdom could feel part of a larger organization and feel a kinship, bestowed by their rank, with others similarly designated. They could take pride in being part of a hierarchy of prestige that came straight from Chola royalty. No doubt, with such a large bureaucratic setup, the situation must have been ripe for intrigue, treachery, and all manner of double-dealings, but we have no records of these, and can only allow our imaginations to fill in the details.[5]

Where there is a bureaucracy there is perforce a hierarchy and the officers were designated perundaram (bigger, or senior) or sirutaram (junior, or smaller). This distinction spanned all sections of the government, and even the military. Attaining perundaram status did not mean that the officers were above transgressive behaviour: there is an inscription that names eight perundaram officers of Rajaraja's court, who were caught in (unnamed) acts of cowardice or misdemeanour, and endowed lamps to the Brihadeeshwara Temple in the fervent hope that divine intervention would save them from the wrath of their king. We have no idea if their strategy worked.[6]

Where were these officers recruited from? We do not know, and scholars have postulated that coming from a family of high birth, wealth, and connections conferred a definite advantage, although they almost certainly needed to prove themselves to further advance their careers. Inscriptions show that nepotism favoured sons of prominent fathers and won them coveted positions.

Rajaraja's economy was a thriving one and revenues obtained from around the kingdom played a key role in funding his administration. The bulk of the revenues came from land tax, and a complex system of land measurements was in place, some of them several centuries old. Even though terms like kuli, veli, ma, and patti, all units of land measurement, were used across the realm, there was little standardization. Different measuring rods were used, adding to the confusion.[7]

Rajaraja, a king who didn't lack for titles, earned the Ulagalanda Perumal (the great king who measured the earth) moniker for a gargantuan land survey and measurement that he commissioned around fifteen years into his rule, in the year 1000. The survey covered his entire kingdom—Cholamandalam, Pandimandalam (former Pandya lands, to the south), Ilamandalam (Ceylon), and Tondaimandalam (former Pallava lands, to the north). He appointed an officer in charge of this mammoth operation, who was awarded the title Senapathi Kuravar Ulagalanda (the general who measured the earth). Dimensions were calculated to the minutest fraction, showing

Rajaraja's focus on detail and accuracy. New standardized measuring rods were introduced. One was called sripadakkol—the revered feet of the king. The royal foot of Rajaraja might well have served as the standard for the measurement.[8]

Thanks to the land survey, myriad discrepancies were cleared up. A new unit of land, the valanadu, was created. Boundaries and borders were clearly demarcated, and the amount of arable land was determined. These were the lands that were taxed, at a standardized rate of 100 kalams (a measure of grain, approximately 29 kilograms by weight) of paddy per veli (approximately 6.6 acres) of arable land.[9] Common grazing lands, the residential areas of lower-caste agricultural workers, artisans, and weavers, the cremation ghats, temple grounds, and the main road of the town or village were all exempted from taxes. This was yet another feat of Rajaraja's—it ensured fair and accurate taxation. It is a shame that most of the original documents, which would have allowed us a deeper understanding of the survey, are now lost. All we have are what we can glean from inscriptions on temple walls and copperplate grants like the Leiden grant.

In order to collect the taxes and other funds, a revenue collection hierarchy was put into place along with a set of procedures that ensured meticulous accounting. Revenue collection was handled by a department called Puravuvari, which employed vast numbers of officers of various ranks, all performing a variety of functions including accounting, collecting, issuing and executing royal orders, and record-keeping.[10] The sheer number of offices and officers at the village, district, and national levels, all spelled out in inscriptions and copperplate grants, points to a well-oiled machine of officialdom.

Tax codes appear to have been as onerous in Rajaraja's time as we find them now. Wading through the thicket of terminology, two types of taxes stand out: they were called kadamai, and kudimai. Both were land taxes, the first, kadamai, was levied on landowners, and the second, kudimai, levied on those who cultivated the land.[11] Agriculture, particularly rice production, was a major part of the Chola economy, especially in the early centuries of their rule.

Further strengthening the argument that Rajaraja's was a planned and well-executed bureaucratic establishment was the fact that the land was broken down into different territorial divisions based on size, and who occupied it. However, some of these arrangements and structures had their roots in the heyday of the Pallava empire, a couple of centuries earlier; it is very likely that rural society began taking shape in ways that coalesced into well-organized forms during the Sangam Chola era, even well before Pallava times. It is mainly from the Pallava inscriptions that we get a sense of how the land was put in order. Chola society was largely agrarian and rural, although it became increasingly urbanized during its centuries in power.

Among the people of the countryside, as in any society, there existed a social hierarchy, with the landowner-cultivators (vellalas, uluvars, or kaaralar), at the top, followed by the cowherds and shepherds, the hunters, various artisans, armed men, and at the very bottom, fisherfolk and scavengers.[12] How exactly this hierarchy played itself out in practical terms is not entirely clear. As the Chola kingdom grew, and as areas that were empty tracts of forest and wild land became settled, society became further stratified. With the movement of people and time, social divisions called valangai (right-hand) and idangai (left-hand) emerged. Using inscriptions as evidence, historians have attempted to make sense of these classes. The valangai (right-hand) division comprised groups related to land ownership and agriculture, and the idangai (left-hand) group was made up of merchants and artisans. The reality is much more muddled, especially when these categories were still new. The valangai–idangai nomenclature was first seen during the reign of Rajaraja, during a period of intense military activity and mobilization of troops for his imperial expansions. Therefore it might have initially been a military classification, and with the passage of time and the evolution of the society, it started to be used for all groups.[13]

The Chola kingdom in Rajaraja's time was spread over a large portion of southern India and beyond, and was a patchwork of villages of farmers, merchants, and Brahmins. These villages, alone or along with a group of others, had their own assemblies and corporations that took care of social, economic, and religious affairs. Presiding over it all from his distant capital was the king, whose roles straddled the practical and the fantastic, the worldly and other-wordly, the divine and the martial.

The Chola country had many territorial and administrative divisions—ur, nagaram, brahmadeya, nadu, valanadu, and mandalam.[14]

The village was the smallest territorial unit and was identified by who lived in them. They fell into three broad categories that were not necessarily watertight: those occupied by farmers and herders; those in which the Brahmins lived; and merchant villages.

The agrarian villages were called ur. These were traditional villages that had been a part of the Tamil countryside for many centuries. Every village had an assembly made up of Vellala landholders, and the assembly was also called ur. The ur members were common landholders of the village. Private ownership was rare. The members of the village assembly met regularly to ensure smooth functioning of its institutions. They discussed matters that were generally of strictly local interest: the temple and its affairs; irrigation; crime and punishment; record-keeping. The Chola village was much like many villages in modern south India. There were the villagers' homes, gardens, wells, and tanks and enclosures for cattle; there was the temple and its grounds; the cremation ground; and all around, the lands under cultivation, with rice as the predominant crop, along with coconut and areca nut, and cottonseed and sesame both prized for the oil from their seeds. There were groves of mangoes and plantains in profusion.

Inscriptions on the walls of the village temples give us information about the goings-on in the assembly. They write about disputes and how they were resolved, how crimes were punished, alliances between local chieftains, and a great deal more. There is a whole lot more detail about the exact size of the village, the extent of taxable and non-taxable land, the different categories of residential quarters, the temples, the tax on paddy and other commodities, and more. The inscriptions also show that land ownership by individuals became more prevalent in the later Chola years (thirteenth century), while shared ownership was more common earlier.

Another category of village, the brahmadeya, came into being during the reign of the Pallavas. Also called agraharam, chaturvedimangalam, mangalam, or brahmadesam, the brahmadeya was a village, most often in very fertile lands, granted to learned Brahmins by the king. The brahmadeya village assembly was made of Brahmin landholders and was called a sabha.[15] The records of the brahmadeya assemblies provide us with some of the most insightful details about local affairs. There were committees (variyam) in charge of the gardens, the tanks, the fields, taxes, and accounts. Fines were imposed on those residents who fell short in a variety of ways. Every social group—the brahmins, accountants, merchants, landowners, cultivators, and other castes—had its own department in charge of levying fines, and these departments could belong to the king's court, the court of justice, the revenue arm, and others. Each group or caste was responsible for paying the fines for its members. Clearly, the psychology of peer pressure and group loyalty was at work here.

Among the most detailed and fascinating inscriptions that take us into the world of the brahmadeya assembly, or sabha, and lay bare all manner of its functioning are those on the wall of the Vaikunta Perumal Temple in the village of Uthiramerur, midway between the great temple city of Kanchipuram to the north and Madurantakam to the south.

Today it is a bustling, mid-sized town but in Chola times, it must have been quite large, just judging from the size of the assembly and the complexity and level of detail that went into its creation and structure. These inscriptions are from the time of Parantaka I and showcase the Chola love for attention to minutiae to ensure the watertight and smooth running of their associations.

Here are some nuggets from the Uthiramerur inscriptions, which serve to illustrate just what lengths the village went to, to ensure the best possible selection of candidates for its assembly. The inscriptions give an astonishing amount of detail about the administrative procedures followed in the villages of Parantaka's time. It describes the formation of committees called variyams, each consisting of six to twelve members, who had executive powers to make decisions on behalf of the village. There were committees in charge of the town's gardens, its tanks, tax assessment, the annual meeting, and even a gold committee. The inscriptions date from 919 and 923. Parantaka was far from being a pioneer in the organization of village administration by committees and assemblies—inscriptions like these have been found several centuries prior to his rule, all over India.[16]

Suitable candidates—men—had to be between the ages of thirty-five and seventy, mature enough, but not too old. They also guaranteed that every eligible man in the village would get a chance in his lifetime to serve on a committee so that no one got to hang on to the position for life. They had to possess a certain amount of immovable property; this ensured they had the experience in dealing with property ownership and everything it entailed. There was also a minimum educational qualification requirement. In addition, the candidates had to be men of good moral character.

Most fascinating was what disqualified potential candidates. Anybody who was lax in submitting proper public accounts was disbarred; taking a bribe, being in any way disruptive to the peaceful life of the village, committing incest, all ensured the loss of right to stand for election, for life. Also excluded were those who had been 'village pests', taken forbidden dishes (primarily, alcohol) or ridden an ass (a punishment for certain offences). And that was not all. Any family member of an eliminated candidate was also out of the running. Even those who administered rites to these sinners became ineligible. High moral conduct and good standing were of supreme importance and a person with any association with a person of ill-repute could not be trusted to be part of the variyam.

The inscriptions then go on to describe the actual election process. The names of suitable candidates were written on palm leaves, which were placed in pots. In the presence of all the village elders, an illiterate boy was tasked with pulling out leaves, one at a time, and that is how the variyam members were chosen. The term was for a year, and elections were held annually. The slightest whiff of misconduct meant the man, and his family, were dismissed, then, and forever after.[17]

An equitable, democratic process, it ensured fair representation by qualified candidates and undercut potential power struggles by feudatory agents.

The painstaking level of detail spelled out in the Uthiramerur inscription regarding who was eligible and who wasn't, to contest in the village assembly elections, was there for good reason. It appears that there were certain former committee members who had brought the village administration to its knees by embezzling funds and indulging in other dishonourable activities. The rules inscribed on the temple wall were meant to ensure that only people of the highest moral calibre would be able to represent their village. Not only were the wayward and disreputable former representatives and 'incorrigible sinners' barred, but also their remotest relatives. Village pests, thieves, those guilty of committing incest, the foolhardy, the unredeemed outcaste who committed the sin of communing with the lower castes, all had doors slammed in the face of any political and bureaucratic ambitions.

The brahmadeyas were not exclusively populated by Brahmins. Along with the Brahmins there were artisans, peasants, and merchants; only the toddy tapper or the Ilava group was forbidden entry into the brahmadeya.

Brahmadeyas were already in existence during the early years of Chola rule, but there was an explosion of land gifts to Brahmins under Rajaraja's regime. Counter-intuitive as it might seem, such lavish giving over of land, privileges, and immunities to Brahmins did not result in a loss of control on the part of the king. Here again was an instance of far-sighted strategic thinking. In spelling out the legal requirements and boundaries for the brahmadeyas, the king was laying the ground for legitimizing the same norms for all villages in the region. If the privileged Brahmins were obliged to abide by certain rules, then it became an easier pill to swallow for everyone. The king's authority was then established in areas where he might have not otherwise been able to do so easily.

At the same time, there was the growing importance of the temple as a major institution that served far more than the religious needs of the community. Temples were the social, cultural, and economic pulse of the area. In this environment the idea of a brahmadeya made perfect sense. Establishing a separate township for Brahmins served multiple purposes. It brought agriculture to a wider area and, consequently, increased the land value of these areas, but perhaps more importantly, given the power and authority that Brahmins held in the minds of the people, the king's own power and authority enjoyed a boost and greater legitimacy; in addition, creating another type of municipality with its own assembly could have served to dilute the control wielded by the councils of the urs and nadus.

The brahmadeya was of vital importance in preserving and disseminating religious knowledge. Brahmins enjoyed a high level of patronage under the Chola rulers and commanded authority, both sacral and otherwise. The Brahmins were responsible for a variety of religion-related activities and functions. Rituals involving recitation from the Vedas, reading aloud from the Mahabharata and the Puranas, teaching these texts to Brahmin students, and deciphering and interpreting the calendar to suggest the most auspicious times and dates for the many different events that made up the life of a village (marriages, ploughing, festivals) were among the most important of them. During the height of Chola rule, the temple, or temples, that were in every brahmadeya, were the site for these activities, and the sabha, or assembly of the brahmadeya, was responsible for the overall supervision. Often these temples were on the pilgrim route and a supplementary economy of merchants and artisans—to serve the pilgrims developed. Many of the bigger brahmadeyas were important centres of learning and were home to muths or seminaries that housed a considerable number of students. Inscriptions made mention of payment to teachers and donations of food for the community, and these are a valuable window into the form and functioning of these villages. Religious education was far from the exclusive focus of the brahmadeya schools. Medicine, basic engineering, astrological, and astronomical computations, the law and judicial procedures, martial arts, and languages were all part of the Brahminical syllabus.

Occasionally, a Brahmin who had distinguished himself or earned the king's highest admiration and appreciation was awarded a brahmadeya all to himself. This was known as an ekabhoga brahmadeya.[18] Sundara Chola's Anbil plates record the gift of such a village to an individual named Aniruddha Brahmadiraja. An elaborate ceremony sanctioned the gifting of the village, with a female elephant marking the boundaries. The grant goes on to give an exhaustive list of everything that was included as part of the village: fruit-yielding trees, gardens, wells, water, open spaces, grazing lands for cattle, anthills, canals, granaries, fish ponds, the places where the iguanas and tortoises crawl, and more. The new owner was free to build halls and dig wells and plant trees. Old tenants were evicted, and the new owner was entitled to any income from a variety of sources specified.[19]

Sometimes confused with the brahmadeya was the devadana village. The devadana was a gift of land—sometimes a portion of a village, and sometimes the entire village—that was given by the king to a temple. The income from these lands was granted to the temple and went towards its upkeep. The wealthier and bigger devadana villages could yield a vast income. More commonly, only a portion of the village was part of the devadana scheme. However, in the case of the Brihadeeshwara Temple, entire villages were granted, ensuring a vast infusion of funds, which were used for the functioning of the temple as well as for loans, which brought in additional income in the form of interest. Under Rajaraja, with the proliferation of newly converted brick-to-stone temples and the construction of the massive Brihadeeshwara Temple, the number of devadanas exploded. Inscriptions of Rajaraja at the Brihadeeshwara Temple mention that all the income from as many as forty devadana villages was transferred to the temple. This was not the case for all devadana villages. There were two categories of such villages, one from which all the land taxes were transferred to the temple; these were designated as a tax-free devadanas or devadana iraiyili. In the other category, called just devadana without any other label, the temple received only a portion of the government tax.

Devadana lands were often marked off by stones engraved with the emblems of the deity of the temple they belonged to. They were administered by temple authorities and supervised by both the village assembly and representatives of the government, to ensure that all was above board. The terms of the devadana lease were often open to negotiation, and inscriptions from both Rajaraja's and Rajendra's time show a flexibility and willingness on the part of the temple authorities and the government to show leniency to the tenants. For the tenant, being of service to the temple was considered an honour.[20]

This level of detail was common in regular brahmadeya and devadana charters as well. No aspect was too small to escape mention. Rajaraja's Anaimangalam grant on the Leiden copperplates explicitly prohibits the climbing of coconut and palmyra trees by the Ilava tribesmen (possibly for toddy tapping purposes).[21] Some grants placed restrictions on the sale or mortgage of the property by the new owners. With this level of detail, the Chola rulers, particularly Rajaraja and Rajendra, ensured the smoothest possible running of what could have been a messy coalition of villages and towns in their realm.

The worlds of the peasants and Brahmins were not mutually exclusive, nor were they always, as one might suspect, exploitative or controlling. Historians such as Burton Stein and D. D. Kosambi have characterized their relationship as one that was reciprocally beneficial. The reality was that Brahmins possessed both religious as well as agricultural knowledge, and, for the most part, did not live in isolated communities; but rather, their brahmadeyas were dispersed through peasant lands.[22]

Merchants and traders had their own towns, villages, and institutions that took care of the centres of commerce and trade. These villages, called nagarams, were where the merchants, like the oil sellers, weavers, goldsmiths, and other shopkeepers, lived. Their administrative assemblies were also called nagarams. The nagarams served as arbiter of all things commerce-related and more for their town or village; they were responsible for an array of tasks like administering all aspects of local market operations, collection of taxes and fees, and dispute resolution. The merchants paid the nagarams a fee for their services which included police protection, garbage collection, and street cleaning. These nagarams were generally established by the merchants themselves, or rather, in many cases, by the guild to which they belonged.

In the early decades of Chola rule, the traders' commercial dynamism was yet to reach its peak and many also had income from agriculture, even if they themselves may not have worked the land. As the Chola empire grew in size and power, so too did the number of nagarams, reflecting the growing importance of commercial activities and the need to corral them under an organizational umbrella.

As trade and trade networks expanded, so did the presence of guilds in a number of towns in which they established their presence. The merchants played a key role in urbanization. These merchants, who were called nagarattar, did not limit themselves to trading; they wielded considerable influence on the socio-cultural-religious ethos of the towns they inhabited. An example of this can be found in inscriptions that detail their revenue collection responsibilities and privileges. Inscriptions also show that certain merchants and artisans were granted special privileges (including tax breaks); the merchants in return played a vital role not just in contributing to economic prosperity of the state, but in enriching social, religious, and cultural life as well. Certain artisans like goldsmiths and weavers were held in high esteem by the royalty. They were major donors to temples across the land.

How were the merchants, many of whom were not Brahmins, allowed to build and donate to temples? This was in large part thanks to the Bhakti movement that began in the seventh century which emphasized the individual and his or her devotion over Brahminical rituals. The movement opened a different set of doors of faith to people across castes and the socio-economic spectrum. Thus the contributions of merchants and artisans to temples were as welcomed and valued as those by the upper castes.

Clusters of villages—ur, brahmadeya, and nagaram—made up the micro-level territorial unit called the nadu. Several nadus together constituted the valanadu, a creation of Rajaraja's; and a group of valanadus formed a mandalam.

The nadu was the most basic—and smallest—unit of agrarian rural society, consisting of a cluster of agrarian villages that depended on a common source of irrigation. The fundamental and enduring unit of south Indian agrarian peasant society, these nadus predated Chola times. They maintained a certain degree of independence, but were also subject to the vagaries and crosswinds of local and larger scale conquests and politics, sometimes getting subsumed into larger territorial units or being grouped with neighbouring villages. The nadu might have been small but it was a key part of the Chola administrative system. A nadu could encompass as small an area as 25 square kilometres, and cover as many as 780 square kilometres. Within each nadu were villages; some had just a handful, while the larger ones had forty or more, and each established its own institutions for trade, politics, and culture. Central to everything was the temple. It was here that surplus grains were stored and redistributed; it was what dictated the role that different societal groups had to play; and it was the meeting place for priests, poets, musicians, and others who shaped the religious life and thinking of the village.

The nadus had assemblies that were responsible for making decisions and taking actions that were hyper-local in their impact. It is estimated that there were around 500 nadus in the lands that came under Rajaraja's overlordship. It seems clear that the Cholas piggy-backed on the existing social and territorial structures and although there are wildly differing opinions on what role these nadus played in the Chola bureaucracy, there is no doubt that they were involved in issues of local governance, besides serving a social role and, most fundamentally perhaps, one that was concerned with agrarian matters. Over time, the Vellalas or farmers who lived in the nadus wielded tremendous economic and political power, thanks to the prosperity they enjoyed from their prowess at controlling irrigation and agriculture.

These urs and nadus were around even in Sangam times, the sole stable organized associations in a world of rapidly shifting allegiances and constant power struggles. One might wonder why a ruler like Rajaraja allowed these village and town assemblies to retain their authority; surely it would be more politically expedient to dismantle them altogether and wield all power from the centre. The calculation is never that simple and a ruler as shrewd as Rajaraja must have realized that even as his own power was consolidated and solidified, he had to remain ever aware of the tenuousness of his position. Upsetting an ancient and well-entrenched system in which the inhabitants of the urs and nadus had the independence and autonomy to make decisions could stir up more problems than it was worth.

Rajaraja introduced a new territorial unit called the valanadu, in-between the nadu and the mandalam. In creating the valanadu, Rajaraja achieved multiple objectives. The traditional nadu had been firmly ensconced since well before Chola times as a part of the territorial division in the region. Many of these had been the long-time fiefdoms of minor chiefs. Some of them were of very ancient lineage and wielded a fair amount of local power and influence. They had their own courts, officers, and troops. Some were wealthy, and patronized local temples with money and land gifts. Rajaraja knew that the power enjoyed by these chiefs in their nadus could very quickly become a real threat. In order to diffuse and rearrange the old power structures, he created a new territorial division, the valanadu, which in size was between the nadu and the mandalam. Some valanadus cut right through old nadu boundaries. The old chiefs were not left entirely bereft. Rajaraja created new roles for some of them in his bureaucracy, as revenue officials for the valanadus, for example. In doing this he vested them with the authority and importance that ensured their involvement and participation in the valanadu administration. This showed brilliant strategic thinking on Rajaraja's part. During his reign, there were ten valanadus in the core Cholamandalam region. He endowed some of them with grandiose names after epithets for himself: for instance, the valanadu around Thanjavur was called Pandikulasanivalanadu.

Major zones in the Chola territory were called mandalams. They were probably equivalent to the states of modern times. The core mandalam, the heart of the empire was Cholamandalam; the old Pallava lands, Tondaimandalam, were renamed Jayankondacholamandalam, and Pandiyamandalam, the former Pandya territory, now became Rajarajamandalam. In the outer boundaries were the lesser mandalams of Nadavilnadu, Kongu, and Gangavadi. During Rajaraja's time, there were eight or nine mandalams, including Ceylon, and this number did not grow during the later Chola years.

Historians like Y. Subbarayulu and Noboru Karashima have done the tedious and painstaking work of combing through endless numbers of inscriptions, subjecting them to statistical analysis, and making meaningful inferences. From this we learn about the many changes that took place in the realm of land ownership over the centuries of Chola rule. A striking case in point: possession of land in an ur and how it differed from the brahmadeya. In the early years, including Rajaraja's time, ur land was held in common by a group of its members, who shared the same task of cultivating it, and the same goal of achieving a good harvest. There are very few inscriptions that mention private ownership of land in an ur; the few instances appear to be restricted to persons like dancers, astrologers, or irrigation specialists, who performed special services for the ur. On the other hand, land in the brahmadeyas was often owned individually, by Brahmins, although the brahmadeya assembly or sabha did also own land as a collective. A century later, this had changed, as the number of individuals owning land in urs swelled; we know this from the number of inscriptions that recorded transfers of land ownership from one individual to another, with both parties mentioned by name. And as this non-Brahmin ownership and real-estate dealing grew, the same could not be said for the Brahmins, as we find fewer inscriptions describing their transactions.

As individual land ownership in the general population grew, some people became medieval real estate tycoons, owning, buying, and selling large tracts of land. How did this come about? As the Chola empire evolved past its turbulent adolescence and into settled maturity, transactions that are a part of any society with a bureaucracy became commonplace here as well. High-ranking officers were granted land as part of their stipends, and also for good service and loyalty. Fertile areas like those around the Kaveri were particularly prized. The landowner was identified by the title udaiyan or kilavan (meaning possessor) along with the name of the ur. Statistical analyses of the titles held by individuals in inscriptions show a marked increase in the number of these titles towards the end of the Chola era. Naturally, once somebody acquired enough land and the land values grew, it made good financial sense to sell it and so the number of individual owners of land grew still larger.

From the Vellalas and Brahmins being the main land-owning communities in the tenth century, the growing number of individual transactions meant that in due course, people from other communities, like the Chettis and Kaikkolas and even those from hill tribes, also started buying and owning land. Eventually, by the twelfth century, unbridled land sales resulted in the state having to issue an order to restrict them, in order to protect the old landholders in the Kaveri delta, who were no doubt displeased with the incursion of the nouveau riche into their old lands. However, these orders did not succeed in squelching the burgeoning real estate transfer market, and eventually entire villages were bought and sold by individuals; temples got in on the action as well, acquiring large parcels of land through grants and purchases.[23]

The shifting social hierarchies, the transition from collective to individual ownership of land, the forced intermingling of formerly discrete groups resulted quite naturally in unrest among those communities that felt disenfranchised by the new developments. The village assemblies that decided on the taxes denied any voice to landless labourers, whose numbers increased in the later Chola years. Often, they bore the brunt of the growing tax burden—lands owned by Brahmins and temples were exempt from taxes, which shifted the onus to others—and protests and revolts broke out as a result. Societal upheaval always comes at a cost and very often with the attitude that the means justified the ends, and it was no different for the Cholas.[24]

Each of these and more—the peasants and cultivators,

the artisans, the Brahmins, the merchants, to name just a few—constituted the social segments of medieval southern India. These basic groups massed together and created local and supralocal organizations (the nadu, the brahmadeya, the nagaram) that were an important tier in the political organization of the empire. And at the very top was the king, who by virtue of his ritual authority, and his status as the Great Conqueror, the Top Devotee of the empire's Top Deity, the Upholder of Dharma and Law, commanded the loyalty and respect of the teeming masses and segments of society that formed a part of his kingdom.

Rajaraja's kingdom-wide land survey, standardization of grain and land measures, reorganizing and streamlining of territorial units, and setting up of bureaucratic posts to carry out revenue and tax collection and much more, served to stabilize and consolidate his political authority and ensure a steady flow of funds. This in turn enabled the Cholas' successful overseas ventures (Sri Lanka, Southeast Asia, and China) which added significantly to the Chola coffers.[25]

The Cholas inherited an unwieldy assemblage of villages and towns, each with their particular mode of self-government, a large conglomeration of traders and their guilds, and their brilliance—particularly that of Rajaraja—lay in how they used these already existing institutions to their advantage by the astute use of propaganda and publicity and by ensuring good human and economic outcomes for them. This was done out of sheer necessity, in order to exert some control over what was often a precariously held together whole. That Rajaraja succeeded to a large extent is testament to his genius.

CHAPTER 12

THE TWAIN MEET

TRADE AND MERCHANTS

From very early times—the start of the Christian era—the entrepots of the eastern and western coasts of southern India had been part of an extensive trade network that stretched from the Greek and Roman empires of the Mediterranean region in the west to China in the far east. As the Chola empire grew, so did south Indian trade networks, both inland, within the borders of the kingdom and beyond, as well as overseas, particularly to countries to their east. We have read how, in the Sangam era, there was active trading between the ports of the Roman empire and those along the western and eastern coasts of India.[1] When the Roman empire collapsed, so too did this trading activity, but that was only temporary. After a lull of a few centuries, with the rise to prominence of the Pallavas, who were both an inland and maritime power, commercial dealings picked up again, and this time there was a difference caused due to the growing power of the merchant guilds.

Training a microscope into the world of the merchants and just the merchants alone, we see that they did what their ilk had always done, transporting, buying, and selling merchandise (including silk, cotton, spices, pearls and other gems, as well as more mundane items like rice and oil). But they were no mere bit players in the world they operated in. They were integral participants in the expansive and vibrant world of international trade. Their influence went far beyond merely shuffling goods about; along with their merchandise went people, ideas, and ideals.

On a larger scale, the dawn of the second millennium saw

Europe emerging from its Dark Age while, at the same time, economic activity in lands to the east moved into high gear. The near-simultaneous rise of the Fatimid dynasty in Egypt, the Khmers in Cambodia, the Song dynasty in China, and of course, our Cholas in southern India, rocked the geopolitical and commercial dynamic of the time which had consequences for the merchants and how they conducted their business.

Sometime in the eighth century, kingdoms along the southeastern coast of India, starting with the Pallavas, grew to be trading powerhouses. A couple of centuries later, as the Chola kingdom expanded, the ports of the Coromandel coast were the centres of a flourishing trading economy. The Tamil region was now part of a wider world of intra and inter-regional trade. Chola ports were recognized as hugely important, and China held them in high esteem as its 'first class' trade partners.[2] From these ports an array of prized products was exported, including coral, pearls, areca nuts, cardamom, and cotton and silk articles. Many of these were crops from interior regions and this resulted in a great expansion in the networks and relationships between these regions and the ports. Itinerant merchants who had, before the consolidation of Chola power, worked in isolation or in a not particularly systematized manner, now aligned themselves in growing numbers to the newly powerful supra-regional guilds, and enabled the flow of merchandise between the hinterlands and the coasts in a far more efficient manner. The scattered and diffused workings of a loose clutter of traders was gathered and brought into a connected and organized network that fed and was fed by an exploding trading economy. The guildsmen grew in wealth and prestige along with their commercial successes and they were a vital link connecting people and goods across the scattered villages of medieval south India.

The guilds arose out of the existing social structure of caste and occupation. The most well-known of them were called Manigramam, Ainuravar, Anjuvannam, and Nanadesi. From inscriptional evidence, specifically the number of inscriptions by the guilds, we know that these guilds came into being around the eighth century, gaining in influence from the eleventh century and growing to their peak in the thirteenth century. The inscriptions recorded donations to temples by individual merchants as well as a collection of them, or by a combination of merchants and landowners/cultivators. Often, they served as guarantors of loans to individual borrowers; the guild served as a loan and donation servicer by accepting loans and donations on behalf of individual merchants and ensuring that the funds were put to the proper, stipulated use.[3]

Although the term 'guild' has been used to describe these groups, there is scant evidence to show that they were organized and structured in any way like the medieval trading guilds of Europe. Unlike the guilds of Europe that were very local and in which the members all practised the same trade, the guilds of south India consisted of itinerant merchants who traded in a diverse array of goods (and services too) across large distances. No set of strict rules or a constitution governed their activities and membership. They describe themselves as samaya, a group created through means of a pact or contract. According to their own inscriptional records, they were governed by a code of conduct they called the bananju dharma, a loose set of rules and regulations. The guilds did not operate in isolation; many records and inscriptions show that their worlds were deeply intertwined with each other.

What is fascinating about these guilds is that they operated autonomously and were entities that wielded power and influence entirely independent of the royal sphere. They even had their own armies. The guild's presence and responsibilities ensured, to the extent possible, an equitable marketplace, the collection of duties and taxes and a fair assessment of the value of the goods that entered and left the marketplace. For all these services and more, they were awarded their fees, or dues. Inscriptions by guild members have been found all over southern India and even in Sri Lanka, Myanmar, Thailand, and Indonesia. Among the most important grants as a source of invaluable information are the Sthanu Ravi plates of Kollam in Kerala that give us a wealth of detail concerning the activities and privileges of two major guilds: Anjuvannam and Manigramam. Fully seventy-two different rights and benefits are spelled out including the entitlement to carry earth and water on the back of an elephant, to ride on the back of an elephant during marriages and other important occasions, to withhold taxes in case of disputes until they were resolved, and perhaps most importantly, jurisdiction over their own affairs.[4] In this way, the merchants were incorporated into the social, religious, and political affairs of their communities.

Among the most important guilds that were created by merchants within southern India were Ainnuruvar and Manigramam.

Ainuravar, or the Five Hundred, was probably the most powerful of the travelling merchant guilds. The town of Aihole, also called Ayyavole, in Karnataka was where it had its beginnings; they were called Ayyavole in Kannada country.[5] Ayyavole was one of the principal cities of the Chalukyas and lay near Manyakheta, the capital city of the old foes of the Cholas—the Rashtrakutas. It is very likely that the armies of the Rashtrakuta king Krishna III marched along the very routes that the traders had been using in earlier times. The earliest inscriptions that mention this guild are from the eighth century, the period when the Chalukyas were fading and the Rashtrakutas were emerging as a force to reckon with.

It is fascinating that their members were not limited to, as one might assume, the Vaishya or trading community. In fact, the founding members of the Five Hundred were a group of Kannada Brahmins and once again, in contrast to the perception of Brahmins as being rigid in terms of where they worked and who they worked with, they moved, travelled, and traded across multiple linguistic and caste lines. Many all-Brahmin communities were actively involved in trading, and that they organized themselves into a large guild is evidence of their far-sighted thinking, ambition, and prowess in the commercial realm.

A more elaborate version of the Ainnuruvar moniker was Nanadesi-Tisai-Ayirattainnurruvar, which translates to the Five Hundred of the Thousand Directions in All Countries. This grand name instantly grants us a vision of the sweeping scope of the world of the Ainnuruvar guild. Their view of themselves as a transregional organization was integral to their group identity as well their world view. Much like the Chola emperors, the Ainnuruvar inscriptions had their own prasasti or eulogical introduction, full of flowery praise for what they were about. They were called 'ornaments on the brow of that great lady, the city of Ahichchatra (Ayyavole)' or the 'five hundred swamis of the illustrious town of Ayyavole'; they claimed descent from the goddess Parameshwari of Ayyavole as well as Bhumidevi, the earth goddess; their bravery was lauded and they were referred to as Vira Valanjiyars, brave merchants. As their power and influence grew, so too did the flamboyance of their eulogies.[6]

They became active in Tamilakam in the tenth century, both in trade as well as important donors to temples and the sociocultural life of the kingdom. The Five Hundred were more active in interior regions. Inscriptions included many of donations to temples or villages by individual merchants. The name of the guild was suffixed to the merchant's name. There were also inscriptions on behalf of a group of guild members, that detailed their donations, or other actions, towards larger causes such as the construction, or protection, of a temple and its tank.

A fascinating testament to the synergies that worked between the merchants and the ruling powers is in the fact that the Tamil segment of the Ainnuruvar guild first set up base in and around Kodambalur in Pudukkottai district, the home of the Irukkuvel chieftains. The earliest inscriptional evidence of this is from the late ninth century.[7] As the chieftains who controlled this area, the Irukkuvels would have naturally taken an interest in the economic and commercial goings-on in their territory and supported the guild and its merchants. The Irukkuvels were a minor dynasty, and their power never grew beyond their borders. However, they were close allies of the Cholas, their fates and lineages intertwined, and they played a vital supporting role in many Chola victories. Theirs was the border zone between the Chola and Pandya lands; sandwiched between these bitter rivals and their territorial ambitions, they chose to ally with the Cholas and their support proved to be of critical importance. Marital alliances ensured and sealed their loyalty. We have read about Vikki Annan, an Irukkuvel who was Aditya Chola's military general who played a big role in Aditya's conquest of the Kongu lands in western Tamilakam. Later, when the Cholas established control over the Irukkuvels and their lands, the latter maintained friendly ties with and continued supporting the merchants and their guild. Clearly, the Cholas were interested in more than merely seizing control; maintaining and boosting economic activity was also a priority. As the Chola empire grew in strength over the centuries, so too did the guilds and their sweep.

A guild as important, large, and as widespread as Ainnuruvar had to hold assemblies and meetings. Much like modern associations record the minutes of their meetings, so, too, did the guilds of a thousand years ago. Meticulous record-keeping ensured that all decisions and transactions were laid out for everyone to see. These records were inscribed along temple walls. Two such major inscriptions, made on behalf of the guild's assembly, are the erivira-pattinam inscriptions in which the merchants record their decision to award the moniker erivira-pattinam to a particular town; the second type are the pattana pagudi inscriptions.

The erivira-pattinam has been variously described as a fortified mart; a market town protected by erivirar (javelin throwing warriors); the place where the heroes of the road conducted trade, mostly in turbulent frontier regions; a royally sanctioned protected trading base. The common thread underlying all these opinions is that the erivira-pattinam was some sort of a protected trading town. But as for where they were located, how they were created, and what relationship they had with the king, there are as many theories as there are scholars.[8]

Recently, however, newly deciphered inscriptions seem to lend some clarity to the matter. Some erivira-pattinams, at least, were so designated in order to honour a warrior who saved his fellow warriors while fighting against the enemies of the merchants. With the merchants travelling around with valuable merchandise, theft and other crimes were always a danger, and they would have had the protection of armed guards. It was to honour these guards that the erivira-pattinams were designated; judging by the number of inscriptions that mention them, they were a significant part of the lives of the merchant community.

The pattana pagudi inscriptions record the decision made in a town assembly meeting of the Ainnuruvar guild members, often along with others like landowners, artisans, and soldiers, to assign a certain share (pagudi) of their income for festivals, temple repairs, or charity. Merchant contributions were often in the form of a quantity of the commodity they traded.[9]

These inscriptions show that the various slices of society—including the farmers, Brahmins, warriors, and traders—did not live in siloed isolation, but that their lives and activities were quite significantly intertwined.

The Great Silk Road, the network of overland trade routes that connected the ancient worlds of Europe in the West to China is well known. Just as lucrative and thriving were the ocean routes—a maritime Silk Road that linked these worlds in trade. The east and west coasts of India, positioned right between the ports of the Mediterranean world to the west, and those of China to the east, have long been at the centre of a thriving maritime trade route. More importantly, these regions were the source of many valuable goods that were in high demand in these faraway places. Ports along both coasts were hives of activity with ships loading and off-loading their precious cargo, and at the hub of all this activity were the merchants.

Long before globalization became a catchword, it was very much a fact of life in medieval times as traders and their wares traversed the world. The tales of Sinbad the Sailor might be fictional, but they were surely based on real-life accounts of itinerant traders from the Middle East. One prominent group of such traders who dealt extensively with ports of the western and eastern coasts of southern India was called Anjuvannam. There are a few copperplate grants from the ninth century that first mention the guild. Among the earliest of these are two that are in the possession of a church and a synagogue in Kerala, and because of this, it is assumed that the Anjuvannam merchants were—at least at some point in time—of the Christian and Jewish faiths. In addition, there is literary evidence from a twelfth-century collection of Tamil Muslim poetry called the *Palchandanamalai*, that indicates that Anjuvannam members included Muslims as well.[10]

What there is general agreement upon is that the Anjuvannam merchants originally came from West Asia and further west, traded, and eventually lived in and established communities along the western and eastern coasts of southern India as well as further afield in Indonesia, networked with other merchant guilds, and were granted many rights and privileges.

Another guild that played a major role in medieval south India's economy was called Manigramam. The earliest mention of this guild in inscriptions is found in the same Sthanu Ravi plates in which the Anjuvannam guild was referred to. Inscriptions related to them have been found from the ninth century onwards, initially in Kerala, but over the next several centuries, in Tamil cities and as far afield as Thailand. (In Tamil Nadu, many Manigramam inscriptions have been found in the

Pudukkottai area.) The Manigramam guild members plied their trade more in ports and coastal towns. Its members came from a wide swathe of social classes.[11] Later, well after the reigns of Rajaraja and Rajendra, even as their trading activity remained strong, Chola monarchs increased their control over institutions that had functioned more autonomously earlier, and the Chola chokehold over their cultural and religious contributions resulted in a decline in the number of inscriptions that detailed their donations to temples.

The life and work of a merchant, which could lead to rich monetary rewards, was nonetheless full of risk and danger. The high seas posed multiple threats—pirates, mutinies, storms, and shipwrecks. Overland trade, too, was rife with hazards; many of the routes were outside the jurisdiction of any ruler and could be very unsafe. Information, such as it was, was scanty and unreliable. Would potential buyers fall upon his merchandise with glee and offer him payment that made it all worthwhile, or would his goods be looked down upon with disdain, or disinterest, or be deeply devalued? The possibilities spanned the entire gamut from profits and great riches to losses, debt, and hardship.

What exactly was the relationship between the Chola court and the merchants? There is little evidence to show that the former ever participated directly in the inter-nation trade that was growing even as its power expanded. That seems to have been mostly the domain of the traders and the guilds; as we have seen, the guilds took care of their own administrative and 'governmental' affairs, managed their own security and safety, and, one imagines, all the nitty-gritty of conducting trade across long distances. The king and his court, on their part, confined themselves, almost exactly like in modern times, to taxation and regulation, and granting concessions and privileges to the traders. Rajaraja, with his broad strategic vision, understood that offering support to the traders would be to the state's benefit as well, and provided tax benefits and residential quarters to the Ainnuruvar. While the Chola administration did not get directly involved in the minutiae of trade, it played a big part in creating an environment and making the connections that best served a successful trade climate, especially from the time of Rajaraja on. But as the 'trade wars' heated up, so too did the direct involvement of the Chola rulers, navigating multiple treacherous political tightropes to ensure the best outcome for themselves. The ties between the Chola rulers, merchant guilds, and temples proved beneficial to all. The conquest of southern Karnataka by Rajendra would have served to secure and open up internal trade routes for the merchant guilds.[12]

For the sake of their survival, the traders operated, for the most part, above the seamy world of politics, adapting themselves to the power in charge. As George Spencer put it so beautifully, the merchant-artisans lived in 'balanced but cautious cooperation' with the royal court.[13] But this is not to say that their worlds remained entirely independent of one another. In reality, the merchants were a source of very useful information about the lands they travelled to and served as a vital information network. A prime example is of the horse-trader who reported back to the court of Rajaraja about the unrest in Sri Lanka, prompting the king to invade the island. In addition, the mercantile regiments that protected the traders and their wares were sometimes deployed by the royal court as the need arose. And as far as the royal treasury was concerned, more trading activity at ports and other centres meant more revenues in the form of taxes and levies.

◆

During the reign of the Cholas, particularly Rajaraja and after, the coastal regions under their control were key centres of trans-oceanic trade. Rajaraja was keenly aware of the revenue potential inherent in his port towns. He did his part to encourage maritime trade through the ports he controlled; there was huge profit to be made from taxing and supplying goods to markets in Song China and the Middle East and the port duties were added incentives.

Two major port cities that were part of the international trade in Rajaraja's time were Mamallapuram, to the north, in former Pallava territory, and Nagapattinam, further south, on the coast near the Chola capital Thanjavur.[14] Mamallapuram was managed by a managaram—a grand nagaram—but inscriptions on the Shore Temple there made during Rajaraja's twenty-fifth regnal year (1010) show that the administrative structure of the place was reorganized by royal command, and the port was assigned to a key officer—a pudukkudaiyan ekadira—which means 'one who is the owner of a new parasol', indicating somebody newly promoted to this position of power. In addition, the inscription tells us, the nagaram levied a tax on traders, artisans, and labourers, probably on royal command. All this goes to demonstrate Rajaraja's intent to exercise his control over Mamallapuram.[15]

The main Chola port was Nagapattinam, 250 kilometres from Mamallapuram, down the Coromandel coast. It was a lively, thriving port during Rajaraja's reign. With Rajaraja's oversight of the ports of his empire, and his conquests in the Maldives and Sri Lanka, the Cholas now had control over the maritime trade in that region. Further east, command over the routes and trade through the seas around the Malay peninsula was the privilege of the Srivijaya kingdom. Maravijayattungavarman, the ruler of the Srivijaya dynasty in the Malay peninsula, saw that it would be prudent to establish friendly relations with Rajaraja in order to protect and maintain his position. The Srivijaya kingdom was caught between two mighty powers of the time—the Song and Chola empires. In an effort to secure the best possible outcome for itself and maintain and protect its position of privilege in the maritime trade of the region, the king had to resort to flattering the Song emperor of China as well as well as establishing strong diplomatic ties with the Chola emperor. Maravijayattungavarman financed the construction of a Buddhist vihara just north of Nagapattinam, named Chudamanivarma Vihara after his father. This would provide Buddhist merchants and pilgrims who visited Nagapattinam a place to worship. Rajaraja, clearly intent on creating as hospitable and friendly an environment as possible for the traders and other visitors, endowed an entire village, Anaimangalam, to support the upkeep of the Buddhist vihara. Strikingly different in intent from his other endowments, this one was very obviously done with diplomatic and commercial considerations, to attract more trade and visitors to Nagapattinam. The Larger Leiden plates from the reign of Rajaraja record this grant.

From the order given orally by the king, a tightly controlled step-by-step system wended its way from its being written down by the official Writer of Royal Orders, signed by multiple Superintendents of Royal Writs, and entered in the royal account books by designated Secretaries and Arbitrators. Officials of the tax department were present as the grant was entered into the state registers. Then came the tasks of drawing up the gift deed, awarding it to the recipient, and making the necessary changes in the village or at the land where the gift was made. A solemn ceremony followed, to mark the boundaries of the land. A female elephant was commissioned for the task of walking along the perimeters of the land, while yet more officials laid stones and other objects to mark the limits. Further ceremonies ensued to acknowledge and receive the royal mandate (the designated officials received it on their heads). Fulfilling all these formalities took a full two years and seventy-two days and the deed was finally completed and presented after that.

The terms of the deed are what are inscribed on the copperplates—in the case of the Leiden grants, it is the village of Anaimangalam, along with a certain value of the paddy crops from there. The details of the actual grant are in Tamil; preceding this is the Sanskrit portion, laying out, as it were, the entire story and history of the magnanimous and big-hearted king making this supremely generous endowment.

The Buddhist temple, the Chudamanivarma Vihara stood along the Coromandel coast a couple of kilometres north of Nagapattinam. The inscription marvels at the height of the structure—so lofty it dwarfed the great Mount Meru. It went by a multitude of names: the Puduveli Gopuram, the Chinese Pagoda, the Old Pagoda, the Jaina Pagoda. In 1878, Sir Walter Elliot wrote about a 'tall, weather-beaten tower, affording a useful landmark to vessels passing up and down the coast.... But save in name it has nothing in common with Hindu or Mahommedan architecture, either in form or in ornament. Tradition is silent as to its origin or purpose, and although it has been the subject of frequent speculations, no satisfactory theory has been formed to account for it.' Earlier, he had described it as a 'somewhat four-sided tower of three stories, constructed of bricks closely fitted together without cement...no trace of sculpture of inscription was visible'.

Sadly, this monument was not to survive. Dismissed as a crumbling old ruin with neither sculpture nor inscription to embellish it, it became the subject of a petition to remove it by a group of Jesuits who had been expelled from Pondicherry and who settled near it in the late 1850s. A spot of bureaucratic back-and-forth ensued and, finally, in 1867, orders were given to demolish it. The bricks were used to build a Christian missionary school.[16]

This vanished icon from a long-ago era grants us a vision of a far-sighted king with far-flung connections and a far-reaching generosity, imagination, ambition, tolerance, and shrewd practicality. A thousand years ago, this devout Saivite king had the largesse, foresight, and astuteness to bequeath land near an important port in his kingdom to a foreigner king who practised a faith different from his own. Alas, the monument he helped fund no longer stands but the inscription, painstakingly etched on copper, has stood the test of time to enlighten and enrich us about this great emperor.

◆

While the Cholas were establishing themselves in southern India, the Song dynasty was making waves in faraway China. The first Song emperor, Taizu, came to power in 960 and succeeded in unifying a country that had been fractured and had witnessed much upheaval during previous regimes. Like Rajaraja, he had a vision beyond mere conquest and, starting early in his reign, he issued a series of orders regulating maritime trade and revenues. The overland trade routes were occupied by semi-nomadic people like the Khitans, Tanguts, and Jurchens who could distrupt trade in the region. So, he focussed instead on developing maritime trade as a way to bring in fiscal revenue. He dispatched missions overseas to lobby 'foreign traders of the South Sea and those who went to foreign lands beyond the sea' to come to Chinese ports, promising special facilities and other incentives.[17] These caused no small ferment in the countries that were part of the trade networks and routes with China, as its markets and ports grew into highly lucrative places for trade and commerce. Chinese porcelain and silk were hot commodities, and there was a brisk market for all manner of goods in China, ranging from spices to horses. Hectic diplomatic manoeuvres ensued as rival kingdoms, especially in Southeast Asia, vied for advantage.

The Chola traders, a vital part of the China trade nexus, were naturally interested in the attractions of the Song markets. Their trading ports and the mercantile guilds that flourished in the Chola lands played a vital role in linking the Chinese markets to the rest of the world. And late in his reign, Rajaraja set in motion an enterprising mission that proved him a trailblazer yet again. He sent, by sea, a delegation of fifty-two people to the Song court, with the obvious intent of cutting a trade deal.[18] They took with them a rich lode of gifts, special tributes intended to flatter and impress: elephant tusks, pearls, frankincense, and perfumes, all commodities valued by the Chinese and subjected to high import taxes.[19] The journey, with several stopovers along the way, including a month-long one at a Srivijaya port, took

1,150 days to complete. They arrived at their destination in May 1015. The Chinese court appears to have known of the arrival of this mission as it sent an Imperial Aide Usher in the role of Lesser Lord of Diplomatic Reception to escort the Chola delegation to the capital.[20]

The group received a warm welcome at the Chinese court. According to the *Wenxian Tongkao*, a publication on Chinese institutional history that was released in the year 1319, 'The kingdom (Chu-lien—Chola) which in antiquity never had communications with the Empire, sent an ambassador for the first time under the dynasty of Song.'[21]

Another Chinese text called *Song Shi*, the official history of the Song Dynasty that was published in 1345 and that drew heavily from the *Wenxian Tongkao*, provides a host of fascinating details. Heading the contingent was someone the Chinese called the ambassador vice minister 'Suo-li San-wen (variously interpreted as Chola Samanta or Chola Samudra), with his deputies the second ambassador Pu-shu, the third ambassador Weng-wu, the guard Ya-le-jia', and others.[22] Alas, we have no Chola records that could enlighten us on their names. Emperor Rajaraja goes by the delightful name of King Luo-cha-luo-zha.

We learn from *Song Shi* that Suo-li San-wen and his deputies entered the audience hall of the Chinese court holding a tray with pearls and green beads, which they scattered in front of the throne. They then presented a letter, written by their king Rajaraja. The letter is a masterpiece of diplomatic sweet-talk and self-effacement. It begins with Rajaraja describing how he learned about the glories of the Song emperor and empire from a merchant who arrived at his country. He wrote, of the Song court, 'The merit of your administration covers Heaven and Earth and the force of your power gives discipline to the universe. Your divine power has never killed, your civility has enlightened, your high virtue has been extended to your subjects, and you worshipped Heaven with submissive mind....'[23]

The letter then moves on to a cringeworthy piece of self-deprecation. 'I presume to consider that as your subject I am a small being like a mosquito and a humble creature like a papier-mâché dog, having been living for generations in a barbarous town. My country is far from Chinese civilization, having not been enlightened and having sent no tribute to your court.... Regrettably I am too advanced in age to proceed to your court personally to offer tribute.... To present the products of my country is like ants and crickets being attracted by mutton, and to pay tribute and serve Your Majesty is like sun-flower and giant hyssop being drawn towards the sun. With respect I send a mission of 52 persons to your court to offer the products of our country as tribute consisting of a robe and a cap both decorated with pearls, 21,000 liang of pearls (around 840 kilos), sixty elephant tusks, and sixty jin (nearly 40 kilos) of frankincense.'[24]

It is impossible to imagine Rajaraja—King of Kings, Jewel of the Solar Dynasty, Three-Crowned King, the Thunderbolt to the Pandyas, the mightiest emperor of the legendary Chola dynasty, the builder of one of the grandest monuments of all time—referring to himself as a small mosquito from a barbarous town. Was this how eleventh-century diplomacy worked? Or was the Chinese narrative as richly embellished and varnished with fantasy and imagination as so many accounts from history are apt to be?

There is also the question, with no certain answer, of how the letter was read and understood in the Song court. It is known that traders from Chola India and Song China travelled to each other's lands, and some even stayed on. Perhaps one such person served as a translator–interpreter, because the language of gestures would certainly not have been enough.

The Song emperor ordered his staff to treat the visiting Chola delegation with great regard and high honours. The group returned to India the following year with an imperial edict and an abundant supply of gifts for Luo-cha-luo-zha. It appears that the leader of the group, Suo-li San-wen, took ill and died on the journey back.

Sadly, Rajaraja never learned of his men's adventures in China. He died before they even reached.

CHAPTER 13

THE NAME OF VALOUR
THE CHOLA ARMY AND NAVY

Medieval empire building happened largely as a result of success in the battlefield; without their military victories, there would be no Chola empire, and naturally, its army and navy have been much vaunted. However, while Chola inscriptions are rich in detail about temple rituals, the religious ethos, and cultivation and agriculture, and provide details about the military and other achievements of the king and other important personnel in the kingdom, data of any meaningful level of detail on the actual army and navy, the equipment they used, and how they were organized, is scant and can only be inferred.

Chola inscriptions mention numerous army units, and their members, by their names. Inscriptions from Rajaraja's time alone mention around thirty military groups. The military had its own hierarchy along with its own set of grandiose titles. Most of these positions had been created by the time Rajaraja came to rule and continued through the end of the Chola empire.

Each unit had the name of the ruler it served, as well as its function. There were archers, cavalrymen, swordsmen, the elephant corps, and foot soldiers. The infantry, especially the archers, swordsmen, and spearmen formed a major part of the Chola army, followed by the cavalry and the elephant corps.[1] The kaikkolar, a prominent weaving community in the post-Chola era, seems to have been an important military group during Chola times. During the reign of Rajaraja, units called the velaikkara figured prominently in inscriptions. Scholars have diametrically opposing views about the nature of these units, based on their etymological interpretation. Some believe they were a mercenary unit, hired for a job (velai) or assignment. In stark contrast, others are of the view that these were loyal and dependable troops ever ready to defend the king, and even sacrifice their lives if the occasion (velai) called for it.[2] Very little is known about the navy, although there is bountiful mention of naval expeditions, especially in the eleventh century.

Inscriptions abound about the loyal and capable senapathis or army generals. They were crucial to the success of the armies, and praise has been lavished on them in multiple inscriptions. The Thiruvalangadu copperplates make frequent mention of generals, their military exploits, as well as their steadfast loyalty. It is unlikely that the king himself led the army in battle, unless it had to be done. It was therefore of utmost importance that their generals be not only of top-notch military calibre, but also of impeccable character and utmost trustworthiness. It is very interesting to note that many of the senior officers of the Chola regiments were Brahmins, and those who achieved high distinction in their military careers were awarded the honorific Brahmadiraja. They enjoyed a remarkable degree of autonomy and were free to grant lands and construct temples in their name.

One of the most touching instances of the intense loyalty felt by a general towards his master is the tale of Vellan Kumaran, told in a set of inscriptions made in 959 at a temple in Tiruvottiyur in north Chennai. Vellan Kumaran was a faithful guard, able general, and close friend of Parantaka Chola's oldest son, Rajaditya. Rajaditya tragically lost his life in the terrible Battle of Takkolam in the year 949. For reasons unknown to us, Vellan Kumaran was not present at this battle, his beloved master's final, fatal mission. Stricken with grief and guilt at not being at Rajaditya's side, feeling himself unworthy of his class, his self, his family, and his master, he renounced all worldly attachments and became a monk in a monastery in Tiruvottiyur.[3]

As the Chola empire expanded, so too did their need for people to fight for them. In particular, the great territorial growth of the Chola empire during the reigns of Rajaraja and Rajendra necessitated an enormous mobilization of military labour. They recruited a number of people from the tribal communities who occupied the hills and fringes of their empire. A number of bowmen came from these areas. As they enjoyed repeated military successes and were rewarded by their monarchs, the tribesmen moved into the plains and became part of that milieu, enhancing their social and economic status. The new wealth and newly wealthy, as the former tribals settled into communities in the delta, resulted in the emergence and growth of private landholding in the region, changing and adding to the social fabric. They also recruited chieftains and other rural elite, as well as Brahmins, into the ranks of the military leadership.

We have a great deal of inscriptional evidence about the military (and other) achievements about the Cholas, but details on the recruitment process, how their military units were set up and the equipment they used, is scant. Unsurprisingly, there is little agreement among scholars about how to interpret these inscriptions.

Over a century ago Rao Bahadur Venkayya, one of India's most eminent epigraphists, listed the names of thirty-three Chola military regiments.[4] They lived in garrisons and cantonments that were called kadagams, and some scholars believe that some form of military training was conducted in them. Starting with this information, scholars have arrived at vastly different conclusions about the Chola army. Theories have been put forward about their being a highly organized, unified body; others have argued the opposite, that the so-called regiments were nothing more than an ad hoc collection of units that came together as the need arose.[5]

As always, inscriptions give us some wonderful details. One, in a village called Tiruvalisvaram, gives an account of the wondrous military successes of a group called the Munrukai Mahasenai or Three-Armed Great Army (three-armed here referred to three sections or divisions). Although the inscription is undated, this unit is believed to have fought during the reigns of Rajaraja and Rajendra. They are praised for their constant worship of Vishnu and Siva, and this is followed by a long list of victories against foes and in battles across a wide swathe of the country. The primary duty and function of these army units might have been fighting battles and wars but that did not stop them from taking a keen interest in civil matters. They made numerous charitable donations, both individually and as a group.[6] Munrukai Mahasenai troops lived in a kadagam (military barracks or garrison) near Tiruvalisvaram, in Tirunelveli, which was once part of the Pandya realm. They took under their eternal protection the temple of Tiruvalisvaram, including its priests, servants, and all its belongings.[7] It is also very likely that military troops were posted in these temples to protect the inscriptions, documents, and titles related to land ownership that were housed within the temple's premises. There are reports of revolts and insurrections, of peasants trying to wreck temples in order to destroy these records and therefore spare themselves the tax burdens.[8]

In spite of many assumptions to the contrary, there is no evidence of a standing Chola navy; rather, much like the peasant armies, it is just as likely that they piggy backed on to the existing maritime infrastructure. Maritime trade had been an ancient tradition, from the days of the Sangam Cholas, and it is very likely that they were well-versed and comfortable with the sea and its challenges. Rajaraja's conquest of Ceylon and the Maldives entailed nautical operations, and the Chola diplomatic delegations to China indicated that they were confident seafarers and equipped with the ships and other necessities for undertaking long sea voyages. This would have served them well in their naval military expeditions.

CHAPTER 14

THE PRICE OF TRANSGRESSION
CRIME AND PUNISHMENT

Sekkilar was a poet and minister who served in the court of the twelfth-century Chola king Kulothunga II. This king was a devout Saivite, but he did display a disturbingly avid interest in a Jain book called *Jivaka Chintamani*. This book had rather more erotica than Sekkilar was happy about, and so in order to wean his king away from it and steer him firmly and completely back into the Saiva fold, he wrote a book on the lives of the great Saiva Nayanmar saints.[1] This book, called the *Periya Puranam*, is a literary masterpiece and is revered as a fifth Veda by Tamilians.

There is a fascinating incident described in the *Periya Puranam*. Sundarar, who would go on to become one of the greatest of the Nayanmar poet saints, was all set to get married, when an old Brahmin interrupted the proceedings and claimed that Sundarar was his slave and that he would not allow the marriage to happen. The two went to the court of the village assembly in order to settle the dispute. They went through an involved and serpentine judicial procedure, going back and forth with the judges who demanded proof, which could include precedent, documents, or eyewitness accounts. Mention was made of a copy of the document, and eventually the original was produced, from the records office of the village. After thorough scrutiny of the contents and signatures of the document it was proclaimed the genuine article; the document recorded that Sundarar's grandfather had pledged himself and all his descendants to eternal slavery to the old Brahmin. Satisfied with the evidence, the judges of the court told Sundarar that he had lost his case, that he was indeed enslaved to the old Brahmin.[2]

The story is of great interest because Sekkilar very likely drew upon his knowledge of contemporary Chola life, which illuminates to us what a village court proceeding might have looked like. Inscriptions of other court cases corroborate Sekkilar's account; the involvement of the village assembly, the wise and knowledgeable judges, the record-keeper and records office all reflect the way justice was meted out in countless Chola villages. The plaintiffs and defendant each argued their own positions. The importance of evidence and the trustworthiness of the documents showed a well thought through judicial system. (For those who are curious, the old Brahmin in the story was actually Lord Siva; that was how Sundarar dedicated his life to his beloved lord.)

Where there are humans living together, there is crime; and where there is crime, there is punishment! And so it was with the Cholas. Crimes ranged from simple thefts (cattle stealing was very common) to murder and were dealt with in a multitude of ways. There was no legislature to speak of; rather, each situation was handled as and when it arose, relying on the wisdom of elders and learned members of the group and the existing social norms to come up with an appropriate solution, much as in Sekkilar's story. The king's royal authority made him not the creator, but the guardian, of the laws of society.

The famous Uthiramerur inscriptions, which are the source of hugely valuable and detailed information on how members were elected to the village assembly, also show that theft, forgery, and adultery were considered serious enough crimes that people found guilty of them were ineligible, for life, for candidature to any committee in the assembly.[3]

Agreements and contracts of all types were recorded on the walls of temples. Some of them included imprecations or threats to those who might dare violate or defy these agreements. These were of an extravagantly dire variety in Pallava royal inscriptions. One such (Pallava) imprecation swore: 'Whoever takes away property (belonging to a Brahmin) given by himself or by others, he shall become a worm in the dung for sixty thousand years.' The Cholas, on the other hand, included no such curses in their royal inscriptions. However, in earlier Chola inscriptions that record charitable donations made by commoners, including grants of land to Brahmins, there are imprecations, although of a much tamer nature. A commonly issued one says 'the person who would give harm to the charity shall incur all the sins committed in the land between the Ganges and Kanyakumari' reflecting, perhaps, the known limits of the country at that time. The gifting of land to Brahmins in the form of brahmadeyas or Brahmin villages, was considered an act of great virtue, and any crimes that contravened an agreement involving Brahmins were considered more heinous than others. Breaching a commitment to burn lamps in a temple was another flagrant violation that foreboded catastrophic consequences.[4]

The nature of the imprecations evolved with time and were given for matters beyond charities to Brahmins or the burning of lamps in temples. Often, the potential wrongdoer was warned that he would be labelled a drohi, or a traitor, and publicly shamed by being branded thus, for all to see and know about, on the temple walls.

The drohi moniker was appended to one of eight possible victims of the treachery: Siva (or god), raja (king), guru (religious teacher), nadu (locality), ur (village), ina (community), and matru (mother). [5]

One of the most fascinating accounts of what befell a trio of drohis is from an inscription from Rajaraja's time, found on the wall of a temple in a village called Udaiyarkudi. In Chola times, it was known as Viranarayana Chaturvedimangalam, which meant it was a brahmadeya, or Brahmin village. The inscription records an endowment of land to the temple by someone named Araiyan Bharathan. The inscription is a short one, a mere eight lines, and begins with a mention of a letter written by Rajaraja to the assembly of Viranarayana Chaturvedimangalam. The contents of the letter are extraordinary. It names three brothers who had been found guilty of treason for the murder of Aditya Karikala, Rajaraja's older brother. And what was the punishment for these drohis, these murderers of the crown prince, the king-in-waiting? Their property, as well as that belonging to a long list of specified relatives, was to be taken away from them and sold at the current going rate, and the proceeds handed over to the treasury of the village assembly.

The land belonging to the drohis and their relatives was bought by Araiyan Bharathan from the village assembly; he then endowed it to the temple of Viranarayana Chaturvedimangalam, which was the impetus for the inscription and its record of the grant.

The Udaiyarkudi inscription is important because it is our only source of information on who killed Aditya Karikala. It is extraordinary for the almost casual way in which it is mentioned, and the perpetrators named, in the larger context of the endowment of land that once belonged to them. We have no idea what became of the three drohis and their relatives. Very likely, stripped of their lands and disgraced as murderers and traitors, they spent the rest of their lives in a pall of disrepute and hardship.[6]

As the years progressed, Chola inscriptions began to include details of actual punishments. Interestingly, no inscriptions mention the death penalty for any crime, even murder. An inscription made during the reign of Rajendra describes the almost laughably lenient punishment, by today's standards, given to a man who had stabbed to death the commander of a regiment. He had to endow ninety-six sheep for a perpetually burning lamp at a local temple.[7] However, Chau Ju Kua (Zhao Rukuo), a thirteenth-century Chinese historian and politician who had not actually travelled to India but who gathered his information from merchants and other travellers to the Song court, had the following to say about the Chola system of justice: 'When any one among the people is guilty of an offence, one of the Court Ministers punishes him; if the offence is light, the culprit is tied to a wooden frame and given fifty, seventy or up to a hundred blows with a stick. Heinous crimes are punished with decapitation or by being trampled to death by an elephant.'[8]

Other inscriptions mention a variety of offences. Most were resolved by the members of the village assembly. The assembly had a committee just for this purpose, and the members were called nyayattar, or dispensers of justice.[9] The most common punishment was the levying of a fine. The fine could be in the form of money, or, very often, a perpetually burning lamp to the temple. In the case of crimes committed against high-ranking officials, or even the royal family, the king took a keen interest and dealt with the matter himself.

CHAPTER 15

O MADMAN WITH MOON-CROWNED HAIR

FAITH AND THE BHAKTI MOVEMENT

Imagine that you are in the lush countryside of Tamil Nadu. You are in the village of Thiruthonipuram, the holy place where heaven and earth and the four Vedas were created. All around you are verdant paddy fields. Bees frolic in the warm sunshine and the ponds are filled with lotus blossoms among which swans float in regal grace.

This is the home of the wondrous black-necked Lord Siva, slayer of Yama, powerful dancer, the almighty deity with the radiant half-moon in his matted hair and the garland of bones on his chest. But, where *is* he? In this bucolic paradise, Siva is nowhere to be seen. However, despair not. There is a way to find him. Just sing this song written by the lotus flower-garlanded Sambandar, and you will reach his heavenly feet.[1]

This is a poem by Sambandar, a seventh-century saint, poet, and ardent devotee of Siva. He is one of the most important of the Nayanmars, who were holy people who dedicated their lives to singing the praises of their beloved Lord Siva. These Nayanmars, along with their Vaishnavite counterparts, the Azhwars, were part of a Bhakti movement that came to life in the Tamil-speaking parts of south India between the sixth and tenth centuries. This was the most significant religious development of this region in this period. The inroads made by Buddhism and Jainism, as well as the stifling social and theological exclusionism of Hinduism as practised by the Brahmin elite made the conditions ripe and ideal for its efflorescence.

In this environment, the popular Hinduism of the Bhakti

saints with their credo of personal salvation through an intimate, deeply emotional, and personal connection to their god came as a breath of fresh air. They wrote meltingly beautiful and soul-stirring songs and poems that provided succour to the struggling human soul, serenity to the devotee, joy and beauty to all, and they are deservedly a significant and celebrated part of Tamil devotional literature. They sang of Siva's many feats and of his irresistible beauty. They described the festivals and processions that celebrated their lord. The most mundane of everyday occurrences made their way into their hymns: a coconut falling, a blundering young buffalo, a little red-legged egret ruffling its feathers with its sharp bill. The poetry of the Nayanmars is collected in twelve volumes called the *Thirumurai*; the first seven of these (that includes the work of Sambandar) are the *Thevaram*. To know these hymns by heart is a virtue, and to this day, public recitation of them, by a class of Vellala priests called odhuvars, takes place in Siva temples all over Tamil Nadu.[2]

The Tamil Bhakti movement was a great equalizer as people from across the social spectrum expressed their devotion, in words that were highly personal and in the language of the everyday. This was an expression of faith by the people, of the people, for the people. Their very accessibility fuelled their popularity. These saint-poets are inseparable from the gods they sang about, and are themselves deemed holy, and worshipped. There are sixty-three Nayanmar poets in all, a motley assortment of men and women from a wide swathe of society: kings and peasants, Brahmins, low caste, and outcaste; from occupations as varied as warriors, chieftains, potters, hunters, and cowherds. Three of them who most captured the popular imagination are called Muvar, or the Three, and are the triumvirate of Sambandar, Appar, and Sundarar. Between them they composed around 700 hymns that form part of the sacred liturgy of Siva temples in Tamil Nadu.[3]

Sambandar is often referred to as a child saint. Legend speaks of his being taken regularly to the Siva temple in his village (probably present-day Sirkazhi, near Thanjavur, and probably near or actually the Thiruttonipuram of his songs) by his father. One day, the story goes, little Sambandar was left on the steps of the temple tank while his father went to take his ritual dip; the child, hungry, began to wail. When the father returned, he was amazed to find his son with milk dripping down his chin, a golden bowl in his hands. When asked about who gave him the milk, the little boy pointed up to the temple where the goddess Uma sat alongside Siva. Sambandar has been immortalized by this tale in the form of bronze icons that depict him as an infant, bereft of clothes, with a bowl in one hand and a finger of the other pointing up, to Uma and Siva.

One of the highlights of Sambandar's life was the time he was summoned to the court of the Pandya king by his queen. It was an interesting marital dynamic: the queen and one of the ministers were devout Saivas; the king himself was in the thrall of the Jain faith and its monks. Sambandar's mandate was to make the king realize the greed and deception of the Jain monks and it was one he fulfilled admirably well against many odds, including having his house set on fire by the devious monks. In the midst of this, the king was struck with a burning fever. The best efforts of the Jain physicians were in vain and, finally, it was the healing powers of Sambandar that restored the king to good health. The king, who had promised Sambandar that he would return to the Saiva faith if he were cured, kept his word.[4]

Much of Sambandar's poetry is filled with rich imagery of the Tamil countryside with its paddy fields, flowering trees, rivers, ponds, and rich variety of flora and fauna. His Siva belongs here, close to his home and hearth, a world away from the distant, snow-clad Himalayas. He was an indefatigable traveller and appears to have visited towns and villages across the length and breadth of the Tamil countryside, and his keen observations find his way into his poems. Amidst the frolicking bees and flowering trees, Sambandar has sharp words for his bitter foes, the Jains. The tenth verse of each of his eleven-verse hymns is reserved for a cutting condemnation of the 'crooked Jains' and 'base Buddhist monks'.[5]

Thirunavukarasar, fondly known as Appar (father), was the most senior of the trio. He was of the Vellala (landowner) caste who became a Jain monk as a teenager. Later, in no small part due to the prayers of his sister, a devout worshipper of Siva, he reconverted to his family's practice of Saivism and started to sing hymns at Siva temples. The ruling Pallava emperor, Mahendravarman, was a Jain and he disapproved of Appar's switching faiths. He summoned him to his court, where he tested his faith with all manner of horrific tortures that included having him trampled by an elephant and tied to a rock and hurled into the sea. Appar emerged unscathed by his ordeals and the king, duly impressed by the faith that stood him such good stead, converted to the worship of Siva and built a temple in his honour. Appar, like Sambandar, minced no words in disparaging 'the weak and filthy Jains with their yellowing teeth'.[6] And like Sambandar, he was a traveller; the two met in the course of their peregrinations. Sambandar, a young lad, addressed Thirunavukarasar as Appar and that is the name by which he is more commonly known today.

Sundarar, the third of the Nayanmar threesome, was not a contemporary of Appar and Sambandar, but lived a century later. Born a Brahmin and brought up in luxury, he took his first step as a full-fledged Siva devotee when his wedding was rudely stopped by a 'madman with moon-crowned hair'—none other than Siva himself—who proclaimed him his slave.[7] Shaken by this unexpected mystical encounter, Sundarar devoted himself from that moment on to the worship of Siva. There are paintings at the great Brihadeeshwara Temple that depict this event. However, his was not a conventionally pure and moral life. He married two women from the lower castes—a temple dancer and a Vellala—and he expounded his myriad problems and unconventional life choices, his continual struggles with poverty, his blindness, in his hymns. Here was a saint that the common man could relate to, in his requests to Siva to give him 'strands of pearls, necklaces of diamonds, and gems to wear'[8] in addition to the more prosaic 'men to carry the grain' that he procured in Kuntayur.[9] Sundarar, too, wrote uncharitably of the 'Jains and Buddhists, no better than demons...with their lies and deception',[10] but not in as unrelenting and caustic a fashion as Sambandar and Appar; perhaps their influence was already waning in his time.

These three itinerant Saiva saint-poets lived in the region of the Kaveri delta in the seventh and eighth centuries, a time of great social and political change, before the emergence to power of the Cholas. For some time before this, in the Pallava lands to the north, the merchant community seemed to lend their support to the Buddhist and Jain monasteries. And to the south too, where the Pandyas ruled, Jains and Buddhists enjoyed royal backing. And between the two, in the Kaveri belt, the Saiva faith gained in strength, slowly but surely. The Vellala landowners in these fertile lands controlled the irrigation channels and with that came increasing wealth and influence. They built temples in their nadus, and as the itinerant hymn poet-saints travelled around and spread their faith through their songs, the practice of Saivism established deep roots. Appar and Sambandar's successes at the court of the Pallava and Pandya kings, respectively, served not only to strengthen the Saiva faith throughout the Tamil region, but also succeeded in dislodging the influence that Buddhists and Jains enjoyed. We think of Buddhism and Jainism today in nothing but the most pacifist of terms, but even the most peace-loving of religions, when entangled with power and politics, can get cast in a menacing light.

Every place visited by the Nayanmars, every temple they wrote about, was anointed with the halo of sacredness and acquired an enhanced holiness. The places they wrote about, the little villages and their temples, became as important as the god who lived there. Every site they wrote about became a home for a specific form of Siva, his very own local habitation in Tamil country. The town where Siva was enshrined under a sacred banyan tree was later called Alangadu—which means sacred banyan tree; Siva's town where the peacocks danced was Mayiladuthurai, and Kurangaduthurai was where the monkeys frolicked around him. These sacred sites became small temples of mud and brick, which the Chola rulers made into bigger, more elaborate, and more permanent edifices of stone. As the empire and the temples grew, they became the nerve centres of their towns and villages. They were a major source of employment and labour, the hub for arts, artists, and artisans, the place where merchants congregated to conduct their business; they functioned as banks, loaning money to all manner of people from the enormous wealth at their disposal, and they often served as hospitals and feeding centres.

This was the faith that inspired the Chola rulers. These were the gods they evoked to sanction their royalty and rulership. As devotees of Siva, they fed off the fervour created by the Nayanmars. Sites that were deemed sacred in their hymns received special attention and care and the shared faith strengthened the bond between the ruler and the ruled. The Cholas, starting with Rajaraja, adopted their already well-known hymns and further encouraged their popularity by ensuring their regular recitation in temples. They were edited and set to music and became an essential part of religious rituals. Alongside, a whole cluster of specialties that were part of the ritual life of the time blossomed into glorious sublimity: architecture, sculpture, painting, music, and dance, all enriching the life and legacy of the Cholas, while drawing together a wider swathe of the populace who embraced Bhakti temple worship.[11]

Worship of Siva followed many tenets, forms, and rituals, dictated in part by the leaders of a variety of Saivite sects. The early Chola rulers followed the teachings of a sect of Saivism whose members were called Pasupatas.[12] These wandering sages who smeared themselves with ash from the crematorium worshipped Siva as the god of death and destruction, an amalgam of the stormy howling Rudra of the Rig Vedas and one, or several, local deities. Their lives and rituals reflected this in their wild and bizarre actions. Their abode was the cremation ground where they embraced the death-ashes, snakes, and skulls. Sadly, we have no records from the Pasupatas themselves that might give us some insight into why they did what they did. Among other things, the Pasupatas are believed to have encouraged the Chola rulers to build sepulchral temples, places of worship built over the remains of religious leaders and rulers. It is likely that prior to having a tomb-temple being built over their remains, the Pasupatas would have conducted their eerie rituals. These sepulchral temples were simple structures but must have been places of tremendous importance in those times. There are at least three that we know of today: the tomb-temple for Aditya, built by his son Parantaka, which is near Kalahasti in present-day Andhra Pradesh; one built by Rajaraja for his grandfather Arinjaya near Ranipet in Tamil Nadu; and one built by Rajaraja's son Rajendra in Patteeswaram, near Kumbakonam, for either his aunt or his stepmother. These temples are called pallipadais, meaning tomb-temple. We know this because inscriptions inform us that this temple is a pallipadai, and who it was built by and for whom.[13]

Over the course of time, another Siva sect took root as a number of Saiva Siddhanta monks arrived in the Chola lands and made their homes there. They embraced the Bhakti hymns of the Nayanmars as an important part of their heritage and lineage. Their influence grew, and that of the Pasupatas waned, and due to a confluence of factors not least among which was its embrace and patronage by Rajaraja, his son Rajendra, and other Chola rulers, this branch of Saivite thinking became the pre-eminent religious philosophy of the Cholas, and the Tamil lands. The Saiva Siddhanta sect emphasized, among other things, the Bhakti path of worship to realize Siva. The Bhakti hymns fit in well with their outlook, and in establishing and systematizing their ideology they instituted the recitation of the *Thevaram* hymns in their muths or monasteries.[14]

When Rajaraja became king, he had as his rajaguru (religious teacher and mentor and head priest of the Brihadeeshwara Temple) one Isanasiva Pandita, who belonged to this sect. For Rajaraja and his realm, being initiated into this sect by Isanasiva had consequences that went far beyond the personal. It was very likely that it was with Isanasiva's go-ahead and guidance that Rajaraja built a place of worship as grand as his Brihadeeshwara Temple. Rajaraja appears to have used the Saiva Siddhanta scriptures to create and maintain his imperial temple system, and thus ensured that this philosophy took hold and prospered under him. It breathed life into the structure, rituals, practices, and festivals of temples across his realm. It was a powerful coming together of royal and philosophical agencies that influenced the religious, social, and political life of the kingdom.

The heart and soul of the Tamil Saiva Siddhanta movement was Chidambaram, an ancient temple town with a fascinating lore and mythology that stitched together people and events from all over the country, establishing it as one of the holiest, most powerful centres for the worship of Siva. Umapati Sivacaryar, one of the most important and prolific of the Tamil Saiva Siddhantas is said to have been a priest at the Chidambaram Temple. The Nayanmar poets too sang about Chidambaram and strengthened the deep connection that the Saiva Siddhantas had with the place. Their hymns, with their simple yet deep roots in the Tamil ethos, spoke to them as they did to all devotees of Siva directly to the heart. They sing of Thillai—one of the names for Chidambaram, after the thillai trees of the mangrove forests nearby; they sing of Nataraja, the Dancing Lord, who is supposed to have performed his Ananda Tandava or Dance of Ecstasy, the dance that shook the heavens and earth, right here.

Chidambaram, one of Siva's most sacred abodes, has been a place of worship for nearly 2,000 years. There is a muddled fable tradition about how the place came into being. Like any mythology, versions vary depending on who is telling the story. Characters show up here who are part of a separate folklore.

The story begins in a forbidding environment, the thillai forest, where this eponymous shrub grows in a thick, impenetrable mass along the banks of the backwater channels of the area. Its branches, a tangled mess, exude a sticky sap that is highly poisonous. A long time ago, a wandering ascetic, in search of the harshest, most hostile environment to conduct his penance in, arrived at this thillai forest near where Chidambaram is today. Pleased with the inhospitable severity of the place, he settled down to worship. In order to be able to pluck the lovely flowers that grew atop the dense canopy, our ascetic grew claws like those of a tiger, that he might get a good grip on the branches, and this earned him the moniker Vyagrapadar, or Tiger Foot. The tiger theme is echoed in the tale of a local goddess Pitari (Kali), who roamed the forests with her tiger. This might be why Chidambaram is also known as Puliyur, or Tiger Town. The tiger on the Chola flag most likely came from here.

In time, Vyagrapadar was joined by an exiled prince from Bengal who, similarly delighted with the spot, invited 3,000 religious scholars to carry out their special worship. In due course, a small hut was built as a place of worship, and from this humble spot grew the massive temple complex that is the great Chidambaram Nataraja Temple today. The hut is now called the Cit Sabha or Citrambalam, and the deity inside is the Dancing Siva or Nataraja, the only temple where this form of Siva is the deity of the central shrine.

Why the Dancing Siva, and why here, at Chidambaram? There are more stories, enchanting and confounding in equal measure that explain this. Many loosely linked story fragments come together here. The stories are fascinating in how they nudge aside, adapt, and incorporate deities and personalities into local lore. Tradition tells of two dances. In one, Siva challenges Kali to a dance contest. The two are evenly matched until, in a coup de grace, Siva raises his leg vertically upwards in what is called the urdhva tandava pose. Feminine modesty prevented Kali from continuing, and Siva won. The story might well serve as a metaphor for how Kali was edged out and how Siva assumed the position of prime deity. Cultural memory still lingers, though, and there are Kali temples that dot the area around Chidambaram, and her tiger lives on in the name that many locals still call the town by—Puliyur.

The second dance took place after Siva and Vishnu, watching from their perch in the heavens, decided that the sages of the thillai forest were becoming too proud of their asceticism, that their austerity was tainted with arrogance. The two descended to earth, Siva as a naked beggar, Bhikshasanan, and Vishnu as a seductive young damsel, Mohini. Their presence wreaked havoc in the village of ascetics as the men went on a lust-filled chase after Mohini, and the women did the same with Bhikshasanan. Once order was restored and the sages realized that they had been tricked, they flew into a rage and attempted to destroy Siva by conjuring up a fierce tiger, snake, and demon. It was a mere moment's work for Siva to subdue them all. Adorning himself with the tiger's skin and the snake, and standing atop the demon, he terrified the sages with a wild dance which evolved into the greatest dance of all, the cosmic dance of life and death and the entire universe, the fearsome and wondrous Ananda Tandavam.

There is another character woven into the story of the cosmic dance—Patanjali. In this story, Patanjali, who shares the name with the Sanskrit grammarian and famous author of the *Yoga Sutra,* is actually Vishnu's snake Ananta, who longs to witness the grand cosmic dance of Siva. He is reborn with the torso of a human and the bottom half of a snake, and makes his way to Chidambaram via an underground path through a complex snake civilization. His fervent wish is fulfilled as he witnesses the greatest dance of all. He is a model devotee, and through him, the south Indian tradition of reverence for snakes and their hidden spiritual power finds expression.[15]

The Chidambaram stories weave together so many facets, human and animal, tiger and snake, the ascetic and the humble devotee, in ways that are powerful and deeply meaningful to those for whom Siva is their universe.

Songs are sung to this day about the 3,000 priests and their unique rites, and it is believed that the present-day priests of the temples, the Dikshithars, are descendants of the original 3,000. The tale of the Bengali prince makes sense if one looks at the architectural style of the Cit Sabha, which does not conform to the style found in southern India at the time but is more along the lines of temples found much further north.

Chidambaram long had a reputation of being an exceptionally holy site. The 3,000 Dikshithar priests enhanced the mystique of the place as they had a status more exalted than that of other priests. Even the Chola kings could not assume that their royal status assured them any favours from the Dikshithars. The lord of this temple, Nataraja, was the one they held in the highest esteem, whose blessings they sought above all.

The Cholas claimed a hoary connection to Chidambaram. Their family genealogies mention a ruler from ancient times, called Kochenganan or the King with the Red Eye. This king was born under unusual circumstances in Chidambaram. His parents went there to pray for a son. The mother did conceive, but the baby was about to be born at an inauspicious time. In order to stall matters till a propitious time came around, the mother had her legs tightly tied and was kept upside down. As a result, the baby, who did arrive after the inauspicious time had passed, was born with the unfortunate flaws of red eyes and skin. This child, Kochenganan, grew up to be a great and devout king.

Many centuries later, the Chola king Aditya, who had great military successes across the Kaveri River valley and the Kongu lands to the west, used the gold collected from his conquests to shingle the roof of the sanctum with gold tiles. Aditya's grandson Gandaraditya wrote a beautiful paean to the temple and its community of priests: 'The Sages there tend the three-tiered fire, perform the Five Sacrifices, know the Six Limbs and the Four Vedas.... They total three thousand, and you, O Lord stand with them on the front platform of your hall!'[16]

The number of tiles on the sanctum's roof is significant. It is believed that an individual inhales and exhales 21,600 times in a twenty-four-hour period. These breaths are an affirmation of life; yogic principles dictate a meaningful distribution of these breaths to various deities and principles. The gilded roof at Chidambaram has 21,600 gold tiles; this number is believed to be derived from this number of breaths.[17]

One of the Chola emperors, most likely Rajaraja, went to the Chidambaram Temple with his court scholar Nambi Antar Nambi to collect the official manuscripts of the hymns of Appar, Sambandar, and Sundarar, which were housed in the temple at Chidambaram. The priests, unimpressed by the stature of their visitors, initially refused, and only relented eventually. After a good many vicissitudes and the invoking of divine intervention, the manuscripts were unearthed from a room in the temple. The hymns were then codified as the *Thevaram*, and their musical notes systematized. They are sung, to this day, in Siva temples around Tamil Nadu, a living legacy from Rajaraja's time.

In the twelfth century, Sekkilar composed the *Periya Puranam*, a legend-soaked narrative of the lives of the Nayanmar saints. In it he recounts an incident that purportedly took place just before the rise to power of Vijayalaya Chola. A petty regional ruler, the chief of Kalandai, wanted the Dikshithars of the Chidambaram Temple to bequeath him a special diadem that would recognize and be a symbol of the power he had gained from his many conquests. The Dikshithars, however, turned him down. They said that only the ancient family of the Cholas, then based in Uraiyur—that is, Vijayalaya and his descendants—were entitled to this high honour.[18] By the time Rajaraja became the monarch, deep faith in the supreme lord of the Chidambaram Temple had completely soaked into the religious ethos of the Chola domain. Bronze and stone icons of Nataraja started appearing all over the land. Rajaraja and his wives visited the temple, an event that found its way into the murals of the Brihadeeshwara Temple. Many royal coronations took place at Chidambaram. The Chola rulers had tremendous reverence and respect for the divine power and stature of the Dancing Lord Siva and nurtured their allegiance and devotion with unremitting fervour and sincerity. They knew the power of faith and they harnessed it to win respect, loyalty, legitimacy, and power. During their time, the merger of religious fervour and royal patronage created an impact that resonated through every aspect of life: religious, political, cultural, economic, and social.

In ninth-century south India, there were two principal centres of Saivism. Chidambaram was one. The other was Thiruvarur, home to an embodiment of Siva called Thyagaraja or Vitankar. Like Chidambaram, Thiruvarur and its lord have many tales associated with them that bring together local deities, folklore, and traditions, like the Tamil god Muruga, snakes, and anthills. And a mythical Chola king is woven in as well. The legend goes that the idol of Thyagaraja at Thiruvarur was brought down to earth by a monkey-faced Chola king named Mucukuntan. Successful completion of his penances in a previous life had won him the favour of Lord Muruga, who dispatched him to the Kaveri delta, where he had many successful conquests, became a king among kings, and established a dynasty—the Chola dynasty, of course. Mucukuntan's nemesis was Lord Indra, who had promised him a precious icon of the Lord Siva as Thyagaraja. When Mucukuntan asked Indra to deliver on his promise, Indra attempted a sneaky dodge. He created six replicas of the idol and asked Mucukuntan to pick out the original one. With a combination of luck and divine intervention, he did, and all seven idols were handed over to him. The original was enshrined at Thiruvarur, and the remaining six went to temples in nearby towns. The idol form in which Thyagaraja was—and still is—worshipped is as Somaskanda: Siva and Uma with their infant son Skanda, or Muruga.[19]

Siva is a multifaceted god with a range of forms that represent the very yin and yang of existence. The Cholas must have worshipped them all, but they had a particular reverence for three of them. One was Siva as Nataraja, and another, Siva as Thyagaraja, also called Vitankar. Both forms are enshrined at Rajaraja's Brihadeeshwara Temple. The third was Tripurantaka, the Destroyer of Three Citadels. This was Siva at his heroic best. He had to contend with three powerful demons and the only way they could be defeated was with a single arrow shot from his bow. Needless to say, he achieved his end with perfection. This Siva had tremendous symbolic value for the Chola rulers—the three demons represented the three major enemy states: the Pallavas, Pandyas, and Rashtrakutas, and his feat mirrored their aspirations and achievements as the ideal warrior-heroes who vanquished their adversaries. This manifestation of Siva truly resonated with the psyche of kings battling for power at a time when war was an incessant fact of life. Rajaraja seems to have been particularly enamoured of Siva as Tripurantaka as there are many carvings of him throughout his grand Brihadeeshwara Temple.

One of the most potent ways for the Chola kings to announce their benevolence, stature, and royal presence was through the network of temples that were scattered all over their realm, particularly in the Kaveri delta. We encounter the kings most frequently, via inscriptions, as they donate land and other goods to temples, or acknowledge the gifts to temples of their subjects, peasants, landowners, merchants, generals, and the nobility. They created substantial networks around their temples that drew in the peasant, Brahmin, and merchant villages with their assemblies as well as the great multitude of people who were linked to the temple in many different ways as accountants, dancers, artisans, and so much more. All of them contributed to the temple economy and benefited from it as well. Their generosity to temples was both an act of religious supplication and political calculation. Nearly every great Tamil temple has a tale involving a Chola king woven into its sthalapurana, or local legendary history.

The faith of the Chola kings was genuine and heartfelt. It was the very bedrock that anchored them and propelled them to greatness.

CHAPTER 16

THE EPONYMOUS TEMPLE
RAJARAJESHWARAM IN THANJAN'S CITY

> Hail! Prosperity! This (is) the edict (*sasana)* of Rajaraja (alias) Rajakesarivarman, which is cherished by the multitude of the diadems of (i.e., which is obeyed by) the crowd of all princes.
>
> On the twentieth day of the twenty-sixth year of the reign of Ko-Rajakesarivarman, alias Sri-Rajarajadeva, who...vouchsafed to say: 'Let the gifts made by us, those made by our elder sister, those made by our wives, and those made by other donors to the Lord of the sacred stone-temple called Sri Rajarajesvara, which we caused to be built at Tanjavur...be engraved on stone on the sacred shrine![1]

These are the words of the very first inscriptions on the grandest of the Chola temples, the Rajarajeshwara or Brihadeeshwara Temple, the magnum opus of Rajaraja, in Thanjavur.

A long time ago, a wicked demon named Thanjan ruled an area of land in the Kaveri delta. Arrogant and ruthless, he struck terror in the hearts of the people there, who appealed to Lord Vishnu for help. Vishnu saw that matters had gotten out of hand and he made his way to Thanjai's realm as Neelamegha Perumal, accompanied by the goddess Parvati as Anandavalli Amman. The struggle that followed was short and swift and Thanjan stood no chance against the combined forces of the gods. As his life ebbed away, Thanjan expressed a dying wish. He wanted to be remembered forever. Name my land after me, he beseeched, and Vishnu, an honourable god, kept his word.

And that is how Thanjavur got its name.[2]

There is another, far more prosaic suggestion, that Thanjavur could have derived its name from the word thanjam, which means refuge.[3]

Thanjavur, the ancient capital of the Cholas, lies in the heart of the Kaveri delta, south of the Kollidam river. The Coromandel coast and the Bay of Bengal frame its eastern boundary; the city of Tiruchirapalli is to its west. In the ninth century, it was a small place from where a clan of chieftains called the Muttaraiyars ruled. And one day, sometime in the mid-ninth century, it made a grand entry to the pages of history when an ambitious young man named Vijayalaya took on the Muttaraiyars and defeated them. His clan or group, such as it was, had been operating out of Uraiyur, some 60 kilometres to the west, and after his victory, he made the decision to establish himself in Thanjavur instead. The Thiruvalangadu plates describe it as being 'picturesque to the sight, as beautiful as Alaka (the abode of the god Kubera), reaching the sky (with its high turrets), the whitewash of whose mansions appeared like the scented cosmetic (applied to the body)'.[4] Here he built a temple to the goddess Nisumbhasudani, a fierce, bloodthirsty goddess who was also compassionate and caring, who single-handedly vanquished two fierce demons. The ideal goddess to protect and bless a fledgling empire in the making. This temple is long gone, although worship of the goddess in her different forms, especially as Kali, continues to be popular there.

It appears that it was a fortified city then, and it continued to be so, as its rulers had to constantly to fend off invaders. Rajaraja's religious guru, Karuvur Devar, composed a poem celebrating the Brihadeeshwara (then called Rajarajeshwara) Temple, in which he made mention of a fort wall and a moat. There is evidence of the moat to this day, surrounding the temple, and walls surround the entire complex.[5]

Rajaraja, with his multiple queens, had several palaces scattered throughout the city. Not a trace of a single one of these palaces remains today, unsurprising considering they were probably built of brick. The palaces were expansive; in addition to the numerous residence buildings, there were halls for eating and bathing. Large numbers of people lived within the palace complex. There were the many wives, their children, and other kin, as well. High-level officials, bodyguards, and some military personnel were also housed within the complex. Then there were the special intimates (anukki) and concubines (poki) and friends (sakhiva), who enjoyed a good deal of prestige and high status. The palace compound must have been a busy, teeming place, full of life and laughter but also plenty of drama and intrigue.

Many of these people travelled as part of the king's retinue or entourage as he toured his kingdom, or shifted to another palace complex.

Near the palaces lived large numbers of palace servants in quarters that were called velams. Many of the velams were named after the ruler or the queen they served. The palace workers were never referred to by name; the women went by the generic pendatti, and the men, panimakan. Many of them were recruited from those captured in battles.

Inscriptions also mention an 'inner' (ullalai) city and an 'outer' (purambadi) city although it is not entirely clear what these might have been. Thanjavur exploded in size and population during Rajaraja's rule, and the purambadi area might have been the newly developed quarters. We know that Rajaraja ordered the granting of the village of Anaimangalam (the subject of his famous Leiden grant) while seated in a hall to the south of his palace called Rajasraya in the purambadi of Thanjavur.[6]

Thanjavur had grown into a city with many big streets, neighbourhoods, shops, and bazaars even before Rajaraja's time. There was the Virasola Street and the Tribhuvana Mahadeviyar bazaar that were well known. The names evoke society as it was then; we learn of a whole host of names of Rajaraja's Thanjavur from the inscriptions on the walls of the Brihadeeshwara Temple.

There is an Anai Atkal Teru (street of the elephant troops), a Gandharva Teru (musician's street), Villigal Teru (street of the archers), and Anaikkaduvar Teru (street of those who cook for the elephants). There are streets named for Chola royals: Jayangondasora Perrunteru (the grand street of Jayangondasora, one of Rajaraja's many names) and a Surasikhamani Perrunteru (another grand street named for a yet-undeciphered Chola).[7]

Just as fascinating was an entire network of over a hundred underground passages that connected the temple to the various palaces and other locations that the king and his retinue frequented. The passages provided shelter from the elements as well as from potential enemies and also afforded them a measure of privacy and a respite from crowds and traffic.

The biggest construction project in Thanjavur was most certainly the Brihadeeshwara Temple. It covered a vast area, and new streets and residences sprang up in its vicinity. The temple inscriptions inform us about the northern and southern Taliccherri streets, home to the 400 temple women Rajaraja brought and settled into Thanjavur from around his kingdom.

And, of course, there were other temples as well. Vijayalaya's Nishumbhasudani Temple must surely have been in use, a reminder of the brave warrior who got the ball rolling on the great Chola empire. Other temples mentioned in inscriptions are the Tanjaimamani and Jayabhima temples. The latter has been mentioned in an inscription by Parantaka in the year 931, and both temples supplied several temple women and other personnel to the Brihadeeshwara Temple.

It was not enough for the citizens of Thanjavur to live, shop, and pray. There was a free dispensary, a vaidyabhoga, named Sundara Chola Vinnagar Atulasalai for Rajaraja's father Sundara Chola, and endowed by his sister Kundavai. The hospital was attached to a Vishnu temple.[8]

Thanjavur then, as now, was a bustling, vibrant city, but it is also a vastly different place from its heyday as the crown jewel in the Chola empire. The Brihadeeshwara Temple is the sole remaining monument from that era, but what a monument it is! It has weathered the passage of time with nary a trace of wear and tear, a fitting and eternal tribute to one of the great kings of history.

◆

Nineteen years into his reign, Rajaraja was in a position no emperor in his region had ever achieved. The years of fighting had yielded results that matched his ambition and fearless heroism. He had done it all in the name of his beloved Lord Siva. Now it was time to build a shrine to him on a scale that nobody, not even the great Siva, had ever seen. It would be a fitting tribute to the God of Gods from the King of Kings.

We do not know exactly when he commenced building the Brihadeeshwara Temple. It has been suggested that this project was initiated in his nineteenth regnal year, 1004.[9] That year, his military prowess proved, his empire robust, his achievements unequivocal, he gave thanks to his beloved Lord Nataraja at Chidambaram, showering the temple with generous gifts. He was rewarded with the title he would be forever known by, Rajaraja, King of Kings. His extraordinary successes had to be celebrated, and the Lord who had watched over him, protected him, and enabled his triumphs had to be acknowledged with the grandeur that matched the scale of Rajaraja's faith, ambition and achievements. The temple was dedicated to Siva, of course, but here, the royal devotee lent the Lord his self-anointed appellation and called it the Rajarajeshwara temple; Rajarajeshwara derives from Rajaraja-ishwara, or the Lord of Rajaraja.

A mere six years later, in the year 1010, the temple was completed with the ceremonial placement of the kudam or water-pot, upon the copper pinnacle.[10] Rajaraja had been king for twenty-five years. That a structure of a scale of such magnificence could be completed in so short a while speaks volumes about the remarkable mobilization of people and resources, and the extraordinary organizational skills of Rajaraja.

The size and scale of operations of this grandest temple of its time were completely unprecedented. It was the tallest building in India at the time, and nothing anywhere in the country remotely approached it in size and complexity. At the time, none of the great cathedrals of Europe had been built. Construction of the cathedral at Pisa began fifty years later and took the better part of three centuries to get completed.

Any visitor to the temple today is struck by the expansiveness of the complex, the sense of immenseness and openness. It stands on the highest point in Thanjavur, which adds to its prominence. Imagine what it must have looked like in the tenth century, when out of the flat countryside, with its rice paddies and modest dwellings and temples, there appeared this colossus soaring to the heavens, evoking the mighty Himalayan abode of Siva! Clearly, the temple was the confident proclamation of a triumphant king at the peak of his power that his Lord Siva was grand and glorious and that he, the king who enjoyed the blessings of the great Lord, was every bit as grand and glorious.

Until Rajaraja, most royal Chola stone temples were either pallipadais: sepulchral, built to commemorate a dead king or ancestor; or those built at sites made sacred by their mention in the hymns of the great Saivite saints, the Nayanmars. In building his Brihadeeshwara Temple at his capital city, Thanjavur, he picked a place that was not part of the holy Saivite world of the Nayanmars, nor one in which resided the memory of a dead ancestor. It came uncluttered with any association, religious or familial, and was a gloriously blank slate upon which Rajaraja poured ambition, money, and an artistic vision grander than anything the country had ever seen.

Rajaraja, a devout Saivite, was guided by the instructions in the Agamas. These were ancient religious texts that covered a range of themes including philosophy, cosmology, and epistemology as well as the design, construction, and functioning of temples.[11] The section devoted to temple building is rather like an instruction manual that brings together architecture, astrology, and theology. Different categories of temples are described. Rajaraja's design of the Brihadeeshwara Temple is of the kind extolled in the Agamas as a great temple of the most excellent type befitting a great king. It is of the 'Meru' design, named after the golden Mount Meru, the fulcrum of the universe, which, according to the Agamas is the pinnacle of temple types.[12] Rajaraja referred to his temple as Dakshina Meru, the Meru of the south, a fitting local abode for the mighty mountain, temple, and its lord. One of the most important deities of the temple is Dakshina Meru Vitankan—Siva as Thyagaraja from Thiruvarur—and Rajaraja even named the standard weights used in the temple after him as Dakshina Meru Vitankan. Other measures were named Adavallan and Rajakesari, after the lord Nataraja, and Rajaraja himself. His religious gurus, Karuvur Devar and Isana Siva Pandita, steeped in these scriptures, played a big role in helping Rajaraja conceptualize, plan, and steer this colossus of a venture. Karuvur Devar composed a set of hymns in praise of Lord Rajarajeshwara and his temple, and they are a rich source of information about the place in its earliest years. There is a small shrine to him, built not so long ago, on the grounds of the complex. Devotees flock to this shrine, believing in his miraculous powers.

The temple is built of granite, a material not found in its immediate vicinity. Local legend holds that the stone was transported by bullock cart from a pair of hills 45 kilometres to the northeast of Thanjavur. Others have suggested that the stone might have been quarried from a place upriver and placed on coracles that ferried them to Thanjavur. Perhaps it was transported by elephants. A temple of this magnitude would have required a colossal quantity of granite, and it is estimated that around 130,000 tonnes of it were utilized. The granite was cut into large blocks which were perfectly hammer dressed to sit one atop another. No cement, stucco, or any form of binding was used. The weight of the stones pressing downwards kept the entire gigantic structure stable. Dowels, sockets, and iron beams were used where necessary for reinforcement. There has been much speculation about how the heavy blocks were lifted to the upper levels of the temple. One theory that appears to have gained traction is that of an inclined earthen ramp that originated in a town around 6 kilometres northwest of Thanjavur, called Sarapallam. Could there have been a scaffold to help hoist the stones up? Perhaps, but there has been no mention of it, and naturally, not a trace of it would have survived.

It was easily the richest temple of the time. Rajaraja showered gifts of huge amounts of land, money, precious gems, and jewels on the temple, and his family, royal retinue, civil, and military officers were also major patrons. Sixty-six metal idols made of gold, silver, and bronze were donated, almost all lost to us today, alas. Four of these were bronze portraits of Chola royalty. Rajaraja's sister, Kundavai, gifted images of her parents, Sundara Chola and Vanavanmadevi, and the temple's manager, Adittan Suryan, commissioned bronze images of Rajaraja and his queen Lokamahadevi. As far as we know, only two of them remain today. One is Siva as Nataraja, in worship at the temple and the other, Siva as Tripurantaka, now in the Tanjore Art Gallery. Booty won from years of successful wars were poured into its coffers, including over 500 pounds of gold and silver each. More money, land, and other riches made their way to the temple from members of the royal family and officers who served the royals.

The brilliant mind of Rajaraja and his far-sighted vision established the temple as not just a place for worship, but as the nerve centre that connected it to the economy of his kingdom. The annual income earned by the fertile lands across his kingdom, even from Sri Lanka, enriched the temple further. The temple sat on a huge amount of cash, which was loaned out at fixed amounts of interest, usually 12.5 per cent. The temple became the centre of a dynamic chain of religio-socio-economic activity that strengthened the royal connections with diverse sectors in the kingdom. Inscriptions provide dozens of examples.

For instance, money endowed to the temple was then loaned to a bazaar which would use the money to buy seeds and flowers that would be used in the bath water for the temple's deities. A very neat and mutually beneficial way of keeping the circle of supply and demand alive. By being directly invested in and involved with the well-being of the temple, his subjects felt a deep connection with it. It was a masterstroke that ensured that the temple thrived, the people thrived, and a sense of national integration was achieved.

The temple was clearly a treasure trove with its rich cache of gold, silver, cash, gemstones, and jewellery, all of which was watched over by a multitude of guards, who were, on Rajaraja's orders, supplied by the brahmadeyas, or Brahmin villages of Cholamandalam. Walls enclosed the entire complex, and a moat ran along the front. The royal palace, made of brick and long vanished, was also situated within the temple grounds, another good reason for the fortifications.

The actual temple and its attendant shrines were an obvious display of Rajaraja's might. But he wanted to further proclaim his largesse and power. Perhaps he had a keen sense of history, of a world beyond that would one day see his temple and wonder: who built this marvel? How did it function? What did its gods look like and wear and how were they prayed to and celebrated? Where did all its stupendous wealth come from? And from whom? All this and so much more was recorded in exhaustive detail in inscriptions all over the temple walls.

The very first inscription, running to 107 verses on the walls of the central shrine, was made in Rajaraja's twenty-sixth regnal year in which he decreed that all donations to the temple made by him, his elder sister, Kundavai, his wives, and other donors, be inscribed on the walls of the temple. He issued this order while ensconced in the royal bathing hall on the eastern side of his palace.[13] Rajaraja gifted a dizzying array of riches, including trumpets and flowers made of gold, water-pots, betel pots, chains, plates, fly-whisk handles, and parasol tops, all of gold. A special double-piped bugle was commissioned by Rajaraja to be played before the deity when taken out in procession. The pipes were inscribed with the names Rajaraja and Sivapadasekara![14] The gesture indicated that Rajaraja and Sivapadasekara (names by which the emperor was known) would go ahead of the Lord as his servants and announce his arrival to the public. He made it known, loud and clear, that the temple was built by him and named Rajarajeshwara. The remaining lines list every item that he gifted, down to the smallest details: the exact weight, measurements, what it looked like, what it was made of, where he got the funds for it (out of treasures seized from defeating the Pandya king, for instance). Temple appraisers had to assign an exact value to every gift, whether it came from war booty or was a fresh creation of a jeweller. Inscriptions inform us, for instance, of the number of pearls in a piece of jewellery, and how many of them were stained, cracked, or worn, all of which went into the final appraisal of its value. They also inform us about the dozen classifications of pearls that existed during Chola times. These included round pearls, roundish pearls, polished pearls, crude pearls, twin pearls, red water pearls, and brilliant water pearls.[15]

Rajaraja meticulously documented every aspect of the workings of his temple. Inscriptions fill the stone walls around the entire structure. They cover the minutiae and specifications of deities, idols, donations, employees, spelling out anything and everything that needed to be known and done to make sure that everything ran smoothly and at the high standards he demanded. To ensure that everything ran like clockwork, he appointed some of his most senior and trusted administrators to manage this gargantuan enterprise.

Only the best and the brightest would do for his temple. Rajaraja gathered people from temples around his realm and brought them to Thanjavur to serve the new deity. Inscriptions on a wall on the northern side of the temple catalogue a long list of men and women who were employed by the temple.

Their number and range are staggering.

In a temple with as rich a ritual life as Brihadeeshwara, dance and music played a vital role. The inscriptions name 400 women who were brought in from other temples from around the realm. The list is fascinating for many reasons, providing us with all manner of information.[16]

How were these women recruited? What did they do? Was there an audition? Were they recommended? Surely there were some favoured ones whose connections won them this prize assignment. What would one give to know! Many of the dancers held the coveted title of talaikkoli, an honorific which in the epic *Shilappadikaram* was awarded to the best dancer in a temple. It has been widely assumed that the women were all primarily dancers, but research undertaken by Canadian historian Leslie Orr on Chola temple women casts doubt on that premise. We will examine the lives of the temple women in greater detail in a later chapter.

The names run on for over 500 paragraphs without a whisper of these details, but they do give us an idea of the names of women. The custom of naming a child after the celebrities of the time was in vogue even then; there are girls called Rajaraji, Rajakesari and Arulmozhi, all clearly named after their beloved ruler; others, like Kundavai and Arinji were probably named after Rajaraja's sister and grandfather (Arinjaya). Names that seem to have been popular then, judging from their appearance multiple times, include Accham, Madevi, Pon, Sundari, and Thiru. These would most likely have been honorifics, or epithets, rather than their actual names. Women from the same village with the same name have descriptors like dark and fair, or elder and younger, to distinguish them from each other. The women's names are preceded with the village or temple they came from, another detail that gives us an idea of the temples already in existence then. Unsurprisingly, the majority are Saivite shrines, but there are a handful of Vishnu temples in the mix. Rajaraja certainly paid meticulous attention to detail!

These women were all allotted homes on three newly built streets directly abutting the temple. This area was called Taliccheri, and the ladies were likely called Taliccheri Pendugal, which means, literally, the women who reside in the streets near the temple. Some of these women might have been assigned to the large granary on the temple premises, doing the back-breaking chore of husking paddy.

The dancers needed teachers, conductors, and musicians, and further on, the wall lists around 200 non-priest employees of the temple. They cover a wide and telling range of duties: dance masters, musicians, drummers, singers, accountants, parasol bearers, lamp lighters, watermen, potters, washermen, barbers, astrologers, tailors, a brazier, carpenters, a goldsmith, and a few more. Here too, there is a whole slew of Rajarajas, Arulmozhis, and Mummudicholas, all very liked named for their royal patron. Just glancing at this list gives you an idea of the scale of operation of the temple, all the functions and people it took for its smooth operation.

The positions were held on a hereditary basis, but fitness for the position was also a prerequisite. All the women received one share of the paddy that was produced in a certain area of land. Then men's allotment ranged from half a share to two shares a piece. Men of the same profession received differing amounts, and the assumption is that this was based on their seniority. There is an accountant who receives a mere half a share; another one receives two, and each of his assistants get three-fourths of a share. Dance masters get two shares each, while musicians receive between three-fourth and one share each. A jewel-stitcher earns one and a half shares while a tailor earns one. While there is variation in how many shares are earned, the range is small.

Rajaraja ensured that his temple employees were well cared for. In addition to the paddy and housing, they were given grants of land. Many people who were recruited to work at the temple were brought from other towns and villages, and he ensured their smooth transition into their lives in the new city. Free food was provided for everyone, regardless of caste. He must have been keenly aware of the benefits of rewarding his people by merit and seniority, not merely caste. A Brahmin accountant received the same two shares as the superintendent of temple women.

The creation of the Brihadeeshwara Temple was a major event and a play, *Rajarajeshwara Nataka*, was produced, to recount the details of its genesis. An inscription by Rajaraja's grandson tells us that special arrangements were made for its performance during a grand festival. The actors in the play were awarded a daily allowance of paddy for their efforts. Alas, the manuscript, which would have been an invaluable, if somewhat embellished, source of information about how the temple came to be, is lost to us.[17]

The temple complex is spread out over a rectangular area of over 40 acres. It is enclosed by a moat wall that likely served as fortification. The entrance is through first one gopuram, called the Keralantakan Tiru Vasal, and then a second, smaller one, named Rajaraja Tiru Vasal for its founder. Two enormous dwarapalakas or door guardians dominate the lower part of this gopuram. The gopurams, particularly the Rajaraja Tiru Vasal are beautifully carved, but modest in size, giving no hint of the soaring temple and vast grounds beyond.

Past the gopurams is a huge courtyard, probably where the people congregated in Chola times, as they do today as well. If the courtyard were divided into halves, there would be two perfect squares. In the exact centre of the square to the front is an open hall or mandapam that is a shrine to Siva's bull Nandi. This was built several centuries later by the Nayak rulers. An essential feature of all Siva temples, there must have certainly been a Nandi installed there in Rajaraja's time, perhaps replaced and enhanced by the Nayaks.

Straight ahead across the Nandi mandapam on a huge raised platform in the rear square, a magnificent vision graces the landscape. This is the crown jewel of Rajaraja, of Thanjavur, indeed of any temple anywhere: the Brihadeeshwara Temple. It is of a lovely ruddy hue, punctuated with a teeming mass of stunning sculptures, its vimana rising into the sky, embellished with more gorgeous carvings. The main shrine to Lord Siva lies in the centre of this square.

The entrance to the temple from the courtyard is up two sets of steps, through a vestibule that leads into a pillared hall that houses images of Rajaraja and Siva as Thyagaraja. The steps bring the height of the temple's base up at least 15 feet, making it stand out even further. Fiercely fanged muscular dwarapalakas guard the entrance. Beyond the hall is a vestibule, the ardhamandapa, and right after, the sanctum sanctorum, the garbhagriha. Here in the heart and soul of this temple, Siva is worshipped in the form of a giant lingam, the central and primary deity, Rajarajeshwaramudayar, named for its creator and benefactor. The lingam, carved from a single piece of granite, is over 12 feet tall and 5 feet wide. The two other main deities of the temple in the form of portable metal images are Siva as the Dancing Lord Nataraja or Adavallan, and Siva as Thyagaraja, named here Dakshina Meru Vitankar.

A passage runs around the central shrine. All around are a series of remarkable paintings. The story of their discovery, over 900 years after they were created, is just as remarkable. In 1930 Mr Govindaswamy, a lecturer in history at Annamalai University, walked around the dark seven-foot-wide passageway that bordered the sanctum sanctorum seeking to examine the paintings he knew adorned the walls. All he succeeded in seeing in the 'dim religious light of a small oil lamp' were a few patches of painting. The fledgling field of the study of the ancient Indian tradition of painting had been stirring to life, which might have piqued Govindaswamy's interest.

The following year, he returned, this time better equipped with a baby petromax lamp. What he saw, however, was a sad disappointment. In his words there were 'paintings of an undoubtedly very late and degenerate age, whose linear contortions and chromatic extravagances shattered in a moment all my wonderful dreams of discovering there the best and the only example of the art of Chola mural painting'. These were from the age of the Nayaks, in the seventeenth century. A few moments later, dejection turned to exhilaration. Govindaswamy noticed that some of the painted plaster on the wall had cracked and peeled off. And beneath the layer of peeling paint another set of paintings revealed themselves, 'palpitating with the life of other days'. He realized then that they were the original Chola paintings that had been painted over by the overzealous Nayaks who probably saw no value in the fading murals of yore.

The following day, an excited Govindaswamy wrote an account of his discovery, which was published in *The Hindu*.[18] The world woke up to the knowledge of just how many more treasures lay concealed within the walls of the temple, and a whole new area of scholarship was born. Alas, Govindaswamy died a few years later at the very young age of thirty-eight, a life of genuine scholarship and discovery cut cruelly short.

Recognizing that special care needed to be taken to preserve and restore the paintings and other treasures of the temple, the Archaeological Survey of India stepped in. It has done a marvellous job, striking the delicate balance of safeguarding both the Chola and Nayak era paintings and ensuring that the work of restoration is done with the utmost caution.

Given Rajaraja's devotion to Lord Siva, it is unsurprising that he is the main motif for the majority of the Chola era paintings. There are paintings of Siva as Dakshinamurthi, and a magnificent one as Tripurantaka, his multiple arms bristling with weapons, ready to take on the evil asuras. There is the dancing Nataraja of Chidambaram, gazed upon with devotion by Rajaraja and his wives. The story of the Nayanmar poet-saint Sundarar is depicted in great detail. Most fascinating of all is a portrait—the only one extant—of a youthful Rajaraja. Full-lipped and lotus-eyed, he stands respectfully behind his revered teacher and mentor, Karuvur Devar. His hair is piled up high, resembling the locks of his beloved Lord Siva. The two stand in worshipful devotion in front of a painted icon of Siva. There is a subtlety and delicacy to the paintings that are full of life and expression, which lends them a special charm.

Around the garbhagriha above the paintings, are sculpture panels representing the 108 karanas or dance poses captured in a moment of action. Only eighty-one have been completed, which suggests a project abandoned, most likely because Rajaraja passed away before it was done. These karanas were lost to time until 1956, when Balakrishnan, an employee of the Archaeological Survey of India was working on the arduous task of pulling out the weeds that had crept up all around the vimana. While working outside the first tier, he discovered a passage that led to the inside. He reported this to his superiors at the Archaeological Survey, and K. R. Srinivasan, the Superintending Archaeologist, attempted to get the passage open. It was found to be choked with what must have been several centuries' worth of bat excreta, solidified to a concrete-like hardness. It took some hard shovelling to remove it, and many workers, walloped by the stench and the backbreaking labour, fell ill.

Eventually, a month of shovelling later, the passage was cleared, and it was then that the beautiful sculptures came to light. It took an expert, the Joint Director General of the Archaeological Survey T. N. Ramachandran, to identify the sculptures as karanas, described in the seminal work on Indian classical dance, the *Natya Sastra*.[19]

Outside, the walls are carved with large figures of Siva. An entire level has been dedicated to depicting him as Tripurantaka, the Victor of Three Forts, while the level below shows his well-known forms of Dancing Nataraja, the Half-Man Half-Woman Ardhanarishwara, Bhikshasanan, Dakshinamurthy, and others.

The crowning glory of the temple is the hollow thirteen-tiered vimana, the tower that tops the sanctum sanctorum. It is unusual among the temples of south India in that it dwarfs the gopurams by a large margin. It climbs upwards to a height of

216 feet, sloping gracefully inwards in the shape of a pyramid. Nearly 200 feet up is an octagonal capstone that sits atop the vimana. Remarkably, its size—24 square feet in area—echoes that exactly of the sanctum sanctorum that lies 183 feet directly below it.[20] It was long believed that the capstone was a single 80-ton slab of granite, but recent restorations have shown otherwise, that it is made up of eight smaller slabs over which a thick layer of brick and stucco were later laid. There has been much speculation about how these made it to the top. Locals like to say that the blocks of granite that made up the capstone levitated their way up, powered by the chants of priests! The more prosaic and realistic answer probably lay in a set-up which used a ramp, rollers, and ropes. Four pairs of Nandis adorn the top of the capstone, facing the four cardinal directions, a lovely touch that shows Rajaraja's attention to detail, even in a spot not easily visible.

The grounds are dotted with many small shrines to a variety of deities. Of these, only the shrine to Chandesa is a contemporary of the original. Chandesa, one of the sixty-three Nayanmar poet-saints, was a cowherd who worshipped Siva while tending to his cows. Every day he built a small lingam from mud, and used the milk of his cows to bathe it. One day, his father, furious at this waste of milk, and at his son's absorption in his worship at the cost of turning a deaf ear to his admonishments, kicked the lingam. Chandesa, unaware that it was his father who had done so, flung his axe at him. In mid-air, the little axe morphed into the mighty axe of Siva, and instantly killed Chandesa's father. At that moment, Siva appeared, blessed his devotee and promised to care for him and protect him as a father would.[21]

Rajaraja was so drawn by this tale that he built a separate shrine for Chandesa and commissioned a set of bronze icons to honour him and his life; sadly, these are missing. The Cholas empowered Chandesa with a new role: that of divine financial agent and guardian. The financial dealings of the temple were all transacted in the name of Chandesa and recorded in hundreds of inscriptions. To this day, it is Chandesa who guards the temples of his beloved Lord Siva, and their possessions. Even today, worshippers clap their hands in front of Chandesa's shrine to show him that they have not taken any temple property and that their hands are empty. Quite a career trajectory for a humble cowherd!

Walls and cloistered corridors enclose the temple grounds. The temple's many bronze images, vessels, and lamps might have been housed here. Parts of them were built by one of Rajaraja's most trusted and senior generals and his chief secretary or olai nayakan, Krishna Raman. He was a signatory on several of Rajaraja's grants, and he was clearly trusted and valued enough that Rajaraja's son, Rajendra, retained him when he became king. Krishna Raman's official name, Mummidisola Brahmamarayan became Rajendrasola Brahmamarayan, revealing his move from one master (Mummidisola or Rajaraja), to the next (Rajendrasola).[22]

Ensuring the smooth running of an enterprise as gargantuan as the Brihadeeshwara Temple would have required an administrative setup that was efficient and free from corruption. Mundane functional matters like revenue administration and personnel management had to coexist with the spiritual and ritual requirements of the temple. The obligations to the spiritual preceptors and rajagurus would have to be respected, along with the pragmatic concerns of the financial trustees. Here, too, Rajaraja showed his genius in successfully juggling these multiple factors, and no doubt, multiple personalities and strong egos to ensure that above all, his temple dazzled like no other.

In managing the temple, Rajaraja appears to have operated on the principle of separating the secular from the spiritual. The person who took charge of the administration of the temple was Adittan Suryan, also known as Tennavan Muvendavelan, who was the headman of Poygainadu. The muvendavelan title was given to certain elite landowners in Chola country; literally, it meant the velan (a member of the landowning Vellala caste) of the three kings (probably the three traditional Tamil kings, Chola, Pandya and Chera (or Pallava)). Appended to the muvendavelan title was the name of the nadu that he owned, and/or the name of the king he served. It is thought that this title was conferred on them (likely beginning from the reign of Parantaka I) to win the confidence and loyalty of the landowning groups of the territory. Adittan Suryan held the title of srikaryam (which literally means sacred duty), the only one for the Brihadeeshwara Temple, and he held this position under both Rajaraja and Rajendra. He must have had his work cut out for him, with 800 people employed by the temple. Adittan Suryan donated generously to the temple, and his name endures on one of the walls of the temple he served so faithfully.[23]

Suryan had an entire establishment including a head supervisor or kankani nayagam, executive officers, taanattars or trustees, accountants, treasurers, officers in charge of paddy supply, inscription engravers, superintendent of temple women, and watchmen to keep the temple operating smoothly.

Taking care of the spiritual affairs of the temple was an elaborate hierarchy of priests and other religious functionaries.

At the top, in the role of chief priest or saivacharya was one of Rajaraja's closest spiritual advisors, Guru Isana Siva Pandita, who ensured that the rituals were conducted according to Agamic prescriptions. Isana Siva Pandita was a person of not just great spiritual eminence. As the chief priest, he had a considerable volume of endowments under his control, and he had administrative duties as well; all royal orders were issued to the srikaryam, the executive officers, as well as the chief priest. He must have been a wealthy man, donating money for a lamp to an image of himself that was installed in the temple.

The actual rituals or pujas were performed by a group of priests called the Panchacharyas. Brahmacharins, or bachelor priests-in-training, recited the Vedic mantras and assisted with the preparations for the pujas. They were never allowed to perform the actual pujas, having to be satisfied with tasks like carrying the holy water for bathing the deity, lighting the lamps, and getting ready the myriad items needed for the rites. A temple like the Brihadeeshwara would have had a large number of pujas, performed daily in addition to the special ones for the big festivals throughout the year. A considerable number of Brahmacharins would have been required and pressed into service. An astronomer, called Perunkani was appointed by Rajaraja. It was his job to pick and announce the auspicious times and days for all the temple's festivals, based on the movements of the stars and planets.[24]

Karuvur Devar, who was also Rajaraja's most trusted religious teacher, who probably had an intimate, day-to-day relationship with him, is said to have been the person who advised Rajaraja to build the temple, and who continued to guide him through his life. He was a Siva Yogin, a holy man who had mastered the practice of yoga as specified in the Agamas. He helped in fixing the giant lingam in the sanctum sanctorum and composed poems in praise of the temple's Lord Rajarajeshwara, which form part of the *Thiruvisaippa*, the ninth volume of the Saivite canon *Thirumurai*. The mural of him and Rajaraja on the inner wall of the passageway around the sanctum shows two men who are clearly very dear to each other. There were 240 Siva Yogins in the temple, and tradition dictated that they be fed in the temple hall on twenty-four festival days. A quantity of paddy was earmarked for their feeding.

It is unclear what became of the Brihadeeshwara Temple once the reign of Rajaraja came to an end. His son Rajendra, who succeeded him, made his own grand statement with his temple at Gangaikondacholapuram, the capital city he created. Thanjavur, which had shone bright and glorious, slipped a bit into the shadows. The winds of history swept through, and the fourteenth and fifteenth centuries were ones when the city sank into further obscurity. The Brihadeeshwara Temple, once such a proud beacon of an empire at its zenith, became an incongruous onlooker over a withering city. With the emergence of the Thanjavur Nayaks, an offshoot of the great Vijayanagar empire, the city rose to prominence again as the capital of this dynasty, and then, that of the Marathas who followed in the seventeenth century. The Nayaks and Marathas both used the temple, adding shrines, paintings, and inscriptions to the complex.

A Manual of the District of Tanjore in the Madras Presidency, published in Madras in 1883, says about the Brihadeeshwara Temple: 'The Hindu temples which dot the whole delta of the Cauvery are in fact almost the only monuments of antiquity in this district. The most celebrated is the great temple of Brihadisvarasvami at Tanjore, which, it is believed, was built by the famous Kulottunga or Viracola in the eleventh century AD.'[25]

So, it was not known then, in 1883, that it was Rajaraja who built the temple!

Many temples have a sthala purana, a mythical history of how they came to be. In the seventeenth century, during what must have been the Nayak era, there appeared one for the Brihadeeshwara Temple, called *Brihadisvara Mahatmya.* It tells a story about how the temple arose, seamlessly fusing fantasy and fact. In it, a great Chola emperor of the past, Karikala, was in misery as he was afflicted with leprosy. He appealed to his guru, Haradatta, a great devotee of Siva, for help. Haradatta fell asleep one day at a Siva shrine, and had a dream in which he was told that his king's leprosy was a punishment for sins he had committed in a previous life. In order to atone and be rid of his suffering, he would have to build a grand temple to Siva, with a tall vimana, and a magical lingam from the Narmada that would grow in size and earn the name Brihadeeshwara. A few other tasks were issued, and once they were all completed, the king would be cured. The king set out to do what Haradatta's dream dictated, and a great many chapters are given over to details on how it was done, and several twists and turns later, the great temple was completed, and the king restored to good health.[26]

Knowing what we now do about how the temple came

about, it is not surprising the historian Nilakanta Sastri had scathing words for the tale. 'The long narration of Karikala's leprosy, the exertions of Haradatta, and the construction of the Brihadishwara temple which apparently forms the central theme of the puranas and gives it one of the two names by which it is known—this legend is not only unsupported by any other account known to us but is given the lie direct by the very inscriptions on the walls of the temple which are cited in his support by the ignorant verifier who indited the *Mahatmya*'.[27]

For such a tale to be written around 600 years after the temple was built must have meant that knowledge about the great emperor who built this magnificent monument had faded from memory. A few stray bits might have lingered, a haze of recollections and rumours of a glorious empire from times past imagined into something else altogether. The inscriptions on the walls were in the Tamil of an earlier era and were probably not understood by the people then.

It wasn't until the nineteenth century, when great epigraphists like Hultzsch and Venkayya began the formidable job of deciphering the inscriptions that the full story of Rajaraja and his temple came to life once again. And that is how we have the immense fortune to know that a king from long, long ago wrote:

> On the twentieth day of the twenty-sixth year of the reign of Ko-Rajakesarivarman, alias Sri-Rajarajadeva, who... vouchsafed to say: 'Let the gifts made by us, those made by our elder sister, those made by our wives, and those made by other donors to the Lord of the sacred stone-temple called Sri Rajarajesvara, which we caused to be built at Tanjavur...be engraved on stone on the sacred shrine!'[28]

CHAPTER 17

RESPLENDENT IN CEREMONIAL DRESS
CHOLA BRONZES

The gods and goddesses of the Cholas lived a life of pomp and splendour, pageantry and celebration. Draped in the finest brightly coloured silks, decked up with exquisite jewellery of gold, rubies, and pearls, smothered in garlands of fragrant flowers, feted with joyous music and jubilant drums, they sat atop richly decorated vehicles, pedestals, and palanquins, giving an audience to their devotees, visiting the riverfront and the beach, calling in at another temple, or simply going around their own temple and its grounds. There were festivals that took place on a daily, weekly, monthly, and annual basis, observing the cycles of the moon, birthdays, weddings, and other occasions that made up the lively and busy lives of the gods.

These gods were portable deities made of bronze. They lived as immovable stone images within the temple and for their forays into the world outside they assumed another form altogether, of richly adorned metal, and became a crucial part of Tamil worship, unique to this region. They ranged in size from small images that could be carried by a single person, most often used for daily rituals and not more than 18 inches in height, to huge ones that were over 4 feet tall weighing over 300 pounds, requiring a small army of men to carry them. Every temple possessed an entire series of bronzes that served specific festival and ritual needs. The image of Siva that was used to celebrate his wedding was different from the one that inspected the temple, and so on.

The tradition of using portable metal images began during the Pallava dynasty a couple of centuries earlier. The Pallava bronzes were small ones, used not for processions, but rather for personal worship And the images used for processions were usually made of wood. The Cholas, and particularly Rajaraja, believed in a larger-than-life approach to anything, and under their patronage, the bronze images attained a standard of beauty that remains unsurpassed. It was not just the royals who commissioned these bronzes. Creating and donating an image to a temple was the ultimate form of reverence to an all-giving god, and people from across the kingdom expressed their devotion and gratitude by commissioning and gifting an image to their temple. Women were active donors, commissioning a wide range of icons and then donating the jewels and other ornaments to further embellish them. The hymns of the Nayanmars and Azhwar Bhakti poets were full of vivid descriptions of temple processions that spurred the creation of the most exquisite images that lived up to the beauty of the poems.

The early period of Chola rule was rather turbulent—there were frequent battles and many losses. And yet, it was in this time that the first of the lovely portable bronze images began appearing in the temples of Chola lands. A much beloved image was that of Siva as Tripurantaka, the Destroyer of Three Citadels, an embodiment of their beloved lord that had particular resonance for the Cholas, as they set out to defeat their three biggest foes (predominantly the Pandyas, Pallavas, and Rashtrakutas) and capture their territory.

It was a fortuitous convergence of many factors that resulted in this glorious efflorescence of Chola bronze art. The technology of metal casting had been worked out, agricultural prosperity was growing in the villages and towns of the Kaveri delta, and the religious fervour ignited by the Bhakti movement was on the rise. Siva was the object of intense religious devotion. Just in the immediate area around Thanjavur and the Kaveri delta, there were over 200 temples to Siva alone out of the roughly 300 temples there. The sheer number of temples built makes the Cholas the greatest temple builders of all of south India, and possibly all of India. The time and circumstances were ripe for the blossoming of bronze art.

The depth of fervour resulted in the creation of the most stunning bronze icons that were housed in these temples. A wide array of men and women from all walks of life made donations in cash and kind so that the activities in these temples could be conducted in utmost splendour. The temples, their priests, and the devotees together created an environment of deep devotion and veneration which spurred the sculptors to ever greater heights.

The Bhakti movement and the Pallavas emerged somewhat in tandem. As the ritual-based form of worship extolled in the Bhakti hymns became popular, so too did icons of the gods for worship at home and in temples. A new class of artisan, the sthapathi, emerged, some say from the third eye of Siva, expert at metal sculpting. It is likely that they were already experienced in wood and stone sculpting, techniques which had been around for a while. The sthapathi enjoyed respect and veneration beyond the ordinary craftsman. This was as a result of the complex nature of his work, his familiarity with the *Shilpa Shastras*, and most important of all, that the fruits of his labour were the ultimate, the unsurpassable, the divine—the gods and goddesses themselves!

The *Shilpa Shastras* are ancient texts that are rather like manuals for arts and crafts and are believed to be divinely sanctioned. Metal casting is covered in a chapter of a section called the 'Manasara Shilpa Shastra' and includes instructions and details on the protocols of form and design for religious icons. They are believed to have been written sometime between the fourth and sixth centuries, just when the Bhakti movement, with its ethos of a very intimate and personal form of devotion to god, was coming alive. To this day, these are the texts studied, followed, and revered by the bronze idol makers of the Kaveri delta.[1]

The men who made the bronze images had a remarkable task: they were creating gods. They were alchemists who transformed a handful of materials—resin, wax, clay, and an amalgam of copper, tin, and lead—with a blast of furnace fire and an abundance of devotion into gods and goddesses of stunning form and beauty that were worshipped and venerated throughout the land. Special rites endowed the portable icons with the same divinity and power as their immovable stone counterparts and enabled them to represent the gods and act on their behalf outside the inner sanctum.

The sthapathis were artists, above all. They were guided by the *Shilpa Shastras* and the requests of their patrons, but a large part of how they envisioned the god they were tasked to create came also from their own faith, their imagination, the inspiration they drew from the wondrous hymns of the Nayanmars and Azhwars.

There have been questions raised, and not entirely satisfactorily answered, about the source of the copper used in making the bronzes. There is no copper ore to be mined in the Kaveri delta region. Vidya Dehejia, one of the world's leading authorities on Chola bronzes, has calculated that bronze image production for temples in just the heartland of the Chola empire would have required around 200 tons of copper. As large processional bronzes became increasingly popular, the rate of copper usage soared. It was used for copperplate inscriptions as well. The biggest sources of copper in India are Rajasthan and Bihar, far away to the north. The *Periplus of the Erythraean Sea*, a Greek sailor's log from the first century, mentions the import of copper into India, and a sixth-century Sanskrit lexicon dubs it mlechha mukha, or foreign-faced, indicating a foreign origin. There are fascinating letters from the *Cairo Geniza*, (medieval documents that offer us a peek into the Middle Eastern and North African worlds of a thousand-year period from the ninth to the nineteenth centuries) in which a Jewish merchant from Aden writes about a shipment of copper to a bronze factory in Mangalore, which he requests to be made into a variety of bronze objects including a tray, a jug, and a candlestick, and shipped back to him. Another possibility suggested by Dehejia is the copper belt near Trincomalee in nearby Sri Lanka. She wonders if this might be one of the reasons for the Chola desire to capture and rule the island. There is evidence of extensive mining of copper in this belt during the first millennium.[2] Scientists have said that determining the source of copper is a devilishly difficult task, but Dehejia has commissioned an important and exciting non-invasive test, using samples from Chola bronzes, to see if their 'signature' matched that of the copper from Sri Lanka. The results of the test suggested that two out of the five pieces tested may have the high cobalt-nickel trace element that is particular to Sri Lankan copper. This means that the copper is likely to have come from more than one source, a fascinating possibility that raises more questions. In order to get more conclusive results, the lab insists that both Sri Lankan and the Chola copper be tested in the same lab, an almost impossible-to-achieve scenario, given the multiple logistical and bureaucratic issues involved.[3]

The bronze idols were made with the direct lost wax process. To this day, they are made in Thanjavur and the villages and towns surrounding it, using almost exactly the same method that has been employed for over a thousand years. Before getting the process underway, the gods had to be propitiated. The creation of divinity had to begin at an auspicious day and time, and astrological calendars were consulted and scrupulously adhered to. The sthapathis conducted pujas and called upon the blessings of a cow, a holy Tulsi plant, and the fire god, and then, on the wings of divine benediction, the process of making the image got underway. The first step involved making a model of the idol out of a special mixture of hard paraffin and soft bees waxes and resin from the local sal tree. For larger images, the different parts of the body were made separately, and then joined together with wax struts. The basic model was made with the harder wax, over which the softer wax was layered, enabling the sthapathi to add in the finer details like jewellery and delicate facial features, and even tweak the shape of the fingernails to perfection. No element was too small.

A baked clay mould was then applied over the wax model. The fine silt of the Kaveri River in and around Thanjavur is especially well suited for making the clay moulds. The qualities of this silt enabled the finest details imprinted on the wax model to be mirrored on to the clay mould, and the application of the first layer was entrusted only to the most skilled craftsman whose expert application of the clay ensured that the work of the wax modeller was perfectly captured. A series of escape channels or holes were made at the bottom of the mould. The clay-mould enshrouded image which revealed no hint of what lay inside was placed in the sun to dry, a process that took from a day to up to several weeks, depending on the mould's size.

Once it was completely dry, it was ready for the alchemy of heat, the incandescence of fire to work their magic. The steps that followed were fraught with risk and peril. Prayers were said, the image was anointed with pastes of vermillion and turmeric, and then it was offered to the fire. The heat melted the wax, which ran out through the channels and holes. The original wax model was lost forever, reduced to a puddle of melted wax, making every icon unique, the only one of its kind. This lent the entire process its name, the lost wax method.

There was now a hollow icon-shaped clay mould and into this was poured red hot molten metal, a mixture of 90 to 95 per cent copper, with equal quantities of tin and lead making up the remainder. This was a fiendishly difficult process that required the precise calibration of a multitude of factors—the temperature of the metal, its composition, the quality of the clay mould, the proper pouring of the hot metal. If any one of these things was not just so, the finished product would be a defective one, unworthy of divinity. The clay mould with its filling of metal was left to dry and set and once the sthapathi had deemed that the time was right, following all the while the mandates of the *Shilpa Shastras*, he smashed the clay mould to smithereens, exposing the metal image within.

The next step was to smooth out rough edges and fine-tune

the details, which were chiselled in by hand. In the hands of an expert sthapathi, minimal work was needed; most Chola-era bronzes from the best workshops emerged from their clay cocoon almost perfectly finished, requiring only minor tweaks. Any connecting rods and protruding bits of metal had to be filed away. The image was bathed in a solution of tamarind and water and buffed to a shine with sand.

The image at this point was a thing of beauty, but it was still merely a thing, an object. What invested it with the halo of sanctity was the Opening the Eyes ceremony, performed in strict accordance to ritual guidelines. Using a golden chisel, the sthapathi awakened the divine in the idol.[4]

This was the moment when man created God.

Every Chola bronze was made with this direct lost wax process, and each one was solid, unique, unreplicable. Each new piece had to be made from scratch. The bronzes of the ancient Greek and Roman worlds were, in contrast, cast hollow and the original model was retained, enabling multiple replicas to be made.

When the bronzes emerged from the mould, they were already richly embellished, with necklaces, earrings, anklets, armlets, waistbands, and amulets carved into their bodies. But these merely set the stage for additional adornment of a dazzling array of real jewellery. Devotees plied the gods with gorgeous and expensive ornaments made of gold, silver, and a variety of precious gems like pearls, rubies, and coral; nothing but the very best would be acceptable. Gifting the deity such treasures surely assured the devotee of the choicest divine blessings.

Some of the most stunning Chola bronzes were commissioned by the remarkable queen Sembiyan Madevi. She was the wife of Gandaraditya, the king with the mysteriously short reign, the mother of Uttama Chola who preceded Rajaraja, and the grand-aunt of Rajaraja. For over sixty years, through the reigns of five emperors, she was responsible for creating fine images of a maturity and sophistication that testified to bronze workshops and craftsmen of high training and ability. She was clearly a connoisseur of the arts and under her patronage both the building of stone temples as well as the making of the deities that were worshipped there flourished and raised the bar for the exquisiteness of Chola bronzes. She set in motion the flowering of an art form that would forever be linked to the Chola name and that revealed to the world that they were not merely after conquests and territory, but were also endowed with a keen sense of beauty.

Chola bronzes are remarkable for their sensuousness, in how they celebrate and flaunt the beauty of the body. Siva is taut, supple, toned, and his wife Uma is unabashedly curvaceous and full-breasted. The Cholas saw no dichotomy between the sacred and the sensuous; indeed, they viewed both as integral parts of the whole, the physical perfection of their bodies a manifestation of their divine inner beauty.

The majority of the bronze images were those of gods, primarily the different forms of Siva, along with his wife Uma. Figures of the sixty-three Nayanmar saints were also popular and were included in the rituals of worship and processions. In addition, images of Rajaraja, Sembiyan Madevi, and other members of the royal family were also commissioned, and were taken out in procession on their birthday. These statues represented the blurring of boundaries between the divine and the royal. So highly respected was Sembiyan Madevi that her image was worshipped alongside those of gods and goddesses.

Inscriptions on the Brihadeeshwara Temple walls tell us that a village headman named Adittan Suryan who served as a manager of the temple, donated a solid image of 'Periya Perumal', or Rajaraja, and his wife Lokamahadevi, along with armlets, earrings, and other jewellery made of gold.[5] These images vanished from the temple some sixty years ago and were believed to have been housed in a museum in Ahmedabad. After a police complaint was registered, the Idol Wing of the Tamil Nadu police launched an investigation and, eventually, the two bronzes were retrieved from the museum. Amid great fanfare and terrific excitement, Rajaraja and Lokamahadevi, immortalized in metal, were reinstalled in their original home, the Brihadeeshwara Temple.[6]

These were the bronze gods and goddesses who were the stars of a multitude of celebrations throughout the year. Festival days brought together the entire village or town. The priests, the deity bearers, the supervisors, the washerman, the food preparers, the tailors, the musicians, the dancers, the accountants, and so many more, were all instrumental in bringing the celebration to life. Every citizen participated with gusto, and the place had the air of an exuberant carnival, full of colour, sound, and light-hearted cheer.

On the day of the temple festival or utsavam an elaborate set of rituals prepared the gods for their foray into the world outside. The occasion could be the daily sribali ceremony, which in some temples took place as many as three times every day, in which the divine couple were paraded around the temple grounds, stopping to offer specially prepared food to the guardian deities dotting the compound. Often, the temple elephant did the honours of carrying the food. There might have been people bearing lamps and incense, and singers, but the key participants without whom there would be no festival, were the drummers, called uvaccar. The uvaccar were present at a variety of critical rituals that made up the festival and procession, from the sacred bath, the food offering, the early morning awakening of the gods and the late night putting them to bed.

The weekly processions, usually also within the temple grounds were often more elaborate, and could include several priests, dancing women, singers, a veena player, flag hoisters, garland bearers and, of course, drummers.

Monthly festivals happened when each month commenced, on new moon days, or the star birthday of a royal or an important donor. Annual festivals were huge affairs; one of the most important ones in Chola country, and particularly at the

Chidambaram Temple was the one that celebrated the holy day of Thaipusam, held during the month of thai (January–February).[7] This was the day that the ascetic Patanjali witnessed the universe-churning cosmic dance of Siva, and the festival was a mega affair, worthy of the grand event it commemorated. Like processional temple festivals all over Tamil Nadu, this is celebrated to this day in Chidambaram. It is a cacophonous, crowded, chaotic madhouse of a scene, the air thick with the passion and fervour of the devotees, and is testament to the amazing power of faith to bring together a diverse and teeming mass of humanity.

As expected, among the grandest of the annual festivals was the one at the Brihadeeshwara Temple, which was called the Periya Thiru Utsavam or the Big Holy Festival. This was a nine-day affair that began with a flag hoisting. Bronze icons were taken out in procession; for three consecutive days, the image of Nataraja was taken out, with five drummers announcing, on the first day, 'For three days from today, Lord Nataraja will come out in procession'. The image of Siva as Thyagaraja—Vitankar—was also paraded. A grand and specially decorated pandal or open-sided shelter was made for carrying the deity, so that he might be shielded from the harsh sun and other elements. Rajaraja's sister Kundavai covered the expenses for this. This temple celebrated a total of thirty-four festivals every year each with special rituals, processions, and food offerings.[8] The life of the temple, the pomp and splendour with which it celebrated its gods, lived up to its grand stature and that of the great king who created it.

Festivals didn't just celebrate the gods. Every month, in temples across his realm, Rajaraja's birthday was celebrated on the day of his star, Sadayam. The Hindu calendar, which follows the lunar cycle, has twenty-seven stars in every month, and each star is allotted a particular day in a month. Since the lunar month is twenty-nine days long, a couple of stars occur twice in each month. One of Rajaraja's queens, Panchavan Madevi, shared the same star as her husband, and an inscription at the Agnisvara Temple in Puhalur lists her endowments for joint celebrations on

Sadayam day every month for her and Rajaraja. The inscription also gives details about how the festival was to be celebrated. A bronze icon of a deity called Tiruvila Elundaralum Tirumenu was specially worshipped and taken out in procession. The deity was bathed in ghee while Brahmins performed purifying rituals. A beautiful golden aureole was fastened around him. Special rice dishes were prepared, with curd and coconut. Garlands were strung to adorn the deity, and perpetually burning oil lamps were kept lit to drive away darkness. At night, another ritual took place that invoked the deity to live in the metal icon and invested it with divinity. The terms used in the inscription were those used in Agamic rites, establishing its prevalence during the rule of Rajaraja.[9]

It was an elaborate and spiritually rewarding ceremony, befitting a great king and his wife.

We have seen that people from across a broad swathe of society donated to temples, from lavish gifts of gold, jewellery, and actual idols to camphor and flowers. Wealthy donors often enjoyed privileges during temple processions. An inscription at Uthiramerur describes the entitlements earned by a temple woman for her sponsorship of numerous repairs to the temple 'that on every occasion when the god goes forth in the temple car on festival days in this temple, she will stand at the front of the car and wave the flywhisk, holding on to the top of the car, the little girls (of her family) to be seated on the upper platform of the car, while other relatives stand behind and perform flywhisk service'.[10] Another generous donor, a man, was granted the right to be one of those carrying the deities in procession. There are instances of temples essentially conducting auctions among temple women for a variety of processional rights and opportunities.

On their peregrinations, the gods and goddesses were serenaded by dancers and musicians and offered betel leaves and areca nuts. Dressed in their finest, weighed down with exquisite jewellery, daubed with fragrant sandalwood paste, they

Top: Karana (dance pose) sculptures inside the first tier of the vimana over the sanctum sanctorum of the Brihadeeshwara Temple.
Middle: A coin from the reign of Rajaraja I.
Bottom: Seal of Rajaraja I's Leiden copperplate grant, now housed at Leiden University in the Netherlands. It includes two fishes, a tiger, fly-whisks, a parasol, and lamps.

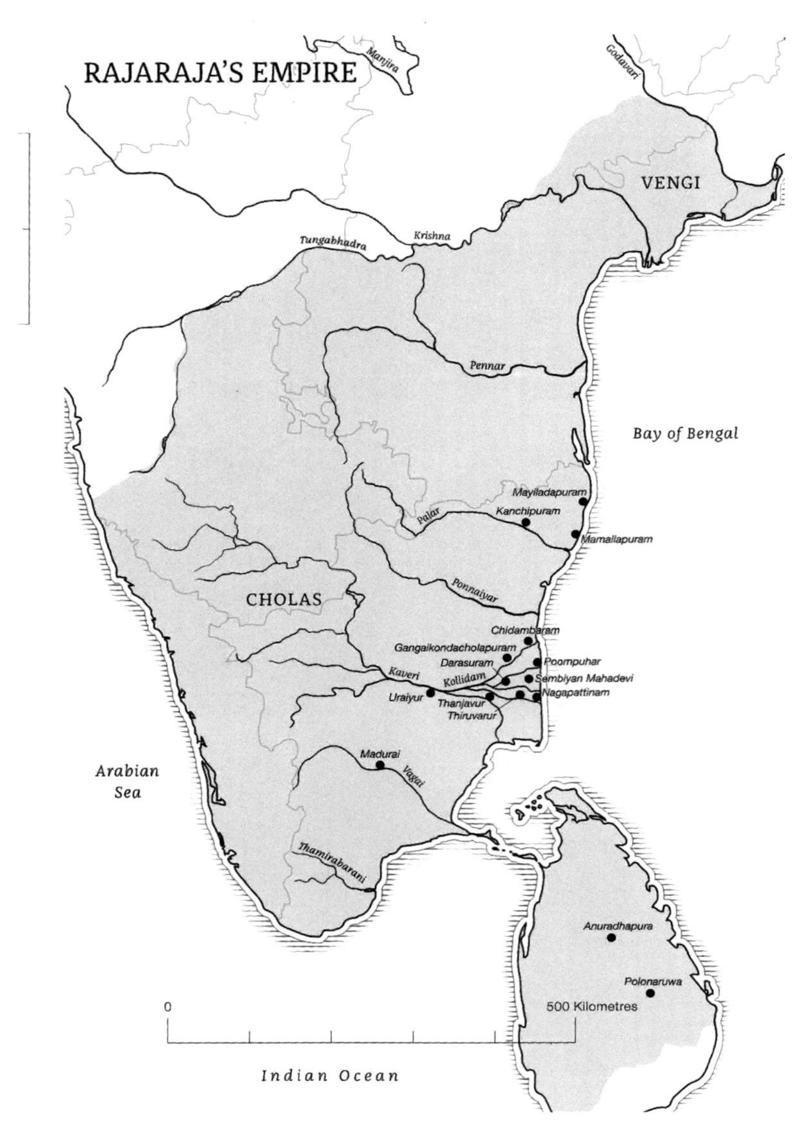

This map has been prepared in adherence to the 'Guidelines for acquiring and producing Geospatial Data and Geospatial Data Services including Maps' published vide DST F.No.SM/25/02/2020 (Part-I) dated 15th February, 2021.

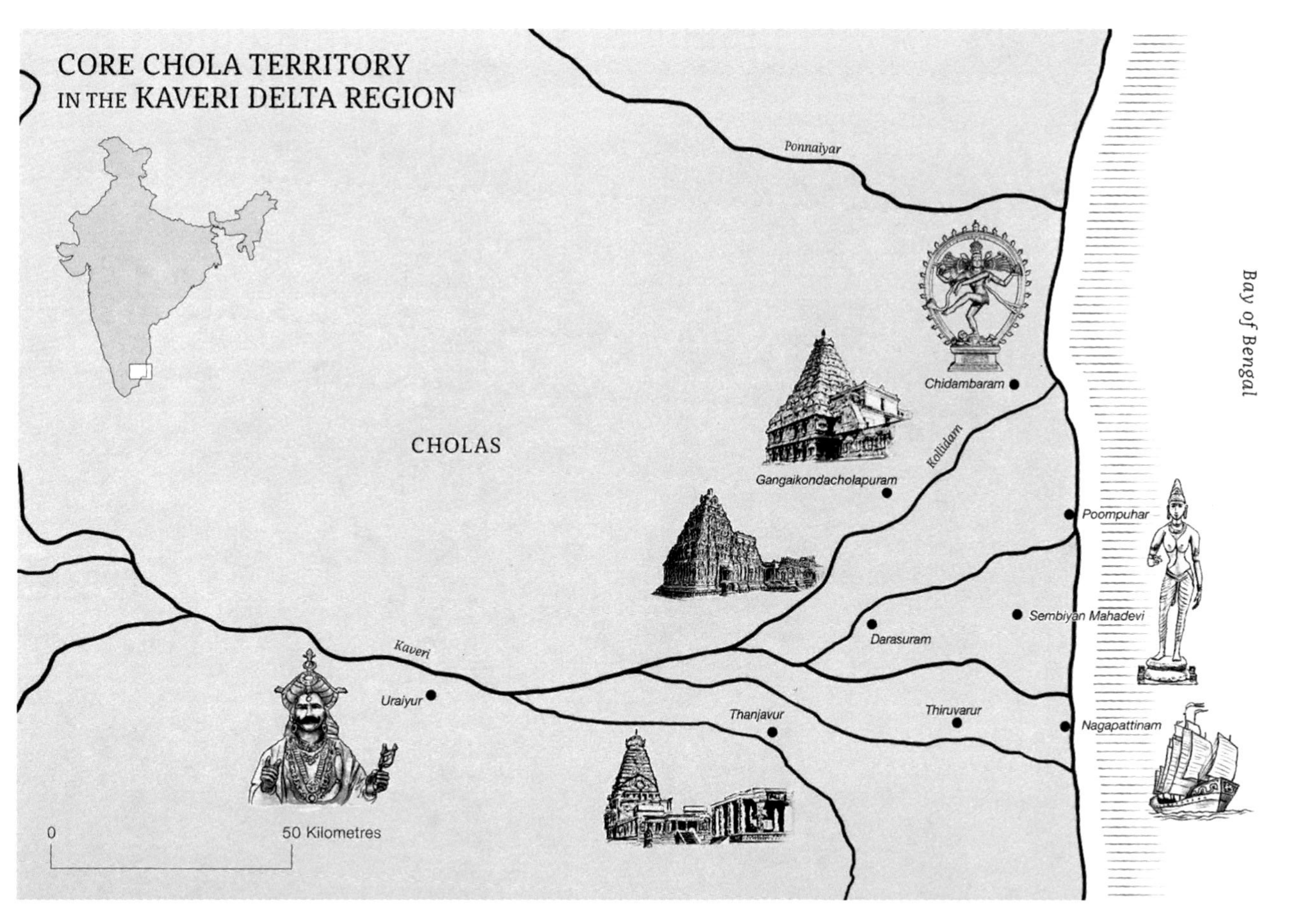

This map has been prepared in adherence to the 'Guidelines for acquiring and producing Geospatial Data and Geospatial Data Services including Maps' published vide DST F.No.SM/25/02/2020 (Part-I) dated 15th February, 2021.

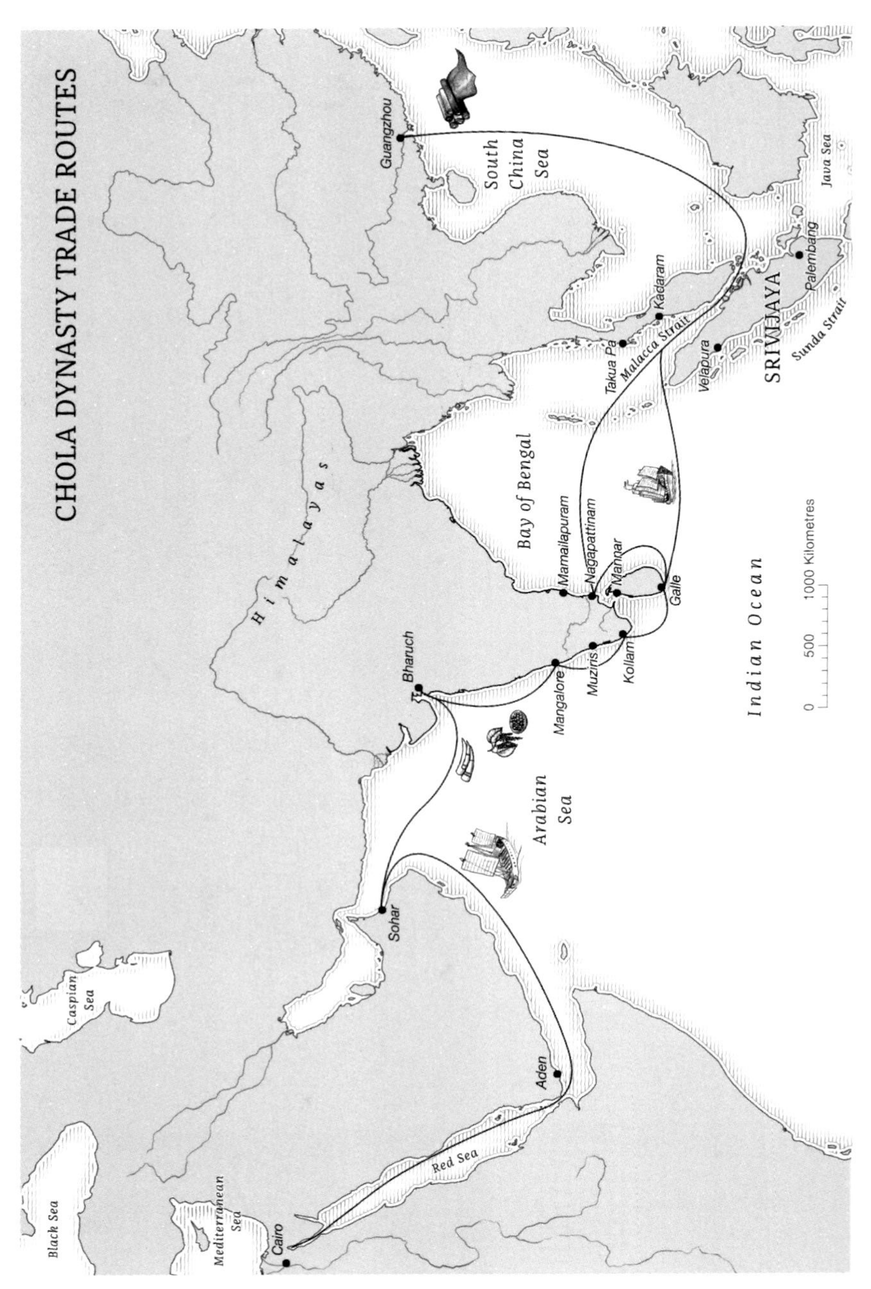

This map has been prepared in adherence to the 'Guidelines for acquiring and producing Geospatial Data and Geospatial Data Services including Maps' published vide DST F.No.SM/25/02/2020 (Part-I) dated 15th February, 2021.

Top: Chidambaram Nataraja Temple and Sivaganga tank. The Chola kings were deeply devoted to the lord of this temple.
Middle: The gilded roof of the Cit Sabha of the Chidambaram Nataraja Temple. Multiple Chola rulers, from Aditya and Parantaka I, claim credit for gilding the roof. Later Chola kings like Kulothunga I, Vikrama, and Kulothunga II invested hugely in the temple's expansion and it grew to its present proportions largely during their reigns.
Bottom: Kampahareshwarar Temple in Tribhuvanam, built by Kulothunga Chola III, 1212 CE.

Top left: Sculptures on the wall at the Gangaikondacholapuram Temple. This exquisite sculpture shows Siva—with goddess Uma-Parvati beside him—conferring his blessings on his devotee Chandesha. Some interpret it as Siva blessing Rajendra.
Top right: Sculpture of Siva as Ardhanarishwara—half-woman, half-man—on a wall at the Gangaikondacholapuram Temple.
Bottom: Rajendra I's Gangaikondacholapuram Temple (1029 CE) from the approach road.

Top: Rajendra Chola's Thiruvalangadu plates. These are in the Government Museum in Chennai.
Middle: Copperplate inscriptions of Rajendra Chola's Thiruvalangadu plates.
Bottom: Carved chariot at Rajaraja II's Airavateshwara Temple, Darasuram, 1150 CE.

Top: Rajaraja Chola's statue in a park in Thanjavur.
Bottom: Modern day bronzes made in Thanjavur by traditional bronze casters following a 1,000-year-old practice.

were installed in their vehicles; a mirror was offered to them to ensure they were satisfied with their appearance. A plate of burning camphor, aromatic and auspicious, made a circular journey in front of the idols, and amid the heart-pounding rhythms of drums and the soaring music of the nadaswaram, they began their journey. The procession stopped at specially erected shelters for a respite from the sun; it then moved on and wound its way around the streets. There might be a ritual dip in the river or the sea. All the while, devotees of every stripe clamoured for a glimpse of their beloved gods and goddesses; the air was filled with joy and festive cheer.

The gods went out both to be seen and to see. People who might not have been allowed into the temple's sanctum could have their fill of divinity regardless of who or what they were. And, these lands belonged foremost to the gods, and a big part of their travels was to survey their kingdom, to make sure all was well, to bless the land. Thus satisfied—the gods and their devotees—they returned home to their sanctum in the temple. The deities would be bathed in milk, butter, honey, and curds upon their return, their clothes changed, and they would be put to bed with a gentle lullaby.

There are no better words than those of our Bhakti poets to describe the joyous sights and sounds of a festival procession. Sambandar wrote of his beloved Lord:

> The Lord of Citticcaram shrine in Naraiyur,
> who has the river in his hair,
> the poison stain on his throat,
> and the Veda on his tongue,
> goes resplendent in ceremonial dress,
> as his devotees and perfected sages
> sing and dance his widespread fame,
> and the sound of festival drums
> beaten on the streets where the temple-car is pulled
> spreads on every side.[11]

CHAPTER 18

IT'S A WOMAN'S WORLD
CHOLA WOMEN

Women in Chola society were active participants in the religious and economic life of their towns and villages. Hundreds of epigraphical records, engraved on stone on temple walls, offer us a glimpse into the world of the temple women of Chola times. Leslie Orr has painted a fascinating picture of their lives. The Brihadeeshwara Temple inscriptions provide us with an extraordinary record of the women who worked there, identifying them by their hometowns and home temples, and the house number and street they lived on near the temple in Thanjavur.

The women who worked at the temple were a distinct social group. They were addressed by titles like devaratiyar (devotee of god), devanar makal (daughter of god), taliyilar (woman of the temple), and some others. These titles were badges of identity that conferred on them the status of temple woman. Most common among these was devaratiyar, an amalgam of devar (god) and atiyar (which means devotee, or servant).[1] This gives the lie to the erroneously and commonly held notion that the temple women were prostitutes. Absolutely *nowhere* is there a hint of this. In fact, what they seem to have had was a connection to a divine, or royal, figure, accorded a good deal of prestige and status.[2]

These appellations started appearing in Tamil in the ninth century, concurrent with the Bhakti movement and the rise of the Cholas. The temple woman received her means of living—land, food, clothing, jewellery—from the temple. Inscriptions recognized her as a woman of a particular temple, or as the devotee of the lord of a certain place. They were distinct from other categories or classes of women who also found mention in inscriptions.

There were the royal women, including the queens, who had titles like deviyar, madevi, or pirattiyar, affixed to their names.[3] They were members of the royal family—the wives, mothers, daughters, or sisters of kings and other royalty. They were extremely active and generous donors, plying the deity with the most expensive jewellery and ritual objects of gold and precious stones. They received gifts of land, money, and jewels from their natal families when they got married as well as gifts from their husbands; these they were free to sell, or donate, as they wished.[4] Most Chola monarchs—with the exception of Gandaraditya, as far as we know—had many wives, part of their strategy to cast a wide net in snagging loyal allies. Rajaraja, for instance, had at least a dozen, possibly more, judging from their inscriptions. His chief wife was Lokamadevi, but it was another wife, Vanavanmadevi (also known as Tribhuvanamadevi) who had the honour of bearing the son who would succeed him as king.[5] Others included Panchavanmadevi, Cholamadevi, and Trailokyamadevi.[6] These were not their birth names, but those awarded or bestowed on them as a mark of royalty. The wives of chieftains, too, were active in Chola temple life.

Then there were the palace women—ladies-in-waiting, palace attendants, and occasionally, mistresses or concubines. They were referred to by the velam (palace) or parivaram (retinue) they belonged to; occasionally they were addressed as anukki (an intimate) or a poki (mistress) of a king or a chief. They enjoyed a position of status in society and some possessed a great deal of wealth. Other women who have been mentioned in inscriptions were the family members of the non-royals: merchants, landowners, farmers, shepherds.

There appear to be a couple of tantalizing exceptions to the separation between palace and temple women norm, that sows a seed of doubt into our notions that the different classes of women were distinct. Inscriptions have revealed at least two women who were likely both queens as well as temple women. One was a lady called Nakkan Akkaranankaiyar, who was both a temple woman of the Agastheeswarar Siva Temple at Melapaluvur in Tiruchirapalli district (identified as such by the devanar makal prefix) and also the wife of a Chera prince.[7] Another was Nakkan Panchavanmadevi, one of Rajaraja's wives. She was also a devanar makal of the same temple.[8] This is as much as we know, and it leaves a whole host of questions unanswered. How did Rajaraja meet and marry her? In an age when marriages were largely alliances with political or economic motives, was this a love marriage? Did the daughters of kings and chieftains become dancers? Her name, Panchavanmadevi indicates a Pandya connection (Panchavan was a Pandya epithet). Rajaraja's inscription at the Agastyesvara temple identifies her as her as his queen Nakkan Panchavanmadevi, the daughter of Avanikandarppapurattu Devanar of Paluvur, and goes on to record her donation of 900 kalams of surplus paddy that was found to be available after a revenue survey. That, alas, is all we know of her.

However, such cases were the exception rather than the rule. In the majority of inscriptions, temple women and palace women maintained their separate identities, and their worlds did not overlap. Nonetheless, we must be conscious that we are imposing our modern mindset in our understanding of these categories and divisions; perhaps they were not entirely relevant in medieval society, and more women than we know of did hold dual or multiple identities.

As the Chola empire grew and matured, the number of inscriptions that involved temple women also grew, indicating a surge in their presence and involvement in temple activities.

Many temple inscriptions record donations by devaratiyars. This was the most common capacity in which they they made their mark in the inscriptions, as temple benefactors. Most of the gifts were of lamps, or of the means to keep them burning perpetually. In this, they were no different from most other donors, whether they were queens, merchants, or landowners. They had access to wealth and their gifts and patronage were acknowledged and documented publicly. The daughters, sons, grandsons, brothers, sisters, and other kin of the temple women mentioned their relationship to the temple women in their own inscriptions; perhaps they hoped that some of her prestige and social standing would rub off on them. Inscriptions marking their gifts are found in temples throughout the Chola region; this is in contrast to the gift-giving by queens and other royal women, who tended to patronize the larger temples in the core Cholamandalam region around Thanjavur.[9]

The gender of the temple donor or patron was of no relevance; people of either sex were free to endow gifts to the temple. It was the devotion and piety behind the act that mattered, and the status it conferred on the donor—that applied equally to men and women.

As the stature and prominence of the temple women became more established in the course of time, they started making 'deals' in return for their endowments to the temple. Although such 'deals' became much more common in post-Chola times, there are several inscriptions that note that the temple received a certain quantity of gold from a devaratiyar, and that in return she got to sing and dance at a festival, or sing the sacred hymns, or enjoy a prominent position in the temple's festival procession.[10]

It is both fascinating and heartening to note that Chola women—some women, at least, and certainly many of the temple women, but others as well—participated freely in land transactions. There are several inscriptions that show them engaging, independently, in the buying and selling of land, from one woman to another, with the full assent of the village assembly and temple authorities, with no male family member interfering. Clearly, women had the right and freedom to own, buy, and sell land on their own names. However, they were by no means as active as men in such transactions. Most unfortunately however, judging from inscriptions, it appears that women—not the temple women, but all others—became less active in the later years of the Chola empire. Also, in later years, male intermediaries, termed mukutan or guardians, appear more often; perhaps this reflected the growing male chokehold over the autonomy of women to transact their own deals. Inscriptions showing donations by non-temple women also decrease in later Chola years, in the twelfth and thirteenth centuries.[11]

A bright spark of light in all this is that the decreasing independence of women was not echoed in the case of temple women. It was quite the opposite, in fact. All other women acquired property and wealth through marriage. The temple women, who lived outside the social system of marriage, often followed a matriarchal structure; their wealth could have been inherited from their mothers and stayed within the family. In addition, being supported by the temple and having the status of temple woman enabled them to acquire wealth; as the temple became the centre of economic activity they reaped the financial rewards of their connection to it. They earned their own income in the form of land, houses, gold, clothing, or jewellery from the temple. Often, they received gifts as special devotees of the temple's deity and, in addition, were paid for their part in ritual tasks (like marriage ceremonies, for instance) performed outside the temples.[12]

And so the post-Rajaraja and Rajendra era saw a growing divide in the status of temple women with respect to other women. Judging from the number of donations to temples alone, it appears that temple women became economically stronger, and more stable and independent; the rest moved in the opposite direction.

Interestingly, and at odds with our ideas about temple women, they were almost never referred to as dancers; also, not all female dancers were temple women. There are inscriptions that refer to women who have been commissioned to perform a particular dance and who are *not* temple women. Just as interesting, early Chola inscriptions reveal that more men than women were employed as temple dancers; inscriptions mention cantikuttars, or dancers, and the majority were male. This is reversed in later Chola years, in the twelfth century and after. Dancing at festivals was therefore not a major part of what the temple women did, and dance per se was not a pivotal part of temple festivals. Dancing at festivals was considered a privilege, though, which would explain why many women 'bought' the right to do it with their donations and gifts. In later Chola years, women became increasingly prominent as temple dancers, effectively nudging the men aside from a role that had been largely theirs a century or two earlier. In due course, and with the passage of a few centuries, dance became a key part of the temple women's identity and specialization.[13]

The nattuvanar, or dance master, on the other hand was always male, and this was an inherited profession, one that could not be 'won' as a privilege with donations and gifts. This did not change during the years of Chola rule, or after.

This is certainly not to say that Chola temple women did not dance. But that was not their principal function, nor was it an exclusively female preserve. So if they were not primarily dancers—or singers—what else did the temple women do? Unfortunately, inscriptions remain rather vague on this point. It appears, judging from the small number of relevant inscriptions, that that they were almost never given any duties that involved a level of accountability or authority, like supervision, administration, tax and fine collection, or anything involving the inner workings of the temple.

Interestingly, the services and functions to be performed by temple men were spelled out in some detail: the exact hymn to be sung or text to be recited, the part of the ritual when the drummers came into play. This is rarely seen in the case of temple women. The identities of the Chola temple women were not tied to any particular functions or specializations. Most of the inscriptions in which women feature prominently are where they play the role of donor and patron. Next most common are those in which women are mentioned as being involved in attending and helping out during rituals and festivals. The women were fly-whisk bearers, gently fanning the deity—this was a highly coveted and prestigious task. Inscriptional evidence indicates that the fly-whisk bearers were most often, although not exclusively, women. Other activities included being the lamp bearer, being present at the festival, and personally attending upon the deity. Oftentimes, these roles were privileges earned by the women for a particularly generous donation; it might not have been what they were hired to do. Such tasks, therefore, were not those that required any particular qualification—in terms of caste, gender, ritual purity, etc.—and might have not been a necessary part of the ritual, but rather, an ornamental one. Being seen in the temple, or in procession, bearing a fly-whisk, could have been a way to advertise the prestige and status earned by the woman. Such services were far from being the exclusive domain of women; inscriptions mention large numbers of men as well.[14]

In general, having your name inscribed on a temple wall was a mark of high honour in Chola times; it meant you were worthy of mention, that you had the means to be a generous patron, generous enough to merit acknowledgement. However, there was another scenario, one devoid of any hint of prestige or distinction, in which women's names have been recorded in inscriptions. This was when they were sold (probably as slaves) to the temple, where they performed menial tasks. These included cleaning the temple's floors and serving in the eating halls. Not a whisper of privilege is in evidence here. Inscribing their names provided a record of the temple's property, much like a grant of land. Such inscriptions are not numerous, but they do date more often from the post-Rajaraja era.

The role of temple women, therefore, was quite different from that of the men. The men far outnumbered them, for one, and women were excluded from many of the critical ritual activities, and from administrative roles in managing the temple. While there were functions that could be done only by men, there were none that were exclusively the realm of temple women. And with the exception of dance, nothing required any special skills or training.

And here is another interesting yet disturbing statistic. The proportion of women who were remunerated in some form was the highest during the reigns of Rajaraja and Rajendra; this proportion dropped precipitously after that, even while the absolute number of temple women burgeoned. This separation of service from compensation could be due to the fact that the number of women negotiating deals with the temple in return for donations increased in this period.

Rajaraja changed the existing dynamic of temple women being attached to a particular temple and deity, usually of their home town. He gathered the best dancers from around his kingdom and installed them in his Brihadeeshwara Temple, providing them with housing and compensation, naming each one, identifying her by name and the town and temple she came from. Did this alter the circumstances and ethos of temple women in the long run? It did not appear to, at least during Chola times. Rajaraja's model was an aberration, a departure from the very local world of the temple woman, but within a century of his death matters appear to have drifted back to women patronizing and working in the temples of their hometowns.

The dancers listed on Rajaraja's inscription at the Brihadeeshwara Temple came from fifty-four towns and villages from around the Chola country. Only around a third of these places have been mentioned in other inscriptions predating Rajaraja's as the homes of temple women. Prominent among these are Kanchipuram, Tiruvarur, Tiruvidamarudur, Takkolam, and Tiruvannamalai. Perhaps these were the major centres that maintained temple women, enough to find their way into inscriptions. Two glaring omissions from this list are the two major temple towns of Chidambaram and Sri Rangam, the chief centres for the worship of Siva and Vishnu, respectively. In general, women tended to donate to and be patrons of smaller and medium-sized temples; perhaps these behemoths were outside the orbit of temple women donors.[15]

The majority of inscriptions that mention temple women identify them as belonging to a particular place, or temple. A mere handful allude to a familial relationship, as the wife, daughter, or sister of somebody. And among these, most of them refer to the mother–daughter tie. There are very few inscriptions where the temple woman's connection to her father is mentioned.

There are several—not many, but they exist, and are significant, as we will see soon—inscriptions in which the temple women are presented as the wife of so-and-so. Some were both temple women and queens. Most prominent among these, of course, was Rajaraja's wife Nakkan Panchavanmadevi, who was both devaratiyar and madeviyar, temple devotee and queen. In Chola India, being a temple woman and marriage were not mutually exclusive, as it appears to have become in later centuries. Temple women were presented as wives and daughters in much the same way as other women were. Nevertheless, there are more inscriptions in which the temple woman herself is the point of reference: others identify themselves as relatives of a particular temple woman, suggesting that while some temple women did marry, many did not, and the community as a whole may have traced their lineage matrilineally.

Ultimately, the temple woman's identity lay with her village, temple, and its deity. Not as a dancer, a wife, or a daughter. All those other affiliations were secondary, at least in how they were characterized in inscriptions.

◆

Many Chola women were actively involved in the life of the towns and villages they lived in, particularly that of the temple. Among the most active temple donors were the royal queens, who gifted extremely generously, particularly to the temples of their home towns. There are some women who stand out for not merely the extravagance of their gift-giving, but also for their impact across multiple spheres of life. They were respected and revered by king and commoner alike. One of the most truly exceptional women from Chola times was Queen Sembiyan Madevi.

This grande-dame of the Chola family, the wife of Gandaraditya, mother of Uttama Chola, the Ruby of the Chola dynasty, Our Lady, Great Queen Sembiyan Madevi was one of the most remarkable women of all time.[16] She was the embodiment of grace and strength and could well be a model for women anywhere, anytime, for how to live a life of dedication and purpose through upheaval and tragedy.

Sembiyan's father was the chief of Malanadu, a region north of the Kaveri. Her birth family were courtiers called Malavaraiyars—they married into the Chola family for obvious political reasons; they were in a subordinate position of giving their daughters away as brides.[17] She married Parantaka's son Gandaraditya when he was the crown prince and had the unusual status of being the only (known) wife of an emperor. She was certainly the sole queenly authority. What a contrast to her father-in-law Parantaka, husband to at least eleven queens that we know of through inscriptions! We have seen that marriage alliances were very often made with an eye to creating or strengthening political affiliations and in these exceedingly volatile and precarious times, could be a key factor in matters of state. Thus, she got her only son, Uttama, married to no fewer than thirteen wives, casting the net of loyalty and protection far and wide.

She became the Chola queen in 949, the year her husband became king after his brother, Rajaditya, was brutally killed at the bloody Battle of Takkolam. He ruled for a mere eight years, until 957, after which he vanished from the pages of Chola history. Did he abdicate? Did he die? The answers have not been discovered to this day. An inscription describes him as 'the lord who rose and went west'. The west was believed to be the direction of death, and thus this inscription has been interpreted by some to mean that he took his own life.

She was widowed young, when she was only twenty-eight years old. She had a son, Uttama Chola, who was too young to become king at the time of the king's death. She no longer held the exalted position of queen, as the throne passed on to her husband's brother Arinjaya (r. 957–61), then to Arinjaya's son Sundara Chola (r. 958–69). At the best of times, in any place and time in history, this would have been the death knell for any hope of a meaningful life for her. She could have well faded into the shadows and be forgotten about. But she was a remarkable woman and truly came into her own with her son's accession to the throne. She regained a good measure of status then; she was in her early forties, not young, but certainly still in the prime of life and determined to make a difference. By the time his reign ended, sixteen years later, she was a woman of great stature who commanded respect, devotion, love, and admiration.

The first temple inscription of her donation to a temple at Uyyakondan Tirumalai was from the year 941; she was the crown princess then, a girl barely matured into womanhood.[18] She continued building, renovating, and endowing temples throughout her life. One of the last temples she built was one at Tiruvakkarai, during the height of Rajaraja's reign, in 1001. Metal-casting was another passion of hers and some of the loveliest bronze images from Chola times were made under her patronage. She made lavish grants of land, gold, jewels, and endowments for temple festivals. She was generous with charity and organized meals to feed large groups of the pious and learned.

She was a strong woman who was held in high esteem by her son, daughters-in-law, and her grand-nephew the great Rajaraja—so much so that her orders carried the same weight and authority as his.[19] She commissioned the building of many temples. Among the best known is the Umamaheshwara Temple in Konerirajapuram, one of the ancient Saivite places of worship mentioned in the Tevaram hymns of the Nayanmars. It was built in the very early years of the reign of her son, Uttama Chola, in the early 970s. On the south wall of the central shrine of this temple is an inscription:

> ...the glorious Sembiyan Madevi, queen of Gandaraditya, constructed in the sacred name of her husband, the glorious Gandaradityadeva, a stone temple to the lord of Tirunallam (which was what Konerirajapuram was called then) when her glorious son the illustrious Madhurantakadeva alias the glorious Uttama Chola was graciously ruling. This is (the image of) the glorious Gandaradityadeva which was made in this sacred stone temple in the posture of worshipping the sacred feet of the lord of Tirunallam.[20]

Above this inscription is a group of sculptures, of Sembiyan Madevi kneeling in a worshipping posture, along with her husband, Gandaraditya, shown with a simple and elegant headdress and strings of pearls. Behind her are her attendants. On another panel nearby is another sculpture of a person that an inscription informs us is Sattan Gunabattan, the builder of the temple. In recognition for his work, he was awarded the title rajakesari muvendavelan.[21]

Queen Sembiyan must have made plans for this temple soon after the death of her husband in 957, and put them into action as soon she had the power to, with her son on the throne. She must have visualized a temple that would be a fitting monument to her beloved husband. The temple was the first to have niches all along the walls of the ardhamandapa, or entrance pavilion to the temple, each of which was adorned with sculptures. A beautiful flower garden adorned its grounds. Some of the most exquisite Chola bronzes of all time were commissioned for this temple by Sembiyan Madevi. Two in particular stand out: the goddess

Parvati as the consort of Siva as Tripurantaka, the Destroyer of the Three Citadels, all grace and soft curves, on which her sharply etched abundance of jewellery stands out; and Siva as Vrishabhavahana, the Rider of the Bull, a commanding figure, immaculately cast, every detail finished to perfection.[22] It must have been a master craftsman, his skill and genius at its pinnacle, who created these treasures. Sembiyan sought out the best and gave them the opportunity to blossom. One imagines her keenly interested and involved in the workshops that produced the stunning bronzes of her era. Nothing less than sublime beauty and outstanding quality would do for her.

Not content with merely building the temple, Queen Sembiyan paid meticulous attention to ensure that every aspect of running it was documented. The level of detail in the inscriptions at this temple is mind-boggling and gives us considerable information about its administration. Every minute detail was made a note of. Just to give an idea of some of what was recorded in the inscriptions: the exact measurements of the lands from which the rice had been obtained in order to ensure the pay of the Brahmins who crushed sandal, those who held the canopy (over the images) and rendered other necessary services; the wages for the temple servants who picked up flowers and strung them, and those who swept the sacred temple and smeared it with cow dung; the payment and what form it was given in to musicians, trumpeters, conch-blowers, watchmen of images, reciters of the *Tiruppadiyam* hymns, the Brahmins who attended to the general management of the temple (kovil-variyam), the temple accountant of the potter caste, the potter who supplied pots, the dyer who dyed the sacred cloth (for the images), the Brahmin who carried the water from the Kaveri for the sacred bath, the official auditor who checked the temple transactions under orders of the king, temple repairs, the monthly sacred baths and the ceremonies on eclipses, renewal of screens and canopies, the purificatory ceremony called Jalapavitra, annual renewal of sacred cloths, the astrologer who recited the astronomical changes every day and carried the calendar with him, the pay (including cost of clothing) of the gardeners and of their assistants, the temple architect, the carpenter, and the blacksmith, special worship for the images of Tripuravijaya, Vrishabhavahana, and Ganapati and the sacred bath with milk, curds, butter, sugar, and honey.[23]

She built many other temples, including in Anangur, Tirukodikaval, Aduturai, Kuttalam, and Vriddhachalam. She was a woman with a mind of her own, a true trailblazer with a vision and sense of purpose that propelled the most important institution of her time, the temple, into new territory. There was no clear style of Chola temples at that point; iconography and many details of ornamentation and layout were very much in a fluid state. Sembiyan Madevi introduced some features that would be replicated across all the temples associated with her in an early efflorescence of a Chola form. Her temples had a style and features that were distinct. In temples built in what has come to be called the Sembiyan style, the number of niche sculptures nestled in the walls of the temples, increased from just a handful to as many as nine, and even sixteen. Here, she incorporated sculptures, including those of the many forms of Siva—as Nataraja, Ardhanareeshwara, as Bhikshasanan (the beggar lord), and as consort of Uma.[24] She must have had a particular fondness for the dancing Lord Nataraja, and every one of the new stone temples she built, as well as those she had rebuilt, had his image carved in stone in a niche on the south wall of the temple's hall of worship. Others who sponsored and patronized temple building in this period followed suit. This ensured that devotees could view and worship their beloved dancing lord close to home in the towns and villages along the Kaveri, without having to make the journey to Chidambaram.[25]

Sembiyan was far-sighted too. She realized that the old temples of brick and wood had a limited lifespan, and she converted many of them into permanent structures of stone, and also commissioned the building of many new stone temples.

Then she lavished her energy and attention on these temples, flooding them with abundant generosity in the form of gifts and endowments, getting involved in the most minute details concerning their operations.

She lived up to a ripe old age, through the reigns of five kings: her husband, Gandaraditya, his brother Arinjaya, Sundara Chola, her son Uttama, and Rajaraja. Through it all she was actively involved in her favourite enterprise of commissioning temples and bronze sculptures. Her own portrait in bronze was commissioned too, during her lifetime, probably by her son. This was the first known image of a Chola royal, and its making must have been testament to the inspiration she invoked with her remarkable personality. She was held in high regard by the members of the royal household.

She rebuilt in stone brick temples, many of great spiritual renown that had been sung and written about by the great Saivite poets. She was not alone, or unique, in doing this. Where she did stand out is that she ordered that the inscriptions from the old brick temples be re-engraved on the walls of the newly built stone temples. The donations mentioned in the inscriptions were meant to last as long as the moon and the sun; by having the inscriptions that made mention of them engraved on to stone, she ensured that they, too, endured as long as the moon and the sun. She had a keen sense of history, correctness, accuracy, of clarifying and saving records for posterity. If an inscription was a copy of an earlier one, she established that they were copies. In the words of an inscription at her temple at Aduthurai: 'While dismantling the earlier part-brick, part-stone structure, the inscribed stones were carefully removed and preserved for the documents engraved on them; and when the new structure was completed, all in stone, this great soul Sembiyan Madevi ordered that the old inscriptions recording grants, donations, etc. of all earlier kings which had been damaged or worn out, be faithfully engraved on the walls of the new structure.'[26] She was pragmatic, too. Inscriptions at Tirukodikaval tell us that she instructed that the old inscriptions be discarded, as they had served their purpose.

In her seventies, as the tenth century drew to a close, she created a Brahmin village that was named after her—Sembiyan Madevi—the name that the village is known by even today. A quiet place some 65 kilometres east of Thanjavur on the Tiruvalur–Nagapattinam road that time has forgotten, it retains no vestige of its ancient grandeur and the vision of its creator. Created as a brahmadeya or Brahmin village, she settled it with highly learned Brahmin scholars who were Chaturvedi Bhattas or knowledgeable in the four vedas. Here, Sembiyan Madevi built the temple of Kailasanathaswami. This temple is the first known one where a stone sculpture of Siva as Nataraja (Adavallan) was carved into a central niche in the temple wall of the entrance hall. That spot had been reserved hitherto, for the most part, for Ganesha. Sembiyan commissioned this image of this form of Siva, which would become the one most revered and worshipped by the Cholas. An inscription by her great-grandnephew, the emperor Rajendra, explains the special arrangements for celebrations for her birthday, which fell during the month of Chithirai (March–April) at this temple. Her bronze image was worshipped, along with the image of Siva with his bull. The inscription also mentions a grand hall—the Sembiyan Madeviyar Periya Mandapam—which might have served as the venue for the celebrations.[27]

Besides the village, a plumeria pleasure garden, a water tank, and a liquid measure have all been named after her.

Queen Sembiyan was not merely a pious lady who was active in temple building and administration. Inscriptions reveal a woman with a very practical intelligence too, involved in matters of irrigation and agriculture. An inscription in a Siva temple from the year 998 details the directive she issued to the village assembly and the temple priests with precise instructions about how certain temple lands should be irrigated. In a village, Gandaradita Chaturvedimangalam, named for her husband, she built a large lake spanning over 400 acres. The lake, called Sembiyan Madevi Pereri, filled up with the overflow from a nearby river and provided the water to irrigate nearly two dozen surrounding villages. Sadly, the lake now is weed-choked, and only a fraction of it is of use to the farmers.

Is it any wonder that the greatest of the Chola emperors, Rajaraja, had the highest esteem and affection for her? The two were kindred spirits, after all, and their relationship was one of mutual regard and genuine admiration. Two trailblazers with a vision that went beyond the norms of their time, brilliant administrators who paid meticulous attention to detail, and who were all about breaking and expanding boundaries.

Sembiyan Madevi died in 1001, but her memory lives on. There is a stunning statue that made its way in 1929 to the Freer Sackler Gallery of the Smithsonian Museum in Washington, DC.[28] It is of a slender, graceful, full-breasted young woman, simply adorned, with fine, delicate features and a soft, serene expression belying an inner strength. Many scholars believe that this is the statue of Sembiyan Madevi that once graced the temple in the village named for her. The cool, quiet air-conditioned room she now stands in is a far cry from the hot and lively world she once was a part of. Lithe and with fine, delicate features, she stands on a pedestal with holes for carrying poles, indicating that she had been taken out in procession, a high honour indeed, respected and worshipped at the same level as the saints and gods revered by the people of the time. Like those very gods and saints, her bronze image was taken in triumphant procession through the streets, bedecked with jewellery, silks, and flowers. Now she is stripped bare of her finery. All she can offer her visitors and admirers is an enigmatic smile. Once upon a time, she seems to say, there was a queen who lived in a faraway land, ruled by a great dynasty called the Cholas.

And in the temple she built in the village she created—Kailasanathaswami Temple in Sembiyan Madevi village—her birthday is celebrated every year. Flowers, silks, and fruits are offered. Recently, a large group of people from fifteen neighbouring villages collected funds to create a bronze image of their ancient queen. It weighs 1,000 kilograms and has been installed in the village.

Queen Sembiyan must have inspired many other women to sponsor and patronize temples. Inscriptions provide ample evidence of women from both the ruling Chola families as well as from the families of the Irrukavels, Muttaraiyars, and others, being involved in temple building. These women put themselves at the forefront of one of the most important aspects of Chola life. Their families had their own styles and traditions of temple building that were largely in the hands of the women of the family. The Cholas (males) took inspiration from them for their own temple building efforts starting later in the tenth century.

◆

The emperor Rajaraja had two older siblings: a brother, Aditya Karikalan, and a sister, Kundavai. Aditya Karikalan was murdered under circumstances that have not been uncovered; shortly after their father, Sundara Chola, died, and their mother, Vanavanmadevi, chose to commit sati and die with him.

Rajaraja and Kundavai were orphaned while they were in their twenties. Growing up, they witnessed the upheavals of the empire, and the tragedies they experienced together must have drawn them close. They had their grand-aunt Sembiyan Madevi in their life, who must have surely inspired both siblings with her combination of piety, grit, generosity, far-sightedness, and can-do determination. All qualities to influence an impressionable young woman.

Ambition and curiosity about the wider world must have been a family trait. Kundavai showed a keen interest in the activities of her father's, brother's, and nephew's affairs, and was an active and generous donor to many temples.

She was married to Vallavaraiyar Vandhiyadevar, who was the chief of a Bana clan. He almost certainly held a position of high status, as Vallavaraiyarnadu, a nadu, or district was named for him. The couple lived in the Chola kingdom, which was quite unusual for the time. Most women married and moved to where their husbands came from. We have no record of when Kundavai got married but given that women married very young in Chola times, it is very likely that she was already married when her brother became king. Besides, it took several years for Rajaraja to consolidate his position. So it could not have been the fact of his power and domination over southern India that allowed her to remain in the domain of her birth. It has been suggested that she was an independent-minded young woman. There is no way of verifying this, but it is an alluring thought, borne out by the depth and breadth of her activities.

She spent much of her married life in a palace at Pazhayarai, a town near Kumbakonam and some 30 kilometres east of Thanjavur. Several Chola monarchs had palaces there, and Pazhayarai seems to have served as a secondary capital in those times. Kundavai was a generous patron of the Siva temple there.[29]

There was a deep bond between Rajaraja and Kundavai. When he built his magnificent Brihadeeshwara Temple, hers was the first name next to his, in the inscriptions recording his donations. He declared using the royal we, 'Let the gifts made by us, those made by (our) elder sister, those made by our wives, and those made by other donors to the lord of the sacred stone-temple, (called) Sri Rajarajesvara—which we caused to be built (at) Tanjavur—be engraved on stone on the sacred shrine (sri-viman).'[30] Kundavai was always referred to as the venerable elder sister. Beyond that, those inscriptions that document the gifts donated by only him and Kundavai are etched in the most sacred part of the temple, the exterior walls of the sanctum sanctorum. Donations by his wives are recorded on pillars and in niches in far less important parts of the temple.

Rajaraja was not obliged to do any of this. His actions must have surely sprung from a well of great respect and love. He had two children that we know of. The best known, of course, was his son Rajendra. The other was a daughter. He named her Kundavai, after his sister.

Kundavai lavished gifts and endowments on temples throughout her brother's realm. She might have been a Siva devotee, but that did not limit her generosity to other sects and faiths. If Vishnu devotees and Jains lived in Chola country, then their places of worship too needed support. She sponsored the building of three new temples including one to Vishnu at Rajarajapuram and then endowed it with land, sheep for ten lamps, vessels of gold, silver, and pearl. The Vishnu temple was named Kundavai Vinnagara Alvar. She provided for a flower garden and the means to feed the Sri Vaishnavas at a muth (monastery) in Uthiramerur. At the foot of a hillock in the Jain town of Tirumalai, Kundavai built a Jain temple named Kundavai Jinalaya. She was sensitive to the particular practices and preferences of different sects; for this Jain temple she specially commissioned paintings for its walls and installed and consecrated images of Yaksha and Yakshini (Jain guardian deities).

There are numerous instances such as this, of Kundavai's largesse and benevolence.

She established a village that was called Kundavai Chaturvedimangalam, which was home to scholars of Vedic studies. She gifted the village to the scholars. We know of two irrigation tanks that she sponsored, one named after herself, and the other, after her father, Sundara Chola.[31]

Kundavai must have taken keen interest in the Brihadeeshwara Temple. Once it was built she contributed vast amounts of gold, jewellery, and utensils, and gave liberally for the rituals, garlands, and clothing for the deities. She deposited money with a variety of village assemblies and used the interest to pay for temple services. She endowed four bronze icons: her father, mother, and the consorts of Dakshina Meru Vitankan and Tanjai Vitankan. Twenty pairs of earrings were made for the image of her mother, as well as beautiful silks and other jewellery. For her father's image, she deposited substantial sums of money in several villages, with the interest to be paid in paddy. Unimaginable quantities of gold and jewellery were bequeathed to the goddesses.[32]

Kundavai must have been a dedicated daughter and ensured that the memory of her parents was kept alive with the pomp and splendour that were their due. She established a dispensary in Thanjavur that she named Sundarachola Vinnagar Atulasalai after her father. Medicines and treatment were dispensed free of cost, thanks to her munificence.

She outlived her beloved brother Rajaraja. She must have been fond of her nephew Rajendra, as she lived out her last years in her palace in Pazhayarai, where Rajendra lived as well.

As with anybody else in Chola times, everything we know of Kundavai is from inscriptions, but even through the cold medium of stone she emerges as a dynamic, big-hearted woman, a devoted daughter and sister who lived life on her terms.

As in any society at any point in time, life for women during Chola times was a mixed bag. They were a part of war booty, the living spoils of plunder and violence that drove home the realities of conquest in brute fashion. They were pawns in the game of networking and alliance-forming. They were undoubtedly sex-slaves to a wide swathe of male society. Those who lost their husbands were pushed into the darkest margins of their community. But to think of them solely as meek and passive and absorbed only in domestic matters is to do them a gross disservice. Even while living largely under the shadow of the patriarchal umbrella, Chola women from all walks of society were actively involved in activities outside the home sphere. These were hardly women on the margins. Thanks to the many inscriptions that allow us a glimpse into their lives, we are granted a fuller picture of the long-ago society they were a part of. Their investment, not just of money, but also of time and spirit, in multiple aspects of the temple, was huge, and important, as this institution was a vital part of the Chola ecosystem. They were involved in philanthropy, funding the establishment of hospitals and rest houses.

As in any society at any point in time and against many odds, the women of the Chola empire contributed to and enriched life around them in a variety of ways.

BOOK FOUR

The Son Also Rises, and the Moon Too

CHAPTER 19

THE DAZZLING SON

PARAKESARI RAJENDRA (R. 1012–1044)

> The king Madhurantaka, who punishes those who do not submit to him, who chastises his enemies, and who possesses a body as handsome as that of Cupid himself, was born as the son of Rajaraja.[1]

Rajendra was Rajaraja's son through his wife Vanavanmadevi, a Chera princess from Kerala. He was a young boy when his father became king and, very early on, he came under the tutelage of his father, along with the best teachers in the realm. Together, they provided him with the training and exposure befitting a future king.

In the year 1012, two years after he completed his magnificent Rajarajeshwara Temple, Rajaraja appointed Rajendra as his yuvaraja and co-ruler.[2] Unlike in his own case, we know of no other contenders to the throne and, besides, Rajendra had more than proved himself on the battlefield and beyond as a worthy successor to his great father. His brilliance and bravery had won the Cholas the Rattapadi territory that belonged to the Western Chalukyas. He had also served as Rajaraja's commander-in-chief of the Vengi and Ganga territories to the north and east of the Chola heartland.

Far too often, we hear about the son of a great man falling short and failing to live up to the father's legacy. But Rajaraja's son had his father's ambition and grand vision. He inherited a large kingdom that enjoyed more stability and cohesiveness than those parts had probably ever seen. He could have sat back and enjoyed the spoils of his father's successes. But he had been groomed at the altar of extraordinary expansionary ambition. Rajendra was a son who would do any father proud, taking the reins of an empire that was more powerful and extensive than it had ever been and steering it to even greater heights. He won every battle he fought and amassed a bushel full of titles.

One of the most valuable sources of information about Rajendra's reign as well as Chola genealogy are the Thiruvalangadu copperplate inscriptions that recorded his grant to the temple of the goddess of Thiruvalangadu. They were discovered by K. V. Subrahmanya Aiyer in 1906. The same court poet, Anantanarayana, who wrote the prasasti for the Leiden plates composed the Sanskrit prasasti portion of these plates and it is a wonder for its high literary quality and wealth of genealogical information, as well as for the attention he has lavished on details about Rajendra's rule. There are thirty-one copper sheets, in Tamil and Sanskrit, the former written at the time of the grant, and the Sanskrit section, with the genealogy, around a decade later. Its main purpose was to record the grant made to the temple of the goddess at Thiruvalangadu. This was the town where one of the Nayanmar poets-saints, a woman named Karaikkal Ammal who starved herself into utter emaciation in order to free herself from the encumbrance of beauty, worshipped Siva as the dancing lord.[3]

Like all Chola genealogies, they are a mix of the fantastic and factual, and are a particularly rich source of information on the earlier Chola kings. A full forty-four kings before Vijayalaya, the founder of the 'Imperial' line, are introduced, before moving on through the kings until Rajendra, full of vivid and lively details about their royal triumphs. The plates bemoan their inadequacy, saying: 'the letters of the alphabet number only fifty; the virtues of the kings of the solar race are resplendent beyond number. How can I describe these virtues with those letters?' They might be excessively embellished, but they are invaluable for their insights into the life and times of the Cholas and often our only sources. Unsurprisingly, there are discrepancies between the genealogies mentioned in various sources. Kings are mentioned here who are missing elsewhere.

About Rajendra himself, these Thiruvalangadu inscriptions paint a picture of a dynamic, fearless, ambitious man whose anger against his enemies resulted in disastrous outcomes for them. And yet, he had a delicate path to tread, stepping out of his father's shadow, asserting his own personality and achievements, without in any way undermining him. Rajaraja had set the bar sky high, and Rajendra had to—and did—resort to extraordinary measures to surpass his father and establish his own credentials.

Very early into his reign, sometime in the year 1018, he appointed his oldest son, Rajadhiraja as his yuvaraja.[4] Just as Rajendra had shared the responsibilities of running the kingdom with his father Rajaraja, so too did Rajadhiraja with Rajendra, for over twenty-five years. Appointing his son so early in his rule was a way to ensure that there was no succession dispute, and also that the next emperor, when he occupied the throne, was a seasoned ruler who would pick up the reins seamlessly. At the same time, Rajendra was smart enough to make the effort to ensure that the other princes, both those directly in the line of succession as well as further degrees of separation away, were kept occupied and would thus be less inclined to intrigue and insurgency. They were given appointments and positions of responsibility and whether it was because they were satisfactorily occupied or that they were disinclined to upset the status quo, but there was no attempt at a coup and Rajendra ruled along with Rajadhiraja with no apparent turmoil.

Rajendra had already amassed a formidable record of victories during his father's rule, and once he became the king, he kept up the pressure on his rivals. He had an exceedingly busy first decade of rule, and among his earliest successes was in the emerald isle of Ceylon, across the waters off the coast.

Rajaraja had launched a serious attack on Ceylon, a far cry from the earlier ad hoc efforts that focussed on short-term gains with minimal involvement in internal affairs. In 1017, Rajendra set out to complete his father's conquest of Ceylon. Aggressive Chola raids into Ceylon were launched southward from Rajarata into Ruhuna. The wild southern region of Ruhuna which had eluded capture by Rajendra's predecessors, now became part of Chola territory. And probably, most gratifying of all, Rajendra was able to collect the long-coveted Pandyan royal regalia which had been left in Lankan safe-keeping around a century ago by the then Pandyan emperor Rajasimha. Rajendra's great-great-grandfather, the great Parantaka, had spared no effort in attempting to secure them for himself, but the Lankan king had escaped into the wilderness of Ruhuna, Pandyan crown jewels in tow.

By his fifth year, Rajendra claimed to have completely conquered Ceylon, a claim that has led some historians to assert that Rajendra 'completed' the conquest Rajaraja had begun. The king, Mahinda, was captured and brought to India, where he eventually died in exile. Saivite temples were built in Polonnaruwa, the Chola headquarters in Ceylon. Taxes and tolls were imposed upon merchants and artisans, but collection was haphazard and not easy to implement. But the Cholas never really consolidated their control over southern Ceylon, and from their faraway headquarters in the Kaveri delta, their control remained always tenuous.[5]

Closer to home, too, Rajendra decided he had to more fully drive home his father's victories in Kerala and the Pandya country, and just a few years into his reign, in 1018, his troops went on a rampage in these lands, seizing treasures, building a palace in Madurai that was so enormous and heavy that its weight 'made the earth unsteady', and appointing his son as his viceroy there, with the title Chola-Pandya.[6] He used his navy to subdue rebellious lords along the Malabar coast, and appointed another son as viceroy of the newly re-tamed Kerala territories. This practice of installing sons as viceroys of conquered territories was first carried out by Rajendra and followed by subsequent Chola monarchs. It ensured that these lands remained submissive and manageable, under the control of a trusted family member.

The Western Chalukyas who ruled over much of the western Deccan, were led at the time by their king Jayasimha. They continued to trouble the Cholas and there was much fighting with both sides resorting to gross exaggerations and declaring minor gains as major victories. There must have been a lot of brutal fighting, many lives lost. The Thiruvalangadu Plates describe it rather alarmingly: 'The sides of the ample breasts of the ladies of the Ratta (Western Chalukya) king who was cut to pieces were destitute of ornaments (as they had been widowed) but nevertheless became as brilliant and beautiful as before with shining pearls (which were their tears).'[7]

There was trouble brewing on the eastern flank as well, in Vengi country. The year was 1019. Rajendra's brother-in-law—his sister Kundavai's husband—Vimaladitya, whose family had gained the Vengi throne thanks to Rajaraja's diplomatic machinations, was no longer king, either because he had died or stepped down. The heir to the throne was Vimaladitya's son Rajaraja Narendra. Rajaraja Narendra was very closely bound to Rajendra in a tight web of familial ties. His mother, Kundavai, was Rajendra's sister, and his wife, Ammanga, was Rajendra's daughter.

The transfer of power to Rajaraja Narendra was anything but smooth. Like almost every king of those times, Vimaladitya had multiple wives and sons. Rajaraja Narendra was his son through the Chola line; he was Rajendra's direct nephew as well as son-in-law and therefore had his complete backing and support. However, there were other sons, too. The Western Chalukya king Jayasimha II who had his ear to the ground saw that he could turn things to his favour. He poured his efforts into placing another son, Vijayaditya, on the Vengi throne. In order to execute his plan, he crossed the Tungabhadra River into Vengi territory and occupied Bellary. His favoured candidate for king, Vijayaditya, captured Vijayawada.

Rajaraja Narendra's ascension to the throne had been thwarted and his prospects looked bleak. Naturally, he appealed to his uncle and father-in-law Rajendra, for help.

Rajendra, who did nothing in half measures, responded with a two-pronged attack, sending armies to both the east and west. Rajendra's armies defeated both Jayasimha's and Vijayaditya's forces, and the Vengi crown was finally handed over to Rajaraja Narendra in 1022. Once on the throne, he ruled for four decades.

Not satisfied with this, Rajendra's army continued north to Kalinga whose ruler had sided with Jayasimha against Rajendra. Revenge had to be obtained. He enjoyed a string of victories along the way as his troops travelled through the Vengi, Kalinga, and Odda (part of modern-day Odisha) kingdoms. After these successes, the army swept further northward on a grand victory march.

Having consolidated the territories closer to him, he set his sights where no Chola army had ventured: northern India. In the most spectacular land expedition undertaken by the Chola forces, his troops made their way all the way to the Ganga, far to the north. Along the way they had victories in Kalinga and over the Pala kingdom of Bengal. Well pleased with their successes, his men collected tank-loads of holy Ganga water and had it transported all the way down to southern India in vessels of gold. This, his 'liquid pillar of victory', was a hugely important and symbolic triumph, the 'conquest' of the holiest river in the land, something that even his great father had not done![8] Rajendra himself did not make the journey to the Ganga. He turned south and met his victorious troops on the banks of the Godavari River. His meykkirtis mention that this event took place in his eleventh year as ruler, which makes it 1023.

Rajendra's triumphal expedition to the Ganga was the reason for the name of his new capital city: Gangaikondacholapuram—the City of the Chola who conquered the Ganga. This was stretching the truth, because he had not actually conquered or captured the river, nor any territory along it. His armies had merely reached the river and brought back enormous quantities of sacred water which he used to consecrate his new capital and a temple, some 60 kilometres to the north and east of Thanjavur. Construction was completed seventeen years into his reign, in 1029. The city was surrounded by a large rectangular wall which, in turn, was surrounded by a moat. The royalty and military and administrative elite lived within the town walls, and everybody else lived outside.

Today, nothing remains of the town except for a large foundation which must have been where the palace stood. It must have been a grand building made of brick, with polished wooden pillars that rested on granite bases.[9] Unfortunately, the bricks used for this palace as well as other buildings in Rajendra's city have been systematically pilfered. In fact, the locals boast that they have never needed a brick kiln, so well supplied have they been with bricks from the grand old city.[10] We can only use our imagination to conjure up the glory of the place, aided by the words of Ottakoothar, court poet to three twelfth-century Chola kings:

> Palace entrance, mansions, avenues,
> temples, pavilions, balconies,
> ornamental gateways,
> windows, verandahs, upper storeys,
> dancing halls and platforms
> were filled with palace women,
> with crowds of people
> so that the very landscape around
> was made invisible to the eye.[11]

Around 300 metres to the west of the town, Rajendra created an enormous artificial lake that was called Chola Ganga. It was 25 kilometres long and 5 kilometres wide, which makes it the largest man-made lake in India to this day. Into this, he poured the water from the Ganga. The water from the nearby Kollidam

River, as well as the rain, fed it, and it was connected to the palace moat.[12]

Gangaikondacholapuram was built on land that was not particularly fertile or well-populated, and was chosen by Rajendra as a place to create his township from scratch, unimpeded by any existing development. It was a place that was unknown, lacking in any significance symbolic or otherwise. Thanjavur had served the Cholas well as their capital city for well over a hundred years. Rajaraja had invested enormous resources to build the grandest temple in the realm, the magnificent Rajarajeshwara or Brihadeeshwara, in the heart of Thanjavur. So why did he choose this location? Speculations abound.

Perhaps this was the place from where his northern campaigns were launched, making its position and name symbolically fitting. Or Rajendra sought a clean slate, an area that was strategically and deliberately removed from the factious politics of Thanjavur. Or, he wanted to make his own mark, untouched by his father's aura and memory and show the world that he, Rajendra, was the greatest king of all.

Gangaikondacholapuram remained the Chola capital, controlling the affairs of a good deal of south India, for over two centuries. It faded into obscurity as the Chola star dimmed. Today it is a dusty little town with little to show for its years of eminence. Surrounding it are paddy fields, and villages that bear names that hold the memories of times and people long gone.

Along with his new city, Rajendra built a monumental temple to Siva which was called Rajendracholiswaram or Gangaikondacholeswaram. This massive undertaking that involved the mobilizing of staggering amounts of money, materials, and labour, came barely two decades after Rajaraja's own mammoth construction.

The Gangaikondacholeswaram Temple stood—and stands—outside the town walls. Like the Brihadeeshwara Temple, it is built of stone and, undoubtedly, the same craftsmen were commissioned to work on both temples.[13] It has been presumed that the town and temple came up at the same time, although there is no epigraphical evidence to prove this. In fact, one of the earliest records that refer to arrangements for the temple comes a full six years after the first reference to the city, in 1035, from an inscription by Rajendra's third son, Virarajendra. From these, we know that Rajendra, and his sons after him, made large grants of land and villages to the temple. A number of these villages had been donated by Rajendra's father, Rajaraja, to his own grand temple at Thanjavur. Clearly, Rajendra meant to sever ties with the old Thanjavur milieu and divert resources to his own newly established temple and town.

Rajendra's Gangaikondacholeswaram Temple was modelled after the grand Brihadeeshwara Temple. While similar in some respects, it has distinct features that set it apart. Its vimana, or tower, over the sanctum sanctorum, rises in a gently curved slope, less dramatic than its sharply soaring counterpart in Thanjavur. The inner shrine has the same dimensions as Brihadeeshwara, but falls short in height at 160 feet, a full 60 feet shorter.[14] The lingam, 13 feet in height, is the tallest in all of India; the ambulatory passage around it is plain, without the rich trove of paintings that tell many a story in Thanjavur. The walls and niches teem with the most wonderful stone sculptures. The impression is one of a soft femininity, compared to the robust masculinity of the Thanjavur Temple.

Rajendra's grand Gangaikondacholeswaram Temple was consecrated by his religious guru, Sarvasiva Pandita. This same guru built a temple in Esalam, a little village near Villipuram in South Arcot district. In 1987, a group of villagers who were doing some renovation work in the grounds of this temple stumbled upon a treasure trove of bronze idols and a copperplate charter, all carefully buried in a deep pit. Scholars believe that they were buried during the invasions by the armies of the Delhi Sultanate between 1310 and 1350 that took place in that area. The copperplate charter, dated 1,036, was issued by Rajendra, and is one of three that have been found so far from his region. It records the creation of a brahmadeya and a gift of money to 1080 Brahmins. This charter is important for all the usual reasons, providing genealogical details and listing military and other exploits. But most of all, it stands out because it contains the only epigraphical evidence from Rajendra's reign about the construction of his new capital city and the Gangaikondacholeswaram Temple.[15] Curiously, there are no inscriptions of Rajendra's on the walls of this temple, at least none that have survived.

The Gangaikondacholeswaram Temple succumbed to the ravages of time and circumstances. When it was first surveyed and documented in the nineteenth century, it was in a state of disrepair, overgrown with vegetation, with parts of the enclosing wall and entrance gopuram broken and missing.

◆

With all his conquests Rajendra had succeeded in suppressing those who posed a threat to his power. However, there was another lurking menace, a major competitor for the profits of the extremely lucrative maritime routes between China and the countries of the Persian Gulf. This was the powerful Srivijaya kingdom, over 3,000 kilometres away across the Bay of Bengal in modern Sumatra, Indonesia.

These were excellent times for sea trade. Two new dynasties had risen to power: the Fatimids in Egypt, and the Song in China, and both were deeply invested in maritime trade. The markets and ports of China became some of the most lucrative places for international commerce, and almost every power in Asia wanted to be a part of it. Chinese porcelain and silk were highly coveted, and the Chinese in turn coveted a range of goods, from horses to spices.[16] Between the two, in prime position right at the centre of the bustling maritime Silk Route was Rajendra, who controlled all the major seaports along the southeastern coast of India. In the early days of this sea trade, ships stopped in the ports of both southern India and Southeast

Asia, to refuel, restock, offload, and sell. These stopovers were a rich source of revenue for the ports. As shipbuilding technology became more advanced, many ships needed to make just one stop on the journey between Egypt and China. They would have to choose between one of the Chola ports and those of Srivijaya kingdom. Naturally, both powers were keen that their ports be utilized, and any semblance of friendship and cooperation was cast aside as tensions arose.

Rajendra was hardly one to avoid head-on confrontations, but he was also adept at playing the diplomatic game, particularly if there were commercial interests involved. There are several inscriptions, from early in his reign, that show that there was at least the facade of friendship and accommodation between him and the Srivijaya kingdom. They record the gifts of an expensive emerald-and-ruby encrusted jewel, several types of lamps, and a deity to Rajendra. The inscriptions seem to suggest that there was a representative of the Srivijaya king who was permanently posted in the Chola kingdom taking care of his king's interests in south India.[17]

Rajendra had his sights set on the maritime trade between China and India as well as the countries to the west. The Srivijaya kingdom, right in the middle of the sea route between coastal China and the Chola ports was, as we've seen, a powerful thalassocracy. It was driven primarily by trade and commerce; it was not an empire that produced grand monuments or soul-melting poetry and until a century ago, scholars were unaware that such a kingdom had existed. Its proximity to and control of the Straits of Malacca, a vital transit sealink connecting the trade routes of the east and west, gave rise to its own shipping industry, and a slew of ports along its coasts. Their own goods, like pine resin, perfumes, and drugs, were coveted, particularly in the courts of China.

The shortest sea route from China to the Chola ports was through the Straits of Malacca, which was under Srivijaya authority. In 1016, soon after Rajendra came to power, the

Srivijaya empire enjoyed a major victory over the Javans. Their capital, Mataram, was seized, and the Sunda Straits, an alternate China–India sea route came under Srivijayan control allowing that kingdom to tax the ships and shipments that stopped along the way.

A web of tension and intrigue, and a veneer of friendship linked these three powers. While presenting lavish gifts to the Cholas, the Srivijayans, realizing that a strong China–Chola relationship was a threat to their own position, took to underhanded moves to undermine the Cholas' status. They insinuated to the Chinese that the Cholas were not quite the great power they were claiming to be, and indeed, were subordinate to them.

Their tactic appears to have worked. Chola trade missions to the Song court were received with the status accorded to tributary kingdoms of second-rate military power. An official in the Song court explained that they wrote to the Chola ruler on 'coarse paper with an envelope of plain stuff' because of his status as a subject of the Srivijaya kingdom.[18] The Song regime treated the various trade and diplomatic missions that made their way to its court according to how they perceived their military strength. The highly ranked ones received favourable trading privileges and enhanced diplomatic status.

Srivijaya engaged the Orang Laut, a tribe of sea nomads who lived along their coasts to patrol the waters and create trouble for the Chola ships that came their way. The Orang Laut forced all passing ships to dock at Srivijaya ports and pay customs taxes and resupply there.[19] Once stocked, ships could continue sailing on to Arab lands and other countries to the west without needing to stop at Chola ports. This deprived the Cholas of valuable income. There was no way that Rajendra would take this lying down. The Srivijayans needed to be taught a lesson and be brought under control.

There were further geopolitical convolutions involved. Srivijaya had an ally in the fellow Buddhist kingdom of

Tambralinga (in southern Thailand). This had not always been the case: Tambralinga had attempted to extricate itself from the Srivijaya chokehold so it could enjoy more of the rewards of trade with Song China, but soon realized that the competition was too intense, and that it was better off hanging on to Srivijaya coat-tails. At the same time, the Angkor kingdom of Cambodia was friendly with the Cholas. Suryavarman, the Angkor king, had presented Rajendra with a war chariot with which he had defeated his own enemies.[20] This grand gesture was probably made to secure Rajendra's friendship and protection.

The Angkor and Tambralinga kingdoms were at loggerheads with each other, and the Angkor king Suryavarman sought Rajendra's assistance. Rajendra was only too happy to oblige, probably well aware of how the situation would unfold. When the Cholas declared war on Tambralinga, the Srivijaya emperor could not stand by quietly. He, in turn, declared war on the Cholas and the Angkor king, matters escalated. This could have been one more reason for Rajendra to launch mighty raids on the Srivijaya ports.

In 1025, Rajendra sent a naval fleet to attack Srivijaya. A small decoy force was sent to the Malacca Strait at the northern end of Sumatra, where they were met by the waiting Srivijaya fleet, which assumed that this was the entire attacking contingent. In the meantime, a second much bigger fleet headed south, and around Sumatra through the Sunda Straits, to the major Srivijaya city of Palembang on the southeast coast. Facing no major opposition, they seized and sacked the city. The ships then sneaked up on the Srivijaya fleet from behind and the combined Chola forces enjoyed an easy victory. They next laid siege to Kadaram, an important administrative and trade centre on the Malay Peninsula and captured it. With the Srivijaya kingdom effectively subdued, the Chola forces took on Tambralinga and brought it into line, to the satisfaction of the Angkor king.[21]

Rajendra's invasion of Srivijaya was brutal. His inscriptions boast about his victories and the sacking of their ports.

An inscription on the walls of the central shrine of the Brihadeeshwara Temple says: 'Having despatched many ships in the midst of the rolling sea and having caught Sangrama-Vijayottunga-Varman, the king of Kadaram, together with his rutting elephants, took the large heap of treasures which that king had rightfully accumulated, the (arch called) Vidhyadhara-torana at the war gate of his extensive city, Srivijaya with the jeweled wicket gate and the gate of large jewels.'[22] The inscription goes on to list twelve more port cities of the Srivijaya kingdom Rajendra's navy had raided.

Interestingly, however, the Chinese did not seem to have been aware of any of this. Srivijaya traders and rulers continued to enjoy enhanced privileges, and the Chola's trading relationship with Song China remained unchanged. In 1033, Rajendra dispatched a trade emissary and a convoy of ships bearing gifts to the Song emperor, in order to strengthen ties. We have no further details about this, but excavations at Gangaikondacholapuram have unearthed porcelain potsherds of the finest quality Chinese porcelain, as well as pieces of glass bangles of various colours; these might have been brought from China by the envoys sent by Rajendra.[23]

It wasn't until nearly a century later that Chola traders were able to establish themselves in China and create a diaspora there, even building a temple to Siva in Quanzhou in the coastal Fujian province in southeastern China.[24]

Whatever the motivations behind Rajendra's attack on the Srivijaya ports—suppressing their growing power and influence on the maritime trade networks, plundering the riches of the kingdom, or flexing his naval muscle—Chola rule was never established over these lands. They set up military garrisons and bullied the now chastened empires into acquiescing to their demands and requirements, but that was it. Their presence and soft power in the region helped the trade guilds from Tamil lands, which thrived and enjoyed growth in trade. There were marital alliances: Rajendra married the Srivijaya king Sangrama

Visaiyottunga's daughter.[25] This was most probably done to seal friendly relationships through familial ties. Half a century later, Rajendra's grandson Kulothunga intervened in a succession dispute in Kadaram, launching a successful attack there and installing a Chola-descended (puppet) king on the throne.[26] No records have been found of Chola presence there, and a few years after Rajendra's raid the two powers drifted back into a state of cordial harmony or, at least, the appearance of it.

Rajendra died in 1044, and would most likely have been content that the kingdom that he worked so hard to grow and maintain was in the good hands of his son Rajadhiraja. One of his queens, Viramadevi, committed sati and was buried with his remains.[27]

It was a commonly held belief in those times that the spirit of a dead person was possessed of an extraordinary thirst that had to be appeased with the presence of a water storage facility like a watershed, tank, or well near their grave. One of Rajadhiraja's inscriptions from 1044 mentions the gift of a piece of land in a village called Brahmadesam in Thiruvannamalai district by a general named Madurantakan Parakesarivelar. This land was to be used to create and maintain a watershed in order to appease the thirsty spirit of the general's sister, Viramadevi. The inscription also mentioned that Viramadevi entered the supreme feet of Brahma (died) in the same tomb in which the body of her husband, the emperor Rajendra Chola, was buried. This is how we know with a fair amount of certainty, that Rajendra Chola died in 1044, that his wife Viramadevi committed sati and her remains were buried with him, and that they were buried in the village of Brahmadesam in Thiruvannamalai district.

Rajendra's modest samadhi in Brahmadesam is maintained today by the Archaeological Survey of India.[28] It lies 26 kilometres west of Kanchipuram, off the Chennai–Bangalore highway. A narrow one-lane road lined with thorny shrubs goes past emerald-green paddy fields and terrain that is mostly devoid of habitation. In this quiet landscape there appears a fence and gate, and beyond, a little mud road that leads to the patch of land, bare but for a scattering of trees, on which stand a small mandapam and temple to Siva. It is a memorial temple, and no religious rituals are performed here. The walls of the temple, made of large blocks of stone, are covered with inscriptions. Inside are two lingams, commemorating the great king and his wife.

This humble, nondescript site, mostly visited by a handful of ardent scholars, is the memorial to one of the world's greatest emperors.

The closing years of Rajendra's reign saw the Chola empire at the peak of its power and prestige. The success that he and his father enjoyed on the heels of the Rashtrakuta collapse resulted in their subjugating the Pandyas and the Cheras, advancing hundreds of kilometres into the Deccan, unseating the rulers of Lanka, the 'conquest' of the Ganga, and his bold operation against Srivijaya. Chola military and naval prowess were renowned. Even so, keeping a tight rein over so many far-flung areas, many of them socially and culturally distinct, was challenging. Loyalties were tenuous and there were attempts to break free by several chieftains who had been corralled into the Chola fold. There were constant outbreaks of fighting that had to be quelled.

CHAPTER 20

THE KING WHO DIED ON THE BACK OF AN ELEPHANT

RAJAKESARI RAJADHIRAJA (R. 1044–1054)

> This king had three sons, comparable with the three fires in a yagna. Of these, the preeminent Rajadhiraja was his first son. He set fire to Kalyanapura and defeated its king....[1]

Rajadhiraja was Rajendra's oldest son. He was appointed yuvaraja very early in his father's reign and spent over quarter of a century as his junior partner. In 1044, when his father died, Rajadhiraja stepped into the role of Chola king. He was the first Chola to be crowned king at Gangaikondacholapuram, which remained the Chola capital till the empire faded away.

Even though he ruled an extensive empire with a large administrative machinery in place, his was a life of constant warfare, and his role was more commander-in-chief than king. He had his hands full keeping together an unwieldy empire that had grown on the backs of an assortment of old ruling clans and chieftains who had never fully reconciled themselves to the role of Chola subordinates.

The Western Chalukyas were the biggest threat to the Cholas at this time; they were led by Ahavamalla Someshwara I. The two kingdoms fought several battles, each side desperately clawing for supremacy.

The battles were brutal and filled with cruel and punitive measures designed to humiliate, disgrace, and crush. In one instance, a high-ranking Chalukya official was dispatched to deliver a hostile message to the Cholas. Two people who accompanied this official were the butt of all manner of crude insults. One was forced to shave his head, leaving behind five tufts of hair; the other was made to dress like a woman. Dubbed the 'miserable Ahavamalli and Ahavamalla' (Queen and King Someshwara)[2] they were sent packing, no doubt to the jeers of the Cholas, along with the high-ranking official.

At a battle fought at Dannada on the banks of the river Krishna, Someshwara's army faced another humiliating defeat and was forced to retreat. Several leading Chalukya warriors were killed, as were a large number of their elephants. Vast amounts of valuable treasure, horses, and elephants fell into Chola hands. More Chola victories followed, with the Western Chalukya capital, Kalyanapuram, falling into Chola hands in 1045. Rajadhiraja's troops destroyed this ancient city and gutted its royal palace. Flushed with triumph, Rajadhiraja anointed himself Vijayarajendra and performed a virabhishekam, an elaborate victory ritual.

Over a century later, some of the spoils of this battle at Kalyanapuram would find their way to the magnificent Airavateshwara Temple built by a later ruler Rajaraja II, at Darasuram. One of them was a door guardian, a dwarapalaka that stood out for being in a style that was distinctly un-Chola-like. Made of black stone, the four-armed guardian leaned on a heavy club up which a lizard crawled. In his hands were a trident and a snake, and all around the figure was a veritable menagerie of animals. Chalukya objects like these, the spoils of war, might have been kept in Rajadhiraja's royal palace, or another temple, until Rajaraja II chose to display these war trophies in his temple at Darasuram. Today that dwarapala stands detached from its former home and is displayed at the Thanjavur Art Gallery, an interloper among the plethora of Chola works of art.[3]

However, the Western Chalukyas still retained vestiges of their power, and continued to create trouble in the eastern Vengi region. One of Someshwara's sons went so far as to call himself Vengi Puravareshwara (lord of Vengi).[4] His inscriptions continued to appear in Chalukya territories along the Tungabhadra.

All this while, there was unrest and trouble brewing across the water in Ceylon. Rajadhiraja's father might have proclaimed that he was successful in annexing the whole of Ilamandalam (Ceylon), but the reality was that the years following his attack were filled with insurrections and counter-reprisals on the part of the Ceylonese subjects and their Chola overlords. The Chola hold over the entire island lasted a mere ten years. Prince Kassapa, the son of the deposed king Mahinda who had been captured by Rajendra and had died in India, had fled into hiding in the southern province of Ruhuna. Here he gave himself a new title: Vikkamabahu I, and ruled the region for several years, all the while managing to elude capture by the Cholas. He poured his efforts into organizing a campaign for the liberation and unification of his island but died before his attempts bore fruit.[5] Every ruler that came after was consumed by the burning desire to rid their domain of the Cholas, and the struggle was particularly intense during the rule of Rajadhiraja. For the most part, matters went badly for the rulers of Ceylon, but there were massive losses of lives on both sides.

In 1054, by which time he was quite advanced in years, Rajadhiraja fought his final battle. This was against the Cholas' long-time foes, the Chalukyas, who were led by their king Someshwara I. What provoked this battle was the Chola invasion, led by Rajadhiraja, of Rattamandalam, the very heartland of the Chalukya kingdom. Following him and leading his southern flank was his brother Rajendra II. The Chola and Chalukya forces met at Koppam, a town near the Tungabhadra River (in modern Karnataka). The battle that was fought there was a hard and bloody one that initially went in Rajadhiraja's favour.

The tide turned swiftly when in one unguarded moment atop his elephant, Rajadhiraja was felled by a volley of arrows from the enemy camp. The terror of the Deccan died a hero's death on the battlefield and he came to be known as the 'king who died on the back of an elephant'.[6]

Panicked and in total disarray, the Chola army beat a

terror-stricken retreat. The Chalukyas seemed assured of a resounding victory, but Rajendra II, who had been bringing up the rear, pressed forward, launching a surprise strike on the attacking Chalukyas. Once again, the combat was fierce and brutal. Rajendra II was badly wounded and he lost some of his best soldiers. Undaunted, he fought on, killing several leading warriors on the Chalukya side and eventually, his fearlessness, determination, and doggedness paid off. The Chalukya army capitulated under the relentless Chola attack. Their king, Someshwara I, fled. It was a brilliant military success for Rajendra II, snatched from the very jaws of disastrous defeat. *Kalingattuparani*, a twelfth-century war poem eulogizing the Chola kings, went so far as to state that with his fierce fighting and victory at Koppam, Rajendra II saved the world.[7] Another war poem (*Vikrama Sola Ula*) added its own touch of hyperbole, declaring that with the aid of a single elephant, he captured a thousand of the enemy's elephants at Koppam.[8]

At this glorious moment of victory, right on the battlefield, Rajendra II crowned himself the next Chola emperor.

CHAPTER 21

THE BATTLEFIELD KING
PARAKESARI RAJENDRA II/RAJENDRADEVA
(R. 1054–1063)

> ....his younger brother, who removed the sorrow of the world, ascended the throne. Rajendra-deva, the monarch, who had arms resembling in shape the snake Adi-Sesha, killed all his enemies.[1]

For three generations, the transfer of power had been from father to son. At this point, it turned patrilateral, from brother to brother. Rajendra II's coronation came at a moment of great personal triumph after he routed the Chalukyas in a brilliant reversal of fortune. That done, he pressed on to Kolhapur where he planted a victory flag, before returning to his capital Gangaikondacholapuram.[2]

Uprisings and battles for independence continued apace in the island province of Ilamandalam (Ceylon) and like his brother and father before him, Rajendra II had to invest considerable effort in suppressing these rebellions. The Cholas adopted ever more savage means of crushing the Ceylonese—decapitation and mutilation, even against the women of the Ceylon royal family, were not uncommon. Rajendra II's inscriptions mention his dispatching an army to Ceylon, where the king Vira Salamegha was decapitated, and his sons taken prisoner. This unfortunate king and his sister, mother, and wife had earlier suffered disgrace and humiliation in the aftermath of a hot battle fought against the forces of Rajendra II's brother, Rajadhiraja.[3]

Chola coins and inscriptions from the reigns of Rajadhiraja and Rajendra II have been found in Ceylon, indicating that for all the relentless fighting, this region was still a Chola province.[4]

The fighting against the Western Chalukyas continued unabated into Rajendra II's reign. The Chalukya king Ahavamalla Someswara was eager to avenge his humiliating defeat at Koppam. The year was 1062. Someswara gathered his forces and advanced to Kudal Sangamam, a place that was likely at the confluence of the Tungabhadra and Krishna rivers. The Chola army included many of its princes, including Rajendra II's son, Rajamahendra, and brother, Virarajendra. Virarajendra's inscriptions boast of how the Cholas slew the army chief, cut off his head, and disfigured the nose and face of his only daughter, who was as lovely as a peacock.[5]

It was a stirring victory for the Chola side. Their inscriptions describe how Ahavamalla Someshwara and his two sons were sent fleeing, with dishevelled hair and battered pride.[6] Someshwara's wives, family treasures, and all the paraphernalia of royalty—the conches, parasols, trumpets, drums, canopies, and more—were seized with glee by the Cholas.

There was a short period during which Rajendra II's son Rajamahendra might have ruled as king or as co-king alongside his father. He might have been earmarked for kingship, but the consensus is that he lost his life in one of the many battles that were fought in his lifetime. The crown went to Rajendra II's younger brother, Virarajendra.

CHAPTER 22

BLOOD AND DIPLOMACY
RAJAKESARI VIRARAJENDRA (R.1063–1070)

> ...Virarajendra, who caused the valour of his enemies to wane, succeeded to the throne with due formality. He conquered not only his outside enemies, but also his own five senses.[1]

Virarajendra was the third son of Rajendra to become king, and his ascension to the throne after years of being dominated by his older brothers, when he was well into middle age, came at a time of crisis and uncertainty. Though short, there wasn't a dull moment during Virarajendra's reign of seven years—a soap-opera style family drama was unfolding. The fates of the Cholas, Eastern Chalukyas (Vengi), and Western Chalukyas were bound together in a web of alliances and intrigue that was knotty and complex and a challenge to keep track of. The Vengis, often pawns in the Chola–Western Chalukya power struggle, bore the brunt.

The Western Chalukya king Someshwara had suffered a mortifying defeat at the battle of Kudal Sangamam and was eager for revenge. Telling himself that it was 'better to die than to live in disgrace' he sent a message to Virarajendra inviting him to battle at the same spot—Kudal Sangamam—where he and his troops had endured the ignominy of annihilation. He added in his message that whoever failed to show up was unworthy of being king, and would be considered a disgraced outcaste.[2]

Virarajendra was greatly pleased to receive this message and, armed and ready, set out for the appointed location, where he waited for a full month beyond the date that had been fixed by Someshwara. Chola accounts claim that the Chalukya king ran and hid himself in the western ocean, while Virarajendra rampaged through the country, setting fire to towns and planting a pillar of victor on the banks of the Tungabhadra. He made an effigy of Someshwara and subjected it to all manner of indignities.[3]

Why would Someshwara issue an invitation to battle and then fail to show up, making him the very subject of the disgrace he had warned of? The only satisfactory explanation, mentioned in a poem by Bilhana, the court poet of Someshwara I's son Vikramaditya, is that Someshwara suffered from an incurable disease and that it was this illness that prevented him from keeping his battlefield appointment with his Chola foe.[4]

Someshwara I died in 1068, and his eldest son, Someshwara II, became king of the Western Chalukyas. His reign lasted for eight years and there was hardly a moment's peace. His younger brother, Vikramaditya, was ambitious, aggressive, and ruthless and wanted the Western Chalukya throne for himself. Many battles were fought among all of them, with fortune favouring first one side, then the other.

To add to Virarajendra's problems, Vikramaditya also had his sights set on the Chola domains. Virarajendra, sensing that matters might end badly for him, sent an olive branch to Vikramaditya, adopting the time-tested method of securing a matrimonial alliance. He offered his daughter in marriage to him. He then helped Vikramaditya wrest a portion of the Western Chalukya kingdom from his brother Someshwara II, who was eventually imprisoned, and possibly executed thereafter.

A truce was reached with the Cholas. Vikramaditya married Virarajendra's daughter and retreated to the Tungabhadra, which was tacitly accepted as the Chola–Chalukya boundary. Vikramaditya, who had been the object of contempt in Virarajendra's inscriptions, was now presented in a more respectable light as befitted someone of favoured royal status. In backing and establishing his own candidate on the Chalukya throne, Virarajendra succeeded in shifting the dynamic with his family's longstanding foes. Finally, after countless battles and innumerable lives lost, glimmers of peace appeared on the Chola–Chalukya horizon.[5]

Virarajendra fought battles in the Vengi region as well, crushing the ruler and capturing much valuable territory. This he put in charge of a Vengi prince called Vijayaditya, securing his loyalty and tightening ties with this region. Virarajendra's crafty manoeuvring between his empire's rivals spoke of a keen political intellect. His actions would have major repercussions for the Cholas in the years to come.

Hardly had this been done than things started to fall apart. Virarajendra died in 1070, a mere eight years into his reign, plunging the Chola state into utter confusion and anarchy. History might have taken a very different course had Virarajendra not died so soon after the Vengi and Western Chalukya settlement.

Virarajendra's court poets took to grandiloquent flights of the imagination in their portrayal of their king as an extraordinary player in the theatres of war and statecraft. His best known inscriptions are on a group of pillars at the ancient seaside temple at Kanyakumari and they record a grant to a goddess at the temple there. These provide a great many details about Chola genealogy, mythical, quasi-historic, as well as historic, and have particulars that are not found elsewhere, outdoing the Thiruvalangadu plates in naming no fewer than fifty-two legendary Chola ancestors. There is an imaginative account of the first Chola king, proposing that he brought the first Brahmins from the Aryan country in the north and settled them on the banks of the Kaveri, thus establishing and reinforcing an ancient Chola connection to the Kaveri delta.

The verses wend their way through a fantastic array of characters and incidents, and the story of the first Chola king to establish himself along the banks of the Kaveri could have been plucked straight out of the Ramayana. It goes thus: once, a long time ago, a king went hunting after a deer who was actually a rakshasa (demon) in disguise. The chase led him far down south to a land filled with forests of tall trees and a great river—the Kaveri. Here the king slew the deer-demon, after which he bathed in the holy waters of the Kaveri. This done, he looked about for Brahmins to confer gifts to, to celebrate his victory, but found none. He then brought some Brahmins down south from Aryavarta, the land of nobles and people of excellence mentioned in ancient Hindu scriptures. These Brahmins proclaimed the Kaveri to be a river of equal if not greater holiness than the Ganga. The king and the Brahmins established themselves in this new domain and the implication is that this king's descendants form the Chola line.[6] This tale brings into its fold all the necessary elements that lay a spiritual foundation for the legitimacy of the Cholas' presence in these lands.

The Kanyakumari inscriptions then proceed to actual history, describing the many victories enjoyed by Virarajendra's ancestors as they elevated Chola glory to ever greater heights. Virarajendra's own achievements are here—the many battles against the Chalukyas (in which he 'saw the back' of Ahavamalla Someshwara no fewer than five times), his victories in Vengi, Kerala, Ceylon, and against the Pandyas.[7]

The earliest inscriptions at the Chola capital's Gangaikondacholeswaram Temple were made by Virarajendra. They go into painstaking detail about the arrangements made by his father ('who was pleased to conquer the eastern country, the Ganga and Kadaram'), and later his brother ('my elder brother, who conquered Kalyana and Kolhapur, and died on the back of an elephant') to corral an extensive network of villages into directing their revenues to maintain and run the great temple at Gangaikondacholapuram. Virarajendra convened a grand darbar at Kanchipuram in early 1069 with a large cohort of the Cholamandalam elite at the ready to perform a range of bureaucratic functions. These inscriptions form the record of that darbar. They are among his longest inscriptions, running to over

200 lines, and provide insights into how Rajendra went about gathering support and finances for his temple since we have no record from Rajendra himself.[8] Most of the lands and villages whose proceeds were to be donated to Gangaikondacholapuram had been assigned for the same purpose by Rajaraja for his grand temple. It seems that his motive was to promote his own temple to the detriment of his father's. The men responsible for carrying out the order were listed, from which we get an idea of the composition of the bureaucracy, which is largely from the Cholamandalam elite, including landowners and Brahmins.

Virarajendra's reign might have been one of bloody battles and unremitting pressure, but that did not mean that he ignored the needs of his subjects. An inscription made five years into his reign at a village called Thirumukkudal mentions the charity works done by the local temple, which included an institution called the Jananatha Mandapa, in which there was a school for Vedic studies, a hostel for its students, and a hospital. The students were well cared for, and were provided with food, bathing oil every Saturday, and oil for their lamps. Similarly, the hospital, called Virasolan after the emperor, had fifteen beds, and was well staffed and provided for. A good quantity of rice was kept for the patients; there was a doctor on staff, a surgeon, servants who fetched drugs and fuel and performed a variety of other services, and maids to care for the patients. Cardamom-scented water was given to everybody in the Jananatha Mandapa, and a supply of cow's ghee for making the traditional medicines of the time was ensured.[9] Temple funds were used not merely for rituals and processions, but these very earthly needs as well.

CHAPTER 23

A FLASH IN THE PAN
PARAKESARI ATHIRAJENDRA
(R. 1070–1070)

Virarajendra must have died thinking that he had set things up to ensure that his son had a smooth succession and would enjoy a peaceful reign. He had done the inconceivable in securing good relations with both the Western Chalukyas and the Vengi rulers.

As it turned out, Athirajendra's reign might have been the shortest in Chola history. There was anarchy in the kingdom after his father died, and Athirajendra's position as ruler was far from secure. His sister was married to the Western Chalukya prince Vikramaditya and, as such, the latter might have felt compelled to lend him his support and assistance. Vikramaditya made his way to Kanchipuram and subdued the rebellion that had broken out after the death of Virarajendra. He succeeded in securing the Chola throne for Athirajendra. That done, he returned to his capital and set about winning the loyalty of several local princes. Eventually, his tactics bore fruit when he defeated and captured his brother Someshwara and became the Western Chalukya king in 1076.[1]

The Chola peace, such as it was, was extremely short-lived. A fresh rebellion broke out in Kanchipuram, and Athirajendra was killed. His stint as king was over almost as soon as it began, lasting barely a few weeks.[2]

With his death came the end of the male line of Tamil Chola rulers. How did he die? Who killed him? Unsurprisingly there is little clarity and several possibilities have been suggested. One was that his killer was the person who became the next Chola ruler—the Vengi king Rajiga—who would go on to assume the name Kulothunga. Another is that he was killed by the Chola military establishment (perhaps on behalf of Kulothunga), who refused to accept him as their ruler because they regarded him as weak and ineffectual. A third theory goes that the great Vaishnava philosopher Ramanuja was persecuted by Athirajendra and his people, and that he was killed during a revolt by the Vaishnavas. That it was his intolerance that cast a curse upon the Cholas, putting an end to that illustrious lineage.[3]

The Chola throne now passed on to a person who, according to the protocol of the day, was not really entitled to it; his was a matrilineal connection, and his true heritage was the Vengi throne. But history often follows its own course and Vengi now became properly and officially a part of the Chola kingdom. Another fertile riverine-agrarian territory, this one surrounding the Godavari River, came into Chola hands.

CHAPTER 24

A LUNAR KING IN THE SOLAR COURT RAJAKESARI KULOTHUNGA I (R. 1070–1120)

> As a young prince of the lunar race, as an infant lord of the solar race, he [Kulothunga] he grew up, the joy of the kings of both races, like the fruit of the virtuous deeds of his ancestors.[1]

For a short and turbulent period in the summer of 1070, the Chola empire had three kings in rapid succession. There is no certainty about what happened, whether the cycling through of kings was precipitated by civil war, political upheaval, or if it was just the natural course of events. The twelfth-century poet Jayankontar[2] who was the bard at Kulothunga's court described the state of affairs in vivid and somewhat chilling detail:

> Brahmans gave up sacrifices; the laws of Manu were not followed; the six sciences were forgotten; and the chanting of Vedic hymns. The castes mixed one with another in wild confusion; and forgetting their rules of conduct, none kept to their ancient customs...the temples of the gods were neglected; the women lost their chastity; and fortresses were destroyed.[3]

At the end of this upheaval, the throne went to one who was not in the line of succession.

From the time of Rajaraja, the daughters of the Chola kings and princes married their father's sister's sons on the Eastern Chalukya (Vengi) side, fusing the two dynasties ever more closely together. Several generations of cross-cousin marriages between the Chola and Vengi dynasties had set the stage for this moment: the ascension of a prince of the Vengi patriline and Chola matriline, crossing the invisible barrier to become the ruler of the Chola dynasty.

This prince, who was named Rajendra for his maternal grandfather, would go on to acquire the royal moniker Kulothunga. He was a prince in the Vengi (Eastern Chalukya) dynasty. His father was the Vengi king Rajaraja Narendra, the grandson of the great Rajaraja Chola, and the nephew and son-in-law of Rajendra Chola. His mother was Ammanga, Rajendra's daughter. Descended from both the moon and sun, the once-adversarial lunar Chalukya and solar Chola dynasties, he was a scion of Telugu and Tamil ancestors. His Chola lineage was from his mother, which, during that time, counted for nothing. By rights, he was a contender to the Vengi throne. And there was no dearth of male Chola heirs. Kulothunga grew up amid fractious family politics and constant internecine fighting involving a dizzying tangle of half-brothers, cousins, uncles, and in-laws from the Vengi, Western Chalukya, and Chola clans.

It took a couple of years for Kulothunga to consolidate his position as the Chola ruler, at the end of which he referred to himself and was referred to by the grand title of the Wheel Turning Emperor of the Three Worlds: Tribhuvana Chakravartikkal.[4] Hand in hand with his consolidation of power over the Chola kingdom came a new royal moniker that sealed and reaffirmed his claim to the Chola lineage: Kulothunga, the Exalter of the Races, the Star of the Family. With his ascension to the Chola throne, the opposing forces of the sun and the moon came together.

It was important that Kulothunga's legitimacy to the Chola crown be established, that he be presented and accepted as a Chola. He might have been from the Telugu-speaking lands around the Godavari River, but literary works published in his court during his reign ensured that his Tamilness was never in doubt.

Tamil poetry has produced some outlandish, if fascinating genres. One of them is the parani, which has its roots in the bardic poem tradition of the Sangam era. This is a type of war poem, 'which has for its hero a warrior who killed 700 or 1,000 male elephants on the battlefield';[5] not only does it extol war and its bloody and gruesome deeds, but also above all, it is a panegyric for the ruling dynasty and its heroic ruler.

Jayankontar was Kulothunga's court poet, and his writings established his patron's credentials both as a great ruler and warrior as well as a rightful heir to the Chola throne. He wrote a parani, a war poem called *Kalingattuparani,* in the waning years of Kulothunga's long reign. One of the earliest surviving works of Chola court poetry, it is a masterpiece of the Tamil literary canon with its expressive and spirited language. The poet's extravagant imagination makes it a poem of great visionary power, full of the comic, the grisly, the majestic, and the sensuous. It would put the modern horror novel to shame, weaving together the unlikeliest of bedfellows. Macabre and murderous demons and devils hungry for a delectable dinner of fresh corpses off the battlefield, a bloodthirsty goddess Kali and her gang of ghouls, and ladies who are ordered to stop sulking and welcome the heroes of the battle to their bed chambers are all a part of this poem. Amid this high drama is nestled the genealogy of the Cholas, where Kulothunga's illustrious ancestors like Karikala, Parantaka, Rajaraja, and, of course, Kulothunga himself, are shamelessly praised. Alongside the bloodlust and the grisly feasts prepared to order for the Brahmin, Buddhist, and Jain ghouls is a full-blown glorification of the emperor, his noble lineage and his expansionist ambitions.[6]

Kulothunga was so pleased with Jayankontar and his poem that he is said to have rolled a golden coconut to the poet's feet after each verse was recited.[7] Broadly, it is about Kulothunga's second military expedition to Kalinga and its conquest, but it also provides a wealth of information about the king's early years, information on the local vassal chiefs, and geographic details. And in this poem, Kulothunga emerges as a full-blooded Chola, solar genealogy, tiger crest and all, the rightful heir to the Chola lineage and legacy, thus far accessible only to those descended from the male line. The poem talks of Kulothunga's childhood spent at the court and palace of his (maternal) grandfather, the great Rajendra. (In reality, he was likely born only towards the very end of Rajendra's reign.) At birth, he was named Rajendra, after his illustrious grandfather. It describes the (Chola) queen's admiration when she beheld the newborn Kulothunga, proclaiming him a worthy scion of the solar line. His mother tongue was, quite literally, Tamil.

The poem tells us that Virarajendra selected and appointed him as his yuvaraja. And then, following a series of heroic conquests in areas to the north, he returned south following the death of Virarajendra, quelled the anarchy that had engulfed the kingdom, and claimed his rightful position as Chola king. Into a world where the 'darkness of Kali spread abroad, like the Sun arisen from the roaring sea to obliterate the great dark, he came, to rescue the world'.[8] Virarajendra's son was deftly omitted from the narrative, obliterated from this version of history.

An altogether different story, far less flattering to Kulothunga, was told by another poet in a rival court. The Kashmiri poet Bilhana, who served for a while in the court of the Western Chalukya emperor Vikramaditya wrote a poem called *Vikramanka Deva Charita*, a work that, naturally, extolled the virtues and exploits of his patron-king. His version of the events that took place after the death of Virarajendra is very different from that of Jayankontar's. In this telling, it was Kulothunga who, with his 'twisted mind', killed Virarajendra's son Athirajendra who had been placed on the Chola throne thanks to Vikramaditya's efforts.[9]

It is almost certain that Athirajendra did rule, for however short a while, as inscriptions in his name, Bilhana's poem, as well as other literary works, all mention Athirajendra as ruler. Jayankontar's version, in which Kulothunga merely accepted that which was offered to him—the Chola throne—was clearly an attempt to legitimize the rule of this quasi outsider, this Vengi interloper with only a matrilineal connection to the Chola seat of power.

In 1063, the year his father, Rajaraja Narendra, died, Kulothunga was anointed the Vengi ruler but fate had a much bigger role in store for him. He was a young man, barely twenty. A mere seven years later, for reasons that records are vague about, Kulothunga transferred the Chalukya sovereignty to his paternal uncle Vijayaditya and 'wishing for, being desirous of, or preferring' the Chola crown, he took over the reins of the great Chola empire.[10] An inscription from very early in his reign states that with just the strength of his arm and his sword, he overcame the treachery of his enemies. At least some of these exploits took place during the seven-year period between his father's death and his own ascension to the Chola throne.[11]

Kulothunga's ascent to the Chola throne did not take place in a sociocultural vacuum, but was, rather, the product of the very complex combination of forces and events that preceded him. He was in control of a superpower that was overextended militarily, had an amalgam of social groups who did not fit into the 'imperial' social structure, and which had a bloated, top-heavy bureaucracy. Incessant warfare, territorial alliances, and shifts in the social structure all laid the ground for an 'outsider' like Kulothunga to gain entry into the Chola universe. It was in the aftermath of a period of military victories, fruitful diplomatic scheming, and court-produced poetic rhetoric, followed by a clear jockeying for power by the cousins Athirajendra and Kulothunga (judging by the number of inscriptions in both their names, particularly in the northern Tondaimandalam region) that Kulothunga succeeded in gaining the throne that had been in the hands of his mother's relatives and ancestors. And in the end, he seized the opportunity that presented itself when the Chola emperor Athirajendra was killed in a rebellion, plunging the kingdom into anarchy and confusion.[12]

Once on the throne, Kulothunga stayed there and ruled for half a century—reigning the longest of all the Cholas.

Kulothunga spent the early years of his reign like every Chola emperor before him: fighting and sorting out the assorted troubles and enemies that beset the kingdom.

Every great king has a rival who brings out both the best and the worst in him. In Kulothunga's case it was the Western Chalukya leader Vikramaditya VI, whose life had eerie parallels with his own. Both were of Chalukya origin—one from the west, the other from the east, and both had married into the Chola network. Both felt that the Vengi lands should be theirs. Neither was the natural contender for the throne, but managed to fight their way through the opposition and went on to rule their kingdoms for half a century. They spent large portions of their reigns waging war against each other, and the first task for Kulothunga as king was to deal with Vikramaditya VI.

Vikramaditya was not pleased with the turn of events that saw Kulothunga sit on the Chola throne. He must have hoped that with marrying Virarajendra's daughter, relations with the Cholas would be good, and would remain so when his brother-in-law, Virarajendra's son Athirajendra, became king. That was not to be, and instead of a friendly face, Vikramaditya had to contend with Kulothunga, who was also too closely aligned with the Vengi kingdom. A clash between these highly ambitious young rivals was inevitable.

Kulothunga sought the friendship and support of Vikramaditya's brother, Someshwara II, who had been divested of a large portion of his kingdom thanks to the machinations of Virarajendra and Vikramaditya.

Wildly differing versions of the battles that ensued have been described in the poems of Vikramaditya's court poet Bilhana and Kulothunga's Jayankontar. Historical accuracy seemed to have been totally beside the point; the aggrandizement and exalting of their respective kings was what was probably expected of them. In Bilhana's telling of the tale, the crooked king (Kulothunga, of course) entered into an evil pact with the older brother of the noble Vikramaditya, pitting brother against brother. In the fierce fighting that ensued, the Chola side was forced to flee the field, and Someshwara was taken prisoner.[13] Vikramaditya was all set to free his brother and give him the throne that was rightfully his, but Lord Siva appeared in his dream one night and bade him assume the position for himself, which he did.[14]

The Chola account, found in inscriptions, told exactly the opposite story. It writes of the battlefield being strewn with the elephants, soldiers, lost pride, and much-vaunted valour of Vikramaditya's side. The Cholas seized much valuable territory and sent the enemy fleeing in disgrace.[15]

Piecing together evidence from inscriptions, we know that the war began with Vikramaditya marching eastwards towards Chola lands until he encountered the Chola army near Kolar (some 60 kilometres east of Bangalore). Much heavy fighting ensued, which went largely in favour of the Chola side. They collected a good deal of booty and captured the surrounding territory. Kulothunga's claim that he won possession of a good part of the Mysore region was not an empty boast, as his inscriptions have been found all over the area.[16] Sadly, poor Someshwara II did not fare as well. He was captured by his brother Vikramaditya and lost his kingdom. What became of him is uncertain; it is possible that he was killed.

In the meantime, the Chola adventure in Ceylon was winding to a close. Keeping a tight lid over the many fractious rivalries between the chieftains of the northern and southern regions (including the infamously difficult Ruhuna region to the southeast) was proving to be more than what the Cholas were able or willing to manage.

It was not a smooth departure. Complicating an already knotty situation was Vikramaditya, who propelled his ambition with crafty scheming and untiring efforts to undermine Kulothunga in any way possible. His next step was to befriend the old Chola foe, the Lanka king. This was Vijayabahu, who had just succeeded in expelling the Cholas from the northern part of his island.

The highly ambitious Vijayabahu rose to prominence in the middle of the eleventh century in the Ruhuna province. While still in his teens he defeated his rivals in the area. That done, he was all set to take on his country's most irksome foes, the Cholas. Both Vijayabahu and the Cholas had to contend with an agglomeration of hostile local chiefs from around the island. It was impossible to know who was on which side as loyalties switched back and forth with dizzying speed.[17]

In the midst of the thick mess of treachery and fighting, Vikramaditya sent his envoys to Vijayabahu, laden with expensive gifts. Greatly pleased, Vijayabahu sent them back with his own envoys and an equally bountiful offering. On their journey back to Vikramaditya's court, his messengers were intercepted by the Cholas, and were horribly maimed—their noses and ears hacked off. When Vijayabahu learned about this, he quite naturally flew into a rage and unleashed the full force of his army on the Cholas.[18]

The resulting battles went one way, then the other. Vijayabahu succeeded in establishing a strong base in the south from where he launched successful attacks on Anuradhapura and Polonnaruwa. The Chola forces fared badly and reinforcements had to be sent in to shore up the flailing troops and to save face from the ignominy of total defeat.

In the end, it was the Cholas who tired of the relentless fighting and constantly shifting loyalties. Besides, they had their hands full closer to home with the Chalukyas. Kulothunga even made his peace with Ceylon, marrying one of his daughters to a Sinhala prince, and made a gift of a perpetually burning lamp to a temple on the island.[19] He decided that Ceylon was not a priority and certainly not worth the trouble to keep fighting over and, during his reign, the Chola sojourn and centuries of intertwined history on the emerald isle of Ceylon came to an end.

The unsettled period preceding and following Kulothunga's ascension to the throne presented the perfect opportunity for the Pandyas and their allies, the Cheras, who never came to terms with their subordinate status, to stir into rebellion. It took all of Kulothunga's efforts to keep that region under control. He must have faced some success, judging from inscriptions that boasted of the head of the Pandya king lying on the ground pecked at by kites.[20] While this might have been an exaggeration to drive home the fact of his victory, multiple other inscriptions, as well as the poetic ulas (processional poems) of kings who succeeded Kulothunga describe the swathe of destruction he left in his wake as he decimated the Pandya and Chera army and lands and erected multiple pillars of victory.

Kulothunga waged two major campaigns to the north against the kingdom of Kalinga. These were the major military expeditions and successes of his reign. The first of them was precipitated because the Kalinga and Vengi rulers banded together, with the former attempting to make Vengi part of his territory. Kulothunga's son Vikrama distinguished himself here, suppressing and subjugating the revolting powers and even succeeding in annexing a portion of the Kalinga country.

The Kalinga region was ruled by an eastern Ganga king called Anantavarman Chodaganga. This ill-fated king had made the egregious error of omitting to present himself, along with a tribute, to Kulothunga and, in addition, was two years in arrears. This was a slight that could not go unavenged, and the second Kalinga war of Kulothunga's reign ensued. He did not fight himself, but appointed a senior army general called Karunakarat Tondaiman to lead his forces. Kulothunga himself stayed behind in Kanchipuram, from where he closely followed and directed operations.

Around 1112, Kulothunga's forces, headed by Karunakarat Tondaiman, set out to launch their attack on Kalinga. They crossed multiple rivers on their journey north: the Palar, the Pennar, the Mannaru, the Krishna, the Godavari, the Pampa, and the Gotami, sowing destruction and terror along the way. The battle that ensued at Kalinga was a resounding success for the Cholas, and Anantavarman Chodaganga fled and was not heard of again. The Chola army returned home with a considerable booty. The port city of Vishakhapatnam, which had been part of both Kalinga and Vengi domains, was named Kulothunga Cholapatnam. It was probably an important place for Kulothunga as he attempted to bring coastal Vengi into the Chola sea-trade network. However, for all the victories he enjoyed over Kalinga, the region did not become a fully Chola domain; there is no inscriptional evidence to show that. Rather, they probably remained under a status of enforced subordination and loyalty.[21]

Jayankontar described the war and its aftermath in gory detail in his war poem *Kalingattuparani*. After the Chola victory, a grisly battlefield ritual to the goddess Kali was performed to celebrate—great numbers of the enemy's elephants were killed, Kali and her retinue of ghouls partook of a feast whose main offering was the dismembered bodies of the enemy corps.

Kulothunga was a ruler who took a great deal of interest in commercial transactions. With the diminishing returns from conquered territories, trade revenues were an attractive alternate source of income for Kulothunga. Good diplomatic relations with the rulers in China and Southeast Asia were important since commerce and the tax revenues it brought in grew in importance during his reign. In order to stimulate trade, he got rid of royal tolls, generating income instead from increased taxes on weavers, goldsmiths, and other craftsmen. Sadly, this sometimes resulted in the craftsmen being forced to pursue other means of livelihood as the tax burden grew too much for them to bear.[22]

Kulothunga went about with renewed vigour to strengthen his position in the Chola–Srivijaya–China Song court nexus. The Chola and Srivijaya rulers continued to be in a pitched struggle for a favoured status with the Song court of China and part of their respective strategies to achieve this end lay in each undermining the other in the eyes of the Chinese. This was an age-old tactic; all that had changed was the players.

A couple of years before Kulothunga became king, his predecessor Virarajendra sent a naval expedition in support of a rival contender to the throne of Kadaram, a major Srivijaya port on the Malay peninsula. The tactic did not have the intended result and even backfired a little. The ruling faction of Srivijaya ensured that this move presented the Cholas in a poor light. When Kulothunga became the Chola ruler, the wily Srivijayans succeeded in misleading the Chinese into believing that the Cholas were their vassals.

Kulothunga knew that he needed grand gestures to win the Chinese emperor over.

In 1077, he sent a mission of seventy people, mostly traders, to the Song court. They were received warmly with the highest honours and were accorded top privileges. In return for the ivory, rhinoceros horns, glassware, asafoetida, cloves, and other tributes they gifted to the Chinese, they were given 81,800 strings of copper cash.[23] His commercial diplomacy found mention in Chinese sources: a stone tablet inscription dated 1079 in a Taoist monastery temple in Canton names him as its benefactor. He bequeathed, among other things, a substantial quantity of gold cash, which won him the title 'Great General Who Supports Obedience and Cherishes Renovations' from the Chinese court.[24]

The Srivijaya court was not pleased at this turn of events and redoubled its efforts with the Chinese; two missions were dispatched, in 1079 and 1088, and these paid off. The Srivijaya missions too were received with the same high honours accorded the Chola missions. It was a tense balancing act fuelled by deception and flattery, but the stakes were high and the rewards and prestige very attractive. And it continued in the years ahead, this diplomatic see-saw, and the Chinese probably had the last laugh.

Kulothunga's grandfather Rajendra had resorted to a frontal attack on the Srivijaya kingdom; there had been no pretence of a friendship. Kulothunga took a less confrontational approach and, whatever his true feelings might have been towards the Srivijaya ruler, maintained friendly relations. His great-grandfather Rajaraja had granted the revenues of a village, Anaimangalam, for the upkeep of a Buddhist vihara in Nagapattinam. This was a gesture of friendship and accommodation, providing a place of worship for the Buddhist traders from the Srivijaya kingdom who stopped at this Chola port. During Kulothunga's reign, the Srivijaya ruler requested that some additional grants be made for the vihara, something that Kulothunga readily acquiesced to, recording the grant in a set of copperplates that are known as the Smaller Leiden plates.[25]

Kulothunga had many sons. Two of them, sons of his Chola cousin-wife and chief queen Madhurantaki (daughter of Rajendra's middle son, Rajendradeva), were named Rajaraja and Virachola. They served as semi-independent rulers or viceroys of Vengi, which was still in the process of being integrated into the Chola kingdom. Vengi would be a good proving ground for these sons, deeply vested and connected as they were in their Vengi patrimony and Chola kingdom. Rajaraja lasted a mere year in this role. He found that 'serving at the feet of his elders' to be far more pleasant and satisfying than the aggravations of kingship, and he returned to the heart of Cholamandalam. Virachola was despatched next. He served for several years before being recalled to his father's court where his desire to be reunited with his parents and brothers was fulfilled, and the 'loveliness of his form was gazed upon'.[26]

Rajaraja and Virachola might have been groomed to succeed Kulothunga, but around twenty years into his reign, in the waning years of the eleventh century, a new chief queen entered the picture. Her name was Thyagavalli—Creeper of Generosity. At around the same time, her son Vikrama is believed to have headed the first of Kulothunga's campaigns in Kalinga. Not much is heard of this prince in the years following this, but the simultaneous rise of Thyagavalli and Vikrama must surely have been more than mere coincidence. Thyagavalli must have been a formidable presence in Kulothunga's circle: she has been described as one 'who by right gave commands that were equal to the Chola's own'.[27] Vikrama was also appointed viceroy of the Vengi region after his brothers' short stints there.

For the first time since the reign of Rajaraja, extensive land surveys were conducted, twice, and new valanadus were created in Tondaimandalam. It is very likely that the assorted landholders and elites of the region benefited as a result of the survey, and that was likely what Kulothunga had in mind in order to strengthen his hold over the land and ingratiate himself with its people.[28]

Kulothunga did not build a statement-making temple like his grandfather Rajendra and great-grandfather Rajaraja, but many temples were built during his reign, often with a certain flamboyant stylistic touch that could be traced, in part, to the Chalukya influence. Voluptuous dancing girls, depicted with exaggerated torsion to suggest movement, and mythical yalis—protective creatures, an amalgam of horse, lion, and elephant—burst forth in exuberant profusion from niches, columns, and platforms that had thus far been more restrained. It was during his reign that the first shrine in the shape of a horse-drawn chariot with wheels was built, a style that saw its magnificent efflorescence in the beautiful temple at Darasuram a half century later.[29]

Kulothunga aligned himself ever more closely with the ancient temple at Chidambaram. The temple had certainly grown from its beginnings as an ascetic retreat but was nowhere close to the size and grandeur of the great temples of Rajaraja or Rajendra. It is believed that it was during the reign of Kulothunga that it began to assume the form and dimensions that we are familiar with today, growing six-fold in the area it covered. Gangaikondacholapuram might have been his capital city, but Chidambaram acquired a status and importance that equalled, perhaps even rivalled, that of the capital. As a quasi-outsider Kulothunga forged a strong connection to the temple most sacred to the Cholas—a deeply symbolic gesture that would go a long way in providing legitimacy. A multitude of inscriptions from his reign document the renewal and expansion that he got underway, much of it done by his illustrious general and chief minister, Naralokaviran. A member of the aristocratic elite of Tondaimandalam (the northern Tamil regions that were formerly Pallava territory), he was an ardent devotee of Siva, full of energy and enthusiasm that fuelled his efforts to enlarge and enhance his beloved Chidambaram Temple.

Verse after verse of Naralokaviran's inscriptions describe the gold and ritual paraphernalia that he donated, the street lamps he erected, the palm trees he planted, the mandapams, the enclosing walls, sacred tank steps, and soaring towers he built. The towers were so tall, one of the inscriptions say proudly, that the flags flying atop them were scorched by the heat of the sun! He was responsible for the construction of the Hall of Hundred Pillars, a separate shrine for the goddess Sivakamasundari, and a shrine for the child-saint Sambandar. He had the hymns of the Saivite saints Appar, Sundarar, and Sambandar engraved on copperplates, a major undertaking, as these hymns numbered in the thousands. With his massive donations, this warlord had an outsized influence in the Chola kingdom in the 1100s and on the fate and prominence of the Chidambaram Temple. Kulothunga's sisters contributed generously to the temple on his behalf. One of them claimed to have gilded the roof, a declaration made by several Chola monarchs, starting with the very early Cholas, Aditya and Parantaka.[30] Later, Kulothunga's son Vikrama too would assert that he had gilded the roof!

Koluthunga made special efforts to strengthen his court's relationship with the Chidambaram Temple and the merchant community associated with it. A piece of land belonging to a nagaram or merchant association was transferred to the temple, for which the nagaram was compensated with gold coins and the assurance that it would continue to have the right to manage the land, making it a de facto part of the temple administration.

In addition, he placed a special ceremonial stone into the wall of a hall in front of the shrine. This stone had been gifted to him by the king of Kambhoja (Cambodia).[31] This gesture was likely made as an act of trade diplomacy, to please his trading partners to the east.

Kulothunga became ruler during a period of chaos and confusion but once he was firmly on the throne he ruled his empire with efficiency. During the course of his reign, the expanse of the Chola kingdom shrank and stayed contained to Tamil lands. The Pandyas to the south continued to seethe under Chola overlordship and made repeated efforts to break free. Many bloody battles were fought between them, and Kulothunga had his hands full keeping this always fractious power under control. Towards the end of his reign, he lost some territory to a growing power, the Hoysalas, in the Gangavadi region (modern Karnataka) as well as in Vengi, to his nemesis Vikramaditya of the Western Chalukyas. His empire was not as extensive as that of his grandfather Rajendra, but he left behind a kingdom that was stable, and that endured for the better part of a century. The frenetic fighting of the earlier era simmered down considerably as the empire settled into maturity.

In June 1118, he appointed his son Vikrama as his yuvaraja and crowned him Parakesarivarman Vikrama.[32] Perhaps it was a case of real life following the story of the mythological Chola ancestors Dasharatha and his sons, where the junior wife prevailed upon her husband to pass on the throne to her son. The real-life story appears to have proceeded more smoothly.

And in Vengi country, the lunar Chalukya dynasty began its descent and gradual eclipse into the night of obsolescence.

CHAPTER 25

THE CONSUMMATE SIVA DEVOTEE PARAKESARI VIKRAMA (R. 1118–1135)

> Vikrama Chola, he whose ornament is victory, the glorious Rajakesarivarma Permanadi (the lord of the earth) as far as the Ganga and the Kaveri, the glorious emperor of the three worlds, Vikrama Choladeva.[1]

Vikrama ruled alongside his ageing father for a couple of years before taking over completely. His was a largely peaceful reign during which he spent a great deal of time and effort on renovating temples. All the fighting that he did appears to have taken place when his father was king. Vikrama was a hero in the first war that his father fought against Kalinga. His court poet Ottakoothar wrote a war poem about this which is unfortunately lost to us. We know of its existence and contents because it finds mention in other poems by the same poet.[2]

When Vikrama took over the Chola throne, he left his post as viceroy of Vengi and moved to the Chola heartland. A Velanadu prince took over as viceroy, and the Western Chalukya ruler Vikramaditya VI, sensing an opportunity, swooped in, forced the Velanadu prince into a subordinate position, and established himself in Vengi. Vikrama had to wait until Vikramaditya VI died, in 1126, to re-establish his authority over the region.[3]

Vikrama claimed much of the credit for the work done to renovate and expand the great Nataraja Temple at Chidambaram. The building of the great Siva Ganga temple tank was his undertaking.[4] A large portion of the tributes paid to him by his feudatories went into work on this temple. Naralokaviran, who had directed a great deal of the work, had begun it while

Kulothunga I was king. Vikrama travelled to Chidambaram for the rededication ceremony when the work was finally completed in 1118. At the time, he was co-ruler with his father, sharing the responsibility of running the kingdom. He issued instructions for his inscriptions in temples throughout his realm while 'in his residence in Chidambaram', which suggests that he might have had a palace there.[5] In addition, he gave orders from his capital, Gangaikondacholapuram, Palaiyaru, and Kattumannarkoyil, showing that he was a king who was regularly on the move, a necessity for ensuring an efficient administration in medieval times.[6]

Vikrama appeared to have been a deeply religious man. His devotion to the lord of Chidambaram was so all-encompassing that it came at the cost of neglecting his military. In the Chola prasasti or verses of praise, it was customary to flaunt the military exploits of the king, but Vikrama chose instead to list his extensive donations to the Chidambaram Temple. One of the enclosing walls and one of the main streets around the temple are named for him.[7]

One of the greatest of the Chola court poets, Ottakoothar, served three kings, starting with Vikrama, and lasting through the reigns of his successor Kulothunga II, and *his* successor, Rajaraja II. He was best known for a genre of poetry that is peculiar to the Tamil language, the ula or processional poem, which was first codified in Chola times. Ottakoothar wrote eponymous ulas for all three kings, another mirror that offers us a particular perspective of their lives.

The inspiration for the ula likely came from the king's survey tours of his kingdom. Here, the king rides his majestic elephant in a procession through the streets of his city, swooned over with lascivious and unreciprocated passion by women of various classes of society and ranging in age from five to forty. The king, impassive and aloof, seemingly oblivious to the amorous women all around him, is introduced in the early verses of the ula where his royal genealogy is laid out in all its hyperbolic glory. The king's relationship with the great gods, particularly the most revered Chola deity, Nataraja of Chidambaram, is described.

The poet's intent was not historical accuracy or chronological veracity but rather to portray the ruler in the most heroic, glowing terms, as the scion of a family of illustrious ancestors whose feats of valour and gallantry were exceptional. The genealogy done, the poet moves on to describe the king's bedroom, his morning rituals, and his dress, a large portion of it is given over to jewellery. The royal elephant is covered next in detail, followed by an account of all the pomp and splendour of the procession itself. We learn about the council of ministers, the nobles, the chieftains, the courtiers, the sartorial styles of the day, the architecture and so much more, which makes for very interesting and insightful reading. Chola kings were heavily invested in displays of power and their poets played a dominant role in creating and spreading word of the omnipotent king and his grand lifestyle. In addition, they allow us to imagine—admittedly a highly hyperbolic version—of the nitty-gritty of Chola society, the richness of their ceremonial lives, the little details that formed a part of their rituals and procedures, what mattered to them, how they viewed themselves and the society they attempted to create and control. We get a sense of the teeming diversity—of nadus, of chieftains, of gods, of taxes and dues, and so much more.[8]

Through the ula we learn of the Chola king's love of the pomp and splendour of courtly processions, his compulsion to present a highly rich and ornamental vision of kingship through the flamboyant and fantastic imagination of the poet. The *Vikrama Sola Ula*, written about Vikrama, is particularly notable for its exhaustive list of ministers, officers, and feudatories who served in his military campaigns as well as administrators, builders of temples, and endowers of charity. It is interesting, and telling, that many of these men were not from the core Cholamandalam area, but from further north, the former Pallava region of Tondaimandalam. Down the road, this would have serious repercussions for the Cholas.[9]

Vikrama Chola chose his son, Kulothunga II, as heir apparent in 1133. He ruled for another two years after that, after which Kulothunga II took over, probably on his father's death.

CHAPTER 26

SIVA SIVA SIVA

RAJAKESARI KULOTHUNGA II (R. 1133–1150)

> The Perumal who covered the sacred Perambalam with gold.[1]

Kulothunga II's years as king were mostly peaceful. Vengi was back in Chola control and the Western Chalukyas were no longer a major threat.

All the Chola kings were religious men and while they had a special place in their hearts for Lord Siva, they were catholic in allowing the worship of other deities. Kulothunga II, however, seemed to have taken his Saivism rather more seriously. He was particularly devoted to Nataraja at the Chidambaram Temple and spent extended periods of time there; he is believed to have had his coronation ceremony there.[2] He apparently ordered that the shrine to Govindaraja (Vishnu) be shut down, a rather extreme measure, especially since his forebears were largely tolerant of Vishnu worshippers. Later Vaishnavite texts exaggerated this occurence, claiming that the 'putrid-necked Chola' (Krimikantha) had thrown a Vishnu image into the sea![3]

Kulothunga II continued the work his father and grandfather had begun, in expanding and improving the Chidambaram Temple complex. He, too, claims to have gilded the roof as well as other parts of the temple![4]

It was a time of peace and prosperity in the realm, and many chieftains and feudatories, flush with wealth and the spirit of devotion, contributed generously to temples around the land. Prominent among these were the Kadavas, a branch of the Pallavas. Over time, their power and influence grew, and they would later prove to be a sharp thorn in the Cholas' side.

Ottakoothar, who had been Vikrama Chola's court poet, continued working at Kulothunga II's court, writing a praise-filled ula, the *Kulothunga Sola Ula*, which described in elaborate detail, among other things, the remodelling efforts at the Chidambaram Temple. He also wrote an imagery-rich pillaitamil about this king. Pillaitamils are a genre of poetry peculiar to the Tamil language. In them, the poet, assuming the roles of a devotee and a mother, addresses the king (or deity, or whoever the pillaitamil is about) as a child. Ten stages of a child's life are described, with ten verses dedicated to each stage.

Kulothunga II, the consummate Siva devotee, commissioned the writing of the *Periya Puranam*, a monumental literary work by Sekkilar that narrated the lives of the sixty-three Nayanmars or Saivite saints.[5] Sekkilar spent a year in the haloed grounds of the Chidambaram Temple composing this masterpiece. It was written in everyday Tamil that made it accessible to all. Along with this came an outpouring of bronze images of the Nayanmars, no doubt inspired by the tales from the *Periya Puranam*, and these holy men became household names.

CHAPTER 27

NAMESAKE OF GREATNESS
PARAKESARI RAJARAJA II (R. 1146–1173)

> Having won the heart of the earth for countless ages, he was pleased to be seated on the throne of heroes made of pure gold, while the Cheras, Pandyas and other kings prostrated themselves before him...this king Parakesarivarman, Sri Rajarajadeva.[1]

Rajaraja II started ruling along with his father Koluthunga II as yuvaraja from 1146. For the most part, he retained the empire he had inherited, which included most of the region around and south of present-day Karnataka and the Vengi region to the northeast, along with the traditional Chola strongholds around the Kaveri delta.

Gangaikondacholapuram continued to be the Chola capital. Rajaraja II, however spent a good deal of time in the subsidiary capital of Pazhayarai, 40 kilometres to the south near Kumbakonam.[2] It was known as Rajarajapuri during his time, and it must have been a sprawling city, encompassing several present-day villages like Palaiyaru, Pazhayarai, Mulaiyar, and Darasuram. Unlike his predecessors who were constantly on the move, splitting their time among different palaces across the kingdom, he essentially stayed put in Pazhayarai, probably lulled into a sense of security and stability. Many feudatory chieftains appear to have taken advantage of this and strengthened their autonomy. They engaged in little wars, and established marital alliances between each other, independent of any Chola intervention. Their growing independence emboldened them, and this would prove detrimental to the Cholas in the coming decades.

His was a reign that was largely peaceful, for the times, and is best known for the abundance of literary activity under his patronage. His court poet continued to be Ottakoothar, who composed yet another ula—*Rajaraja Sola Ula* which provides a wealth of information about his reign and times.

Ottakoothar's works make ample mention of Rajaraja II's temple building activities. While his immediate predecessors Kulothunga II and Vikrama focussed largely on embellishing and renovating existing temples, Rajaraja II built some magnificent ones of his own.

Around 1150, he built the richly sculpted temple at Darasuram, where he spent a great deal of his time. He named it Rajarajeshwaram, after himself, just as his renowned namesake-ancestor had done over a century ago. The main temple itself was built on a smaller scale than those in Thanjavur and Gangaikondacholapuram, but the temple complex was expansive, extending to several structures.[3]

There is a porch in front of the temple that is designed to look like a chariot on wheels, complete with caparisoned horses, a feature that places it squarely in the twelfth century. Scholars believe that the architects of the famous Sun Temple in Konark, Odisha, built over a century later, took their inspiration from the Darasuram Temple.[4] The porch is approached up a set of steps with ornately carved railings. These steps are special, as they produce musical notes of different frequencies, and are known as the singing steps. All around are pillars that teem with exquisitely detailed carvings that depict mythological tales. There are lovely jalis or trellis windows carved with floral and other motifs, a feature that was popular in the Chalukya monuments to the north, but hitherto unseen in Chola architecture. The base mouldings brim with an abundance of sculpted dancers and musicians. There are also little carved vignettes that depict the stories of the sixty-three Nayanmars. The growing popularity of these saints was very likely spurred by the royal attention given to them, and Sekkilar's *Periya*

Puranam which had been very recently commissioned during the reign of Rajaraja II's father.

Stunning stone sculptures of Siva as Bhikshasanan (the mendicant) and as the slayer of the elephant-demon Gajasura, all inspired by the beautiful poetry of the Nayanmar saints, once adorned Darasuram; they are now displayed in The Art Gallery in Thanjavur. The poet Ottakoothar was so inspired by this temple that he composed a parani, a war poem, called *Takkayagapparani*. It is different from the traditional parani, in which the king is the hero; here, it is none other than Lord Siva himself, specifically, the Siva of the Rajajeshwaram Temple built by Rajaraja II. Siva had been slighted by his father-in-law Daksha, an event that led to the terrible death-by-self-immolation of his wife (Daksha's daughter) Sati, and he wrought a fury-filled revenge on him. The poem celebrates his victory, and the poet's patron king Rajaraja II basks in the reflected glory of having built and consecrated the grand temple for this lord.[5]

A second temple, also called Rajarajajeshwaram, was built by one of his principal ministers at Pallavarayanpettai, 40 kilometres upriver to the north and east of Darasuram. This temple contains some fascinating inscriptions that tell the tale of how the next Chola emperor came to be.[6]

Two decades into his reign, Rajaraja II was an ageing monarch with no male heirs. He was acutely aware that it was a situation that was ripe for instability and intrigue, and that a succession plan had to be put in place. After evaluating the potential candidates, it was decided that the most fitting person to be the next king was Edirilipperumal, a grandson of Vikrama Chola, the son of one Neri Udai Perumal (presumed to be Vikrama Chola's younger son; some scholars have suggested that Neri Udai Perumal was in fact his daughter). He was appointed yuvaraja in 1166 and ruled alongside Rajaraja II for around six years. A senior official, a close and trusted confidante of Rajaraja II known as Pallavarayan (his name was Kulatturan Tiruch Chirrambalam Udayan Perumal Nambiyan; Pallavarayanpettai is named for him) was entrusted with ensuring a smooth succession, and that Rajaraja II's family members would be taken care of.[7]

A couple of years later, Rajaraja II had two sons. He died in 1172, an old king with infant children aged one and two, both far too young for the throne; besides, a succession plan was in place and was followed through. The new king took his place on the Chola crown. The infant sons were spirited away to safety in Rajarajapuram (today's Darasuram) by Pallavarayan, leaving behind a whole host of questions to which we have no certain answers: what became of them, who they were being protected from, why was Pallavarayan so invested in their safety and welfare? It has been suggested that they were his grandchildren: the infants' mother was Pallavarayan's daughter who was Rajaraja II's wife.[8]

CHAPTER 28

AN IMPOSSIBLE TANGLE
RAJAKESARI RAJADHIRAJA II (R. 1166–1178)

> King Rajakesarivarman Rajadhirajadeva, the emperor of the three worlds...(where) the Goddess of the Earth, the Goddess residing in the flower (Lakshmi), the Goddess of War and the Goddess of Prosperity all lived in amity...and such kings as the Pandyas, the Cheras and the Singhalese came carrying tribute and made their obeisance to him.[1]

Born Edirilipperumal, he took on the royal moniker Rajadhiraja II four years into his reign with the consent and approval of his council of officers.[2] He was not the natural heir, and there were rumblings of dissent and discontent about his ascension to the throne, but Pallavarayan, who had effected his rise to the throne, maintained control in the kingdom while also keeping a close guard over Rajaraja II's infant royal heirs.

Very early into Rajadhiraja II's reign, a Pandya prince called Kulasekhara Pandya, an aspirant to the Pandya throne, was ousted and forced into exile by a rival called Parakrama Pandya, who was backed by the Ceylonese king (who, interestingly, and adding to the confusion, shared his name: Parakramabahu) and his forces. Kulasekhara appealed to Rajadhiraja II for help. The latter was only too happy to oblige, and his efforts were successful. Parakrama Pandya, his wife, and several of his children were killed.

The mood was jubilant, and preparations were in full swing for the coronation of Kulasekhara when, most unfortunately, Pallavarayan fell ill and died. He had been a trusted and loyal adviser, and Rajadhiraja made sure that his family was well taken care of and issued a royal order to gift tax-free lands to many members of his family. Another Pallavarayan–Palayanur Udaiyan Vedavanam Udaiyan Ammanayyapan—took over the position of the duties of the deceased minister. He was entrusted with the task of distributing the gifted lands to the relatives of his late predecessor.

The Pandya succession battle was far from over, and the saga took a series of dizzying twists and turns. The Ceylonese king Parakramabahu was smarting under his loss to the Cholas and sent in reinforcements. The tide began to turn in favour of the Ceylon–Pandya alliance, and Vira Pandya, one of the sons of the slain Parakrama Pandya, was installed on the throne by the general in charge of the Ceylonese troops. In due course, the Chola forces picked up steam and dealt the enemy forces a resounding defeat. In a gory display of vicious revenge, the heads of the defeated Ceylonese generals were nailed to the gateway of the Pandya capital city of Madurai. Following a triumphant return to the city, Kulasekhara was crowned the king of the Pandyas.

The celebratory joy was short-lived. The Chola general Pallavarayan got wind of news that Parakramabahu, a vindictive king who was determined to avenge his losses, was preparing for another attack. The crafty general resorted to the age-old practice of supporting the enemy's enemy—a competing aspirant to the Ceylon throne. This was a nephew of Parakramabahu's, Srivallabha. An attacking force headed by Srivallabha was dispatched, and a multitude of places in Ceylon were destroyed. Parakramabahu, at his wit's end with the never-say-die Cholas, effected a stunning and sneaky about-turn and declared himself an ally and supporter of Kulasekhara. The two former bitter enemies now joined forces against the Cholas.

The Cholas wasted no time in changing their allegiance. A fresh round of fighting ensued, this time it was the Cholas against the joint forces of Kulasekhara and Parakramabahu. Once again, the Cholas proved too strong a force. Kulasekhara was driven into exile, Parakramabahu's dreams of installing a friendly face on the Pandya throne were crushed, and Vira Pandya was made ruler of the Pandyas, thanks in large part to the Chola efforts and the Pallavarayan chieftains.

It was fully 1177 by the time this chapter of the Chola–Pandya–Ceylon saga came to a close. The entirety of Rajadhiraja's short reign was devoted to battling this tangled web of duplicity and constantly changing loyalties.[3]

CHAPTER 29

THE BEGINNING OF THE END
PARAKESARI KULOTHUNGA III
(R. 1178–1218)

> This king Parakesarivarman, who was pleased to be seated on the throne of heroes of pure gold, alias the emperor of the three worlds, Sri Kulottunga Soladeva who was pleased to take Madurai....[1]

Who exactly was Kulothunga III, the ruler who took over after Rajadhiraja II? What were the circumstances in which he ascended the throne?

As with so much about the Cholas, there are no clear answers, only speculation. Rajadhiraja II was still alive when Kulothunga III became king, and it has been suggested that he was one of the sons of Rajaraja II who had been groomed for the position as yuvaraja. This seems a bit far-fetched as the lad would have been barely six years old at the start of Rajaraja II's rule, but perhaps this indeed was the case.[2]

Kulothunga III turned out to be the last of the great Chola rulers. He took over a kingdom that was extensive, well-administered, and relatively peaceful for a spell in the later years of his reign before everything started to fall apart.

After all that had gone into installing Vira Pandya on the Pandya throne, it would be natural to assume that matters had finally settled into stability there. But the merry-go-round of loyalties and alliances started spinning again. For reasons unknown, the Cholas now allied themselves with Vikrama Pandya, a close relative of Kulasekhara, the treacherous defector to the Sinhala side.

Vikrama Pandya sought the help of Kulothunga III to oust Vira Pandya and establish his position as king. Kulothunga III marshalled his forces, routed the Pandyan army, and drove the Sinhala troops into the sea (in the words of the inscription at the Chidambaram Nataraja Temple describing this event).[3] Vira Pandya's son was killed in the fierce fighting. Madurai was captured, and a pillar of victory was erected there. This was the first of the Pandyan wars of his reign. Around 1187, Vikrama Pandya was crowned the Pandya king.

Vira Pandya, the dethroned Pandya king, was grief-stricken at the loss of his son and incensed by his defeat and was determined to seek revenge. He approached the kings of Ceylon and the Cheras, as well as several neighbouring Chola feudatories and asked for their help to crush the execrable Cholas. He gathered together a large fighting force and a violent battle was fought in Nettur in 1193. Once again, the Pandyas faced a total mauling. Kulothunga III's second Pandyan war was a triumph. Vira Pandya's ambitions took a colossal blow. However, all was not lost for him. Kulothunga III, in a devilishly expansive mood, gifted Vira Pandya a vast tract of land which he would rule over as a subordinate, with the Chola king (Kulothunga III himself) as his overlord. The Chera king, who had taken the Pandya side, begged for Kulothunga III's forgiveness and he retained his crown, as a lesser power.

Kulothunga III turned his attention next to Ceylon, defeated the army there, and boasted that he placed his foot on the crown of the king of Ceylon.

In the meantime, major trouble was brewing on his northern frontier, as anarchy and dissent broke out among the Pallava and Telugu feudatories. The Kakatiyas, a rising power in the Warangal region around the lower Godavari River, were creating problems in Vengi lands. A major fighting force was sent north and, again, Kulothunga enjoyed a string of victories.

After this, peace finally descended upon the kingdom. It lasted for all of a decade.

During this peaceful lull, Kulothunga III was actively engaged in building activities in which he took a personal interest, and he was a generous donor to temples and charitable institutions. Large numbers of Saiva muths flourished during his time and after.

After ten peaceful years, the Pandyas, who had been seething under their Chola masters, decided that enough was enough. This time, the troublemaker was Jatavarman Kulasekhara, the son of Vikrama Pandya. Restless and displeased with his insubordinate status, he declared himself the independent ruler of Madurai. Kulothunga III retaliated with a fierce attack on Madurai and its surroundings and defeated both the Pandyan and supporting Chera forces, sowing mayhem and destruction along the way. He seized Madurai and crowned himself the Chola-Pandyan. Madurai was renamed Mudittalai-konda-Solapuram (the city of the Chola who took the Pandyan crown); the Pandya lands were now called Chola-Pandyamandalam and in 1205 he christened himself Tribhuvana Viradeva, the victor over the three worlds—the Pandya, Chera, and Ceylon kingdoms—the name that would grace his great temple.[4] The war booty enriched his newly built temple, the hallowed Nataraja Temple at Chidambaram, as well as the Thyagaraja Temple at Tiruvarur.

The last great Chola temple was completed in 1212 in Tribhuvanam (near Kumbakonam) and named Tribhuvana-Virishwaram, after his self-anointed title of Tribhuvana Viradeva—Victor of the Three Worlds—echoing the Tripurantaka aspect of Siva. After his third victory over the Pandyas, he held a grand celebration in their capital city of Madurai and bequeathed himself this grand moniker. The temple, with its 126-foot tall vimana, was built in celebration and gratitude for his triumphs. Along its walls run a beautiful series of Ramayana reliefs. Its shrine was described as having a 'brilliant, tall and excellent *vimana* which interrupts the sun'.[5] As at Darasuram, an extension off the main shrine took the form of a chariot on wheels. A unique feature of this temple is that shrines for Devi and Sarabhamurthi (a form of Siva that is part-man, part-lion, and part-bird) were built at the same time as the main shrine.

Today, it is known as the Kampahareshwarar Temple and, sadly, only the axle beams and a lone wheel remain of that chariot. In building his signature temple, Kulothunga III was following in the footsteps of his esteemed ancestors Rajaraja, Rajendra, and Rajaraja II, selecting a place that had no prior religious significance whatsoever, thus making a grand statement about his personal power and royal status.

In a strange gesture of placation, Kulothunga III installed the thoroughly crushed and humiliated Jatavarman Kulasekhara on the Pandya throne, a toothless and impotent monarch whose royal status meant nothing.

Kulothunga III would pay for the ignominy and disgrace he subjected the Pandyas to.

After Jatavarman Kulasekhara died, embittered and miserable, his brother, the dynamic and powerful Maravarman Sundara Pandya became the new ruler in 1216. In the short space of two years, he amassed a huge army and invaded the Chola lands. He razed Thanjavur to the ground, destroyed palaces, forts, towers, and buildings, filled the rivers and lakes with blood, and performed a triumphant victory ritual. His troops succeeded in going as far north as Chidambaram, where he paid homage to the supreme Lord of the Cholas, Nataraja. It is not known if he captured and/or destroyed the capital, Gangaikondacholapuram.

Kulothunga III had been hiding in the outskirts of the city of Ponnamaravati. Cowed and utterly disgraced, he offered to name his son, Rajaraja III, after the Pandya.

In what must have been the customary and ceremonial means of humiliating the defeated enemy, Maravarman Sundara Pandya bestowed the Chola kingdom back to Kulothunga, but he was now stripped of any real status and prestige. Kulothunga suffered the same fate he had so triumphantly subjected his Pandya rivals to just a decade earlier.[6]

This marked the beginning of the end of the great Chola empire. Kulothunga III did not live long after this humiliating defeat and was succeeded by his son Rajaraja III who inherited not much more than the name from his brilliant ancestor of over two centuries ago. His rule was inefficient and weak, a disaster for a kingdom that was already tottering.

CHAPTER 30

A SERIES OF UNFORTUNATE EVENTS
RAJAKESARI RAJARAJA III (R. 1216–1246)

> The Chola no longer considered it proper course to owe allegiance to the ruler who had bestowed the crown on him on a former occasion...and declined to do the usual honour to the commands (of the Pandya), refused to pay the usual tribute, but instead despatched a large army and an advance guard.[1]

Rajaraja III's reign was full of unpleasant and humiliating experiences as the once-great empire disintegrated around him. He was forced to seek the help of those who had sought help and protection from his forebears.

Trouble was brewing all around. To the north, the Kadava–Pallava chieftain Kopperunchinga, aided by his fellow Kadavarayars, started establishing his independence in no uncertain terms. In response, the Hoysala king who was friendly with the Cholas (possibly because of marital alliances), stepped in on behalf of Rajaraja III to keep them under control. He captured the Kadava stronghold Kanchipuram, which became part of Hoysala territory.

There was growing agitation and unrest closer to the Chola home base as well. And in the midst of all this, as if he didn't have enough trouble on his hands, Rajaraja III, resorting to the age-old practice of provoking the Pandya king, refused to pay the agreed-upon tribute. This ill-advised move was nothing short of imprudence and Rajaraja III was punished in brutal fashion.

Maravarman Sundara Pandya's army came roaring into the

heart of Chola country, wreaking havoc and destruction. The chief Chola queen and senior ladies of her retinue were forced to carry the auspicious water-pots and other ritual items for the grand Pandya victory ceremony. The beleaguered Rajaraja III was hounded out of his capital Gangaikondacholapuram where the Pandya king established his authority by having his inscriptions added to its temple walls and instituting a special worship in his name.

Rajaraja III fled northwards, hoping for friendly refuge with the Hoysala emperor in Mysore. But he was was captured by Kopperunchinga and held prisoner. The Hoysala emperor, Vira Narasimha, proved to be a true friend. He succeeded in freeing Rajaraja III from the clutches of Kopperunchinga, and also managed to defeat the Pandya emperor down south. The Hoysalas now made their way into Pandya territory, as far south as Rameshwaram. However, they didn't actually control it; instead, they chose the more pacific route of establishing marital alliances. Rajaraja III and Maravaram Sundara Pandya both married daughters of the Hoysala king Vira Narasimha. Maravarman continued to rule for two more decades, after which his son, Maravarman Sundara Pandya II took over.

Rajaraja III was recrowned Chola emperor at Gangaikondacholapuram. The capital remained an important Chola centre, although it must have suffered destruction during the recent wars. Further north, the Kadava–Pallava chieftain Kopperunchinga took full advantage of the havoc wreaked by the Chola–Pandya tug-of-war and declared himself an independent ruler, free of Chola shackles.[2]

Rajaraja III ruled over a sadly truncated empire that was barely bigger than what had been established by the dynasty's founder, Vijayalaya. As his tenuous hold over his lands and people became ever more fragile, anarchy and disorder spread over the fractured kingdom, and instances of treason against the king (rajadroham) became common.[3] After thirty years of the worst reign of the great Chola empire, he handed the throne over to his son, Rajendra III. He lived another ten years after this, perhaps as co-ruler, a broken and haunted man, watching a once-great world crumble around him.

CHAPTER 31

SUNSET AND DARKNESS
PARAKESARI RAJENDRA III
(R. 1246–1279)

> Rajendra Choladeva, whose sword was clever in cutting off the crowned head of the Pandya king...and on whose leg Vira Someshwara placed the anklet of heroes.[1]

Rajendra III inherited a sadly decimated empire that was badly frayed at the edges. Rajendra III was a far more able ruler than his father. An inscription hints at bad blood between them which has led some historians to conclude that the two were brothers, rather than father and son.[2] Whatever the actual relationship was, it certainly points to an empire riven with some amount of dissent and infighting. Treason, disorder, and open defiance of royal orders were rampant.

He made a valiant effort to shore up the crumbling empire. The Hoysalas were a growing power over much of southern India; this was fine as long as they were allied with the Cholas. The Pandyas, who had chafed under Chola overlordship and refused to come to terms with their subordinate status, continued to create major trouble for the Cholas. Rajendra, in time-honoured fashion, attempted to address the situation. Besides, the utterly humiliating defeats that his father had endured at the hands of the Pandyas had to be avenged.

The Pandya ruler was Maravarman Sundara Pandya II. He was a rather weak and colourless character compared to his father, and his hold over his kingdom was feeble. It was a good time to attack, and Rajendra did, successfully. Between 1238 and 1250, Chola power steadied and strengthened, thanks in large part to the help of their loyal feudatories, the Telugu Codas of Nellore.[3] This appears to have alarmed Someshwara, the Hoysala king who decided that the growing Chola power needed to be kept in check. He switched allegiances and took the side of the Pandya ruler. Several battles were fought between the Hoysalas and the Cholas, each claiming victory over the other, each claiming that the other fell at his feet seeking mercy.[4]

And then, in 1251, Jatavarman Sundara Pandya became the Pandya king. He was a great warrior and leader, a brilliant star in the Pandya firmament. A mere seven years after becoming king, he set out on an ambitious digvijaya—victory in every direction—campaign. And what a victory campaign it was! Across the length and breadth of southern India he rampaged with his troops, defeating the kings of Kerala and Ceylon, driving the Hoysala Someshwara back to his heartland around the Mysore plateau, striking terror into the hearts of a multitude of chieftains and feudatories. Kopperunchinga, the ambitious Kadava-Pallava chieftain was stripped of his territory, army, and treasure.[5]

Sundara Pandya captured vast expanses of territory and amassed colossal quantities of war booty. He offered his thanks at the Chidambaram Nataraja Temple, to which he donated generously. He drove home the fact of his Chola conquest with an inscription in the great temple at Gangaikondacholapuram, the Chola capital. He established a special worship at this temple that was called Sundara Pandyan sandhi, to be performed daily.[6]

By this time, Rajendra III was likely already a ruler whose power and domains were badly constrained, judging from the paucity of his inscriptions outside the core Chola territory. The last inscription from outside his heartland is in Kurnool (modern Andhra Pradesh), dated 1261.[7]

Sundara Pandya died in 1268 and was succeeded by another great Pandya ruler, Maravarman Kulasekhara. His responsibilities as king were shared by several Pandya princes, a common arrangement for them. At the time, the Hoysala ruler was Ramanatha, who was a close ally of Rajendra III. In 1279 there a battle was fought at Kannanur between the Pandyas on one side, and the Hoysala and Chola forces on the other.[8]

Maravarman Kulasekhara defeated them and possibly killed Rajendra III at Kannanur.

This is the last we hear of Rajendra III. There is no mention of another Chola successor. Maravarman Kulasekhara took over all the Chola territories and the Chola kingdom was completely swallowed up by the Pandyan empire, more completely than the Pandyas had ever been a part of the Chola empire. The walls of the great temple of Gangaikondacholapuram, the Chola capital, now narrated another history, that of a different dynasty, as Kulasekhara's Pandya inscriptions were added to its rich annals.

After over four hundred years of brilliant successes and harrowing failures, battles fought over steadily expanding territory, exploits and adventures of breathtaking ambitiousness and daring, creating works of stunning beauty amidst almost constant warfare and bloodshed, propelled by abiding faith in their beloved Lord Siva and conviction of their eminence, the sun set on this glorious empire.

In the end, the Cholas fell victim to their own success. The limits to their control over their vast territory became increasingly apparent as the regions in its outer boundaries were never fully integrated into the Chola ethos, and breakaway movements started popping up all over. For all its glitter and grandeur, the Chola state was never ever truly stable and secure; the wonder was that it grew as big and lasted as long as it did.

EPILOGUE

It has been over a thousand years since Rajaraja ruled the Cholas, and there is still so much we don't know about him, many questions that remain unanswered.

All over the world are magnificent mausoleums and memorials built for emperors and their families. There is the beautiful Humayun's Tomb in Delhi, commissioned by the Mughal emperor's wife, Bega Begum. Further afield, the First Qin emperor's mausoleum in Xi'an, China, boggles the mind with its thousands of terracotta soldiers. And there are so many, many more. But what about Rajaraja Chola—King of Jewels, Incomparable Chola, Great Saviour, Jewel of the Solar Dynasty, Lion Among Kings? Where is his burial shrine? How and where did he die?

After having ruled for twenty-nine years as one of the most ambitious and powerful monarchs of his time, and making the word 'Chola' synonymous with grandeur and glory, Rajaraja died.[1] He had shared the reins of power with his son Rajendra for exactly two years, and the yuvaraja was ripe and ready to assume full control of the Chola throne.

A spot of sleuthing using a combination of astrological, astronomical, and plain old arithmetical computing determines that Rajaraja died between 10 July 1013 and 28 June 1014.[2]

History has been silent about how and where Rajaraja died. He was sixty-seven, which might have been considered an acceptable age to die. There was no mention of illness and certainly nothing along the lines of what befell his brother Aditya Karikala nearly half a century earlier. So it is very likely that Rajaraja died a natural death.

But then what became of him? The Chola tradition, which Rajaraja followed, was to build a type of memorial shrine temple called a pallipadai over the remains of the deceased person. Rajaraja had built one for his grandfather Arinjaya near Ranipet, and his great-grandfather Parantaka had done the same for his father, Aditya.[3]

Wouldn't Rajendra have commemorated his father in a similar way?

The village of Udaiyalur (population 3,000) is 30 kilometres east of Thanjavur and 6 kilometres south of Kumbakonam. A few years ago, a stone lingam was found in an area of Udaiyalur called Ottathoppu, half-buried in a thatched roof open-sided shed that stood in the middle of a field. There was much excited speculation that this could be the burial stone of Rajaraja, and that beneath the lingam lay his mortal remains. There was absolutely no evidence to confirm or deny this. But to this day, the residents of the area revere this as Rajaraja's burial spot.

In April 2019, a team of government archaeologists took up the mystery, determined to find out if Udaiyalur was indeed where Rajaraja was buried. They surveyed an area of nearly 10 acres, including the Ottathoppu shed. They made use of drones and remote sensing. A report was to have been submitted within a couple of weeks, but, so far, we have not heard anything.

In the meantime, a scholar of Chola history and temples, Professor G. Deivanayagam, announced that his research has led him to believe that Rajaraja's burial site is indeed in Udaiyalur. But not at the Ottathoppu shed. In a narrow lane in Udaiyalur is the Kailasanatha Temple. This, Professor Deivanayagam is convinced, is Rajaraja's final resting place. He cites a litany of reasons to bolster his case.

When Rajaraja died, Rajendra, who lived in nearby Pazhayarai, built a brick-and-mortar temple with a memorial stone for his father in Udaiyalur. It was called the Kailasanatha Temple, and lasted barely a hundred years. In 1112, Rajaraja's great-grandson, the Chola emperor Kulothunga, renovated the temple in stone to its present structure. This information can be gleaned from an inscription at the Paalkulathu Amman Temple, across the street from Kailasanatha. It also tells us that Rajaraja became a Sivapadasekara, someone who attained the feet of Siva, in other words, salvation. There are sculptures inside the temple that Deivanayagam believes are those of Rajaraja as a Siva devotee and Sivapadasekara.

For a structure to be considered a pallipadai or tomb temple, it must satisfy certain Agamic principles, and the Kailasanatha Temple does that perfectly, further confirmation that it is indeed a pallipadai.

What of the half-buried lingam in the Ottathoppu shed?

There are several very convincing reasons for it *not* to be Rajaraja's burial stone, says Deivanayagam. It is a lingam without a pedestal—this is called a bhanalingam. Such a lingam is made only for those who died an unnatural death. In addition, the top cylindrical portion of the bhanalingam faces west, yet another sign that it is memorial stone for someone who did not die of natural causes. The memorial lingams of those who die a natural death face east towards the rising sun, a symbol of grace. Bhanalingams also do not have a temple constructed around them.

That lingam in the shed, Deivanayagam speculates, might be the burial stone of Rajaraja's murdered brother Aditya Karikala.[4] If this is indeed true, what a coincidence it is that the brothers came to rest so close to each other!

We do not have a definite answer as yet but Deivanayagam and his team would like the government archaeologists to conduct a deep radar survey of the Kailasanatha Temple. That might clear up the mystery and let us discover the truth.

We owe that to Rajaraja.

◆

There are rare moments in history when an amalgam of factors comes together to forge greatness. Rajaraja and the Cholas were, for several hundred years, the shining light of India and the legacy they left behind, both tangible and otherwise, lingers to this day. They were deeply involved in a world that stretched far beyond the Tamil country, from China in the Far East to the Arab lands and beyond in the West.

Tamil Nadu is an intensely religious state that loves its festivals with all their pomp and splendour. They are joyous, rambunctious affairs that bring together throngs of people, often an entire town, on the streets, enjoying the fresh air and glimpses of their beloved deity as all around them a carnival-like atmosphere explodes into life. These processional festivals had their genesis in Chola times and a time-traveller from that period might well feel right at home today seeing the lavishly dressed idols, inhaling the fragrance of incense and flowers, listening to the music of the nadaswaram and tavil, savouring the special foods prepared in the temple kitchens. Bronze idols for these temple festivals are made to this day in several towns and villages in the Kaveri delta, following the same lost-wax method that has been employed for over a thousand years. There are bronze-casting families that trace their ancestors all the way back to Chola times, the precious skills handed down from generation to generation. Today, those bronze idols are in demand around the world, and the bronze workshops are kept busy supplying this need.

There is a dark side to this, too. Bronzes made during Chola times are now a prized part of the international art market and command huge sums of money. Alas, this means they have caught the attention of the seamy world of art thievery and an entire chain of operatives, from humble diggers to upscale dealers, has been involved in stealing these priceless gems. There has been brazen thievery from temples; in some cases, a replica has been sneaked in and the priceless original spirited away.

Where do these bronzes belong? Back in their original homes, the temples, where they will be lavished with deep love and care by their circle of devotees in out of the way places? Or in the sterile glass cages of museums in wealthy cities around the world where they will be gazed at with a different kind of adoration and devotion?

Clearly, the answer depends upon the reader's values and inclinations.

The most concrete, commanding Chola legacies are undoubtedly their temples. Rajaraja's Brihadeeshwara Temple vaulted Tamil temple architecture—quite literally—to new heights; this temple, along with Rajendra's Gangaikondacholapuram and Rajaraja II's Airavateshwara Temple in Darasuram have been recognized as Great Living Chola Temples by UNESCO, praising them as exemplars of outstanding creative achievement and as an exceptional testimony to the development of the architecture of the Chola Empire and the Tamil civilization in southern India.[5]

The Cholas recognized that the Kaveri River had enormous potential and from very early on harnessed, controlled, and channelled its waters to their benefit. They transformed the deltaic region of the river into one of great fecundity that led to tremendous agricultural prosperity. This wealth played a big role in the dynasty's success and to this day, the Kaveri River delta remains one of the most fertile regions in India.

During the reign of Rajaraja, the beating heart of the subcontinent was in the Chola lands in south India. His achievements spanned the gamut—battlefield victories, administrative organization, grand temple with its rich life and far-reaching impact, stunning bronze idols, daring and far-sighted maritime expeditions—and have not been matched by many rulers since. He built his empire through hard-fought heroic successes on the battlefield but understood that mere military might was not sufficient, and that in order to truly capture the hearts of his people, and to bring together and integrate a populace that worshipped different gods, belonged to different ethnic and tribal groups, he needed to draw them into a grand dream, a vision of something wondrous and touched by divinity. His soaring magnum opus, the Brihadeeshwara Temple did just that, bringing together Lord Siva, Rajaraja, his chosen deputy on earth, and the entire, squabbling mass of people who lived on his lands.

Today, Rajaraja is firmly a part of popular Tamil culture, a huge source of Tamil pride. In 1950, the Tamil magazine *Kalki* started publishing weekly instalments of a historical novel based on the life and times of Rajaraja and the Cholas. It was called *Ponniyin Selvan* (the son of Ponni, or the Kaveri) and the author was 'Kalki' R. Krishnamurthy, a well-renowned writer and freedom fighter. For four years between 1950 and 1954, tens of thousands of readers eagerly awaited the weekly and *Kalki*'s subscriptions swelled to undreamed-of heights. *Ponniyin Selvan* is considered one of the best Tamil novels of all time and, to this day, is one of the most celebrated and bestselling works of Tamil literature. It made Rajaraja and the Cholas household names in Tamil-speaking lands around the world. In 1973, he was further immortalized in the movie *Rajaraja Cholan*, starring Sivaji Ganesan in the lead role. It is impossible to conjure up an image of Rajaraja without Sivaji's bright-eyed, fiercely moustachioed, benevolently smiling, jewel-bedecked visage swimming into view. The Chola world will come alive once again on cinema, with a star-studded adaptation of Kalki's *Ponniyin Selvan* slated for release in 2022.

It's interesting to see how Rajaraja has made a place for himself in popular imagination. He was a brilliant blend of humility and chutzpah, a devout worshipper who was also devoutly worshipped. He was an excellent organizer with a passion for grand projects and a keen sense of the ceremonial and symbolic. A canny publicist, he believed in his own greatness and ensured that his subjects believed too. He viewed himself as a more elevated royal than any of his peers or foes and anointed himself with grandiose titles far loftier than anything his ancestors had used. He established a cult of god-king—and what more impressive way to announce this than the mighty Brihadeeshwara Temple—that permeates the sociopolitical ethos of Tamil Nadu to this day. This personality cult is something that we still see in Tamil Nadu. Political leaders might be venal and corrupt, and yet they inspire a cult-like devotion through their munificence that is considered divine by their adoring subjects. It has eerie parallels with how Rajaraja operated, tapping into a primal human need for a benevolent hero who would watch over them as the people's own divine agent right here in their realm. After all, who would not want a god-king in their lives, one who protects them, takes care of their every need, and grants them a vision of splendour and greatness?

Over a thousand years ago, for a few glorious decades, Rajaraja was just that. And today, people yearn to recreate and relive that dream, and like all dreams of the past, the moonstruck, sentimental imaginings brush aside the cruelty and the brutality, the suffering and the injustice, and see only a world of beauty and benevolence.

Southern India under the rule of Rajaraja, and the Chola monarchs who succeeded him, underwent great social, economic, and religious changes. During this time, this region evolved into a plural, complex society that embraced multiple alien cultures and drew them into its fold, blending together the synergies of priests, merchants, agriculturalists, and warriors, the peoples of upstream highlands and downstream river valleys, the rural and the urban, involving them all in the workings of the kingdom. Major developments and changes in trade and commerce, the growth and empowerment of urban centres, with the temple at their nucleus, the expansion of agricultural communities into previously undeveloped areas all changed the social fabric of the land.[6]

Unsurprisingly, there were strains as happens when people with different beliefs, habits, and backgrounds begin living together. The transitions and changes resulted in a shifting of social hierarchies resulting in tensions and, sometimes, protests and revolts. Land ownership moved from the collective to the individual, and as more Brahmins and rich Vellalas bought and sold land in their own names, the number of landless labourers burgeoned. Resentment grew in tandem with the increased tax burden on small cultivators and others, while the brahmadeya and devadana lands belonging to Brahmins and the temples enjoyed tax-free status. Inscriptions tell us about villages refusing to pay taxes, campaigning to oppose certain taxes, and medieval versions of labour strikes, with villagers refusing to sow their crops, or enter their own villages, until taxes were reduced. They conducted their own human rights campaigns, fighting for those who had been defrauded and oppressed by the Brahmins and rich Vellala landowners, and imposing sanctions on the oppressors.[7]

Great empires rise on the backs of brutal wars, exploited citizenry, raped women, oppressive taxation. The turmoil and brutality of the battlefield is often mirrored in the everyday lives of ordinary people. After all, it is no simple task to weave new territory into the old; the complexities are enormous and too often, brute force was the most efficient way to effect change. It was no different for the Cholas, and to be fair to them, they operated in a world in which this was the modus operandi. They were bold, brave, brutal, driven. They had gargantuan egos and the smallest slight enraged them into merciless retaliation.

As the old adage goes, 'all that glitters is not gold' and that is certainly the case with the Cholas. To think of them as above critique and reproach, as a force of unalloyed good power and the face of a mythical golden age of perfection is to do them a disservice, not to mention inaccurate. It reduces them to monochromatic one-dimensionality where in reality their story is a brilliant, technicoloured thriller, a theatrical masterpiece that is true to the messy reality of life and history. To view history through only a rose-tinted lens is to deny ourselves perspective and the opportunity to truly understand and learn from our past.

This is not to say that they were evil. They were rulers of their time. There was never a moment when they could sit back and enjoy the fruits of their hard-won victories. The loyalties they cobbled together were lightweight things bobbing along on shallow waters, readily switching directions the moment the currents of fortune turned. There was always trouble brewing somewhere, and yet through it all their vision and belief in themselves as ones anointed by Siva, the greatest of the great gods, propelled them to seek and attain something sublime, luminous with grace and divinity.

This commands both admiration and introspection.

ACKNOWLEDGEMENTS

When I was a child, there was a range of things I wanted to become when I grew up. These included astronaut, zoo-keeper, the best musician in the world, under-sea explorer, dog trainer, and author. By any count, I am fully grown up now, and at last I can say that at least one of my childhood dreams has come true. I can actually say that I am an author!

This is not the book I imagined I would write. But write it I did, loving and hating the process, swearing I would never do this again, through all manner of ups and downs, a major health crisis and a pandemic. I was hugely fortunate to have the help and support of so many people. To them, I offer my heartfelt gratitude.

Benoy K. Behl, Peter Frankopan, Manfred Sommer, M. Swaminathan, and Thomas Voorter for their generous sharing of photographs that add a beautiful pictorial counterpoint to the deluge of words in this book. Girish Arora for all the maps, providing visually appealing spatial context for the Chola world.

David Davidar and Simar Puneet at Aleph for putting their faith in me and daring me to dream big. Pujitha Krishnan, a dream editor for any writer, with an ethereal magic touch that sculpted an unwieldy mass into a finely chiselled product. Saba Nehal and the rest of the Aleph team for their help in making this book ready for its entry into the world.

Saskia Kersenboom, my companion and guide on a magical trip through Thanjavur and its environs, during which we forged a lifelong friendship and I bonded with a very special group of fellow Yatris.

Aditi Sriram, whose enduring enthusiasm and encouragement opened a very crucial door, along with so much more. Subramani Aiyar, Chitra Andrade, Pradeep Chakravarthy,

Vidya Dehejia, Deepa Ganesh, R. Kannan, Nanditha Krishna, Chithra Madhavan, Bhamini Narayanan, Ramani Natarajan, Vijaya Sharada Ramakrishnan, Shyamala Raman, Girija Ramanathan, Keerthik Sasidharan, G. Sundar (Roja Muthiah Library)—who have each been a vital link in the chain of events that led to this book.

My dear friends and fellow musicians of the Navatman Music Collective, whose love, laughter and music fuelled me in so many ways and nourished something vital, deep inside me.

Karthik Narayanan Uncle (C. V. Karthik Narayanan) and Muthiah Uncle (S. Muthiah) who provided so much enthusiastic support when I was embarking on this endeavour. I am saddened that they are no longer with us.

Sekar and Ambika, always there, steady, calm, my anchors in Madras.

My children, the lights of my life, who give colour, meaning and purpose to everything, beyond anything I imagined possible. Aditi and Rohan, words fail me when I try to say what I want to, because what I feel transcends the realm of mere words. You are brilliant sunlight and iridescent moonshine. Yin and yang. Laughter and tears. Darkness and light. Classical and rap. You make me reach for the stars, you keep me grounded. I'll stop now before I embarrass myself, and you, any further.

Vijay, husband, lover, best friend, my unshakeable rock, champion teleporter, what a roller coaster journey we have been on together (and the ride's not stopping any time soon!), and I cannot think of a better companion than you, holding my hand through it all. For the belief in me, the encouragement, the infinite patience, the kindness, the generosity, the understanding, the joy, the fizz and sparkle, the unflagging support, the unwavering focus on what matters, the endless lectures on e-bikes and lunatic mayors and so much more. With you by my side, all's well with my world.

My parents, Raja and Vasanta. You gave me everything and more, and Mummy, you continue to do so, no matter what. You enriched my life with the best gifts: music, dance, books, but most importantly, all the tools to live a rich and meaningful life. You are the exemplars for a life well lived, and if I reach even half as high, I will consider my life a success. Your zest for life, your passion for stories and story-telling, your ability to see and attract goodness, your warmth and genuine interest in people, and so much more are such an inspiration and I am truly blessed and fortunate. Appa—you sparked my love of history and followed this project with such eagerness, and now you are no longer with us to see it to completion. You were my muse through it all.

IMAGE CREDITS

The River Kaveri at Tiruchirapalli. Courtesy British Museum.

Mural of the Kaveri River at the Panchanadishwara Temple, Thiruvaiyaru. Courtesy Thomas Voorter.

Palm leaf manuscript from the Sangam era. Courtesy Wikimedia Commons.

Map of the Kaveri. Courtesy Girish Arora.

Core areas of the major dynasties of medieval south India. Courtesy Girish Arora.

Vijayacholeshwara Temple, Narthamalai. Courtesy M. Swaminathan.

Moovar Koil, Kodumbalur. Courtesy M. Swaminathan.

Stone carvings and inscriptions at the Brahmapurishwara Temple. Courtesy M. Swaminathan.

Bronze idol of Queen Sembiyan Madevi. Courtesy Freer Gallery of Art and Arthur M. Sackler Gallery, Smithsonian Museum.

Konerirajapuram village. Courtesy M. Swaminathan.

Rajaraja I's Brihadeeshwara Temple, Thanjavur. Courtesy the author.

The Rajaraja Tiruvasal or entrance gateway (gopuram) at the Brihadeeshwara Temple. Courtesy the author.

Mural of Siva as Nataraja in the sanctum sanctorum of the Brihadeeshwara Temple. Photograph by Benoy K. Behl (2001).

Mural in the sanctum sanctorum of the Brihadeeshwara Temple. Courtesy Wikimedia Commons.

Karana (dance pose) sculptures in the sanctum sanctorum of the

AUTHOR'S NOTE

Let me begin with a disclaimer. I am not a historian. I have studied many things, but history is not one of them. And—a confession. For the longest time, I didn't even *like* history. But life goes down strange and unexpected paths and here I am, the author of a book—a *history* book, no less. Paraphrasing the words of the great Isaac Newton, I was able to journey into the world of the Cholas only by standing on the shoulders of giants.

This is my small tribute to some of those giants and their work and most importantly, the Cholas themselves.

How do we know what we know about Rajaraja and the other Cholas?

The Cholas left behind a permanent record of their times in the form of thousands of inscriptions. A priceless source of information, they are akin to the news bulletins of modern times, a mix of the macro and the micro, a cataloguing of mundane details presented with a dose of historical context and a coating of mythological shimmer. These inscriptions run and up and down temple walls, base mouldings, and trellis windows, around sculptures and recesses, and across huge, heavy copperplates, lines and lines of text covering all manner of details and information. They are a meticulous record of matters that covered the administrative, political, judicial, military, economic, agricultural, and socio-religious realms and left us a vast open book that brings their world alive to us. Modern-day plaques that list donors and other benefactors that are found in hospitals and other institutions are shorter, more matter-of-fact versions of the Chola inscriptions.

Inscriptions are not historical documents, but without them we would be without even the most rudimentary information about the life and time of the Cholas.

Among the most important inscriptional sources of information on the Cholas are four copperplate grants issued by four different Chola rulers: the Anbil, Leiden, Thiruvalangadu, and Kanyakumari grants. These are the only epigraphical sources known so far with the genealogy of the Cholas. It is largely thanks to these that we know anything at all about the kings who established and consolidated the newly risen line of Cholas. Each of the grants has a portion on the genealogy of the Cholas, from the mythical to the protohistoric to the current lineage; each was written by a different author, and therefore tell a somewhat different tale, reflecting the imagination and inclinations of the author.

The Cholas might have lived a thousand years ago, but it was just a little over a hundred years ago that epigraphists started deciphering the thousands of lines of squiggles that covered so many of their temple walls. And that is when we started to learn what we now know about them.

The field of Indian epigraphy was born in the eighteenth century, as Indology became an area of study. The earliest epigraphic publications consisted only of translations; there was no accompanying commentary, no text of the inscription in the original language. In the dawn of this new era, mistakes and misinterpretations abounded, about the dates as well as the actual meaning of the inscriptions. How could this *not* be, as they were dealing with languages long dead or radically different from their present form, dating protocols that were yet to be deciphered, and so much more. In due course, success was achieved in decipherment, and this resulted in a bursting open of the floodgates of epigraphy.

The epigraphists laboured in challenging conditions. It was an era when transportation and accommodations were primitive and technology non-existent. Even a seemingly simple matter like the entry into temples, especially for foreigners, could necessitate all manner of convoluted machinations.

In 1888, the first edition of the *Epigraphia Indica* was

published. Further editions came in regular succession, covering the constant flood of newly discovered and deciphered information in the world of Indian epigraphy. *Epigraphia Indica* became *the* premier journal for Indian epigraphy, and deservedly so. The closing decades of the nineteenth century were a golden age for this area of study, a true classical age of Indian epigraphy. When the twentieth century dawned, epigraphy was a well-established field of study. The scattershot mode of the early years evolved into a systematic and planned one, as the scholars learned more and gained a broader perspective. Some of the most prominent epigraphists who studied Chola inscriptions were Eugen Hultzsch, Rao Bahadur V. Venkayya, and Rao Bahadur Krishna Sastri. The modern seeker of historical knowledge is hugely fortunate: the *Epigraphia Indica*s have been digitized and are available online, at no cost. These volumes have been my lifeline while doing my research for this book.

Of the over 10,000 inscriptions that cover the walls of Chola temples, only around a thousand have been translated into English and published. For another couple of thousand, only a brief synopsis is available. The remaining are unwieldy rolls of rubbings taken directly from the temple walls, or painstakingly copied by hand, stored in the offices of the Epigraphical Survey of India. Today, the work of reading through these inscriptions is tedious enough; just imagine what the early epigraphists had to deal with, and there is simply not enough awe and admiration that is adequate to the sheer brilliance and magnitude of what they have achieved.

This book would never have come to fruition without the work of scholars like Nilakanta Sastri, Noboru Karashima, Y. Subbarayalu, Vidya Dehejia, Indira Vishwanathan Peterson, R. Champakalakshmi, R. Nagaswamy, Chithra Madhavan, Whitney Cox, and many others. They lend honor, dignity, and sheen to the label 'historian' and elevate it to greatness. To all of them, my debt of gratitude is immense and beyond measure.

NOTES AND REFERENCES

THE DYNASTY DIRECTORY

1 Noboru Karashima, *A Concise History of South India*, New Delhi: Oxford University Press, 2014.

PROLOGUE

This section describes a fictionalized set of events based largely on the following sources:

1 K. A. Nilakanta Sastri, *The Colas*, Madras: University of Madras, 1955, p. 12.

2 Rao Sahib H. Krishna Sastri (ed.), 'Thiruvalangadu Plates of Rajendra Chola, Verses 68, 69, 72', *South Indian Inscriptions Volume 3*, Part 3, New Delhi: Archaeological Survey of India, 1920, p. 421.

INTRODUCTION

1 F. W. Thomas (ed.), 'Hottur Inscription of Satyasraya, lines 1–7', *Epigraphia Indica Volume 16, 1921–1922*, New Delhi: Archaeological Survey of India, 1983, pp. 74–75.

2 Wilhelm Gieger (trans.), *Culavamsa: Being the More Recent Part of the* Mahavamsa, *Part 1*, Oxford: Oxford University Press, 1929, pp. 186–87.

3 See David Shulman, *Tamil: A Biography*, Cambridge, Massachusetts: Belknap Press of Harvard University Press, 2016, p. 165. Sastri, *The Colas*, p. 5.

4 Sastri, *The Colas*, p. 27.

5 Ibid., p. 26.

6 C. R. Kannan, *Rajaraja Cholan* (Tamil), Chennai, 2010, p. 124. See also Dhanalekshmi V., *Administration under the Imperial Cholas 850 to 1070 AD*, Tirunelveli: Manonmaniam Sundaranar University, 2017, p. 268.

7 Many sources mention this.

8 Rao Sahib H. Krishna Sastri (ed.), 'Thiruvalangadu Plates of Rajendra Chola, verse 4', *South Indian Inscriptions Volume 3, Part 3*, New Delhi: Archaeological Survey of India, 1920, p. 413.

9 F. W. Thomas (ed.), 'Anbil Plates of Sundara Chola, verse 11', *Epigraphia Indica Volume 15*, 1919–20, New Delhi: Archaeological Survey of India, 1982, p. 67.

10 John Ralston Marr, *The Eight Anthologies: A Study in Early Tamil Literature*, Tiruvanmiyur: Institute of Asian Studies, 1985, p. 107.

11 R. Swaminatha Aiyar, 'The Aryan Element in Dravidian Vocabularies', *Dravidian Theories*, Delhi: Motilal Banarsidass, 1987, p. 31.

12 N. P. Chakravarti (ed.), 'The Larger Leiden Plates of Rajaraja I, verse 7–8', *Epigraphia Indica, Volume 22, 1933–34*, New Delhi: Archaeological Survey of India, 1938, p. 255.

13 Romila Thapar, *Early India from the Origins to 1300*, Berkeley: University of California Press, 2002, p. 121, 319.

14 '....And this (conquest) has been won repeatedly by Devenampriya both (here) and among all (his) borderers, even as far as at (the distance of) six hundred *yojanas* where the Yona king named Antiyoga (is ruling), and beyond this Antiyoga,

(where) four—4—kings (are ruling), (viz, the king) named Tulamaya, (the king) named Antekina, (the king) named Maka, (the king) named Alikyashudala, (and) likewise *towards the south, (where) the Chodas and Pandyas (are ruling), as far as Tamraparni.*' (emphasis mine). E. Hultzsch (trans.), 'Thirteenth Rock-Edict: Kalsi', *Inscriptions of Asoka*, Oxford: Clarendon Press, 1925, p. 48.

15 *History of the World Map by Map*, New York: DK Publishing, 2018, p. 364, 376, 475.

16 Alain Daniélou, *A Brief History of India*, trans. by Kenneth F. Hurry, Vermont: Inner Traditions-Bear and Company, 2003, p. 168, 183.

CHAPTER 1: THE MOOVENTAR (OR THREE CROWNED KINGS): A STORY

1 Lt Col. Colin Mackenzie and H. H. Wilson Esq., *The Mackenzie Collection*, Calcutta: Asiatic Press, 1828, p. 184; William Taylor, *Examination and Analysis: The Mackenzie Manuscripts Deposited in the Madras College Library*, Calcutta: The Asiatic Society, 1838, pp. 49–56.

CHAPTER 2: BEHOLD THIS KAVERI, GRACEFULLY FLOWING

1 Ilango Adigal, *Shilappadikaram*, trans. by Alain Daniélou, New Delhi: Aleph Book Company, 2016, p. 36.

2 Shulman, 'The Tale of Agastya, Lopamudra and the Kaveri', *Tamil: A Biography*, p. 25.

3 Adigal, *Shilappadikaram*, p. 36.

4 T. Janakiraman and Chitti, *Eternal Kaveri: The Story of a River*, trans. by K. Krishnamurthy, Madras: Bookventure, 2020.

5 Vidya Dehejia, '65th A.W Mellon lectures in the Fine Arts', Washington D. C.: National Gallery of Art, April–May 2016.

6 Adigal, *Shilappadikaram*, p. 55.

CHAPTER 3: RED EARTH AND POURING RAIN: SANGAM LITERATURE

1 Shulman, *Tamil: A Biography*, pp. 32–33.

2 Kamil Zvelebil, *The Smile of Murugan: On Tamil Literature of South India*, Leiden: E.J. Brill, 1973, p. 46.

3 A. K. Ramanujan, *Poems of Love and War: From the Eight Anthologies and the Ten Long Poems of Classical Tamil*, New York: Columbia University Press, 2011, p. x.

4 Zvelebil, *The Smile of Murugan*, p. 28.

5 Meeting of Swaminatha Iyer with Ramaswamy Mudaliar. A.R. Venkatachalapathy, 'In Print, On the Net: Tamil Literary Canon in the Colonial and Post-Colonial Worlds', *Globalization in India: Contents and Discontents*, ed. by Suman Gupta, Tapan Basu, and Subarno Chattarji, New Delhi: Pearson Education, 2010, p. 161.

6 Shulman, *Tamil: A Biography*, pp. 98–104.

7 Ramanujan, *Poems of Love and War*, p. 3; David Dean Shulman, *The King and the Clown in South Indian Myth and Poetry*, Princeton: Princeton University Press, 1985, p. 6.

8 Ramanujan, *Poems of Love and War*, p. xi.

CHAPTER 4: THE KING WITH THE CHARRED LEG AND OTHER EARLY CHOLAS

1 Marr, 'Possibility of two Karikalas, grandfather and grandson', *Eight Anthologies*,

p. 97.

2 Sastri, *The Colas*, pp. 31–37.
3 Paranar, 'Puram 4' quoted in Marr, *Eight Anthologies*, p. 94.
4 Quoted in Sastri, *The Colas*, p. 32.
5 Marr, *Eight Anthologies*, p. 97.
6 'Porunaatruppadi' is a 248 line poem in praise of king Karikala Chola, and mentions his victory over the Pandya and Chera rulers at the battle of Venni. Vaidehi Herbert (trans.), *Patthupaat–Porunaatruppadai*, 129–48, https://sangamtranslationsbyvaidehi.com/a-porunaratruppadai/.
7 These lines, written about the Chera king Cheraman Peruncheralathan, are from the only poem written about this particular king. *Purananuru* is an anthology of 400 Puram poems, mostly in praise of kings and chieftains, and their battles and other exploits. Kalaittalaiyar, 'Purananuru verse 65'.
8 Adigal, *Shilappadikaram*, p. 19.
9 Herbert (trans.), 'Hospitality of the King', *Patthupaatu–Porunaatruppadai*, 74–83.
10 Karunkulal Athanar, 'Purananuru 224', quoted in V. Kanakasabhai Pillai, *The Tamils Eighteen Hundred Years Ago*, Asian Educational Services, 1904, 1979, p. 72.
11 Kovur Killi, 'Purananuru 44', quoted in Pillai, *The Tamils Eighteen Hundred Years Ago*, p. 74.
12 Kovur Killi, 'Purananuru 45', quoted in Ramanujan, *Poems of Love and War*, p. 121.
13 Jovur Killi, 'Purananuru 46', quoted in Ramanujan, *Poems of Love and War*, p. 122.
14 Sastri, *The Colas*, p. 43. Pillai, *The Tamils Eighteen Hundred Years Ago*, p. 76.
15 E. Hultzsch (ed.), 'Killi-Valvan, the Naga princess and their son Tondai', *South Indian Inscriptions Volume 3, Part 1*, Madras: Archaeological Survey of India, 1929, p. 3.
16 Alattur Kilar, 'Purananuru 69', quoted in Ramanujan, *Poems of Love and War*, p. 128.
17 Thomas, 'The Anbil Plates of Sundara Chola, verse 13', p. 68.
18 Paul Younger, *The Home of Dancing Sivan*, Oxford: Oxford University Press, 1955, p. 129; Sastri, *Colas*, p. 51.

CHAPTER 5: BEFORE DAWN: SOUTH INDIA ON THE EVE OF THE CHOLA RESURGENCE

1 Hermann Kulke and Dietmar Rothermund, *A History of India*, London: Routledge, 2004, p. 105.
2 Sastri, *The Colas*, p. 102.
3 Ibid.; Avvai Duraiswamy Pillai, 'Verses 154–157', *Tamil Navalar Caritai*, Tinnevelly: South India Saiva Siddhanta Works Publishing Society, 1949, p. 126, 128.
4 Rao Bahadur H. Krishna Sastri (ed.), 'Velvikudi Grant of Nedunjedaiyan, verse 39', *Epigraphia Indica Volume 17, 1923–24*, New Delhi: Archeological Survey of India, 1983, p. 306.
5 Sailendra Nath Sen, *Ancient Indian History and Civilization*, New Delhi: New Age International (P) Limited Publishers, 1999, p. 446, 455.
6 Samuel Beal, 'Chu-Li-Ye (Chulya or Chola)', *Chinese Accounts of India: Volume 4*, Calcutta: Susil Gupta (India) Private Ltd., 1958, p. 428. The li has varied over time. Today it is considered 500 metres. During the Tang dynasty it was likely around 320 metres.
7 Ibid., pp. 428–29.

8 Sastri, *The Colas*, p. 106.

CHAPTER 6: A GLIMMER ON THE HORIZON: PARAKESARI VIJAYALAYA (R. 850–871)

1 Thomas, 'The Anbil Plates of Sundara Chola, verse 16', p. 68.
2 Sastri, *The Colas*, pp. 111–12.
3 Krishna Sastri, 'Thiruvalangadu Plates of Rajendra Chola, verses 44–45', p. 418.
4 Rao Bahadur H. Krishna Sastri (ed.), 'The Kanyakumari Inscription of Virarajendra, verse 53–54', *Epigraphia Indica Volume 18, 1925–26*, New Delhi: Archeological Survey of India, 1983, p. 52.
5 V. Kanakasabhai Pillai, 'Tamil Historical Texts: The Vikrama-Cholan-Ula', *Indian Antiquary: A Journal of Oriental Research, Volume 22*, Delhi: Swati Publications, June 1893, p. 142.
6 Krishna Sastri, 'Thiruvalangadu Plates of Rajendra Chola, verse 46', p. 418.
7 'Then came king Rajakesarin, who conquered all (his) enemies. After him came Parakesarin, who was bent on destroying the towns of hostile kings.' Also 'The name of Rajakesarin and (that) of this Parakesarin became alternately the order of kings born in their family.' Chakravarti, 'The Larger Leiden Plates of Rajaraja I, verse 7–8', *Epigraphia Indica Volume 22,* p. 255.

CHAPTER 7: BUILDING TOWARDS GREATNESS: RAJAKESARI ADITYA (R. 870–907)

1 Krishna Sastri, 'The Kanyakumari Inscription of Virarajendra, verse 55', p. 52.
2 The Takkolam inscription that mentions the eclipse in Aditya Chola's twenty-fourth year is on the west wall of the Jalanatheshwara temple in Takkolam. The translated inscription reads: 'Hail, prosperity! On the day of the solar eclipse which occurred on the first moon in the month of Ani in the 24th year (of the reign) of king Rajakesarivarman, Piridipadiyar (Prithvipati) son of Maramaraiyar (Marasimha) presented a silver can with a spout weighing 317 *kalanju* to the temple of Mahadeva at Thiruvural (Takkolam). This (gift shall be under) the protection of all Maheshwaras.' See Hiranandani Sastri (ed.), *Epigraphia Indica Volume 19, 1927–28*, Delhi: Archeological Survey of India, 1983, p. 84.
3 This is a copperplate grant issued by Prithvipati I's grandson Prithvipati II, converting the village of Udayendiram into a brahmadeya (Brahmin village). E. Hultzsch, 'Udayendiram Plates of Prithvapati II, verse 18', *South Indian Inscriptions Volume 2*, New Delhi: Archaeological Survey of India, 1991, p. 387.
4 Madras Literary Society, *Madras Journal of Literature and Science*, Vol. 7, 1838, p. 3.
5 Madras Literary Society, *Madras Journal of Literature and Science*, Vol. 14, 1847, p. 14.
6 '...the king named Rajakesari who had great glory and fortune, (and) by whom the row of large temples of Siva, as it were banners of his own victories, lofty and unacquainted with defeat (collapse), was built of stone on the two banks of the (river) Kaveri from the Sahya mountain, inhabited by the lordly elephants whose cheeks dripped with (their) temple juice incessantly flowing, even to the ocean....' Thomas, 'Anbil Plates of Sundara Chola, verses 17–18', p. 68.
7 The milk of the sheep was used to make butter/ghee which was used to illuminate the lamp.

8 Thomas, 'Anbil Plates of Sundara Chola, verses 17–18', p. 68.
9 Hultzsch, 'Udayendiram Plates of Prithvipati II, verse 5', p. 386.
10 Aditya gilding the roof at Chidambaram. Nambi Antar Nambi, a poet and scholar who recovered and compiled the hymns of some of the Saivite Nayanmar poet-saints wrote a memoir about the sixty-three Nayanmars; in writing about one of them, Idangazhi, who was a Velir chieftain, he mentioned that this Nayanmar-chieftain was 'an ancestor of the family to which also belonged Aditya who covered the roof of the Chidambaram temple with gold obtained from Kongu'. This is repeated by later poet-scholars like Sekkilar and Umapati Sivacharya.
11 Krishna Sastri, 'The Kanyakumari Inscription of Virarajendra, verse 55', p. 52.
12 Krishna Sastri, 'Thiruvalangadu Plates of Rajendra Chola, verse 47', p. 418.
13 E. Hultzsch, 'Sholinghur Inscription of Parantaka 1, verse 2', *Epigraphia Indica Volume 4, 1896–97*, New Delhi: Archaeological Survey of India, 1979, p. 224.
14 S. R. Balasubrahmanyam, *Early Chola Temples*, Delhi: Orient Longman, 1971, pp. 101–103; Padma Kaimal, 'Early Cola Kings and Early Cola Temples', *Artibus Asiae*, Vol. 56, No. 1/2, 1996, p. 57.

CHAPTER 8: THE GRAND OLD MAN: PARAKESARI PARANTAKA (R. 907–955)

1 Krishna Sastri, 'The Kanyakumari Inscription of Virarajendra, verse 56', p. 52.
2 Professor F. Killborn, 'Dates of Chola Kings', *Epigraphia Indica Volume 8, 1905–06*, ed. by E. Hultzsch, New Delhi: Archaeological Survey of India, 1981, pp. 260–61.
3 Hultzsch, 'Udayendiram Plates of Prithvipati II, verse 20', p. 388.
4 E. Hultzsch, 'Sholinghur Inscription of Parantaka I, verse 8', *Epigraphia Indica Volume 4, 1896–97*, New Delhi: Archaeological Survey of India, 1981, p. 225.
5 Rao Sahib H. Krishna Sastri, 'Rajasimha's Sinnamannur Inscription, line 123', *South Indian Inscriptions Volume 3, Part 3 and 4*, New Delhi: Archaeological Survey of India, 1920, p. 461.
6 Krishna Sastri, 'Kanyakumari Inscription of Virarajendra, verses 56–60', p. 52.
7 Wilhelm Geiger (trans.), *The Mahavamsa of The Great Chronicle of Ceylon*, London: Oxford University Press, 1929, pp. 139–41.
8 Hiranandani Sastri, *Epigraphia Indica Volume 19, 1927–28*, p. 81.
9 Chakravarti, 'The Larger Leiden Plates of Rajaraja I, verse 20', p. 256.
10 E. Hultzsch (ed.), 'Atakur stone inscription of Krishna III and Butuga II, line 20', *Epigraphia Indica Volume 6, 1900–01*, New Delhi: Archaeological Survey of India, 1981, p. 52, 57.
11 The reference to Krishna III is in Pushpadanta's *Mahapurana*, a Jain text composed in the tenth century. P. L. Vaidya, *The Mahapurana of Puspadanta: Volume 1*, Bombay: Manikchand Digambara Jaina Granthamala, 1937, p. 5. See also V. R. Deoras, 'Fresh Light on the Southern Campaigns of the Rashtrakuta Emperor Krishna III', *Proceedings of the Indian History Congress*, Vol. 20, 1957, p. 135.
12 Chakravarti, 'The Larger Leiden Plates of Rajaraja I, verse 17', p. 256.
13 Krishna Sastri, 'Thiruvalangadu Plates of Rajendra Chola, verse 50', p. 419.
14 'He caused to be excavated hundreds and thousands of deep channels with clear water in order to make the earth very fertile'. K. G. Krishnan, 'Verse 21', *Karandai Tamil Sangam Plates of Rajendrachola I*, New Delhi: Archaeological Survey of India, 1984, p. 196.
15 'The Inscriptions at Uthiramerur', *Annual Report of the Archaeological Survey of*

India, 1904–5, Calcutta: Superintendent Government Printing, 1908, pp. 131–45.
16 Thomas, 'The Anbil Plates of Sundara Chola, verse 20', p. 68.

CHAPTER 9: CHAOS AMIDST CHAOS: GANDARADITYA TO UTTAMA CHOLA (R. 950–985)

1 Sastri, *The Colas*, p. 140.
2 Chakravarti, 'The Leiden Plates of Rajaraja I, verse 21', p. 256.
3 Balasubrahmanyam, *Early Chola Temples*, p. 75; N. P. Chakravarti (ed.), *Epigraphia Indica Volume 26, 1941–1942*, New Delhi: Archaelogical Survey of India, 1985, p. 84.
4 Suganthy Krishnamachari, 'A millennium gone but this chola queen is remembered', *The Hindu*, 7 March 2019.
5 Krishna Sastri, 'The Thiruvalangadu Plates of Rajendra Chola, verse 55', p. 419
6 Thomas, 'The Anbil Plates of Sundara Chola, verse 23', p. 68.
7 Chakravarti, 'The Larger Leiden Plates of Rajaraja I, verse 23', p. 256.
8 The only proof apart from the Leiden grant that Arinjaya ruled at all is an inscription that mentions the two queens of Arinjigaivarman who died at Aatrur. Another inscription by his grandson Rajaraja records his building a pallipadai or memorial shrine temple to his grandfather who died at Aatrur. In any event, his reign was too short, and very likely too uneventful, to find meaningful mention in inscriptions. This evidence is as thin as it gets, but Arinjaya's accession was important because it moved the Chola line of rulers to his branch of the family; had Arinjaya not reigned, and had he not been succeeded by his son Sundara Chola, the great Rajaraja would have been very hard-pressed to make a claim to the throne.
9 E. Hultzsch (ed.), 'Melpadi Inscriptions, line 1', *South Indian Inscriptions Volume 3, Part 1*, New Delhi: Archaeological Survey of India, 1929, p. 23.
10 Krishna Sastri, 'Thiruvalangadu Plates of Rajendra Chola verse 58', p. 419.
11 Ibid., pp. 68–69.
12 Krishnan, 'Verse 24–25', *Karandai Tamil Sangam Plates of Rajendrachola I*, p. 196.
13 Chakravarti, 'The Larger Leiden Plates of Rajaraja I, verse 25', p. 256.
14 There is a mass of conflicting and confusing inscriptional, astrological, and other information on the date Aditya Karikala might have been appointed yuvaraja, as well as how long he held this position before he died, while his father still reigned. According to the opinions of some of the most respected scholars his coronation as co-regent could have taken place any time between 956 and 966. In far less dispute is the year of his death, which several scholars agree happened in the year 969.
15 Krishna Sastri, 'Thiruvalangadu Plates of Rajendra Chola, verse 68', p. 420.
16 Bhumi Vikramakesari turned the waters of the Kaveri red. Inscription on the south wall of the central shrine of the Muvarkoil temple in Kodumbalur. G. V. Srinivasa Rao (ed.), *South Indian Inscriptions Volume 23*, New Delhi: Archaeological Survey of India, 1979, p. 101.
17 Aditya Karikala's death is mentioned in an inscription at Udaiyarkudi, found on the west wall of the central shrine of the Anantiswarasvasvamin temple. The inscription is Rajaraja Chola's, from the year 988. 'Soman...his younger brother Ravidasan (alias Panchavan), Brahmadhirajan, and his younger brother Parameshvaran (alias Irummudicchola Brahmadhirajan) have been guilty of treason as they murdered Karikalasola who took the head of the Pandya.' Hirananda Sastri (ed.), *Epigraphia Indica Volume 21, 1931–32*, New Delhi: Archaeological Survey of India, 1984, p. 171.
18 There are several inscriptions that refer to Sundara Chola in his 'Pon Maligai'

(golden palace); Thunjinadeva means the lord who died. One of these inscriptions is on the north wall of the central shrine in the Manikanteswaram temple in Thirumalpuram. This is dated Sundara Chola's fourteenth regnal year. The inscription gives details of his grant to a cluster of villages, which he dictates from the first floor of his golden palace in Kanchipuram.

19 Krishna Sastri, 'Thiruvalangadu Plates of Rajendra Chola, verse 65', p. 420.

20 'The mass of people believe this king to be Manu, who, out of love for the (good) conduct which was set forth by himself, has come to the earth once again to establish his law which had become lax under the influence of the Kali (age).' Krishna Sastri, 'Thiruvalangadu Plates of Rajendra Chola, verse 57', p. 419.

21 'Out of affection.... To this brahmana who belongs to the Jaimini sutra and the Avenika gotra, the king, out of affection, gave the village called Karunakara Mangalam, consisting of ten velis of land, in Nalvilankudi in the great province of Alundur, inclusive of the taxes....together with tanks, trees, pleasure gardens, wells, anthills and ponds, with the boundaries marked by the circumambulation of a female elephant and endowed with all privileges.' Thomas, 'The Anbil Plates of Sundara Chola, verses 38–41', p. 68.

22 T. A. Gopinatha Rao 'Introduction to the Anbil Plates of Sundara Chola', *Epigraphia Indica Volume 15, 1919–20*, ed. by F. W. Thomas, New Delhi: Archaeological Survey of India, 1982, pp. 44–46.

23 Chakravarti, 'The Larger Leiden Plates of Rajaraja I, verse 29', p. 256.

24 'When that chief of kings went to heaven, the son of Gandaraditya, (king) Madurantaka (another name for Uttama Chola), he of powerful arms and famous as Mahendra, protected the earth which had the ocean for its girdle.' Ibid.

25 'Applying his mind to the devotion of Siva, utilizing his wealth in the act of performing his worship, employing all his retinue in the construction of houses (temples) for him and directing his subjects to regularly perform his festive processions, showing his wrath only in the killings of his enemies and distributing his riches among virtuous Brahmins, that king (Madurantaka) bore on his shoulder the weight of the earth.' Krishna Sastri, 'The Thiruvalangadu Plates of Rajendra Chola', p. 420.

26 'Though requested by the subjects to occupy the Chola throne in order to destroy the persistently blinding darkness of the powerful Kali age, Arulmozhivarman who understood the essence of royal conduct desired not the kingdom for himself even in his mind, while his paternal uncle coveted his (Arulmozhivarman's) dominions.' Ibid.

27 Sastri, *The Colas*, p. 159.

28 Walter Elliot, *Coins of Southern India*, Varanasi: Prithivi Prakashan, 1970, p. 132.

29 Rao Bahadur H. Krishna Sastri (ed.), 'Madras Museum Plates of Uttama Chola', *South Indian Inscriptions Volume 3, Part 3 and 4*, New Delhi: The Archaeological Survey of India, 1920, pp. 264–68.

30 Ibid., p. 272.

31 Sastri, *The Colas*, p. 160.

32 Ibid.

CHAPTER 10: THE KING OF KINGS: RAJARAJA CHOLA (R. 985–1014)

1 Krishna Sastri, 'Thiruvalangadu Plates of Rajendra Chola, verse 72', p. 421.

2 Ibid.

3 Sastri, *The Colas*, p. 168.
4 Krishna Sastri, 'Thiruvalangadu Plates of Rajendra Chola, verse 68', p. 420.
5 Hirananda Sastri (ed.), 'The Udaiyargudi Inscription of Rajakesarivarman', *Epigraphia Indica Volume 21, 1931–32*, New Delhi: Archaeological Survey of India, 1984, p. 170.
6 Krishna Sastri, 'Thiruvalangadu Plates of Rajendra Chola, verse 69', p. 420.
7 Ibid.
8 N. Sethuraman, *Raja Raja, the Great: Seminar Proceedings*, Bombay: Ananthacharya Indological Research Institute, 1987, pp. 28–38.
9 Krishna Sastri, 'Thiruvalangadu Plates of Rajendra Chola, verse 76', p. 421.
10 Sastri, *The Colas*, p. 189.
11 E. Hultzsch (ed.), 'Inscription in the Sthanunatha Temple at Suchindram', *Epigraphia Indica Volume 5, 1898–99*, New Delhi: Archaeological Survey of India, 1984, p. 45. See also *Journal of the Andhra Historical Research Society, Volume 10*, Rajahmundry: Andhra Historical Research Society, 1937, p. 43.
12 T. S. Subramanian, 'Unearthed Stone Ends Debate', *The Hindu*, 27 November 2009.
13 Krishna Sastri, 'Thiruvalangadu Plates of Rajendra Chola, verse 78', p. 421.
14 Hultzsch, 'Inscription in the Sthanunatha Temple at Suchindram', p. 46.
15 S. R. Balasubrahmanyam, *Middle Chola Temples*, Thomson Press (India) Ltd, 1973, pp. 201–202.
16 'Annual Report on South Indian Epigraphy for the Year Ending 31st March 1928', Madras: Government Press, 1928, p. 52.
17 'He who conquered the Malai Nadu, (i.e., most probably the Kongu and Chera countries) and killed 18 princes in retaliation for the insult offered to his envoy'. Pillai, 'Tamil Historical Texts: The Vikrama-Cholan-Ula', p. 142.
18 Krishna Sastri, 'Thiruvalangadu Plates of Rajendra Chola, verse 76', p. 421.
19 Usha R. Vijailakshmi, 'Tamil Migration into Karnataka (The Period of Chola Conquest of Southern Karnataka and the Consolidation of Power from 850–1279 A.D)', *Proceedings of the Indian History Congress*, Vol. 66, 2005–2006, p. 241.
20 Chithra Madhavan, *History and Culture of Tamil Nadu*: *Volume 1*, New Delhi: DK Printworld, 2013, p. 72, 81, 88, 151.
21 B. V. Krishna Rao, 'Conjeevaram Inscription of the Telugu Chola King Jatachola Bhima', *Journal of the Andhra Historical Research Society, Volume 10*, p. 50.
22 Dr S. Krishnaswami Aiyangar, 'The Chola Rajaraja I and the Eastern Chalukya alliance', *Journal of the Andhra Historical Research Society, Volume 10*, p. 183.
23 B. Lewis Rice, 'Mulbagul Taluq', *Epigraphia Carnatica Volume 10*, Manglore: Basel Mission Press, 1905, p. 108.
24 'Just as God Isvara received (controlled) the Ganga rushing down (falling fast) from the heavens in his own matted locks, so also Rajaraja mounted on a horse and alone having made to return his own army that resembled (in vastness) the (very) ocean of the (time of the) end of the Age (Kalpa), withstood by (means of) his thin sword (alone) as if by sport, the onrushing army of Satyasraya.' Krishnan, 'Verse 29', *Karandai Tamil Sangam Plates of Rajendrachola I*, p. 196.
25 Krishna Sastri, 'Thiruvalangadu Plates of Rajendra Chola, verse 81', p. 421.
26 F. W. Thomas, 'Hottur Inscription of Satyasraya', *Epigraphia Indica Volume 16, 1921–22*, New Delhi: Archaeological Survey of India, 1983, p. 74, 75.
27 K. V. Subrahmanya Aiyer (ed.), *South India Inscriptions Volume 6*, New Delhi: Archaeological Survey of India, 1986, p. 49; N. Lakshminarayan Rao and D. C.

Sircar, *Epigraphia Indica Volume 30, 1953–54*, New Delhi: Archaeological Survey of India, 1987, p. 248.

28 Rao and Sircar, *Epigraphia Indica Volume 30*, p. 248.

29 Ibid.

30 Geiger, *The Mahavamsa*, pp. 186–87.

31 George W. Spencer, 'The Politics of Plunder: The Cholas in Eleventh-Century Ceylon', *Journal of Asian Studies*, Vol. 35, No. 3, May 1976, p. 414.

32 Krishna Sastri, 'Thiruvalangadu Plates of Rajendra Chola, verse 80', p. 421.

33 Geiger, *The Mahavamsa*, p. 188.

34 Sastri, *The Colas*, p. 183.

CHAPTER 11: THE LAND BENEATH THE CHOLA SUN: ORGANIZATION

1 Maurice Walshe, 'Aggnana Sutta: On Knowledge of Beginnings', *The Long Discourses of the Buddha: A Translation of the Digha Nikaya*, Boston: Wisdom Publications, 1987, pp. 407–15.

2 Sastri, *The Colas*, p. 462, 463.

3 Burton Stein, *Peasant State and Society in Medieval South India*, Delhi: Oxford University Press, 1980, pp. 256–65.

4 Hermann Kulke, 'Fragmentation and Segmentation Versus Integration? Reflections on the Concepts of Indian Feudalism and the Segmentary State in Indian History', *Studies in History*, Vol. 4, 1982, pp. 237–63.

5 Y. Subbarayalu, *South India Under the Cholas*, New Delhi: Oxford University Press, 2012, pp. 224–27.

6 Sastri, *The Colas*, p. 463.

7 Subbarayalu, *South India Under the Cholas*, p. 77, 83, 84.

8 Ibid., p. 84, 88, 101; Noboru Karashima, *South Indian Society in Transition: Ancient to Medieval*, New Delhi: Oxford University Press, 2009, pp. 91–92.

9 Subbarayalu, *South India Under the Cholas*, p. 100.

10 Ibid., pp. 226–27.

11 Ibid., pp. 10–11, 92–93.

12 Stein, *Peasant State and Society in Medieval South India*, p. 71.

13 Subbarayalu, *South India Under the Cholas*, pp. 167–69.

14 Karashima, *A Concise History of South India*, p. 135; Subbarayalu, *South India Under the Cholas*; Stein, *Peasant State and Society in Medieval South India*, p. 90. All three books have extensive discussions on the ur, nadu, valanadu, mandalam, and other territorial categories.

15 Stein, *Peasant State and Society in Medieval South India*, pp. 141–70.

16 Kenneth R. Hall, *Networks of Trade, Polity and Societal Integration in Chola-Era South India*, New Delhi: Primus Books, 2014, p. 7; Subbarayalu, *South India Under the Cholas*, p. 140.

17 'Annual Report of the Archaeological Survey of India, 1904–05', Calcutta: Superintendent Government Printing, 1908, pp. 131–45.

18 Sastri, *The Colas*, p. 577.

19 Thomas, 'Anbil Plates of Sundara Chola', pp. 66–72.

20 Subbarayalu, *South India Under the Cholas*, p. 65.

21 Chakravarti, 'Larger Leiden Plates of Rajaraja I, Verse 20', p. 256.

22 Stein, *Peasant State and Society in Medieval South India*, p. 6.

23 Noboru Karashima, 'Epigraphical Study of Ancient and Medieval Villages in the

Tamil Country', *Review of Agrarian Studies*, Vol. 1, Issue 2, December 2011.

24 M. D. Rajkumar, 'Struggles for Rights during Later Chola Period', *Social Scientist* Vol. 2, No. 6/7, Jan-Feb 1974, pp. 29–35.

25 Hall, *Networks of Trade, Polity, and Societal Integration*, p. 241.

CHAPTER 12: THE TWAIN MEET: TRADE AND MERCHANTS

1 Ibid., pp. 21–23.

2 Ibid.

3 Herman Kulke, K. Kesavapany, Vijay Sakhuja, *Nagapattinam to Suvarnadwipa: Reflections on the Chola Naval Expeditions to Southeast Asia*, Singapore: Institute of Southeast Asian Studies, 2009, p. 54.

4 Ibid., p. 149, 159.

5 Meera Abraham, 'The History of the Ayyavole Association', *Two Medieval Merchant Guilds of South India*, Delhi: Manohar Publications, 1988.

6 Ibid., p. 42. See also Sastri, *Epigraphia Indica Volume 19*, p. 80.

7 Abraham, *Two Medieval Merchant Guilds of South India*, p. 51, 52, 87.

8 Subbarayalu, *South India Under the Cholas*, pp. 188–99.

9 Kulke, et al., *Nagapattinam to Suvarnadwipa*, p. 139.

10 Subbarayalu, *South India Under the Cholas*, pp. 176–85.

11 Ibid., p. 7, 44; Abraham, 'The Manigramam Guild of Traders', *Two Medieval Merchant Guilds of South India*.

12 Geoff Wade, 'An Early Age of Commerce in South East Asia, 900–1300 CE', *Journal of Southeast Asian Studies*, Vol. 40, No. 2, 2009, p. 237.

13 'In a loosely integrated political system like the Chola dynastic state, it was inevitable that merchant–artisan alliances, like other communities and institutions, should have existed in balanced but cautious cooperation with the royal court.' Spencer, 'Politics of Plunder', p. 414.

14 Hall, *Networks of Trade, Polity, and Societal Integration*, pp. 106–107.

15 Hultzsch, *South Indian Inscriptions Volume 1*, pp. 63–66.

16 Chakravarti, 'Larger Leiden Plates of Rajaraja I, pp. 213–66.

17 Kulke, et al., *Nagapattinam to Suvarnadwipa*, p. 5.

18 Ibid., p. 151.

19 Tansen Sen, 'Maritime Contacts between China and the Cola Kingdom', *Mariners, Merchants and Oceans: Studies in Maritime History*, ed. by Kuzhippalli Skaria Mathew, New Delhi: Manohar Publishers, 1995, p. 38.

20 Ibid.

21 Kulke, et al., *Nagapattinam to Suvarnadwipa*, p. 8.

22 Ibid., pp. 292–300.

23 Ibid.

24 Ibid.

CHAPTER 13: THE NAME OF VALOUR: THE CHOLA ARMY AND NAVY

1 Krishna Sastri, 'Thiruvalangadu Plates of Rajendra Chola, verse 79', p. 418.

2 Subbarayalu, *South India Under the Cholas*, p. 198.

3 Dr B. CH. Chhabra and N. Lakshminarayan Rao (eds.), *Epigraphia Indica Volume 27, 1947–48*, New Delhi: Archaeological Survey of India, 1985, pp. 292–98, 303.

4 Sastri, *The Colas*, p. 454; Rao Bahadur V. Venkayya, 'Introduction', *South Indian Inscriptions Volume 2*, ed. by E. Hultzsch, New Delhi, Archaeological Survey of

India, 1991.

5 The eminent historian Nilakanta Sastri believed that the Chola army was a highly structured entity. In spite of Venkayya's terming them regiments and the structure imagined by Sastri's description of them, scholars like George Spencer say they were very unlikely to have been a unified, organized army with all these different subdivisions. Rather, he suggests, they were an ad hoc collection of units that came together as and when the occasion required. Their names reflected their geographic origins, and sometimes their being part of a particular peasant community. Burton Stein has said that many of these peasant units, formed for the protection of certain localities, might have been recruited by the Cholas for larger military expeditions. See Sastri, *The Colas*, p. 454; George Spencer, 'The Politics of Plunder', p. 407; Stein, *Peasant State and Society in Medieval South India*, p. 124, 125.

6 Sastri, *The Colas*, p. 455.

7 Ibid., p. 456.

8 Rajkumar, 'Struggles for Rights during Later Chola Period', p. 30.

CHAPTER 14: THE PRICE OF TRANSGRESSION: CRIME AND PUNISHMENT

1 Ibid., p. 675.

2 Ibid., p. 474.

3 'Annual Report of the Archaeological Survey of India, 1904–05', pp. 131–45.

4 Noboru Karashima, 'The Past as Known From Tamil Inscriptions: Village Community and Challenge to the Caste System', 8 February 2016, p. 11, 12.

5 Ibid.

6 Sastri, 'The Udaiyargudi Inscription of Rajakesarivarman', p. 171.

7 Sastri, *The Colas*, p. 477.

8 Ibid., p. 480.

9 Ibid., p. 513.

CHAPTER 15: O MADMAN WITH MOON-CROWNED HAIR: FAITH AND THE BHAKTI MOVEMENT

1 The wondrous black-necked Lord Siva. From the Sambandar Tevaram Vantaranga Punarkamala by Vijaya Sharada Ramakrishnan.

2 Indira Viswanathan Peterson, *Poems to Siva: The Hymns of the Tamil Saints*, Princeton: Princeton University Press, 1989.

3 Vidya Dehejia, *Chola: Sacred Bronzes of Southern India*, London: Royal Academy Books, 2007, p. 95.

4 P. Sundaram Pillai, 'The Age of Tirunanasambandha', *Indian Antiquary, Volume 25*, ed. by Richard Carnac Temple, Bombay: Education Society's Press, 1896, pp. 113–25.

5 Peterson, *Poems to Siva*, p. 276.

6 Ibid., p. 287.

7 Ibid., p. 303.

8 Ibid., p. 315.

9 Ibid., pp. 313–15.

10 Ibid., p. 231.

11 Hall, *Networks of Trade, Polity, and Societal Integration*, p. 248.

12 Lokeshwarri S. K., 'Thanjavur's Chola Mystery', *Hindu Business Line*, 29 November

2019; Sastri, *The Colas*, p. 648.
13 Sastri, *The Colas*, p. 453.
14 Karen Pechilis Prentiss, 'A Tamil Lineage for Saiva Siddhanta Philosophy', *History of Religions*, Vol. 35, No. 3, February 1996, pp. 231–57.
15 Younger, *Home of the Dancing Sivan*, pp. 163–76.
16 Ibid., p. 215.
17 Rajeshwari Ghose, *The Tyagaraja Cult in Tamilnadu*, New Delhi: Motilal Banarsidass Publishers, 1996, p. 122.
18 Younger, *Home of the Dancing Sivan*, p. 120.
19 Ghose, *Tyagaraja Cult in Tamilnadu*, pp. 79–82.

CHAPTER 16: THE EPONYMOUS TEMPLE: RAJARAJESHWARAM IN THANJAN'S CITY

1 Hultzsch, *South Indian Inscriptions Volume 2, Part 1*, p. 8.
2 Pillai, *The Great Temple at Tanjore*, p. 1.
3 H. A. Newell, *Tanjore (The City of the Mammoth Bull)*, Madras and Bangalore: Higginbothams, 1900, p. 1.
4 Krishna Sastri, 'Thiruvalangadu Plates of Rajendra Chola, verse 45', p. 418.
5 Karuvur Devar's poem. Thiruvissaipu, part of the 9th book of the Thirumurai, a twelve book compendium of Saiva poems. Quoted in Sastri, *The Colas*, p. 449.
6 Ibid.
7 Venkayya, 'Introduction', *South Indian Inscriptions Volume 2.*
8 Balambal, 'Kundavai—A Chola Princess', pp. 79–82
9 Vidya Dehejia, *Art of the Imperial Cholas*, New York: Columbia University Press, 1990, p. 51.
10 Ibid.
11 Geeta Vasudevan, *The Royal Temple of Rajaraja*, New Delhi: Abhinav Publications, 2003, p. 101.
12 Kapila Vatsyayan (ed.), *Concepts of Space, Ancient and Modern*, New Delhi: Abhinav Publications, 1991, p. 304, 305.
13 Hultzsch, *South Indian Inscriptions Volume 2, Part 1*, p. 8.
14 Dr R. Nagaswamy, 'Saivism Under Rajaraja – A Study', *Raja Raja the Great: Seminar Proceedings*, Bombay: Ananthacharya Indological Research Institute, 1987, p. 51.
15 Hultzsch, *South Indian Inscriptions Volume 2, Part 1*, pp. 35–36.
16 Krishna Sastri, *South Indian Inscriptions Volume 2, Part 3*, pp. 278–97.
17 Ibid., p. 306.
18 A. Srivathsan, 'An Exciting Discovery and a 1931 Scoop for The Hindu', *The Hindu*, 3 February 2010.
19 T. S. Subramanian, 'How karana sculptures in Big Temple were discovered', *The Hindu*, 23 September 2010.
20 Dehejia, *Art of the Imperial Cholas*, p. 54, 55.
21 Ibid., p. 56.
22 Balasubrahmanyam, *Middle Chola Temples*, p. 22, 23, 47.
23 Ibid., p. 48.
24 Vasudevan, *The Royal Temple of Rajaraja*, pp. 48–58.
25 T. Venkasami Row, *A Manual of the District of Tanjore in the Madras Presidency*, Madras: Lawrence Asylum Press, 1883, p. 243.
26 J. M. Somasundaram Pillai, *The Great Temple at Tanjore*, Tanjore: Tanjore Palace

Devasthanams, 1935, pp. 39–43.
27 Ibid., p. 43.
28 Hultzsch, *South Indian Inscriptions Volume 2, Part 1*, p. 8.

CHAPTER 17: RESPLENDENT IN CEREMONIAL DRESS: CHOLA BRONZES

1 Thomas E. Levy, et al., *Masters of Fire: Hereditary Bronze Casters of South India*, Bochum: Die Deutsche Bibliothek, 2008, p. 18, 26, 30, 49.
2 Dehejia, '65th A.W Mellon lectures in the Fine Arts'.
3 Results of the lab test for the source of copper. Email from Professor Vidya Dehejia to me, dated 22 February 2021.
4 Levy, et al., *Masters of Fire*, pp. 49–82.
5 Balasubrahmanyam, *Middle Chola Temples*, p. 48.
6 Yogesh Kabirdoss, '1,000-year-old stolen idols of Rajaraja Chola return to TN from Gujarat', *Times of India*, 31 May 2018.
7 Younger, *Home of the Dancing Sivan*, p. 69, 70.
8 Nagaswamy, 'Saivism Under Rajaraja', pp. 58–60.
9 Ibid., p. 58.
10 Leslie C. Orr, 'Processions in the medieval South Indian temple: Sociology, sovereignty and soteriology', *South-Indian Horizons: Felicitation volume for François Gros on the occasion of his 70th birthday*, Jean-Luc Chevillard and Eva Wilden (eds.), Pondicherry: Institut Français de Pondichéry, 2004, p. 451.
11 Peterson, *Poems to Siva*, p. 183.

CHAPTER 18: IT'S A WOMAN'S WORLD: CHOLA WOMEN

1 Leslie C. Orr, *Donors, Devotees, and Daughters of God: Temple Women in Medieval Tamilnadu*, Oxford: Oxford University Press, 2000, p. 37.
2 Ibid., p. 50.
3 Ibid., p. 40, 41.
4 Ibid., p. 72.
5 Sastri, *The Colas*, p. 186.
6 Venkayya, 'Introduction', *South Indian Inscriptions Volume 2*.
7 G. V. Srinivasa Rao (ed.), *South Indian Inscriptions Volume 13*, New Delhi: Archaeological Survey of India, 1952, p. 81.
8 'Annual Report on Indian Epigraphy 1924–1925', New Delhi: Archaeological Survey of India, 1925; Rao, *South Indian Inscriptions Volume 13*, p. 81.
9 Orr, *Donors, Devotoees and Daughters of God*, p. 66.
10 Ibid., p. 75, 76.
11 Ibid., p. 72.
12 Ibid., p. 73.
13 Ibid., p. 104.
14 Ibid., p. 112.
15 Hultzsch, *South Indian Inscriptions Volume 2*, Part 1, pp. 278–97.
16 Dehejia, '65th A.W Mellon lectures in the Fine Arts'.
17 Padma Kaimal, 'A Man's World? Gender, Family and Architectural Patronage in Medieval India', *Archives of Asian Art*, Vol. 53, 2003, p. 46.
18 Dehejia, *Art of the Imperial Cholas*, p. 33, 34.
19 For instance, an inscription dated 988 (during Rajaraja's reign) at a Siva temple in

Tirukodikaval tells of a royal directive from Queen Sembiyan giving insturctions on how certain temple lands should be irrigated). See Vidya Dehejia, *The Thief Who Stole My Heart: The Material Life of Sacred Bronzes from Chola India, 855–1280*, Princeton: Princeton University Press, 2021 p. 92.

20 Krishna Sastri, *South Indian Inscriptions Volume 2, Part 3*, p. 296.
21 Ibid., p. 297.
22 S. R. Balasubrahmanyam, *Early Chola Temples*, New Delhi: Orient Longman, 1971, p. 172.
23 Ibid., pp. 168–69.
24 Dehejia, *Art of the Imperial Cholas*, p. 2.
25 Dehejia, *The Thief Who Stole My Heart*, p. 118.
26 Balasubrahmanyam, *Early Chola Temples*, p. 173.
27 Ibid., p. 181.
28 Dehejia, '65th A.W Mellon lectures in the Fine Arts'.
29 V. Balambal, 'Kundavai—A Chola Princess', *Proceedings of the Indian History Congress*, Vol. 39, 1978, pp. 77–78.
30 Hultzsch, *South Indian Inscriptions Volume 2, Part 1*, p. 8.
31 Balambal, 'Kundavai—A Chola Princess', pp. 79–82.
32 Hultzsch, *South Indian Inscriptions Volume 2*, pp. 17–18.

CHAPTER 19: THE DAZZLING SON: PARAKESARI RAJENDRA (R. 1012–1044)

1 Krishna Sastri, 'The Kanyakumari Inscription of Virarajendra, verse 68', p. 53.
2 Sastri, *The Colas*, p. 194.
3 Krishna Sastri, 'Introduction to the Thiruvalangadu Plates of Rajendra Chola', *South Indian Inscriptions Volume 3*, p. 385, 426.
4 Sastri, *The Colas*, p. 196.
5 Spencer, 'Politics of Plunder', p. 416, 417.
6 Sastri, *The Colas*, p. 202.
7 Krishna Sastri, 'Thiruvalangadu Plates of Rajendra Chola, verse 103', p. 423.
8 Dehejia, *Art of the Imperial Cholas*, p. 79.
9 Daud Ali, 'The Epigraphical Legacy at Gangaikondacholapuram: Problems and Possibilities', *New Dimensions in Tamil Epigraphy: A Multi-Disciplinary Approach*, ed. by Appasamy Murugaiyan, Chennai: Crea Publishers, 2012, p. 5.
10 Dehejia, *Art of the Imperial Cholas*, p. 79.
11 Verses 79–81 of the 'Rajaraja Sola Ula' by Ottakoothar quoted in R. Nagaswamy, *Gangaikondacholapuram*, Tamil Nadu: State Department of Archaeology, 1970, p. 57. Translated in Dehejia, *Art of the Imperial Cholas*, p. 71.
12 Dehejia, *Art of the Imperial Cholas*, p. 79.
13 Ibid., p. 80.
14 Ibid.
15 R. Nagaswamy, 'Archaeological Finds in South India: Esalam Bronzes and Copperplates', *Bulletin de l'Ecole Francaise d'Extreme Orient*, Tome 76, 1987, p. 9.
16 Kulke, et al., *Nagapattinam to Suvarnadwipa*, pp. 1–7.
17 Ibid., p. 69.
18 Ibid.
19 Barbara Watson Andaya, *A History of Malaysia*, Honolulu: University of Hawai'i Press, 2001, p. 26.

20 Kulke, et al., *Nagapattinam to Suvarnadwipa*, p. 183.
21 Ibid., pp. 85–88.
22 Hultzsch, *South Indian Inscriptions Volume 2, Part 1*, p. 109.
23 Kulke, et al., *Nagapattinam to Suvarnadwipa*, p. 84, 100.
24 Risha Lee, *Constructing Community: Tamil Merchant Temples in India and China, 850–1281*, New York: Columbia University Press, 2012, p. 134; Kulke, et al., *Nagapattinam to Suvarnadwipa*, p. 287.
25 There is no consensus on whether Rajendra actually married the Srivijaya king's daughter. The Sejaru Malaya, a chronicle of the Malacca kings of the fifteenth century, wove the Cholas into the ancestory of these kings (along with Alexander the Great and the kings of Srivijaya). George Spencer, *The Politics of Expansion: The Chola Conquest of Sri Lanka and Sri Vijaya*, Madras: New Era Publications, 1983, p. 147.
26 Kulke, et al., *Nagapattinam to Suvarnadwipa*, p. 11, 72.
27 'Annual Report on Epigraphy, 1915–1920', New Delhi: Department of Archaeology, 1896.
28 'Annual Report on Epigraphy, 1915–1920', p. 118; '1,000-year-old chola monument remains obscure', *The Hindu*, 25 January 2020.

CHAPTER 20: THE KING WHO DIED ON THE BACK OF AN ELEPHANT: RAJAKESARI RAJADHIRAJA (R. 1044–1054)

1 Krishna Sastri, 'The Kanyakumari Inscription of Virarajendra, verse 73', p. 54.
2 Sastri, *The Colas*, p. 254.
3 Richard H. Davis, *Lives of Indian Images*, Princeton: Princeton University Press, 1997, pp. 51–53.
4 Sastri, *The Colas*, p. 256.
5 Spencer, 'Politics of Plunder', p. 417.
6 'Annual Report on South Indian Epigraphy for the year 1924–25', p. 83.
7 Sastri, *The Colas*, p. 261.
8 Pillai, 'Tamil Historical Texts: The Vikrama-Cholan-Ula', p. 148.

CHAPTER 21: THE BATTLEFIELD KING: PARAKESARI RAJENDRA II/ RAJENDRADEVA (R. 1054–1063)

1 Krishna Sastri, 'The Kanyakumari Inscription of Virarajendra, verse 74', p. 54.
2 Hultzsch,, *South Indian Inscriptions Volume 3, Part 1*, p. 112.
3 Ibid., p. 63; Sastri, *The Colas*, p. 252.
4 Sastri, *The Colas*, p. 253.
5 Krishna Sastri, *South Indian Inscriptions Volume 3*, p. 37.
6 Sastri, *The Colas*, p. 263.

CHAPTER 22: BLOOD AND DIPLOMACY: RAJAKESARI VIRARAJENDRA (R. 1063–1070)

1 Krishna Sastri, 'The Kanyakumari Inscription of Virarajendra, verse 75', p. 54.
2 Sastri, *The Colas*, p. 268; Krishna Sastri, *South Indian Inscriptions Volume 3*, p. 69.
3 Krishna Sastri, *South Indian Inscriptions Volume 3*, pp. 64–65, 69.
4 Sastri, *The Colas*, p. 269.
5 Whitney Cox, *Politics, Kingship and Poetry in Medieval South India*, Cambridge: Cambridge University Press, 2016, p. 64, 65.

6 Krishna Sastri, 'The Kanyakumari Inscription of Virarajendra, verses 28–35', p. 51.
7 Ibid., p. 54.
8 Cox, *Politics, Kingship and Poetry in Medieval South India*, p. 65, 66; Also in Tamil in Rao Bahadur H. Krishna Sastri, *South Indian Inscriptions Volume 4*, Madras: Superintendent Government Press, 1923, p. 157.
9 Virarajendra's hospital. Government of Madras Home Department, (Miscellaneous) G.O. #99, p. 119, 29 August, 1916.

CHAPTER 23: A FLASH IN THE PAN: ATHIRAJENDRA (R. 1070–1070)

1 Sailendra Nath Sen, *Ancient Indian History and Civilisation*, New Delhi: New Age International Publishers, 1999, pp. 385–86.
2 This is a matter that is still in dispute. According to Whitney Cox, a recent epigraphical discovery puts his date of ascension to the throne as June 1068, which would obviously render this statement untrue. He might have ruled along with his father as yuvaraja from 1068, and as sole ruler for a short couple of months. Cox, *Politics, Kingship and Poetry in Medieval South India*, p. 77.
3 Sastri, *The Colas*, p. 295, 296.

CHAPTER 24: A LUNAR KING IN THE SOLAR COURT: RAJAKESARI KULOTHUNGA I (R. 1070–1120)

1 V. Kanakasabhai Pillai, 'Tamil Historical Texts: The Kalingattu Parani', *Indian Antiquary: A Journal of Oriental Research, Volume 19*, ed. by J. F. Fleet and Richard Carnac Temple, Bombay: Education Society's Press, 1890, p. 332.
2 Jayankontar was Kulothunga's court poet, best known for his *Kalingattuparani*, a war poem on his patron's battles in Kalinga.
3 Pillai, 'Tamil Historical Texts: The Kalingattu Parani', p. 332.
4 Cox, *Politics, Kingship and Poetry in Medieval South India*, p. 5.
5 Kamil Zvelebil, *Tamil Literature*, Leiden: Brill, 1975, p. 186.
6 Shulman, *Tamil: A Biography*, p. 155.
7 Ibid.
8 Cox, *Politics, Kingship and Poetry in Medieval South India*, p. 165.
9 Ibid., p. 129.
10 Sastri, *The Colas*, p. 288.
11 Cox, *Politics, Kingship and Poetry in Medieval South India*, pp. 72–74.
12 J. F. Fleet, 'The Chronology of the Eastern Chalukya Kings', *Indian Antiquary, Volume 20*, ed. by J. F. Fleet and Richard Carnac Temple, Delhi: Swati Publications, 1985, pp. 276–78.
13 Cox, *Politics, Kingship and Poetry in Medieval South India*, pp. 126, 129, 131–132.
14 Sastri, *The Colas*, p. 306.
15 Krishna Sastri, *South Indian Inscriptions Volume 3*, p. 147.
16 Sastri, *The Colas*, p. 308.
17 Spencer, 'Politics of Plunder', pp. 417–19.
18 From an account in the Mahavamsa quoted in Sastri, *The Colas*, p. 314.
19 Sastri, *The Colas*, p. 316.
20 Ibid., p. 312.
21 Cox, *Politics, Kingship and Poetry in Medieval South India*, pp. 153–56.
22 Kenneth R. Hall, 'International Trade and Foreign Diplomacy in Early Medieval South India', *Journal of the Economic and Social History of the Orient*, Vol. 21, No.

1, January 1979, p. 91, 92.
23 Kulke, et al., *Nagapattinam to Suvarnadwipa*, p. 11, 12.
24 Hall, 'International Trade and Foreign Diplomacy in Early Medieval South India', p. 95.
25 N. P. Chakravarti, 'The Smaller Leiden Plates of Kulothunga I', *Epigraphia Indica Volume 22, 1933–34*, Delhi: Government of India, 1938, pp. 267–76.
26 Cox, *Politics, Kingship and Poetry in Medieval South India*, p. 140.
27 Ibid., p. 169.
28 Ibid., p. 176.
29 Dehejia, *Art of the Imperial Cholas*, p. 95, 96.
30 Cox, *Politics, Kingship and Poetry in Medieval South India*, pp. 182–84.
31 Younger, *Home of Dancing Sivan*, pp. 137–38.
32 Cox, *Politics, Kingship and Poetry in Medieval South India*, p. 150.

CHAPTER 25: THE CONSUMMATE SIVA DEVOTEE: PARAKESARI VIKRAMA (R. 1118–1135)

1 E. Hultzsch (ed.), *Epigraphia Indica Volume 6*, New Delhi: Archaeological Survey of India, 1902, p. 227.
2 Sastri, *The Colas*, p. 342, 343.
3 S. R. Balasubrahmanyam, *Later Chola Temples*, Faridabad: Madgala Trust, 1979, p. 161.
4 Dehejia, *Art of the Imperial Cholas*, p. 99.
5 Younger, *Home of Dancing Sivan*, p. 103.
6 Sastri, *The Colas*, p. 346.
7 Younger, *Home of Dancing Sivan*, p. 139.
8 Shulman, *Tamil: A Biography*, pp. 155–58.
9 Cox, *Politics, Kingship and Poetry in Medieval South India*, p. 99, 243; Sastri, *The Colas*, p. 247.

CHAPTER 26: SIVA SIVA SIVA: RAJAKESARI KULOTHUNGA II (R. 1133–1150)

1 Paraphrased from Balasubrahmanyam, *Later Chola Temples*, p. 208.
2 Sastri, *The Colas*, p. 348.
3 Younger, *Home of the Dancing Sivan*, p. 111, 155.
4 Balasubrahmanyam, *Later Chola Temples*, p. 208.
5 Younger, *Home of the Dancing Sivan*, p. 140.

CHAPTER 27: NAMESAKE OF GREATNESS: PARAKESARI RAJARAJA II (R. 1146–1173)

1 Hultzsch, *South Indian Inscriptions Volume 3, Part 1*, p. 81.
2 Balasubrahmanyam, *Later Chola Temples*, p. 221.
3 Dehejia, *Art of the Imperial Cholas*, pp. 106–107.
4 Balasubrahmanyam, *Later Chola Temples*, p. 233.
5 Ibid., pp. 231–32.
6 Ibid., p. 227, 228.
7 Sastri, *Epigraphia Indica Volume 21*, pp. 184–89.
8 Sastri, *The Colas*, p. 358.

CHAPTER 28: AN IMPOSSIBLE TANGLE: RAJAKESARI RAJADHIRAJA II (R. 1166–1178)

1 Sastri, *Epigraphia Indica Volume 21*, p. 191.
2 Balasubrahmanyam, *Later Chola Temples*, p. 264.
3 Sastri, *The Colas*, pp. 366–69; Balasubrahmanyam, *Later Chola Temples*, pp. 263–68.

CHAPTER 29: THE BEGINNING OF THE END: PARAKESARI KULOTHUNGA III (R. 1178–1218)

1 Hultzsch, *South Indian Inscriptions Volume 3, Part 2*, p. 212.
2 Sastri, *The Colas*, p. 375.
3 'While by an army despatched by the request of Vikrama Pandya the son of Vira Pandya was subdued....the Singala soldiers had their noses cut off and rushed into the rolling sea...he attacked Vira Pandya, took Madurai and the throne, set up a pillar of victory, was pleased to bestow Madurai, the throne and the country on the Pandya who had taken refuge with him....' Hultzsch, *South Indian Inscriptions Volume 3*, p. 213.
4 Chola-Pandyan and Mudittalai-konda-Solapuram; Balasubrahmanyam, *Later Chola Temples*, p. 291.
5 Dehejia, *Art of the Imperial Cholas*, p. 122.
6 Balasubrahmanyam, *Later Chola Temples*, p. 292, 293.

CHAPTER 30: A SERIES OF UNFORTUNATE EVENTS: RAJARAJA III (R. 1216–1246)

1 Balasubrahmanyam, *Later Chola Temples*, pp. 361–62.
2 Ibid., pp. 359–65.
3 Sastri, *The Colas*, p. 426.

CHAPTER 31: SUNSET AND DARKNESS: RAJENDRA III (R. 1246–1279)

1 Inscription in the temple at Srirangam. Paraphrased from Sakkottai Krishnaswami Aiyangar, *South India and her Muhammadan Invaders*, New Delhi: Asian Educational Services, 1991, p. 37.
2 S. Krishnaswami Aiyangar, *South India and Her Muhammadan Invaders*, London: Oxford University Press, 1921, p. 37.
3 Sastri, *The Colas*, p. 435.
4 Balasubrahmanyam, *Later Chola Temples*, p. 381.
5 Ibid., p. 382, 383.
6 Nagaswamy, G*angaikondacholapuram*, p. 57.
7 Sastri, *The Colas*, p. 437.
8 Ibid., p. 436.

EPILOGUE

1 Dehejia, *Art of the Imperial Cholas*, p. 49.
2 Sethuraman, *Raja Raja the Great, Seminar Proceedings*, pp. 28–38.
3 Sastri, *The Colas*, p. 453.
4 Lokeshwarri S. K., *Thanjavur's Chola Mystery*.
5 UNESCO World Heritage List, https://whc.unesco.org/en/list/250.

BIBLIOGRAPHY

6 Hall, *Networks of Trade, Polity, and Societal Integration in Chola-Era South India*, p. xi.
7 M. D. Rajkumar, 'Struggles for Rights during Later Chola Period', *Social Scientist*, Vol. 2, No. 6/7, Jan–Feb 1974, pp. 29–35.

LIST OF INSCRIPTIONS AND PLATES

Anbil Plates of Sundara Chola: Thomas, F.W. (ed.), *Epigraphia Indica Volume 15, 1919–20*, New Delhi: Archaeological Survey of India, 1982.

Atakur Stone Inscription of Krishna III and Butuga II: Hultzsch, E. (ed.), *Epigraphia Indica Volume 6, 1900–01*, New Delhi: Archaeological Survey of India, 1981.

Conjeevaram Inscription of the Telugu Chola King Jatachola Bhima Rao: B. V. Krishna, *Journal of the Andhra Historical Research Society, Volume 10*, Rajahmundry: Andhra Historical Research Society, 1937.

Hottur Inscription of Satyasraya: Thomas, F. W. (ed.), *Epigraphia Indica Volume 16, 1921–1922*, New Delhi: Archaeological Survey of India, 1983.

Inscription in the Sthanunatha Temple at Suchindram: Hultzsch, E. (ed.), *Epigraphia Indica Volume 5, 1898–99*, New Delhi: Archaeological Survey of India, 1984.

Inscriptions at Uthiramerur: 'Annual Report of the Archaeological Survey of India, 1904–5', Calcutta: Superintendent Government Printing, 1908.

Kanyakumari Inscription of Virarajendra: Sastri, Rao Bahadur H. Krishna (ed.), *Epigraphia Indica Volume 18, 1925–26*, New Delhi: Archeological Survey of India, 1983.

Karandai Tamil Sangam Plates of Rajendrachola I: Krishnan, K. G., *Karandai Tamil Sangam Plates of Rajendrachola* New Delhi: Archaeological Survey of India, 1984.

Larger Leiden Plates of Rajaraja I: Chakravarti, N. P. (ed.), *Epigraphia Indica Volume 22, 1933–34*, Delhi: Government of India, 1938.

Madras Museum Plates of Uttama Chola: Sastri, Rao Bahadur H. Krishna (ed.), *South Indian Inscriptions Volume 3, Part 3 and 4*, New Delhi: Archaeological Survey of India, 1920

Melpadi Inscriptions: Hultzsch, E. (ed.), *South Indian Inscriptions Volume 3, Part 1*, New Delhi: Archaeological Survey of India, 1929.

Rajasimha's Sinnamannur Inscription: Sastri, Rao Sahib H. Krishna, *South Indian Inscriptions Volume 3, Part 3 and 4*, New Delhi: Archaeological Survey of India, 1920.

Sholinghur Inscription of Parantaka I: Hultzsch, E. (ed.), *Epigraphia Indica Volume 4, 1896–97*, New Delhi: Archaeological Survey of India, 1981.

Smaller Leiden Plates of Kulothunga I: Chakravarti, N. P. (ed.), *Epigraphia Indica Volume 22, 1933–34*, Delhi: Government of India, 1938.

Thirteenth Rock-Edict: Kalsi: Hultzsch, E. (trans.), *Inscriptions of Asoka*, Oxford: Clarendon Press, 1925.

Thiruvalangadu Plates of Rajendra Chola: Sastri, Rao Sahib H. Krishna, *South Indian Inscriptions Volume 3, Part 3*, New Delhi: Archaeological Survey of India, 1920.

Udaiyargudi Inscription of Rajakesarivarman: Sastri, Hirananda (ed.), *Epigraphia Indica Volume 21, 1931–32*, New Delhi: Archaeological Survey of India, 1984.

Udayendiram Plates of Prithvapati II: Hultzsch, E. (ed.), *South Indian Inscriptions Volume 2*, New Delhi: Archaeological Survey of India, 1991.

Velvikudi Grant of Nedunjedaiyan: Sastri, Rao Bahadur H. Krishna (ed.), *Epigraphia*

Indica Volume 17, 1923–24, New Delhi: Archeological Survey of India, 1983.

BOOKS

Adigal, Ilango, *Shilappadikaram*, trans. by Alain Daniélou, New Delhi: Aleph Book Company, 2016.

Aiyangar, S. Krishnaswami, *South India and Her Muhammadan Invaders*, London: Oxford University Press, 1921.

Aiyer, K. V. Subrahmanya (ed.), *South India Inscriptions Volume 6*, New Delhi: Archaeological Survey of India, 1986.

Andaya, Barbara Watson, *A History of Malaysia*, Honolulu: University of Hawai'i Press, 2001.

Balasubrahmanyam, S. R., *Early Chola Temples*, Delhi: Orient Longman, 1971.

———, *Later Chola Temples*, Faridabad: Madgala Trust, 1979.

———, *Middle Chola Temples*, Thomson Press (India) Ltd, 1973.

Chakravarti, N. P. (ed.), *Epigraphia Indica Volume 22, 1933–34*, Delhi: Government of India, 1938.

———, *Epigraphia Indica Volume 26, 1941–1942*, New Delhi: Archaelogical Survey of India, 1985.

Champakalakshmi, R., *Trade, Ideology and Urbanization: South India 300 BC to AD 1300*, New Delhi: Oxford University Press, 1996.

Chhabra, Dr B. CH. and Rao, N. Lakshminarayan (eds.), *Epigraphia Indica Volume 27, 1947–48*, New Delhi: Archaeological Survey of India, 1985.

Cox, Whitney, *Politics, Kingship and Poetry in Medieval South India*, Cambridge: Cambridge University Press, 2016.

Daniélou, Alain, *A Brief History of India*, trans. by Kenneth F. Hurry, Vermont: Inner Traditions-Bear and Company, 2003.

Davis, Richard H., *Lives of Indian Images*, Princeton: Princeton University Press, 1997.

Dehejia, Vidya, *Art of the Imperial Cholas*, New York: Columbia University Press, 1990.

———, *Chola: Sacred Bronzes of Southern India*, London: Royal Academy Books, 2007.

———, *The Thief Who Stole My Heart: The Material Life of Sacred Bronzes from Chola India, 855–1280*, Princeton: Princeton University Press, 2021.

Elliot, Walter, *Coins of Southern India*, Varanasi: Prithivi Prakashan, 1970.

Geiger, Wilhelm (trans.), *Culavamsa: Being the More Recent Part of the* Mahavamsa, *Part 1*, Oxford: Oxford University Press, 1929.

———, *The Mahavamsa of The Great Chronicle of Ceylon*, London: Oxford University Press, 1929.

Ghose, Rajeshwari, *The Tyagaraja Cult in Tamilnadu*, New Delhi: Motilal Banarsidass Publishers, 1996.

Hall, Kenneth R., *Networks of Trade, Polity and Societal Integration in Chola-Era South India*, New Delhi: Primus Books, 2014.

History of the World Map by Map, New York: DK Publishing, 2018.

Hultzsch, E. (ed.), *Epigraphia Indica Volume 4, 1896–97*, New Delhi: Archaeological Survey of India, 1979.

———, *Epigraphia Indica Volume 5, 1898–99*, New Delhi: Archaeological Survey of India, 1984.

———, *Epigraphia Indica Volume 6*, New Delhi: Archaeological Survey of India, 1902.

———, *South Indian Inscriptions Volume 2*, New Delhi: Archaeological Survey of India, 1991.

———, *South Indian Inscriptions Volume 3, Part 1*, Madras: Archaeological Survey of India, 1929.

Janakiraman, T. and Chitti, *Eternal Kaveri: The Story of a River*, trans. by K. Krishnamurthy, Madras: Bookventure, 2020.

Kannan, C. R., *Rajaraja Cholan* (Tamil), Chennai, 2010.

Karashima, Noboru, *A Concise History of South India*, New Delhi: Oxford University Press, 2014.

———, *South Indian Society in Transition: Ancient to Medieval*, New Delhi: Oxford University Press, 2009.

Krishnan, K. G., *Karandai Tamil Sangam Plates of Rajendrachola I*, New Delhi: Archaeological Survey of India, 1984.

Kulke, Herman, Kesavapany, K., and Sakhuja, Vijay, *Nagapattinam to Suvarnadwipa: Reflections on the Chola Naval Expeditions to Southeast Asia*, Singapore: Institute of Southeast Asian Studies, 2009.

Kulke, Hermann and Rothermund, Dietmar, *A History of India*, London: Routledge, 2004.

Lee, Risha, *Constructing Community: Tamil Merchant Temples in India and China, 850–1281*, New York: Columbia University Press, 2012.

Levy, Thomas E., et al, *Masters of Fire: Hereditary Bronze Casters of South India*, Bochum: Die Deutsche Bibliothek, 2008.

Madhavan, Chithra, *History and Culture of Tamil Nadu: Volume 1*, New Delhi: DK Printworld, 2013.

Marr, John Ralston, *The Eight Anthologies: A Study in Early Tamil Literature*, Tiruvanmiyur: Institute of Asian Studies, 1985.

Nagaswamy, R., *Gangaikondacholapuram*, Tamil Nadu: State Department of Archaeology, 1970.

Newell, H. A., *Tanjore (The City of the Mammoth Bull)*, Madras and Bangalore: Higginbothams, 1900.

Orr, Leslie C., *Donors, Devotoees and Daughters of God: Temple Women in Medieval Tamilnadu*, Oxford: Oxford University Press, 2000.

Peterson, Indira Viswanathan, *Poems to Siva: The Hymns of the Tamil Saints*, Princeton: Princeton University Press, 1989.

Pillai, Avvai Duraiswamy, *Tamil Navalar Caritai*, Tinnevelly: South India Saiva Siddhanta Works Publishing Society, 1949.

Pillai, J. M. Somasundaram, *The Great Temple at Tanjore*, Tanjore: Tanjore Palace Devasthanams, 1935.

Pillai, V. Kanakasabhai, *The Tamils Eighteen Hundred Years Ago*, Asian Educational Services, 1904.

Ramanujan, A. K., *Poems of Love and War: From the Eight Anthologies and the Ten Long Poems of Classical Tamil*, New York: Columbia University Press, 2011.

Rao, G. V. Srinivasa (ed.), *South Indian Inscriptions Volume 13*, New Delhi: Archaeological Survey of India, 1952.

———, *South Indian Inscriptions Volume 23*, New Delhi: Archaeological Survey of India, 1979.

Rao, N. Lakshminarayan and Sircar, D. C. (eds.), *Epigraphia Indica Volume 30, 1953–54*, New Delhi: Archaeological Survey of India, 1987.

Rice, B. Lewis (ed.), *Epigraphia Carnatica Volume 10*, Manglore: Basel Mission Press, 1905.

Row, T. Venkasami, *A Manual of the District of Tanjore in the Madras Presidency*, Madras: Lawrence Asylum Press, 1883.
Sastri, Hirananda (ed.), *Epigraphia Indica Volume 19, 1927–28*, Delhi: Archeological Survey of India, 1983.
———, *Epigraphia Indica Volume 21, 1931–32*, New Delhi: Archaeological Survey of India, 1984, p. 170.
Sastri, K. A. Nilakanta, *The Colas*, Madras: University of Madras, 1955.
Sastri, Rao Bahadur H. Krishna (ed.), *Epigraphia Indica Volume 17, 1923–24*, New Delhi: Archeological Survey of India, 1983.
———, *Epigraphia Indica Volume 18, 1925–26*, New Delhi: Archeological Survey of India, 1983.
———, *South Indian Inscriptions Volume 3, Part 3 and 4*, New Delhi: The Archaeological Survey of India, 1920.
———, *South Indian Inscriptions Volume 4*, Madras: Superintendent Government Press, 1923.
Sen, Sailendra Nath, *Ancient Indian History and Civilisation*, New Delhi: New Age International Publishers, 1999.
Shulman, David Dean, *The King and the Clown in South Indian Myth and Poetry*, Princeton: Princeton University Press, 1985.
Shulman, David, *Tamil: A Biography*, Cambridge, Massachusetts: Belknap Press of Harvard University Press, 2016.
Spencer, George, *The Politics of Expansion: The Chola Conquest of Sri Lanka and Sri Vijaya*, Madras: New Era Publications, 1983.
Stein, Burton, *Peasant State and Society in Medieval South India*, Delhi: Oxford University Press, 1980.
Subbarayalu, Y., *South India Under the Cholas*, New Delhi: Oxford University Press, 2012.
Swaminathan, S., *The Early Cholas: History, Art and Culture*, New Delhi: Sharada Publishing House, 1998.
Thapar, Romila, *Early India from the Origins to 1300*, Berkeley: University of California Press, 2002.
Thirumurai, a twelve book compendium of Saiva poems.
Thomas, F.W. (ed.), *Epigraphia Indica Volume 15, 1919–20*, New Delhi: Archaeological Survey of India, 1982.
———, *Epigraphia Indica Volume 16, 1921–22*, New Delhi: Archaeological Survey of India, 1983.
V., Dhanalekshmi, *Administration under the Imperial Cholas 850 to 1070 AD*, Tirunelveli: Manonmaniam Sundaranar University, 2017.
Vaidya, P. L., *The Mahapurana of Puspadanta: Volume 1*, Bombay: Manikchand Digambara Jaina Granthamala, 1937.
Vasudevan, Geeta, *The Royal Temple of Rajaraja*, New Delhi: Abhinav Publications, 2003.
Vatsyayan, Kapila (ed.), *Concepts of Space, Ancient and Modern*, New Delhi: Abhinav Publications, 1991.
Younger, Paul, *The Home of Dancing Sivan*, Oxford: Oxford University Press, 1955.
Zvelebil, Kamil, *Tamil Literature*, Leiden: Brill, 1975.
———, *The Smile of Murugan: On Tamil Literature of South India*, Leiden: E.J. Brill, 1973.

CHAPTERS IN BOOKS

Abraham, Meera, 'The History of the Ayyavole Association', *Two Medieval Merchant*

Guilds of South India, Delhi: Manohar Publications, 1988.
Aiyar, R. Swaminatha Aiyar, 'The Aryan Element in Dravidian Vocabularies', *Dravidian Theories*, Delhi: Motilal Banarsidass, 1987.
Ali, Daud, 'The Epigraphical Legacy at Gangaikondacholapuram: Problems and Possibilities', *New Dimensions in Tamil Epigraphy: A Multi-Disciplinary Approach*, ed. by Appasamy Murugaiyan, Chennai: Crea Publishers, 2012.
———, 'War, Servitude and the Imperial Household: A Study of Palace Women in the Chola Empire', *Slavery and South Asian History*, ed. by Indrani Chatterjee and Richard M. Eaton, Bloomington: Indiana University Press, 2006.
Beal, Samuel, 'Chu-Li-Ye (Chulya or Chola)', *Chinese Accounts of India: Volume 4*, Calcutta: Susil Gupta (India) Private Ltd., 1958.
Hultzsch, E. (trans.), 'Thirteenth Rock-Edict: Kalsi', *Inscriptions of Asoka*, Oxford: Clarendon Press, 1925.
Killborn, Professor F., 'Dates of Chola Kings', *Epigraphia Indica Volume 8, 1905–06*, ed. by E. Hultzsch, New Delhi: Archaeological Survey of India, 1981.
Nagaswamy, Dr R., 'Saivism Under Rajaraja – A Study', *Raja Raja the Great: Seminar Proceedings*, Bombay: Ananthacharya Indological Research Institute, 1987.
Orr, Leslie C., 'Processions in the medieval South Indian temple: Sociology, sovereignty and soteriology', *South-Indian Horizons: Felicitation volume for François Gros on the occasion of his 70th birthday*, Jean-Luc Chevillard and Eva Wilden (eds.), Pondicherry: Institut Français de Pondichéry, 2004.
Rao, T. A. Gopinathan, 'Introduction to the Anbil Plates of Sundara Chola', *Epigraphia Indica Volume 15, 1919–20*, ed. by F. W. Thomas, New Delhi: Archaeological Survey of India, 1982.
Sen, Tansen, 'Maritime Contacts between China and the Cola Kingdom', *Mariners, Merchants and Oceans: Studies in Maritime History*, ed. by Kuzhippalli Skaria Mathew, New Delhi: Manohar Publishers, 1995.
Sethuraman, N., 'Date of Birth Date of Coronation and the Last Day of Raja Raja Chola', *Raja Raja, the Great: Seminar Proceedings*, Bombay: Ananthacharya Indological Research Institute, 1987.
Venkatachalapathy, A.R., 'In Print, On the Net: Tamil Literary Canon in the Colonial and Post-Colonial Worlds', *Globalization in India: Contents and Discontents*, ed. by Suman Gupta, Tapan Basu, and Subarno Chattarji, New Delhi: Pearson Education, 2010.
Venkayya, Rao Bahadur V., 'Introduction', *South Indian Inscriptions Volume 2*, ed. by E. Hultzsch, New Delhi, Archaelogical Survey of India, 1991.
Walshe, Maurice, 'Aggnana Sutta: On Knowledge of Beginnings', *The Long Discourses of the Buddha: A Translation of the Digha Nikaya*, Boston: Wisdom Publications, 1987.

ARTICLES

'1,000-year-old chola monument remains obscure', *The Hindu*, 25 January 2020.
Aiyangar, Dr S. Krishnaswami, 'The Chola Rajaraja I and the Eastern Chalukya alliance', *Journal of the Andhra Historical Research Society, Volume 10*, Rajahmundry: Andhra Historical Research Society, 1937.
Ali, Daud, 'The Service Retinue of the Chola Court: A Study of the Term Velam in Tamil Inscriptions', *Bulletin of the School of Oriental and African Studies*, Vol. 78, No. 3, 2007.
Balambal, V., 'Kundavai—A Chola Princess', *Proceedings of the Indian History Congress*, Vol. 39, 1978.
Deoras, V. R., 'Fresh Light on the Southern Campaigns of the Rashtrakuta Emperor

Krishna III', *Proceedings of the Indian History Congress*, Vol. 20, 1957.
Fleet, J. F., 'The Chronology of the Eastern Chalukya Kings', *Indian Antiquary, Volume 20*, ed. by J. F. Fleet and Richard Carnac Temple, Delhi: Swati Publications, 1985.
Hall, Kenneth R. 'International Trade and Foreign Diplomacy in Early Medieval South India', *Journal of the Economic and Social History of the Orient*, Vol. 21, No. 1, January 1979.
Kabirdoss, Yogesh, '1,000-year-old stolen idols of Rajaraja Chola return to TN from Gujarat', *Times of India*, 31 May 2018.
Kaimal, Padma, 'A Man's World? Gender, Family and Architectural Patronage in Medieval India', *Archives of Asian Art*, Vol. 53, 2003.
———, 'Early Cola Kings and Early Cola Temples', *Artibus Asiae*, Volume 56, Number 1/2, 1996.
Karashima, Noboru, 'Epigraphical Study of Ancient and Medieval Villages in the Tamil Country', *Review of Agrarian Studies*, Vol. 1, Issue 2, December 2011.
———, 'The Past as Known From Tamil Inscriptions: Village Community and Challenge to the Caste System', 8 February 2016.
Krishnamachari, Suganthy, 'A millennium gone but this chola queen is remembered', *The Hindu*, 7 March 2019.
Kulke, Hermann, 'Fragmentation and Segmentation Versus Integration? Reflections on the Concepts of Indian Feudalism and the Segmentary State in Indian History', *Studies in History*, Vol. 4, 1982.
Mackenzie, Lt Col. Colin and Wilson, H. H., *The Mackenzie Collection*, Calcutta: Asiatic Press, 1828.
Madras Literary Society, *Madras Journal of Literature and Science*, Volume 7, 1838.
———, *Madras Journal of Literature and Science*, Volume 14, 1847.
Nagaswamy, R., 'Archaeological Finds in South India: Esalam Bronzes and Copperplates', *Bulletin de l'Ecole Francaise d'Extreme Orient*, Tome 76, 1987.
Pillai, P. Sundaram, 'The Age of Tirunanasambandha', *Indian Antiquary, Volume 25*, ed. by Richard Carnac Temple, Bombay: Education Society's Press, 1896.
Pillai, V. Kanakasabhai, 'Tamil Historical Texts: The Kalingattu Parani', *Indian Antiquary: A Journal of Oriental Research, Volume 19*, ed. by J. F. Fleet and Richard Carnac Temple, Bombay: Education Society's Press, 1890.
———, 'Tamil Historical Texts: The Vikrama-Cholan-Ula', *Indian Antiquary: A Journal of Oriental Research, Volume 22*, Delhi: Swati Publications, June 1893.
Prentiss, Karen Pechilis, 'A Tamil Lineage for Saiva Siddhanta Philosophy', *History of Religions*, Vol. 35, No. 3, February 1996.
Rao, B. V. Krishna, 'Conjeevaram Inscription of the Telugu Chola King Jatachola Bhima', *Journal of the Andhra Historical Research Society, Volume 10*.
S. K., Lokeshwarri, 'Thanjavur's Chola Mystery', *Hindu Business Line*, 29 November 2019.
Spencer, George W., 'The Politics of Plunder: The Cholas in Eleventh-Century Ceylon', *The Journal of Asian Studies*, Vol. 35, No. 3, May 1976.
Srivathsan, A., 'An Exciting Discovery and a 1931 Scoop for The Hindu', *The Hindu*, 3 February 2010.
Subramanian, T. S., 'How karana sculptures in Big Temple were discovered', *The Hindu*, 23 September 2010.
———, 'Unearthed Stone Ends Debate', *The Hindu*, 27 November 2009.
Taylor, William, *Examination and Analysis: The Mackenzie Manuscripts Deposited in the Madras College Library*, Calcutta: The Asiatic Society, 1838.

Vijailakshmi, Usha R., 'Tamil Migration into Karnataka (The Period of Chola Conquest of Southern Karnataka and the Consolidation of Power from 850–1279 A.D)', *Proceedings of the Indian History Congress*, Vol. 66, 2005–2006.

Wade, Geoff, 'An Early Age of Commerce in South East Asia, 900–1300 CE', *Journal of Southeast Asian Studies*, Vol. 40, No. 2, 2009.

REPORTS AND ONLINE RESOURCES

'Annual Report of the Archaeological Survey of India, 1904–05', Calcutta: Superintendent Government Printing, 1908.

'Annual Report on Epigraphy, 1915–1920', New Delhi: Department of Archaeology, 1896.

'Annual Report on Indian Epigraphy, 1924–1925', New Delhi: Archaeological Survey of India, 1925.

'Annual Report on South Indian Epigraphy for the Year Ending 31st March 1928', Madras: Government Press, 1928.

Dehejia, Vidya, '65th A.W Mellon lectures in the Fine Arts', Washington D. C.: National Gallery of Art, April–May 2016.

Herbert, Vaidehi (trans.), *Patthupaat-Porunaatruppadai*, https://sangamtranslationsbyvaidehi.com/a-porunaratruppadai/.

INDEX